# Autonomic Systems

The Autonomic Systems series aims at creating a platform of communication between universities and industry by publishing research monographs, outstanding PhD theses, and peer reviewed compiled contributions on the latest developments in the field. It covers a broad range of topics from the theory of autonomic systems that are researched by academia and industry. Hence, cutting-edge research, prototypical case studies, as well as industrial applications are in the focus of this series. Fast reviewing provides a most convenient way to publish latest results in this rapid moving research area.

For further volumes:
http://www.springer.com/series/8123

Wolfgang Reif • Gerrit Anders • Hella Seebach •
Jan-Philipp Steghöfer • Elisabeth André •
Jörg Hähner • Christian Müller-Schloer •
Theo Ungerer

Editors

# Trustworthy Open Self-Organising Systems

 Birkhäuser

*Editors*

Wolfgang Reif
Institute for Software and Systems
  Engineering
University of Augsburg
Augsburg, Germany

Hella Seebach
Institute for Software and Systems
  Engineering
University of Augsburg
Augsburg, Germany

Elisabeth André
Human-Centered Multimedia
University of Augsburg
Augsburg, Germany

Christian Müller-Schloer
Institute of Systems Engineering
University of Hannover
Hannover, Germany

Gerrit Anders
Institute for Software and Systems
  Engineering
University of Augsburg
Augsburg, Germany

Jan-Philipp Steghöfer
Department of Computer Science
  and Engineering
Chalmers University of Technology |
University of Gothenburg
Gothenburg, Sweden

Jörg Hähner
Organic Computing Group
University of Augsburg
Augsburg, Germany

Theo Ungerer
Systems and Networking Group
University of Augsburg
Augsburg, Germany

Autonomic Systems
ISBN 978-3-319-29199-4      ISBN 978-3-319-29201-4    (eBook)
DOI 10.1007/978-3-319-29201-4

Library of Congress Control Number: 2016941940

Mathematics Subject Classification (2010): 68T42, 68T37, 68T20, 68T05, 68W15, 68W27, 68N30

Printed on acid-free paper

This book is published under the trade name Birkhäuser
The registered company is Springer International Publishing AG Switzerland
(www.birkhauser-science.com)

# Foreword

OC-Trust, this is an acronym representing a research cooperation that addressed one of the core challenges of the emerging digitalisation of almost every facet of our professional and private lives. How can we develop trust into the widely autonomous provisioning of digital functionality and associated services? We expect those services to know what we want them to provide, but we are not physically capable and do not want to programme those multitudes of devices explicitly. So, we increasingly depend on their capability to self-configure, self-optimise, self-heal and self-protect, to name a few of the many so-called self-* properties. But how do we know to what extent they will actually satisfy our expectations? They should be aware of our personal preferences, but will they respect our privacy? If agents act autonomously, how can their operating environment distinguish between trustworthy and malicious agents? This kind of almost contradictory questions and requirements is concerned with the trustworthiness of artefacts that are meant to be self-organising and widely autonomous but nevertheless capable to adapt to potentially changing requirements of their execution environment. Research initiatives like autonomic computing and organic computing have emphasised from the beginning that trustworthiness should be seen as one of the key requirements, but they more or less focused on the development of generic architectures and methodology for providing desired functionality and organic behaviour in the best possible way. So, the German priority programme on organic computing successfully addressed fundamental system concepts supporting controlled self-organisation, as summarised in the compendium on "Organic Computing – A Paradigm Shift for Complex Systems". But it needed the additional initiative of research groups at Augsburg and Hanover to establish this complementary DFG research unit on "OC-Trust – Trustworthiness of Organic Computing Systems".

Wolfgang Reif, the spokesperson of this research unit, continued his work on software design for organic computing systems but focused now on "Formal Analysis and Software Architectures for Trustworthy Organic Computing". Christian Müller-Schloer, one of the core initiators of the organic computing research programme, and Jörg Hähner concentrated on top-down and bottom-up approaches to the "Generation of Self-organising Trust Communities". Theo Ungerer, another core member of the Organic Computing Initiative, investigated "Trust Relationships in Between the Autonomous Units of OC Systems". Finally, since the interaction between man and machine is one of the key aspects of trustworthiness, Elisabeth André joined the research unit with her topic "HCI Design for Trustworthy Organic Computing". Looking at the research unit's record of meetings, workshops and special spring schools, it is obvious that they have been extremely active and productive. The TSOS workshop series on "Trustworthy Self-Organising Systems" as well as its successor, the SASO$^{ST}$ Workshop, were essential for significant international recognition and provided a forum for exchange of ideas with other research groups. The "International Spring Schools on Trustworthy Self-Organising Systems" added specific input from international experts for the doctoral researchers in this research unit with a significant outreach to other research groups. This book now summarises the major results of this research unit on a topic that might prove to become most decisive for the public acceptance of technologies that are developed under a range of different, but highly related, headlines like "Internet of Things", "Cyber Physical Systems", "Industry 4.0" and "Smart City" (including energy and traffic systems as well as all kinds of citizen services), to name a few.

An interesting aspect of this book is the fact that it extends beyond the members of the research unit by including external experts on topics that are of interest for a more complete view on trustworthiness.

So, the DFG research unit OC-Trust not only generated a range of interesting concepts and results on trustworthiness of and within self-organising systems, but they also had a significant impact on the international research community and clearly showed the necessity and benefits of a transdisciplinary approach for a thorough understanding of the role of trustworthiness.

Karlsruhe, Germany                                                          Hartmut Schmeck
November, 2015

# Preface

Our technological landscape is ever-changing. Interconnected devices interact with other devices as well as people in an increasingly autonomous fashion. This core idea manifests itself in several aspiring areas of technology – from the "Internet of Things" to "Industry 4.0". It seems all too obvious that these entities cannot be controlled by individuals or even organisations but rather require sophisticated self-organisation mechanisms to implement various self-* properties without centralised control. This scientific challenge led to initiatives such as autonomic computing or organic computing that proposed important basic architectures, models and algorithms. Particularly in terms of robustness towards failures, these systems show the potential of outperforming conventional, rigid systems. When widening the scope of application of self-organising systems to critical domains that are more open and consist of heterogeneous participants, an essential question accompanies the more widespread adoption: How can we make these systems *trustworthy*?

More specifically, in 2009 the DFG[1] research unit "Trustworthiness of Organic Computing Systems" (OC-Trust) set out to develop methods to construct self-organising multi-agent systems that are deemed trustworthy by their users, by other systems interacting with them and by authorities and even organisations that certify and deploy systems in safety- or mission-critical environments. Positive aspects of self-organisation, such as increased robustness or other positive emergent effects, shall, however, not be sacrificed. The common denominator of the bundled research efforts is the scientific treatment of various facets of *trust* in technical systems. Trust manifests itself in the system design, e.g. by countermeasures against ill-behaving or little predictable agents, and helps to reduce the impact of such entities on the overall system performance. Among technical systems benefiting from trust management, one particular system class is selected to serve as a prominent representative. It can be roughly categorised as *open, heterogeneous, self-organising, multi-agent systems* and is visualised in Fig. 1. Systems in this class share several features that require individual attention:

---

[1]German Research Foundation (*Deutsche Forschungsgemeinschaft*)

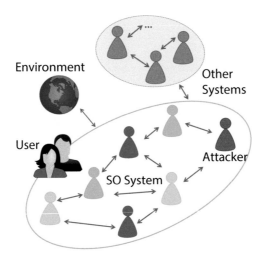

**Fig. 1** Open self-organising multi-agent systems composed of heterogeneous agents. Examples thereof are detailed in subsequent chapters

- Components are represented by agents that interact via a self-organised communication and collaboration structure to, e.g. avoid excessive broadcasting and enable effective problem decomposition.
- The system interacts with other systems, and a single agent may even act on behalf of a larger subsystem in a systems-of-systems approach.
- Due to its deployment as an autonomous entity in a dynamic environment, uncertainty about interaction partners (and their possibly malicious intentions in the case of attackers) and exogenous factors is omnipresent – hence, the benevolence assumption is abandoned.
- Users are present "in the loop" and constantly interact with the software surrounding them – as long as they trust it.

Clearly, these diverse challenges require a collaborative effort that is reflected in the projects the research groups undertook and whose results of 6 years of research form the core of this book. Chapter 1 provides an overview of the properties of computational trust and its different uses. These are concretised in the subsequent chapters. Wolfgang Reif and his group (see Chap. 2) investigated methods that enable scalable, robust optimisation to control systems subject to strong environmental influences and physical constraints. Christian Müller-Schloer (see Chap. 4) and his team provided means to incentivise cooperative or to sanction malicious behaviour in a group of agents. In this context, Jörg Hähner (see Chap. 5) and his team devised mechanisms to form groups of agents that mutually trust each other. Theo Ungerer (see Chap. 6) established with his group how various self-* properties can be efficiently monitored and allowed for selective service placement in middlewares for parallel algorithms and distributed systems, in general. To accommodate the users' interests, in particular its trust in a self-organising system,

Elisabeth André (see Chap. 3) and her team worked on explicit user trust models that capture the effects of system actions on the users' experienced trust and take these factors into consideration. Measuring, formalising and interpreting various facets of trust as well as the incorporation of this knowledge into decision-making is a common theme that transcends all OC-Trust projects. Many of the concepts and algorithms were developed in close cooperation of the project partners, reflected by 35 joint publications. More than 20 internal project meetings over the course of 6 years offered room and time for the fundamental discussions that led to those results.

To illustrate the developed techniques and to instantiate the system class, three jointly used case studies were devised. All of them are based on the Trust-Enabling Middleware that offers communication interfaces and access to a generic infrastructure for application-specific trust metrics. The *Trusted Desktop Grid* deals with open, social agent environments that jointly process computing tasks. As a self-organised collaboration structure, the concept of trusted communities consisting of trustworthy agents is in the focus. Trust-based *Autonomous Virtual Power Plants* allow for a self-organised, robust and scalable control of a large number of power plants in a hierarchical way. Uncertainty introduced by volatile energy sources poses tremendous challenge to the system which has to keep supply and demand of power in balance at all times. *Multi-user multi-display environments* have users interact with a system on both public and private devices. With several participants at the same device, privacy and usability concerns become relevant when it comes to deciding which content should be shown. User preferences guide these decisions which are evaluated at runtime on a dynamic user trust model.

Certainly, the research unit did not work in isolation on these fundamental topics but rather built on top of established theories, models and algorithms and extended the literature substantially. This fact is reflected by the structure of this book which includes three invited contributions by selected experts from the domain of trust in multi-agent systems. Jeremy Pitt (see Chap. 7) discusses formal models of several social processes for open distributed systems and, in a sense, removes the restriction on the social concept of trust otherwise so prominent in this book. Cristiano Castelfranchi and Rino Falcone (see Chap. 8) add various other factors to the discussion on trust in self-organising, sociotechnical systems. Natasha Dwyer and Stephen Marsh (see Chap. 9) conclude the book by asking the interesting and relevant question whether a digital environment empowered users to proceed on their own terms.

These contributions are witness to the fact that the research unit enjoyed great visibility in the scientific community and put serious efforts into the dissemination of its results. Papers that resulted from the projects were regularly presented at international conferences such as the IEEE International Conference on Self-Organising and Self-Adaptive Systems (SASO), the International Conference on Autonomic Computing (ICAC) or the International Conference on Architecture of Computing Systems (ARCS), to name a few. Especially at SASO, nine editions of workshops on topics related to OC-Trust were held, comprising the workshops on trustworthy self-organising systems (TSOS), sociotechnical concepts (SASO$^{ST}$) and quality assurance for self-organising systems (QA4SASO). These workshops turned out to be valuable regular additions to the programme of SASO and led to fruitful discussions. But of course, until sound publications can be written, doctoral students need to be exposed to and guided towards recent scientific work. It is for this cause that the research unit conducted two spring schools on "trustworthy self-organising systems" and three gender workshops to invite prominent researchers and foster future cooperations. Furthermore, due to this encouraging culture, several doctoral researchers were already invited to personally serve in programme committees or panels at both conferences and workshops. Additionally, the 10th edition of SASO will be held in Augsburg in 2016 with demonstrations of the OC-Trust projects.

Besides these community-oriented activities and OC-Trust-internal cooperations, some of the results emerged from collaborations with external partners. Especially papers at the frontiers of trustworthy self-organising systems that could benefit from input from other disciplines were written with OFFIS at the University of Oldenburg, the Imperial College London, the Max-Planck-Institute in Tübingen and the KU Leuven. Interesting meetings took place with NEC Laboratories, the University of Calgary, the University of Duisburg-Essen and the LMU in Munich. Additionally, invited talks at the Stadtwerke Munich, Phoenix Contact, the SORules workshop in London and the Helmholtz centre in Munich showed increased interest from both industry and academia. Wolfgang Reif and Christian Müller-Schlöer furthermore spent sabbatical terms at NICTA in Australia and Telecom ParisTech, respectively, to work intensively on related topics. All shall be mentioned to value their feedback that influenced and shaped the research unit.

Results of OC-Trust found their way into three courses at the universities of Augsburg and Hanover. Therefore, motivated students were well-prepared to conduct their own research in self-organisation in their thesis works. Many of those results found their way into proper publications. Finally, 13 doctoral researchers found challenging questions to complete their dissertations in the research unit. It is due to their continuous efforts that the project succeeded the way it did, in answering some questions but *asking* many important new ones. As a starting point for new directions, a Dagstuhl seminar on "Social Concepts in Self-organising Systems" was initiated by the research unit in December 2015. We are confident that the achieved results presented in this book show great promise for both research and applications and look forward to an increasing number of trustworthy self-organising systems in our future environment.

Finally, many thanks go to the contributing authors, in particular of the invited contributions that enriched the book tremendously. We are indebted to the German Research Foundation for sponsoring the research unit OC-Trust (FOR 1085).

Augsburg, Germany                                        Wolfgang Reif (head of OC-Trust)
January, 2016                                                          Alexander Schiendorfer
                                                                                 Hella Seebach
                                                                                 Gerrit Anders

# Contents

# List of Contributors

**Gerrit Anders** Institute for Software and Systems Engineering, University of Augsburg, Augsburg, Germany

**Elisabeth André** Human-Centered Multimedia, University of Augsburg, Augsburg, Germany

**Yvonne Bernard** Institute of Systems Engineering, Leibniz Universität Hannover, Hannover, Germany

**Cristiano Castelfranchi** Institute of Cognitive Sciences and Technologies, National Research Council, Roma, Italy

**Natasha Dwyer** College of Arts, Victoria University, Melbourne, VIC, Australia

**Benedikt Eberhardinger** Institute for Software and Systems Engineering, University of Augsburg, Augsburg, Germany

**Sarah Edenhofer** Organic Computing Group, University of Augsburg, Augsburg, Germany

**Rino Falcone** Institute of Cognitive Sciences and Technologies, National Research Council, Roma, Italy

**Jörg Hähner** Organic Computing Group, University of Augsburg, Augsburg, Germany

**Stephan Hammer** Human-Centered Multimedia, University of Augsburg, Augsburg, Germany

**Jan Kantert** Institute of Systems Engineering, Leibniz Universität Hannover, Hannover, Germany

**Lukas Klejnowski** Institute of Systems Engineering, Leibniz Universität Hannover, Hannover, Germany

**Oliver Kosak** Institute for Software and Systems Engineering, University of Augsburg, Augsburg, Germany

**Stephen Marsh** Faculty of Business and Information Technology, University of Ontario Institute of Technology, Oshawa, ON, Canada

**Christian Müller-Schloer** Institute of Systems Engineering, University of Hannover, Hannover, Germany

**Nizar Msadek** Systems and Networking Group, University of Augsburg, Augsburg, Germany

**Jeremy Pitt** Department of Electrical and Electronic Engineering, Imperial College London, London, UK

**Wolfgang Reif** Institute for Software and Systems Engineering, University of Augsburg, Augsburg, Germany

**Alexander Schiendorfer** Institute for Software and Systems Engineering, University of Augsburg, Augsburg, Germany

**Hella Seebach** Institute for Software and Systems Engineering, University of Augsburg, Augsburg, Germany

**Florian Siefert** Institute for Software and Systems Engineering, University of Augsburg, Augsburg, Germany

**Jan-Philipp Steghöfer** Department of Computer Science and Engineering, Chalmers University of Technology | University of Gothenburg, Gothenburg, Sweden

**Sven Tomforde** Organic Computing Group, University of Augsburg, Augsburg, Germany

**Theo Ungerer** Systems and Networking Group, University of Augsburg, Augsburg, Germany

**Michael Wißner** Human-Centered Multimedia, University of Augsburg, Augsburg, Germany

# Chapter 1
# The Social Concept of Trust as Enabler for Robustness in Open Self-Organising Systems

**Gerrit Anders, Hella Seebach, Jan-Philipp Steghöfer, Wolfgang Reif, Elisabeth André, Jörg Hähner, Christian Müller-Schloer, and Theo Ungerer**

**Abstract** The participants in open self-organising systems, including users and autonomous agents, operate in a highly uncertain environment in which the agents' benevolence cannot be assumed. One way to address this challenge is to use computational trust. By extending the notion of trust as a qualifier of relationships between agents and incorporating trust into the agents' decisions, they can cope with uncertainties stemming from unintentional as well as intentional misbehaviour. As a consequence, the system's robustness and efficiency increases. In this context, we show how an extended notion of trust can be used in the formation of system structures, algorithmically to mitigate uncertainties in task and resource allocation, and as a sanctioning and incentive mechanism. Beyond that, we outline how the

G. Anders (✉) • H. Seebach
Institute for Software and Systems Engineering, University of Augsburg, Augsburg, Germany
e-mail: anders@isse.de; seebach@isse.de

J.-P. Steghöfer
Department of Computer Science and Engineering, Chalmers University of Technology |
University of Gothenburg, Gothenburg, Sweden
e-mail: jan-philipp.steghofer@cse.gu.se

W. Reif
Institute for Software and Systems Engineering, University of Augsburg, Augsburg, Germany
e-mail: reif@isse.de

E. André
Human-Centered Multimedia, University of Augsburg, Augsburg, Germany
e-mail: elisabeth.andre@informatik.uni-augsburg.de

J. Hähner
Organic Computing Group, University of Augsburg, Augsburg, Germany
e-mail: jorg.hahner@informatik.uni-augsburg.de

C. Müller-Schloer
Institute of Systems Engineering, University of Hannover, Hannover, Germany
e-mail: cms@sra.uni-hannover.de

T. Ungerer
Systems and Networking Group, University of Augsburg, Augsburg, Germany
e-mail: theo.ungerer@informatik.uni-augsburg.de

© Springer International Publishing Switzerland 2016
W. Reif et al. (eds.), *Trustworthy Open Self-Organising Systems*,
Autonomic Systems, DOI 10.1007/978-3-319-29201-4_1

1

users' trust in a self-organising system can be increased, which is decisive for the acceptance of these systems.

**Keywords** Computational trust • Uncertainty • Self-organisation • Open MAS • Robustness

## 1.1 Trust as a Measure of Uncertainty in Open Self-Organising Systems

In open self-organising systems, different participants, such as autonomous agents, human users, and other systems, work together with a strong influence of the environment. These participants communicate and cooperate at runtime in unforeseeable ways and do not always follow the intent of the system designers. They can pursue different goals, and it cannot be assumed that they are intrinsically motivated to contribute towards a common system goal [1, 2]. Beyond that, a participant's behaviour can vary over time. As there is also limited knowledge about and control over the behaviour of the participants in the system, only weak assumptions about them can be made – in particular, we have to abandon assumptions of benevolence of the autonomous agents. The system participants therefore have to deal with both unintentional as well as intentional misbehaviour of others. This situation is aggravated by additional factors that increase uncertainties as they influence the system in unpredictable ways. These factors comprise the environment, other systems the agents interact with, or the users. Another form of openness often regarded in multi-agent systems (MAS) research is present when agents can arbitrarily enter and leave the system [3]. Especially in safety- or mission-critical domains, such as manufacturing or power management, these challenges have to be taken very seriously.

In this chapter, we argue that trust – as a measure of uncertainty – is a key concept for achieving robustness and efficiency in open self-organising systems. The classic notion of *computational trust* in the MAS community is focused on the credibility of agents, i.e. the degree to which they fulfil their commitments. This view stems mainly from psychological and sociological research [4] and boils down to the selection of interaction partners in order to maximise the utility of individual interactions. Economic [5, 6] and computer science [7, 8] literature characterise trust as instrumental to manage *expectations* about others. In computer science, the term "computational trust" is used to stress that the trust in a system or a system's part, such as an agent, is assessed by means of a well-defined metric. Since both (a part of) the system or a human being can act in the role of the trustor, we can differentiate between system-to-system and user-to-system trust. Often, a strong connection between trust and risk is emphasised [9] since interactions that incur a high risk for the participating agents require a high expectation of the others' willingness to contribute in a beneficial manner. An empirically justified expectation reduces the *uncertainty* about the behaviour of another agent [10]. In computing systems, this is often captured by a numerical *trust value* [11].

For these reasons, trust is an essential constituent of ensembles of cooperating agents, be they human or technical systems. Game-theoretical considerations show that trust can help to avoid getting trapped in the tragedy of the commons. Kantert et al. [12] provide such lines of thoughts in the context of Desktop Grid Computing. In general, trust induces a probability distribution over types of interaction partners of different trustworthiness in a Bayesian game. In this setting, agents have to choose their actions given probabilistic knowledge about each other's trustworthiness.

As mentioned above, we claim that trust is a key concept for achieving robustness. In this chapter, we define robustness in two dimensions. The first dimension of robustness addresses a system's ability to resist internal or external disturbances. Such disturbances result from (un)intentional misbehaving agents, for instance. A system exhibiting this type of robustness promises to remain in acceptable states and thus to maintain its functionality despite detrimental influences. The second dimension of robustness considers a system's ability to return into an acceptable state after a disturbance occurred that caused the system to leave the acceptance space. This type of robustness characterises a system's ability to restore its functionality. Consequently, the magnitude of disturbances the system can cope with (first dimension) and the duration of the deviation from acceptable states (second dimension) can be used to quantify the robustness. Both dimensions of robustness quantify the system's ability to fulfil its tasks. In contrast to a mere passive resistance, self-organising systems can actively increase their robustness by means of reactive or proactive measures. In open systems, these measures can be based on participants' trustworthiness, which allows the system to anticipate different sources of uncertainties.

In this chapter, we give an overview of the uses of computational trust (see Sect. 1.3) to deal with uncertainties arising in open self-organising systems. We show that these uses extend the classical use of selecting interaction partners and are based on the same life-cycle describing how trust values evolve over time (see Sect. 1.2). In detail, we demonstrate how trust models can be used to inform self-organisation processes (see Sect. 1.3.1); to optimise for critical or likely situations in uncertain environments (see Sect. 1.3.2); to sanction or incentivise agents in normative systems (see Sect. 1.3.3); and to represent the social relationships of the system's users (see Sect. 1.3.4). Section 1.4 concludes the chapter by emphasising that trust proves to be very useful to increase robustness and efficiency in open self-organising systems.

## 1.2  Computational Trust

Trust is usually measured as a numerical value, often normalised to values between 0 and 1. In [13], an agent's trust value is either very high or very low if the agent is either always expected to behave beneficially or never; if the value is between these extremes, the agent behaves in an unpredictable fashion and thus interactions with it are afflicted with a high uncertainty. Such a simple representation of trust is used

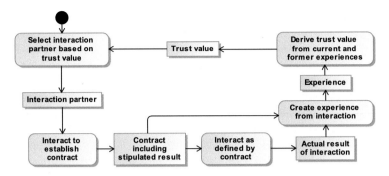

**Fig. 1.1** The life-cycle of trust values derived from experiences (adapted from [OCT3])

in many trust models (for an overview, see, e.g. [14]). However, numerous other interpretations and representations of trust exist. Anders et al. [OCT1], for instance, regard a trust value as an expected deviation from a prediction or promise. The lower an agent's trust value, the higher the expected deviation from its predictions or promises. A supplementary value, called *predictability*, quantifies the variance in the agent's behaviour and is used to indicate the certainty that the expected deviation actually occurs. Other representations based on more complex data structures (e.g. trust-based scenarios [OCT2] or elaborate reputation systems [15]) are able to capture further properties, such as time-dependent behaviour in the sense that an agent's behaviour depends on the time of day or that its behaviour depends on those it showed in previous time steps. Before discussing the general properties of trust, we illustrate the life-cycle of trust values which can be transferred to most of the other representations of trust.

*The Life-Cycle of Trust Values.* There is a general way of thinking about the origin of trust values that is independent of the way they are used (see Fig. 1.1). Two or more parties commit to a (potentially implicit) *contract* [16] that defines an *interaction* (possibly composed of several distinct steps) as well as its *stipulated result*. The *actual result* of the interaction can be compared to what was stipulated in the contract, thus yielding an *experience* for each party [17]. Ultimately, an agent uses its experiences and a trust metric to derive a *trust value* for each of its interaction partners. The trust values, in turn, inform future interactions.

Falcone et al. [18] criticised that many trust models are void of semantics of how the generated trust values have to be interpreted. It is, e.g. often not defined what a trust value of, say, 0.5 actually expresses or which trust value should be assigned to a new agent (the problem of *initial trust*, see, e.g. [19]). If a trust model has precise semantics, meaning a clearly defined way to interpret generated trust values, such an abstracting quantification can still be valid, though.

*Properties of Trust.* The life-cycle shows why trust values are *subjective*. As each agent makes its own experiences with others, it forms a personal opinion (i.e. a trust value) based on these unique experiences. Thus, the experiences of two agents with the same partner can vary tremendously. Additionally, agents can use different metrics to assess trust values and apply different requirements to the behaviour of others, thus implementing different trust models. The same arguments can be used to argue against *transitivity* of trust [20]. An exception are recommendations as a form of *indirect trust* or *reputation* (see discussion below) that have to be based on a mutual understanding of the valuation of an agent's behaviour.

Further, it is crucial to consider the *context* in which interactions occur. The context includes, e.g. the roles the agents play in the interaction, its contract, or environmental circumstances. Comparing experiences to each other in different contexts is difficult: You might trust your doctor to fix you, but not necessarily to fix your car. Falcone et al. [18] relate to context when they mention the "competence belief" an agent has about another. Competence is specific to a certain goal that the trusting agent believes the potential partner is capable to pursue. Agents that are deemed competent for one goal can be incompetent for another. Other authors use, e.g. "circumstance" [21] or "domain of interaction" [22] to denote context.

A trust value can also be supplemented by a measure of *confidence* [OCT4] or *certainty* [23, 24] that indicates the degree of certainty that a trust value describes the actual observable behaviour of an agent. Such an additional value can be based on several criteria, such as how many experiences were used for the calculation of the trust value, how old these experiences are, or how much the experiences differed. It is also possible to take the social relationships between the agents into account [25] or to distinguish short-term and long-term behaviour in order to identify changing behaviour. As with trust values themselves, the initialisation of confidence can be problematic. In human interactions, different trust dispositions are common where people approach newcomers differently and are willing to put more initial trust in them than others [26]. The experiences made by these trusting individuals can then be used by others to judge newcomers. Such a mechanism is especially useful during the exploratory phase after the start of a system [19].

*Reputation.* In open self-organising systems, interaction partners can change often, e.g. due to alterations in system structure or inclusion of new agents. Since the agents' benevolence cannot be assumed, they might not be willing to communicate their true intentions [27]. To deal with this situation, a reputation system can be used which combines the opinions of agents and generates recommendations [7]. This enables cooperation between agents that do not know or have only little experience with each other. To make adequate decisions, agents can rely on a combination of direct trust and reputation. To this end, several approaches [15, OCT5] propose to use confidence or similar metrics to dynamically weigh the influence of direct trust and reputation, e.g. depending on the number of direct experiences. Due to the subjective nature of trust and because agents might lie about the trustworthiness of others, it is often also desirable to weigh the impact a recommending agent, called *witness*, has on the reputation value. The *neighbour trust metric* [OCT6] as well as

*DTMAS* [28] propose to increase the influence of a witness with the similarity of the provided valuation to the one of the requesting agent. If the difference is too large, the witness can even be excluded from the calculation. This allows the system to deal with false reports. Further approaches that incentivise agents to provide truthful reports are discussed in Sect. 1.3.3. Providing reputation data can also be regarded as a special context in which witnesses are assessed according to the quality of their recommendations. In an even more fine-grained system, the context can also include information for which kind of interaction the recommendation is given. Whenever a reputation system is used, there has to be a consensus among the agents about the meaning of trust and reputation values. A common trust model can fulfil this purpose.

*Accountability, Deceit, and Collusion.* Open systems with little control over the agents are prone to exploitation from egoistic or malevolent agents. Therefore, special measures have to be taken to provide accountability of the agents and to prevent collusion. For an overview of attacks on trust and reputation management systems, see, e.g. [29]. Specific countermeasures are often system- or domain-specific, such as those presented for mobile ad-hoc networks in [30] or electronic markets in [31]. An important part of fraud prevention is a well-designed incentive system in combination with efficient monitoring facilities [32].

## 1.3   Different Uses of Trust in Open Self-Organising Systems

As discussed in Sect. 1.1, trust is traditionally used for selecting appropriate interaction partners. Bernard et al. [OCT7] call an agent's set of preferred interaction partners whose trust value is above a predefined threshold its *Implicit Trusted Community* (iTC). From the local view of a single agent, its interaction partners are selected through an implicit formation process. Note that this process is fully decentralised and thus not governed or controlled by an explicit authority. Because the agents do not coordinate their selections, the members of an iTC do not necessarily mutually trust each other. Yet this simple approach successfully excludes notoriously untrustworthy agents from most interactions.

In the following, we give an overview of four different uses of trust that extend this traditional use. First, we consider the trust-based formation of explicit organisations that allow large-scale open systems to deal with untrustworthy agents (see Sect. 1.3.1). Second, robust task and resource allocation promises to improve the system's stability and efficiency in uncertain environments (see Sect. 1.3.2). Third, uncertainties resulting from intentional misbehaviour can be reduced by means of appropriate incentives – employing trust as a sanctioning mechanism is one of several possibilities (see Sect. 1.3.3). Fourth, we outline measures how user trust in open environments can be increased (see Sect. 1.3.4).

## 1.3.1 Trust to Structure Large-Scale Open Systems

In essence, self-organisation enables a system to autonomously form and adapt a structure that supports its objectives under changing conditions. The main reasons for agents to form organisations are to achieve scalability and promote cooperation in order to accomplish their own or the system's goals [33]. While scalability is the result of the accompanying problem decomposition, cooperation is necessary due to the agents' limited resources and capabilities. There are a multitude of paradigms and algorithms for establishing organisations in literature, such as *teams* [33] and *coalition formation* [34]: While teams assume altruistic behaviour, coalition formation is used in systems consisting of self-interested and individually rational agents.

The participants of open systems might not only show self-interested behaviour but also lie about their capabilities, the utility of performing an action, etc. Consequently, the selection of suitable cooperation partners becomes even more important. Since suitable coalition structures depend on the agents' promised contributions, the system has to make sure that these promises are kept and all coalition members pursue a common goal. To this end, extensions of coalition formation incorporating trust into the agents' decisions have been presented in [35, 36]. In contrast to coalitions, *clans* [37] are long-lived. Given that cooperation is likely to be most beneficial and least uncertain with trustworthy agents, clans are groups of agents that mutually trust each other. A similar concept, called *Explicit Trusted Communities* (eTCs), for the domain of Desktop Grid Computing has been proposed in [OCT8]. The main difference to clans and coalitions is that each eTC is represented by an explicit manager which administrates memberships, deals with conflicts, and governs the participating agents with norms. By preferring interactions with trustworthy agents (or even restricting them to these agents), clans and eTCs incentivise untrustworthy agents to change their behaviour (see Sect. 1.3.3 for incentive mechanisms and norms). Ultimately, this procedure aims at a more efficient and robust system – at least with regard to the members of clans or eTCs. While these types of organisations are not necessarily limited to intentional misbehaviour, they assume that agents can be excluded from other parts of the system without jeopardising the overall system's stability and efficiency. This is why trustworthy agents can form exclusive groups.

However, there are situations in which untrustworthy agents can or should not be excluded from the system, e.g. if the system depends on their resources or if they can provide them in a particularly cost-efficient way. In power management systems, for instance, although the output of solar power plants is difficult to predict (their volatility is mirrored in low trust values), they should not be turned off because of their low-cost generation. If, in such a situation, scalability requires the agents to self-organise into subsystems, other types of organisations are needed to deal with untrustworthy agents. One possibility is the formation of *homogeneous partitionings* [OCT9] where organisations are as similar as possible with respect to certain criteria that have been identified as supporting the system's goals (including their mean trustworthiness). This idea is based on the assumption that a centralised system imposes an upper bound on the ratio between trustworthy and untrustworthy agents: Given the uncertainties introduced by untrustworthy agents, the centralised control over trustworthy agents allows the system to fulfil its task as well as possible. If all organisations exhibit similar characteristics with respect to the identified criteria, such as a similar ratio between trustworthy and untrustworthy agents, they approximate the corresponding ratio of the centralised system. Consequently, they also inherit its positive properties. Ideally, this results in an organisational structure in which each organisation can deal with its untrustworthy agents internally without affecting or involving other organisations. In such situations, homogeneous partitioning increases the system's robustness and efficiency, and should be preferred to organisations consisting of homogeneous agents. A similar goal has been pursued in [38] where agents mitigate uncertainties originating from unintentional misbehaviour by forming coalitions in a way that they cancel each other out.

## 1.3.2   Trust as a Basis for Robust Task or Resource Allocation

In many applications, a MAS has to solve a task or resource allocation problem in which a set of tasks is to be allocated to agents, or a set of the agents have to provide a certain amount of resources in order to satisfy a given demand [39]. Due to the agents' limited resources and knowledge, they usually have to cooperate in order to achieve the goal. In open systems, finding an adequate allocation is even more difficult since agents might not provide resources or fulfil the task as promised and the actual demand that has to be satisfied or the resources required to perform a task might not be known exactly beforehand. Both types of uncertainties can be attributed to unintentional or intentional misbehaviour of the system's participants or its environment [OCT1]. If the system's stability or efficiency hinges on how well the agents fulfil the tasks or meet the demand – e.g. think about the demand of electric load in a smart grid application – techniques for robust task or resource allocation have to be regarded. In general, the way a robust allocation can be obtained depends on the type of misbehaviour.

*Unintentional misbehaviour* is introduced by external forces, such as current weather conditions. While this type of misbehaviour cannot be actively reduced, trust can be used to quantify and anticipate the uncertainties [10]. Incorporating trust into the decision-making process allows the system to optimise for *expectations*, such as the expected probability of success [40]. In [OCT10, OCT11], a self-organising middleware incorporating a trust-aware load-balancing mechanism assigns important services to trustworthy nodes in order to increase the services' expected availability. Similarly, participants of a Desktop Grid Computing system delegate the calculation of jobs to trustworthy agents, i.e. to members of their eTC, to improve their expected outcome (see Sect. 1.3.1). If the *predictability* (cf. "confidence") of an agent's behaviour depends on its state, allocations can also be made in a way that promotes predictable behaviour [OCT1]. For highly volatile environments in which dependencies in a sequence of observed behaviour have to be captured, a more expressive trust model, called *Trust-Based Scenario Trees* (TBSTs), has been proposed in [OCT2]. Basically, each TBST represents an empirical probability mass function that approximates the observed stochastic process. In contrast to trust models that capture the expected uncertainty or its variation, a TBST holds multiple possible scenarios, each with a probability of occurrence, of how the uncertainty might develop over a sequence of time steps. As opposed to the concept of *scenario trees* as known from the domain of operations research [41], TBSTs make only few assumptions about the underlying stochastic process. Further, they have been developed with the purpose of being *learned online* by agents with possibly low computational power. Combined with the principle of *stochastic programming* [42], agents can obtain robust allocations dynamically at runtime.

*Intentional misbehaviour* can be ascribed to agents that lie about some private information needed to decide about an adequate allocation, such as the cost or probability of performing a task successfully [40, 43]. Contrary to unintentional misbehaviour, uncertainties originating from intentional misbehaviour can be avoided. The field of *mechanism design* [40] studies how a system has to work in order to *incentivise* its self-interested, strategic, and individually rational participants to tell the truth. Further details concerning this matter are discussed in the following section.

### 1.3.3  Trust as a Sanctioning and Incentive Mechanism

Employing the techniques of *mechanism design* (MD) can guarantee efficiency (maximisation of the agents' overall utility), individual rationality (the agents' utility of participating in the scheme is non-negative), and incentive compatibility (the agents are best off revealing their true type) [44]. The latter property is of particular interest in open systems when agents have to be incentivised to disclose their private information needed to make decisions. In other words, MD can be used to incentivise individually rational agents to behave benevolently, that is, to ensure their trustworthy behaviour. *Fault-Tolerant MD* [43] and *Trust-Based MD* [40] address the issue of agents that have a probability of failure – quantified by a trust value – when performing an assigned task. Both approaches investigate the problem that reasonable task allocations depend on truthfully reported trust values. While each agent calculates and reports its own trust value in Fault-Tolerant MD [43], reputation values stemming from subjective trust measurements are considered in Trust-Based MD [40]. The ideas of MD have been adopted in various market-based approaches in which pricing mechanisms prevent agents from gaming the system [38, 45]. Depending on the regarded problem, it is often hard to devise a proper mechanism guaranteeing incentive compatibility, though, especially in case of unintentional misbehaviour. In these cases, it is still possible to use penalty schemes to increase the agents' risk that providing false reports or promises that cannot be kept is detrimental to their utilities [44, OCT1]. Often, corresponding incentives can rely on the agents' trustworthiness. In electronic markets, trustworthy agents can obtain price premiums or price discounts [6]. In [OCT1], for instance, agents showing well-predictable behaviour can demand higher payments. Preferring trustworthy interaction partners or creating groups of trustworthy agents that benefit from a mutual increase in efficiency (cf. eTCs discussed in Sect. 1.3.1) also incentivises benevolent behaviour. These examples illustrate that trust in the sense of benevolent behaviour yields and, at the same time, embodies a form of *social capital* [46].

While the rules employed in these mechanisms are created at design time, open systems often have to be able to define, adjust, and implement behavioural guidelines in response to environmental and internal conditions at runtime. Such an adaptability is akin to Ostrom's principle of "congruence" that states that sustainable management of commons requires to "match rules governing use of common goods to local needs and conditions" [47]. While stemming from economic and sociological research, these Ostrom's principles have been recognised as the foundations for self-organising electronic institutions as well [48]. In *normative MAS* [49], *normative institutions* enact and enforce *norms* [50] to influence the agents' behaviour indirectly. Each norm describes a behavioural rule and a sanction that is imposed if the rule is not followed. A sanction might be punitive fines or a (temporary) reduction of the violator's reputation value. The latter type of sanction treats reputation in the sense of social capital such that its reduction incentivises trustworthy behaviour in the long run. If an agent did not violate a norm on purpose, if it compensates for the violation, or if the violation was inevitable, the institution might also abstain from a sanction, which introduces a form of *forgiveness* [51, 52]. Essentially, norms have to contribute to reaching the system's goal. In eTCs (see Sect. 1.3.1), managers take on the role of normative institutions. If a manager detects an attack, it defends its community by adjusting the set of norms, e.g. by regulating the delegation and the acceptance of jobs in case of a trust breakdown – a situation in which even the reputation of benevolent agents declines [OCT12]. To enforce norms, an institution must not only be able to react with sanctions but also to detect their violation. Since monitoring an agent's behaviour comes at a price, Edenhofer et al. [OCT13] proposed to couple the effort put into surveillance to the number of received accusations. Especially when regarding trust as the basis of delegation [18], norms can also be understood as social laws governing the delegation of institutional power [53]. In this case, norms represent explicit permissions that have to be acquired before a specific action may be performed.

### 1.3.4   Increasing User Trust in Open Environments

Beyond the use of trust to qualify the relationships between software agents (cf. system-to-system trust in Sect. 1.1), it can also be applied to describe the social relationships between the users and the system (cf. user-to-system trust). Recent advances in sensor technologies and context recognition enable us to capture the users' physical context continuously and to personalise information and services to them in real-time. Apart from simply providing information, context-aware systems can also allow users to manipulate or share data or even act autonomously on their behalf. Combined with advances in display and wireless technologies, users can employ these systems basically anytime and anywhere. While these so-called ubiquitous environments offer great benefits to users, they also raise a number of challenges. In particular, they might show a behaviour that negatively affects user trust. Examples include (1) highly dynamic situations where the rationale behind the system's actions is no longer apparent to the user [54], (2) implicit interactions through proxemic behaviour where the user no longer feels in control [55], or (3) privacy issues [56]. Hence, there is an enormous need for sophisticated trust management in ubiquitous environments in order to ensure that such environments will find acceptance among users.

While most work in the area of computational trust models aims to develop trust metrics that determine, on the basis of objective criteria, whether a system should be trusted or not, not much interest has been shown towards trust experienced by a user when interacting with a system. A system may be robust and secure, but nevertheless be perceived as not very trustworthy by a user, e.g. because its behaviour appears opaque or hard to control. Following the terminology by Castelfranchi and Falcone [57], a focus is put on the affective forms of trust that are based on the user's appraisal mechanisms. Therefore, the objective must be to develop a computational trust model that captures how a system – and more specifically a ubiquitous environment – is perceived by a user while interacting with it.

Many approaches found in literature aim to identify trust dimensions that influence the user's feeling of trust. This is an extension to the trust models as discussed in Sect. 1.2, even though facets of trust play a role in open self-organising systems as well [OCT14]. Trust dimensions that have been researched in the context of internet applications and e-commerce include reliability, dependability, honesty, truthfulness, security, competence, and timeliness, see, e.g. [58, 59]. Tschannen et al. [60], who are more interested in the sociological aspects of trust, introduce willing vulnerability, benevolence, reliability, competence, honesty, and openness as the constituting facets of trust, although their work does not focus on trust in software. Researchers working on adaptive user interfaces consider transparency as a major component of trust, see, e.g. [61]. Trust dimensions have formed the underlying basis of many conceptual models of trust. However, incorporating them into a computational model of trust is not a trivial task.

With the *User Trust Model* (UTM) [62], such a computational model of trust was introduced, along with a decision-theoretic approach to trust management for ubiquitous and self-adaptive environments. The UTM is based on Bayesian networks and, following ideas put forward by Yan et al. [63], assesses the users' trust in a system, monitors it over time, and applies appropriate system reactions to maintain users' trust in critical situations. In a smart office application, for example, the system could automatically switch off the lights because it senses that it is bright enough outside, but might actually decide against it if it assesses that such an action would have a negative impact on the user's trust due to a lack of control and transparency.

## 1.4   Conclusion

The potential of computational trust in open self-organising systems is substantial. As we outlined in this chapter, trust models can increase a system's fitness by providing a means to optimise for the most likely or most risky future states; they can decrease information asymmetry; they can be used in combination with sanctioning and incentive mechanisms in normative frameworks codifying behavioural guidelines; and they can enable the formation of a system structure supporting the functions of the system optimally. If trust models are used to represent the social relationships of a system's users [OCT15], the system can, for instance, even make robust decisions with regard to the users' privacy. The basic principles are the same for all of the uses shown here. They can all be applied on the basis of an understanding of trust that puts the concepts of interactions, contracts, and experiences at its core and is compatible with many trust models available in the literature.

In all cases, trust increases the efficiency and robustness of open self-organising systems by mitigating uncertainties originating from a system's unknown participants and the environment it is exposed to.

**Acknowledgements** This research is partly sponsored by the research unit *OC-Trust* (FOR 1085) of the German Research Foundation.

## References

1. Pasquier, P., Flores, R., Chaib-draa, B.: Modelling flexible social commitments and their enforcement. In: Gleizes, M.-P., Omicini, A., Zambonelli, F. (eds.) Engineering Societies in the Agents World V, vol. 3451, pp. 898–898. Springer, Berlin/Heidelberg (2005). ISBN:978-3-540-27330-1
2. Artikis, A., Pitt, J.: Specifying open agent systems: a survey. In: Artikis, A., Picard, G., Vercouter, L. (eds.) Engineering Societies in the Agents World IX, vol. 5485, pp. 29–45. Springer, Berlin/Heidelberg (2009). ISBN:978-3-642-02561-7
3. Cossentino, M., Gaud, N., Hilaire, V., Galland, S., Koukam, A.: ASPECS: an agent-oriented software process for engineering complex systems. Auton. Agents Multi-agent Syst. **20**, 260–304 (2010).
4. Boon, S., Holmes, J.: The dynamics of interpersonal trust: resolving uncertainty in the face of risk. In: Hinde, R., Groebel, J. (eds.) Cooperation and Prosocial Behaviour, pp. 190–211. Cambridge University Press, Cambridge (1991)
5. Rousseau, D., Sitkin, S., Burt, R., Camerer, C.: Not so different after all: a cross-discipline view of trust. Acad. Manag. Rev. **23**, 393–404 (1998)

6. Ba, S., Pavlou, P.: Evidence of the effect of trust building technology in electronic markets: price premiums and buyer behavior. MIS Q. **26**, 243–268 (2002)
7. Mui, L., Mohtashemi, M., Halberstadt, A.: A computational model of trust and reputation. In: Proceedings of the 35th Hawaii International Conference on System Sciences (HICSS'02), Big Island, pp. 188–196 (2002)
8. Corritore, C., Kracher, B., Wiedenbeck, S.: On-line trust: concepts, evolving themes, a model. Int. J. Hum.-Comput. Stud. **58,** 737–758 (2003)
9. Koller, M.: Risk as a determinant of trust. Basic Appl. Soc. Psychol. **9**, 265–276 (1988)
10. Ramchurn, S., Huynh, D., Jennings, N.: Trust in multi-agent systems. Knowl. Eng. Rev. **19**, 1–25 (2004)
11. Marsh, S.P.: Formalising trust as a computational concept. PhD thesis, University of Stirling Digital Repository (1994)
12. Kantert, J., Edenhofer, S., Tomforde, S., Hähner, J., Müller-Schloer, C.: Normative control – controlling open distributed systems with autonomous entities. In: Reif, W., Anders, G., Seebach, H., Steghöfer, J.-P., André, E., Hähner, J., Müller-Schloer, C., Ungerer, T. (eds.) Autonomic Systems, vol. 7, pp. 87–123 (2016)
13. Mayer, R.C., Davis, J.H., Schoorman, F.D.: An integrative model of organizational trust (English). Acad. Manag. Rev. **20**, 709–734 (1995). ISSN:03637425
14. Yu, H., Shen, Z., Leung, C., Miao, C., Lesser, V.: A survey of multi-agent trust management systems. IEEE Access **1**, 35–50 (2013)
15. Sabater, J., Sierra, C.: Social regret, a reputation model based on social relations. ACM SIGecom Exch. **3**, 44–56 (2001)
16. Ramchurn, S.D., Jennings, N.R., Sierra, C., Godo, L.: Devising a trust model for multiagent interactions using confidence and reputation. Appl. Artif. Intell. **18**, 833–852 (2004)
17. Jonker, C., Treur, J.: Formal analysis of models for the dynamics of trust based on experiences. In: Garijo, F., Boman, M. (eds.) Multi-agent System Engineering, vol. 1647, pp. 221–231. Springer, Berlin/Heidelberg (1999). ISBN:978-3-540-66281-5
18. Falcone, R., Castelfranchi, C.: Social trust: a cognitive approach. In: Castelfranchi, C., Tan, Y.-H. (eds.) Trust and Deception in Virtual Societies, pp. 55–90. Kluwer Academic, Norwell (2001). ISBN:0-7923-6919-X
19. McKnight, D., Cummings, L., Chervany, N.: Initial trust formation in new organizational relationships. Acad. Manag. Rev. **23**, 473–490 (1998)
20. Jøsang, A., Pope, S.: Semantic constraints for trust transitivity. In: Proceedings of the 2nd Asia-Pacific Conference on Conceptual Modelling, vol. 43, pp. 59–68. Australian Computer Society, Newcastle (2005). ISBN:1-920-68225-2
21. Good, D.: Individuals, interpersonal relations, and trust. In: Gambetta, D. (ed.) Trust: Making and Breaking Cooperative Relations, pp. 31–48. Department of Sociology, University of Oxford (2000)
22. Jones, K.: Trust as an affective attitude (English). Ethics **107**, 4–25 (1996). ISSN:00141704
23. He, R., Niu, J., Zhang, G.: CBTM: A trust model with uncertainty quantification and reasoning for pervasive computing. In: Pan, Y., Chen, D., Guo, M., Cao, J., Dongarra, J. (eds.) Parallel and Distributed Processing and Applications, pp. 541–552. Springer, Berlin/Heidelberg (2005). ISBN:978-3-540-29769-7
24. Wang, Y., Singh, M.P.: Formal trust model for multiagent systems. In: Proceedings of the 20th International Joint Conference on Artifical Intelligence, pp. 1551–1556. Morgan Kaufmann Publishers Inc., San Francisco (2007)
25. Kuter, U., Golbeck, J.: Using probabilistic confidence models for trust inference in web-based social networks. ACM Trans. Internet Technol. **10**, 8:1–8:23 (2010). ISSN:1533-5399
26. Marsh, S.: Optimism and pessimism in trust. In: In Proceedings of the Ibero-American Conference on Artificial Intelligence (IBERAMIA '94), Caracas. McGraw-Hill Publishing (1994)
27. Schillo, M., Funk, P., Rovatsos, M.: Using trust for detecting deceitful agents in artificial societies. Appl. Artif. Intell. **14**, 825–848 (2000)

28. Aref, A.M., Tran, T.T.: A decentralized trustworthiness estimation model for open, multiagent systems (DTMAS). J. Trust Manag. **2**, 1–20 (2015)
29. Jøsang, A.: Robustness of trust and reputation systems: does it matter? In: Proceedings of IFIPTM International Conference on Trust Management (IFIPTM 2012), Surat. Springer (2012)
30. Sun, Y., Han, Z., Liu, K.: Defense of trust management vulnerabilities in distributed networks. IEEE Commun. Mag. **46**, 112–119 (2008). ISSN:0163-6804
31. Yao, Y., Ruohomaa, S., Xu, F.: Addressing common vulnerabilities of reputation systems for electronic commerce. J. Theor. Appl. Electron. Commer. Res. **7**, 1–20 (2012)
32. Grossi, D., Aldewereld, H., Dignum, F.: Ubi Lex, Ibi Poena: designing norm enforcement in E-institutions. In: Noriega, P., Vázquez-Salceda, J., Boella, G., Boissier, O., Dignum, V., Fornara, N., Matson, E. (eds.) Coordination, Organizations, Institutions, and Norms in Agent Systems II, vol. 4386, pp. 101–114. Springer, Berlin/Heidelberg (2007). ISBN:978-3-540-74457-3
33. Horling, B., Lesser, V.: A survey of multi-agent organizational paradigms. Knowl. Eng. Rev. **19**, 281–316 (2004)
34. Shehory, O., Kraus, S.: Methods for task allocation via agent coalition formation. Artif. Intell. **101**, 165–200 (1998)
35. Breban, S., Vassileva, J.: Long-term coalitions for the electronic marketplace. In: Proceedings of the E-Commerce Applications Workshop at the Canadian AI Conference, Ottawa (2001)
36. Breban, S., Vassileva, J.: A coalition formation mechanism based on inter-agent trust relationships. In: Proceedings of the First International Joint Conference on Autonomous Agents and Multiagent Systems: Part 1, pp. 306–307. ACM, New York (2002). ISBN:1-58113-480-0
37. Griffiths, N., Luck, M.: Coalition formation through motivation and trust. In: Proceedings of the 2nd International Joint Conference on Autonomous Agents and Multiagent Systems, pp. 17–24. ACM, Melbourne (2003). ISBN:1-58113-683-8
38. Chalkiadakis, G., Robu, V., Kota, R., Rogers, A., Jennings, N.R.: Cooperatives of distributed energy resources for efficient virtual power plants. In: Proceedings of the 10th International Conference on Autonomous Agents and Multiagent Systems. International Foundation for Autonomous Agents and Multiagent Systems, Taipei, vol. 2, pp. 787–794 (2011). ISBN:0-9826571-6-1, 978-0-9826571-6-4
39. Chevaleyre, Y., Dunne, P.E., Endriss, U., Lang, J., Lemaître, M., Maudet, N., Padget, J., Phelps, S., Rodríguez-aguilar, J.A., Sousa, P.: Issues in multiagent resource allocation. Informatica **30**, 3–31 (2006)
40. Dash, R.K., Ramchurn, S.D., Jennings, N.R.: Trust-based mechanism design. In: Proceedings of the Third International Joint Conference on Autonomous Agents and Multiagent Systems, vol. 2, pp. 748–755. IEEE Computer Society, Washington, DC (2004)
41. Shapiro, A., Dentcheva, D., Ruszczyński, A.: Lectures on Stochastic Programming: Modeling and Theory. Society for Industrial and Applied Mathematics (SIAM), Philadelphia (2014)
42. Hentenryck, P.V., Bent, R.: Online Stochastic Combinatorial Optimization. MIT Press, Cambridge/London (2009)
43. Porter, R., Ronen, A., Shoham, Y., Tennenholtz, M.: Mechanism design with execution uncertainty. In: Proceedings of the Eighteenth Conference on Uncertainty in Artificial Intelligence, Edmonton, pp. 414–421 (2002)
44. Dash, R., Vytelingum, P., Rogers, A., David, E., Jennings, N.: Market-based task allocation mechanisms for limited-capacity suppliers. Syst. Man Cybern. Part A: IEEE Trans. Syst. Hum. **37**, 391–405 (2007)
45. Vytelingum, P., Voice, T., Ramchurn, S., Rogers, A., Jennings, N.: Agent-based micro-storage management for the smart grid. In: Proceedings of the 9th International Conference on Autonomous Agents and Multiagent Systems, Toronto, vol. 1, pp. 39–46 (2010)
46. Pitt, J., Nowak, A.: The reinvention of social capital for socio-technical systems [Special Section Introduction]. IEEE Technol. Soc. Mag. **33**, 27–80 (2014)
47. Ostrom, E.: Governing the Commons: The Evolution of Institutions for Collective Action. Cambridge University Press, Cambridge/New York (1990)

48. Pitt, J., Schaumeier, J., Artikis, A.: Axiomatization of socio-economic principles for self-organizing institutions: concepts, experiments and challenges. ACM Trans. Auton. Adapt. Syst. (TAAS) **7**, 39 (2012)
49. Boella, G., Pigozzi, G., van der Torre, L.: Normative systems in computer science – ten guidelines for normative multiagent systems. In: Boella, G., Noriega, P., Pigozzi, G., Verhagen, H. (eds.) Normative Multi-agent Systems. Schloss Dagstuhl, Leibniz-Zentrum fuer Informatik (2009)
50. Conte, R., Castelfranchi, C.: Norms as mental objects. From normative beliefs to normative goals. In: Castelfranchi, C., Müller, J.-P. (eds.) From Reaction to Cognition, vol. 957, pp. 186–196. Springer, Berlin/Heidelberg (1995). ISBN:978-3-540-60155-5
51. Vasalou, A., Pitt, J.: Reinventing forgiveness: a formal investigation of moral facilitation. In: Herrmann, P., Issarny, V., Shiu, S. (eds.) Trust Management, vol. 3477, pp. 39–90. Springer, Berlin/Heidelberg (2005). ISBN:978-3-540-26042-4
52. Marsh, S., Briggs, P.: Examining trust, forgiveness and regret as computational concepts. In: Golbeck, J. (ed.) Computing with Social Trust, pp. 9–43. Springer, London (2009). ISBN:978-1-84800-356-9
53. Artikis, A., Sergot, M., Pitt, J.: Specifying norm-governed computational societies. ACM Trans. Comput. Log. (TOCL) **10**, 1 (2009)
54. Rothrock, L., Koubek, R., Fuchs, F., Haas, M., Salvendy, G.: Review and reappraisal of adaptive interfaces: toward biologically inspired paradigms. Theor. Issues Ergon. Sci. **3**, 47–84 (2002)
55. Müller, J., Exeler, J., Buzeck, M., Krüger, A.: ReflectiveSigns: digital signs that adapt to audience attention. In: Proceedings of 7th International Conference on Pervasive Computing, pp. 17–24. Springer, Berlin/Heidelberg (2009)
56. Röcker, C., Hinske, S., Magerkurth, C.: Intelligent privacy support for large public displays. In: Proceedings of Human-Computer Interaction International 2007 (HCII'07). Beijing, China (2007)
57. Castelfranchi, C., Falcone, R.: Trust Theory: A Socio-Cognitive and Computational Model. Wiley, Hoboken (2010)
58. Grandison, T., Sloman, M.: A survey of trust in internet applications. IEEE Commun. Surv. Tutor. **3**, 2–16 (2000)
59. Kini, A., Choobineh, J.: Trust in electronic commerce: definition and theoretical considerations. Proc. Hawaii Int. Conf. Syst. Sci. **31**, 51–61 (1998)
60. Tschannen-Moran, M., Hoy, W.: A multidisciplinary analysis of the nature, meaning, and measurement of trust. Rev. Educ. Res. **70**, 547 (2000)
61. Glass, A., McGuinness, D.L., Wolverton, M.: Toward establishing trust in adaptive agents. In: Proceedings of the 13th International Conference on Intelligent User Interfaces (IUI '08), pp. 227–236. ACM, New York (2008)
62. Hammer, S., Wißner, M., André, E.: A user trust model for automatic decision-making in ubiquitous and self adaptive environments. In: Reif, W., Anders, G., Seebach, H., Steghöfer, J.-P., André, E., Hähner, J., Müller-Schloer, C., Ungerer, T. (eds.) Autonomic Systems, vol. 7, pp. 55–86 (2016)
63. Yan, Z., Holtmanns, S.: Computer Security Privacy and Politics: Current Issues, Challenges and Solutions, pp. 290–323. IGI Global. Hershey, USA (2008)

# References Originating from the OC-Trust Project

OCT1. Anders, G., Schiendorfer, A., Siefert, F., Steghöfer, J.-P., Reif, W.: Cooperative resource allocation in open systems of systems. ACM Trans. Auton. Adapt. Syst. **10**, 11:1–11:44 (2015)

OCT2. Anders, G., Siefert, F., Steghöfer, J.-P., Reif, W.: Trust-based scenarios – predicting future agent behavior in open self-organizing systems. In: Elmenreich, W., Dressler, F., Loreto, V. (eds.) Self-Organizing Systems, vol. 8221, pp. 90–102. Springer, Berlin/Heidelberg (2014). ISBN:978-3-642-54139-1

OCT3. Steghöfer, J.-P., Reif, W.: Die Guten, die Bösen und die Vertrauenswürdigen–Vertrauen im Organic Computing. Informatik-Spektrum **35**, 119–131 (2012) (in German)

OCT4. Kiefhaber, R., Anders, G., Siefert, F., Ungerer, T., Reif, W.: Confidence as a means to assess the accuracy of trust values. In: Proceedings of the 11th IEEE International Conference on Trust, Security and Privacy in Computing and Communications (TrustCom-2012), Liverpool, pp. 690–697. IEEE (2012)

OCT5. Kiefhaber, R., Jahr, R., Msadek, N., Ungerer, T.: Ranking of direct trust, confidence, and reputation in an abstract system with unreliable components. In: Ubiquitous Intelligence and Computing, 2013 IEEE 10th International Conference on and 10th International Conference on Autonomic and Trusted Computing (UIC/ATC), Sorrento Peninsula, Italy, pp. 388–395 (2013)

OCT6. Kiefhaber, R., Hammer, S., Savs, B., Schmitt, J., Roth, M., Kluge, F., Andre, E., Ungerer, T.: The neighbor-trust metric to measure reputation in organic computing systems. In: 2011 Fifth IEEE Conference on Self-Adaptive and Self-organizing Systems Workshops (SASOW), Ann Arbor, pp. 41–46 (2011)

OCT7. Bernard, Y., Klejnowski, L., Hähner, J., Müller-Schloer, C.: Towards trust in desktop grid systems. In: IEEE International Symposium on Cluster Computing and the Grid, pp. 637–642. IEEE Computer Society, Los Alamitos (2010). ISBN:978-0-7695-4039-9

OCT8. Klejnowski, L.: Trusted community: a novel multiagent organisation for open distributed systems. PhD thesis, Leibniz Universität Hannover (2014). http://edok01.tib.uni-hannover.de/edoks/e01dh11/668667427.pdf

OCT9. Anders, G., Siefert, F., Reif, W.: A Heuristic for Constrained Set Partitioning in the Light of Heterogeneous Objectives. In: Agents and Artificial Intelligence. LNAI. Lisbon, Portugal (2015)

OCT10. Msadek, N., Kiefhaber, R., Ungerer, T.: A trustworthy fault-tolerant and scalable self-configuration algorithm for organic computing systems. J. Syst. Archit. **61**(10), 511–519 (2015)

OCT11. Msadek, N., Kiefhaber, R., Ungerer, T.: Trustworthy self-optimization in organic computing environments. Architecture of Computing Systems – ARCS 2015, pp. 123–134. Porto, Portugal (2015)

OCT12. Kantert, J., Scharf, H., Edenhofer, S., Tomforde, S., Hähner, J., Müller-Schloer, C.: A graph analysis approach to detect attacks in multi-agent-systems at runtime. In: 2014 IEEE Eighth International Conference on Self-Adaptive and Self-Organizing Systems, pp. 80–89. IEEE, London (2014)

OCT13. Edenhofer, S., Stifter, C., Jänen, U., Kantert, J., Tomforde, S., Hähner, J., Müller-Schloer, C.: An accusation-based strategy to handle undesirable behaviour in multi-agent systems. In: 2015 IEEE Eighth International Conference on Autonomic Computing Workshops (ICACW). Grenoble, France (2015)

OCT14. Steghöfer, J.-P., Kiefhaber, R., Leichtenstern, K., Bernard, Y., Klejnowski, L., Reif, W., Ungerer, T., André, E., Hähner, J., Müller-Schloer, C.: Trustworthy organic computing systems: challenges and perspectives. In: Xie, B., Branke, J., Sadjadi, S., Zhang, D., Zhou, X. (eds.) Autonomic and Trusted Computing, vol. 6407, pp. 62–76. Springer, Berlin/Heidelberg (2010). ISBN:978-3-642-16575-7

OCT15. Kurdyukova, E., Bee, K., André, E.: Friend or foe? Relationship-based adaptation on public displays. In: Proceedings of the Second International Conference on Ambient Intelligence, pp. 228–237. Springer, Amsterdam (2011). ISBN:978-3-642-25166-5

# Chapter 2
# Specification and Design of Trust-Based Open Self-Organising Systems

Gerrit Anders, Florian Siefert, Alexander Schiendorfer, Hella Seebach,
Jan-Philipp Steghöfer, Benedikt Eberhardinger, Oliver Kosak,
and Wolfgang Reif

**Abstract** In open multi-agent systems, we can make only little assumptions about the system's scale, the behaviour of participating agents, and its environment. Especially with regard to mission-critical systems, the ability to deal with a large number of heterogeneous agents that are exposed to an uncertain environment becomes a major concern: Because failures can have massive consequences for people, industries, and public services, it is of utmost importance that such systems achieve their goals under all circumstances. A prominent example are power management systems whose paramount goal is to balance production and consumption. In this context, we tackle challenges comprising how to specify and design these systems to allow for their efficient and robust operation. Among other things, we introduce constraint-based specification techniques to address the system's heterogeneity and show trust models that allow to measure, anticipate, and deal with uncertainties. On this basis, we present algorithms for self-organisation and self-optimisation that enable the formation of scalable system structures at runtime and allow for efficient and robust resource allocation under adverse conditions. Throughout the chapter, the problem of balancing production and consumption in decentralised autonomous power management systems serves as a case study.

G. Anders (✉) • H. Seebach
Institute for Software and Systems Engineering, University of Augsburg, Augsburg, Germany
e-mail: anders@isse.de; seebach@isse.de

F. Siefert • A. Schiendorfer • B. Eberhardinger • O. Kosak
Institute for Software and Systems Engineering, University of Augsburg, Augsburg, Germany
e-mail: siefert@isse.de; schiendorfer@isse.de; eberhardinger@isse.de; kosak@isse.de

J.-P. Steghöfer
Department of Computer Science and Engineering, Chalmers University of Technology |
University of Gothenburg, Gothenburg, Sweden
e-mail: jan-philipp.steghofer@cse.gu.se

W. Reif
Institute for Software and Systems Engineering, University of Augsburg, Augsburg, Germany
e-mail: reif@isse.de

© Springer International Publishing Switzerland 2016                                                       17
W. Reif et al. (eds.), *Trustworthy Open Self-Organising Systems*,
Autonomic Systems, DOI 10.1007/978-3-319-29201-4_2

**Keywords** Open MAS • Self-organisation • Robust optimisation • Trust models • Constraint optimisation • Resource allocation

## 2.1 Open Systems: From Correctness to Optimality

Self-organising systems are mainly investigated due to their increased flexibility and robustness to failures which allows them to cope with a wide range of circumstances. Instead of having human operators dealing constantly with ongoing issues, the ability to restore a valid state is implemented in self-* algorithms. A paramount goal is the increased productivity of a variety of systems, such as adaptive production cells, many-core systems, or learning robots [1]. Applications that have been regarded in this context target a rather closed setting with a manageable number of components known to designers, making their analysis feasible [2] by extensive simulation or mathematical tools – albeit at possibly high efforts.

First attempts at a software engineering methodology tailored to self-organising systems focused on specifying valid and invalid states and explicitly modelling the adaptive aspects added to the conventional system. In the *Restore Invariant Approach* [3], an invariant (a logical formula), separates invalid from valid states, i.e. those inside the *corridor of correct behaviour* (see Fig. 2.1a). Structurally, the invariant is a conjunction of constraints that have to be satisfied by the system variable assignment induced by a state. For instance, having a robot assigned to a role "drilling" presupposes that a functioning driller is available to it. Should the driller break (invalidating the current assignment), a reorganisation aiming for another valid role assignment is initiated to guide the system back into the corridor. A governing idea is that the system delivers its *correct* functionality as long as the invariant over the individual participants and the organisational structure (i.e. the communication and collaboration networks) holds. In case of software or hardware failures of individual components, the organisational structure and software agents

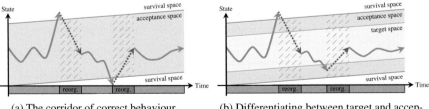

(a) The corridor of correct behaviour.            (b) Differentiating between target and acceptance space (adapted from [4]).

**Fig. 2.1** Once a violation of the corridor of correct behaviour is detected, the system triggers a reorganisation that re-establishes compliance with the invariant (see (**a**)). Refining the corridor by means of a target space allows the system to preserve its efficiency by triggering a reorganisation before it leaves the acceptance space (cf. the second reorganisation in (**b**)). In this case, reorganisations aim at bringing the system back into an optimal state

adapt to keep the system working. In fact, this architecture enables proving some properties about the correctness of the obtained system. Similarly, [4] proposed a distinction of states into the *acceptance space* (correct states, e.g. feasible role assignments), the *target space* (optimal states, e.g. throughput-maximising role assignments), and the *dead space* for irreversibly faulty states (e.g. a necessary tool is no longer available). See Fig. 2.1b for an illustration. Both views follow a rather *reactive* paradigm.

Some interesting application areas for self-organisation principles, however, call for extending this view to *open* systems [5] in which individual software agents are assumed to be programmed by different (and possibly competitive) developers. A prominent example is given by distributed power management systems in which energy producers and consumers have to work together to keep supply and demand in balance at low overall costs and resource usage, e.g. fossil fuels. A very dynamic environment results from the interactions of possibly volatile heterogeneous participants as well as other stochastic influences including weather and consumer behaviour. These characteristics give rise to uncertainties that manifest in the form of deviations between promised and actual supply or demand. The stable operation of such mission-critical supply systems becomes a major concern because failure can have massive consequences for people, industries, and public services. Consequently, the approved reactive approaches to self-organisation mentioned above would lead to extraordinarily high reorganisation costs since they can only perform control actions after the system detects that it is in a bad state.

When moving from closed self-organising systems to open ones in more dynamic environments, the notion of correctness in the momentary state fades out. Instead, *proactive* actions have to be made in pursuit of satisfactory future states. Otherwise, the system might not react fast enough to disturbances or do so at very high cost. Pictorially speaking, we thus aim to keep the system in a state far away from its acceptance boundaries to anticipate possible future violations of an invariant early enough. Changes caused by the more dynamic and volatile environment are also more likely to invalidate current configurations without the system adapting its structure. In such situations, the system is passively "moved out of the corridor", so to speak. In terms of [4], we aim at *weakly robust* systems, i.e. systems that, once being in the target space, cannot be forced to leave the acceptance space by external disturbances. Clearly, this cannot be achieved by putting the system in an arbitrary valid state. Instead, the system now has to solve multiple interconnected optimisation problems (e.g. finding optimal system structures or optimally scheduling control actions) in order to find states that allow it to deal with a wide range of disturbances.

These challenges imposed by the system class necessarily lead to a shift from correctness to *optimisation* that has to be built into the design of open self-organising systems. In this chapter, we address these challenges based on a vision of self-organised and robust resource allocation in large-scale open technical systems (see Sect. 2.2). To be able to find adequate allocations, detailed agent models in terms of their controllability are required (see Sect. 2.3). To deal with uncertainties when solving the resource allocation problem and to increase the system's robustness, we devise predictive models of the agents' possibly deviating behaviour and integrate them with robust optimisation techniques (see Sect. 2.4). Due to the systems' large scale, there is also a need for adequate organisational structures supporting the system's stability (see Sect. 2.5). In all these aspects, the concept of *computational trust* [5] serves as a common denominator to quantify and anticipate uncertainties. Throughout the chapter, we illustrate our findings by means of a case study from the field of decentralised autonomous power management systems. While developing the power management system and through analysis of several other open self-organising systems, we gained a lot of insights into the difficulties of engineering such systems. To make these insights accessible to a broader community, we embedded them in a methodology for the principled design of open self-organising systems. More details concerning this **P**rocess for **o**pen **s**elf-**o**rganising **M**ulti-**A**gent **S**ystems (PosoMAS) [6] are available online.[1]

## 2.2 Vision: Self-Organised and Robust Resource Allocation in Open Technical Systems

An important representative of open systems influencing our daily life is the class of supply systems. Systems of this class have in common that their task is to solve a *resource allocation problem* (RAP). That is, their goal is to stipulate the *supply*, i.e. the contribution, of the system components in a way that their sum satisfies a given *demand* that is imposed by the environment or other components in the system. Neither surplus nor shortage is desirable and, often, even feasible without risking to damage the system's infrastructure. In gas pipeline and water supply systems, for instance, the challenge is to maintain the system's pressure at a certain level [7, 8]. Regarding district heating systems, the network temperature has to be kept between specific bounds [9].

Similarly, the main task in power management systems (PMSs) is to maintain the balance between power production and consumption at all times [10]. This problem is an instance of a *one-good RAP without externalities* [11] in which the RAP's demand corresponds to the so-called *residual load*. The residual load is defined as the difference between the overall non-dispatchable load (the term "non-dispatchable" refers to load and supply that cannot be controlled) and the accumulated output of non-dispatchable power plants (see Fig. 2.2).[2] In other words, it is the fraction of the overall non-dispatchable load that has to be fulfilled by dispatchable prosumers (we use the term "prosumer" to refer to producers as well as consumers). Consequently, the goal is to find an allocation of the individual dispatchable prosumers' contributions such that, in each time step $t$, their sum

---

[1] http://posomas.isse.de

[2] Note that we specify the output of non-dispatchable power plants to be part of the system's demand. That is because their supply cannot be controlled.

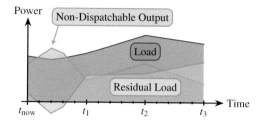

**Fig. 2.2** The residual load is the difference between the overall non-dispatchable load and the overall output of non-dispatchable power plants. It has to be satisfied by the dispatchable power plants and the dispatchable consumers. Note that the residual load is negative if the non-dispatchable output exceeds the non-dispatchable load

matches the residual load as accurately as possible. While the satisfaction of the residual load is paramount, this goal should be achieved at minimal costs.

An important characteristic of PMSs is that it is not feasible to hold the balance between power production and consumption by only reactively adapting the supply of dispatchable prosumers. This is due to heterogeneous types of inertia, such as limits in ramping up and down. Most types of power plants are specialised to take on specific tasks: Peaking power plants like gas turbines, for instance, are able to adjust their output very quickly but cause high costs. On the other hand, base load power plants, such as coal power plants, are designed for operating very efficiently in specific output ranges but their cold and hot start-up behaviour as well as minimal and maximal up-times become additional decisive factors for control actions.

Hence, to take account of the different types of inertia, the contribution of dispatchable prosumers has to be specified *proactively* in the form of *schedules* for a fixed time span $H$ in advance. This means that schedules are created on the basis of *predictions* of the future residual load. A recalculation of the schedules is needed at least after the time span $H$ elapsed since the last schedule creation. For each schedule creation, the time span $H$ defines a so-called *scheduling window* $\mathcal{W} = \{t_{now} + i \cdot \Delta\tau \leq t_{now} + H \mid i \in \mathbb{N}_{\geq 1}\}$ that, depending on the *schedule resolution* $\Delta\tau$ (defined as a multiple of the difference $\Delta t$ between two successive time steps $t$ and $t+1$), comprises $N = H/\Delta\tau$ time steps. Consequently, the system's success in solving the RAP (in terms of balancing supply and demand) depends on its success in solving a *scheduling problem*. In PMSs, this problem is also known as *economic load dispatch* [12] or *unit commitment* [13]. The idea of satisfying the residual load by repeated schedule creation follows the principle of receding horizon control [14], which is illustrated in Fig. 2.3. Solving the scheduling problem introduces two central and interconnected challenges:

1. **Scalability:** Solving the scheduling problem is NP-hard [15]; both with regard to the number $|\mathscr{D}|$ of dispatchable prosumers involved and time steps $N$ schedules

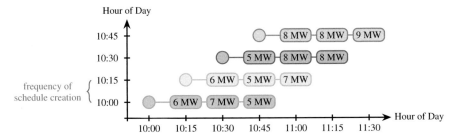

**Fig. 2.3** Schedules stipulate the dispatchable prosumers' output on the basis of residual load predictions (cf. the numbers in the boxes) for a specific time span in advance. Here, schedules cover a time span of $H = 45$ min and are created with a resolution of $\Delta\tau = 15$ min. Hence, each schedule comprises $N = 3$ time steps. At 10:00, for instance, schedules are created for the scheduling window $\mathscr{W} = \{10:15, 10:30, 10:45\}$. As predictions become more accurate as a future point in time approaches, schedules are periodically revised (here, every 15 min). Each schedule creation is depicted in a different colour

are created for in advance.[3] We therefore have to assume a worst-case complexity of $O\left(2^{|\mathscr{D}|\cdot N}\right)$.

2. **Uncertainty:** The dispatchable prosumers have to fulfil the residual load in spite of erroneous predictions of its development. Fluctuations in the residual load originate from changing weather conditions and stochastic consumer behaviour, among others. As for unexpected events, dispatchable prosumers might not be able to comply with their schedules in the light of technical difficulties. In terms of the RAP, uncertainties manifest in the form of deviations between actual and predicted demand, as well as deviations between actual and scheduled supply.

With regard to scalability, a too fine-grained schedule resolution $\Delta\tau$, which unnecessarily increases the number of time steps $N$ in $\mathscr{W}$, should be avoided due to the exponent $N$ in the scheduling problem's computational complexity. In the synchronous grid of Continental Europe, for instance, schedules are typically created with a resolution of $\Delta\tau = 15$ min (see Fig. 2.3), whereas imbalances have to be detected and compensated for within seconds (e.g. $\Delta t = 3$ s) to ensure the grid's stable operation [10]. At the same time, a too fine-grained schedule resolution is not useful because, given that residual load predictions tend to become more accurate as a future point in time approaches, uncertainties require that schedules are periodically revised at runtime.

For many years, PMSs consisted of relatively few and well-predictable power suppliers that faced a large number of pure power consumers. The deregulation of the electricity market as well as climate protection goals have been just a few of various driving forces changing this situation. Nowadays, the wide-spread installation

---

[3]Since dispatchable prosumers show discrete modes of operation (e.g. on/off), the knapsack problem (i.e. choosing which prosumers should contribute at all) can be seen as a special case of the scheduling problem.

of weather-dependent power plants as well as the advent of new consumer types, such as electric vehicles, put a lot of strain on power grids [16]. Additionally, small dispatchable power plants (e.g. biogas plants) owned by individuals or cooperatives feed in power without external control. To save expenses, gain more flexibility, and deal with uncertainties, future *autonomous* PMSs have to take advantage of the full potential of dispatchable prosumers by incorporating them into the scheduling scheme. Especially, the ability to deal with uncertainties introduced by non-dispatchable prosumers becomes a major concern. Although the output of weather-dependent power plants is difficult to predict, simply turning them off is not feasible because the system might depend on their resources at on-peak hours and benefits from their low-cost generation. Utilising the output of renewable energy sources is further incentivised by legal regulations, such as the German Renewable Energy Act.[4] To ensure the system's stable and efficient operation, uncertainties therefore have to be anticipated when creating schedules and compensated for locally to prevent their propagation through the system.

A natural approach to designing autonomous PMSs is to represent each prosumer by a software agent that is able to proactively participate in the creation of schedules and in maintaining the stability of the grid. In [17], we presented the concept of *Autonomous Virtual Power Plants* (AVPPs) as an approach to meet the challenges of future PMSs. AVPPs represent self-organising groups of two or more power plants of various types. Each AVPP has to satisfy a fraction of the overall residual load by periodically calculating schedules for its dispatchable power plants. The overall residual load is the sum of the AVPPs' *local demand*, i.e. local residual load. An AVPP's local demand originates from its non-dispatchable prosumers. Depending on its composition, its local demand is either positive or negative.[5] To avoid affecting other parts of the system, each AVPP's dispatchable power plants have to reactively compensate for deviations resulting from fluctuations of the uncertain local demand.

To cope with the vast number of dispatchable power plants, we proposed a self-organising *hierarchical* structure of AVPPs that decomposes the overall set of dispatchable and non-dispatchable power plants $\mathscr{A}$ into several hierarchically arranged AVPPs (see Fig. 2.4). In this hierarchical environment, each AVPP acts as an *intermediary* $\lambda \in \mathscr{I}$ between its superior AVPP and its subordinate[6] power plants $\mathscr{A}_\lambda \subset \mathscr{A}$. Since an intermediary $\lambda$ represents the subsystem $\mathscr{A}_\lambda$, it can be viewed and treated as one large (dispatchable) power plant that subsumes the behaviour of its collective (thus $\mathscr{I} \subset \mathscr{D} \subseteq \mathscr{A}$). As the hierarchy constitutes a tree, the sets of subordinate power plants are pairwise disjoint. We refer to the root of the hierarchy as the top-level intermediary/AVPP $\Lambda \in \mathscr{I}$.

In this hierarchical system structure, AVPPs autonomously create schedules in a regionalised and top-down manner, meaning that each AVPP redistributes its

---

[4]http://www.gesetze-im-internet.de/eeg_2014/index.html

[5]An AVPP's local residual load is negative, for instance, if its local environment only consists of photovoltaics, leading to a surplus of production.

[6]"Subordinate" power plants are those an AVPP is *directly* responsible for, i.e. those on its next lower level in the hierarchy.

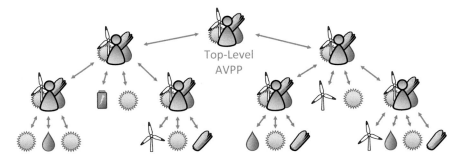

**Fig. 2.4** Hierarchical system structure of a future autonomous and decentralised power management system: Power plants are structured into systems of systems represented by AVPPs that act as intermediaries to decrease the complexity of control and scheduling. AVPPs can be part of other AVPPs. The left child of the top-level AVPP, for instance, controls a solar power plant, a storage battery, and two subordinate AVPPs

own assigned demand to its subordinate dispatchable power plants $\mathscr{D}_\lambda \subseteq \mathscr{A}_\lambda$ (note that these might contain subordinate AVPPs). Even in such a *regio-central approach* where AVPPs *assign* schedules to subordinates, the complexity of solving the scheduling problem is reduced because each AVPP controls only a subset of all dispatchable power plants (recalling the complexity $O\left(2^{|\mathscr{D}|\cdot N}\right)$, AVPPs thus have to deal with smaller exponents $|\mathscr{D}_\lambda|$ instead of $|\mathscr{D}|$). Assuming perfect parallelisation, the time needed to solve the overall scheduling problem is the maximum of the aggregated scheduling times of each branch in the hierarchy. Given an adequate hierarchical structure, this results in shorter scheduling times for the overall system in comparison to a centralised approach. While hierarchical problem decomposition has been proposed as a generic approach to deal with large-scale systems prohibiting a centralised solution [18, 19], our self-organising hierarchy of AVPPs is a means to *autonomously* decompose the scheduling problem *at runtime*. This allows the AVPPs to adapt their organisational structure in response to changes in the environment or the agents' internal state, and thereby to maintain an appropriate compromise between solution quality and runtime performance.

Such a setting imposes several challenges we address in the remainder of this chapter: (1) To ensure that schedules comply with the physical capabilities of heterogeneous power plants, the dynamic behaviour of dispatchable power plants has to be specified in the form of *control models* (see Sect. 2.3.1). (2) To reduce the complexity of creating schedules on higher levels in the hierarchy, the control models of AVPPs have to be abstracted (see Sect. 2.3.2). (3) To take account of the individual preferences of physical prosumers and organisations, their preferences have to be specified and incorporated into the schedule creation (see Sect. 2.3.3). (4) To quantify and anticipate uncertainties stemming from different sources, the AVPPs have to create predictive models of their subordinate prosumers (see Sect. 2.4.1). In our approach, we use the social concept of trust as a metaphor to measure the accuracy of predicted demand and scheduled supply. A prosumer's trustworthiness is the higher, the more it complies with its predictions or promises. (5) To promote the system's robustness, the scheduling problem has to be devised in a way that incorporates anticipated uncertainties and allows for reactive compensations for deviations at runtime (see Sect. 2.4.2). (6) To obtain robust schedules in large systems, appropriate heuristics have to be employed (see Sect. 2.4.3). Since they can provide high-quality schedules in shorter time than the regio-central approach sketched in this section, they allow for more frequent updates of the schedules. (7) To promote both stability as well as efficiency, new types of organisations have to be considered when forming AVPPs (see Sect. 2.5.1). (8) To create and maintain such structures at runtime, new self-organisation algorithms have to be developed (see Sect. 2.5.2). (9) To establish hierarchical structures that feature an appropriate trade-off between scheduling times, system stability, and efficiency, the system has to trigger the right control actions at the right time (see Sect. 2.5.3).

While we focus on power generation in this chapter, both dispatchable and non-dispatchable power consumers can easily be integrated into our concept of AVPPs and the techniques we present in this chapter.

## 2.3  Dynamic Creation of Compositional Control Models and Preference Specification

As mentioned before, power plants modelled as agents exhibit heterogeneous physical behaviour that restricts valid ways to control them. Some are subject to minimal start-up times, others may need to run for a minimal number of time steps once they are on. All are bounded by their maximum output. In Sect. 2.3.1, we discuss how to specify control models that capture typical heterogeneities faced in our case study in order to be able to calculate feasible schedules. Moreover, in our proposed self-organising hierarchy, an intermediary $\lambda$ acts on behalf of its subordinate agents $\mathscr{A}_\lambda$. Since $\lambda$ will itself get assigned a schedule *before* it re-assigns that schedule to its subordinates, the *joint* capabilities of the agents $\mathscr{A}_\lambda$ need to be described adequately. Only considering the Cartesian product of the agents will inevitably lead to a fully centralised, highly complex optimisation problem at the top level. Therefore, we propose some techniques to calculate abstracted models of a set of agents at runtime in Sect. 2.3.2. Besides mere physical restrictions, we also aim for a language that captures *preferences*, i.e. optional yet desirable properties of schedules. For instance, a power plant could specify to preferably be operated in a certain economically good range. Section 2.3.3 illustrates these considerations.

Moreover, these models form the deterministic basis of the more elaborate, uncertainty-aware scheduling problem discussed in Sect. 2.4. As such, they are intended to comply with existing *constraint-based* technology, i.e. constraint programming and mixed integer programming [20].

## 2.3.1   Specifying Optimisation Problems Using Control Models

In designing control models, we search for a layer of abstraction that is flexible enough to capture commonly occurred prosumers yet specific enough to be of use to generate code in a modelling language amenable to optimisation solvers.

For illustration, consider two power plants $a$ and $b$ where $b$ has to run at least two time steps, once it is switched on but $a$ does not show that physical limitation. Both are constrained by minimal and maximal production when on and constant maximal rate of change. For illustration, assume $a$ may provide between two and five units if it is on (written as the closed interval $[2,5]$), zero if it is off, and may change the contribution only by one unit in one time step. In [21], we introduced *supply automata* as a formalism to describe feasible trajectories and generate optimisation model code in the *optimization programming language* (OPL) [22]. Supply automata capture guarded transitions between *modes* (e.g. on or off) and integer- or real-valued state variables (e.g. contribution or up-time). Consideration of a real-valued *supply* variable $S$ is mandatory. Figure 2.5 illustrates the idea on the previous example regarding power plant $b$. Each system participant specifies its control model as a supply automaton.

This formalism allows for a clear description of the possible physical behaviour due to inertia and gives an operational view that is useful for simulation and testing of the control models. In terms of constraint models for discrete optimisation solvers, however, the only primitives are decision variables, parameters, and constraints, i.e. relations that specify consistent variable assignments. We thus need to move to a *declarative* view of the feasible trajectories. It is straightforward to "flatten" an automaton-based specification to a constraint model, as was done in [21].

To illustrate some of the complications incurred when sticking to a conventional, parametrised constraint model, we sketch the flattening steps for the minimal up-time constraint that could be generated from Fig. 2.5. Assuming that decision variables for the supply at time $t$, $S_b[t]$ exist, we need additional decision variables for bookkeeping. We use a boolean variable $\text{isOn}_b[t]$ to store whether $b$ is on.

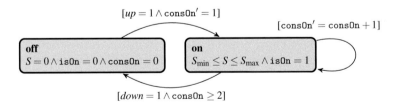

**Fig. 2.5** Supply automaton to model a minimal up-time of 2 for agent $b$. A local variable $\text{isOn}$ is constrained according to the modes of the automaton. Another local variable $\text{consOn}_b[t]$ counts the number of consecutive time steps $b$ is on. Switching from on to off is only possible if $\text{consOn}_b[t] \geq 2$. Expressions in brackets denote jump predicates, invariants are inside the modes, and primed variables indicate values after a transition

Assume for the sake of this example that $\mathrm{isOn}_b[t] \leftrightarrow S_b[t] > 0$ holds. We then define an additional variable $\mathrm{consOn}_b[t]$ for the number of consecutive time steps a plant is on. These variables are constrained with a case distinction:

$$\neg\mathrm{isOn}_b[t] \wedge \mathrm{isOn}_b[t+1] \rightarrow \mathrm{consOn}_b[t] = 0 \wedge \mathrm{consOn}_b[t+1] = 1 \qquad (2.1)$$

$$\mathrm{isOn}_b[t] \wedge \mathrm{isOn}_b[t+1] \rightarrow \mathrm{consOn}_b[t+1] = \mathrm{consOn}_b[t] + 1 \qquad (2.2)$$

$$\mathrm{isOn}_b[t] \wedge \neg\mathrm{isOn}_b[t+1] \rightarrow \mathrm{consOn}_b[t+1] = 0 \qquad (2.3)$$

$$\neg\mathrm{isOn}_b[t] \wedge \neg\mathrm{isOn}_b[t+1] \rightarrow \mathrm{consOn}_b[t] = 0 \wedge \mathrm{consOn}_b[t+1] = 0 \qquad (2.4)$$

One can write this more succinctly by noting that $\mathrm{consOn}_b[t] = 0 \leftrightarrow \neg\mathrm{isOn}_b[t]$ holds, simplifying (2.1), (2.3), and (2.4). For clarity, we used the verbose formulation. These variables allow us to to specify the minimal up-time:

$$\mathrm{isOn}_b[t] \wedge \neg\mathrm{isOn}_b[t+1] \rightarrow \mathrm{consOn}_b[t] \geq 2 \qquad (2.5)$$

However, these constraints do not matter for power plant $a$ which has no minimal up-time. The conventional, parameterised approach in modelling languages would require adding the decision variables $\mathrm{isOn}_a[t]$ and $\mathrm{consOn}_a[t]$ to our constraint model. The constraints (2.1), (2.2), (2.3), and (2.4) would still have to be managed for $a$ even if (2.5) is ignored. This unnecessarily increases the constraint model leading to possibly higher solving efforts. Consider, e.g. an optimisation problem intended to schedule 10 plants for 4 time steps, as faced by an AVPP and assume that only 3 of them are of type $b$. Due to the minimal up-time constraint, $3 \times 2 \times 4 = 24$ additional boolean variables have to be introduced. Simply adding $\mathrm{isOn}_a[t]$ and $\mathrm{consOn}_a[t]$ for all 10 agents leads to $10 \times 2 \times 4 = 80$ Booleans. Hence, 56 superfluous variables are added. More severely, in a propagation-based solver, we also add at least 56 unnecessary constraint propagators to keep $\mathrm{isOn}_a[t]$ and $\mathrm{consOn}_a[t]$ consistent.

Clearly, stating these and more involved inertia constraints directly in a modelling language is prone to errors (consider, e.g. forgetting case (2.4)). We therefore move these tedious yet straightforward "flattening" tasks to a code generator and have modellers focus on the system they are trying to describe.

### 2.3.2 Model Abstraction: Dynamic Creation of Compositional Control Models

Once control models are specified as supply automata for physical power plants, we need to address the task of describing the *composite* behaviour for the intermediary. We obtain a precise model of the joint contributions by taking the Cartesian product of several automata, leading to a fully centralised top level optimisation, as mentioned before. Instead, for the sake of scalability, we can choose to sacrifice exact optimality by using abstracted models of collectives, i.e. an intermediary $\lambda$ abstracts all models of $\mathscr{A}_\lambda$ to a single one. Coarse decisions about schedules at a higher level are based on these abstracted models and get refined when the assigned residual load is redistributed. The goal of abstraction is to find composite supply automata that are comparable in calculation efforts to those of physical plants but represent a whole collective instead. We presented algorithms to calculate these abstractions in [21, 23, 24] and revisit the core concepts.

More specifically, we need to calculate the states and transitions of a composite automaton. First, the joint space of feasible contributions has to be found as they represent the *states*. Since each mode constrains feasible contributions according to its invariant (e.g. a positive minimal contribution if the plant is on), we have to combine all possible modes. Consider again the two plants $a$ and $b$ which both can be turned off but contribute in the intervals $[2, 5]$ and $[8, 15]$, respectively, if they are on. For the collective $\{a, b\}$, we get $[0, 0]$, if both $a$ and $b$ are off, $[2, 5]$, if only $a$ is on, $[8, 15]$, if only $b$ is on, and $[2, 5] + [8, 15] = [10, 20]$, if both $a$ and $b$ are on.[7] Since at a higher level it does not matter whether, e.g. 10 is obtained by assignment $\langle 2, 8 \rangle$ or $\langle 0, 10 \rangle$, we can merge overlapping intervals. This results in a normalised, sorted list of non-overlapping intervals, e.g. $\langle [0, 0], [2, 5], [8, 20] \rangle$. We identified $(0, 2)$ or $(5, 8)$ as "holes". This procedure naturally extends to multiple modes (e.g. start-up, shut-down, . . . ). Similarly, we obtain lists of feasible intervals for collectives of $k = |\mathscr{D}_\lambda| > 2$ agents. In the worst case, however, $O(m^k)$ intervals are calculated where $m$ is the largest number of distinct intervals a single plant has. Our application scenario typically leads to $m = 2$ at lower hierarchy levels since plants contribute $[0, 0]$ if they are off and in $[S^{\min}, S^{\max}]$ with $0 < S^{\min} \leq S^{\max}$ when on. Some plants may however be so-called must-run plants [25], leading to a singleton list $\langle [S^{\min}, S^{\max}] \rangle$. Hence, if all plants must run, $m = 1$ and thus this single contribution interval of the collective can be found in time linear in $k$. The situation is ameliorated by applying the binary combine-and-merge operation incrementally.

In addition to the contribution ranges that map to the distinct states, we need to consider inertia in the abstract model as well – corresponding to the *transitions* of the supply automation of the collective. Moreover, other relationships between the variables of a collective are needed such as a cost function mapping joint production to total (minimal) costs. In the previous example, schedules $\langle 2, 8 \rangle$ and $\langle 0, 10 \rangle$ could lead to substantially different costs. Fortunately, the constraints obtained from supply automata give us a way to determine the best costs for, e.g. production level 10 by solving an optimisation problem. We exploit this capability of point-wise calculating a function of interest (e.g. "production to costs" or "production to maximal next production") in a *sampling* approach to model abstraction. With enough points of the function, we aim for approximations that interpolate sufficiently accurate in unknown ranges of the function such that a simpler representative

---

[7]Recall that $b$ further has a minimum up-time constraint but this does not concern the generally feasible contributions relevant at this point but rather dynamic behaviour.

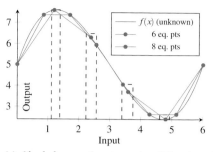
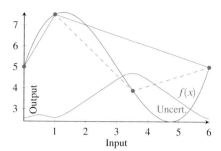

(a) *Shaded areas* denote parts of the domain where less equidistant points (6) are closer to $f(x)$ than more equidistant points (8).

(b) An approximation of $f(x)$ (*solid line*) is improved at its most uncertain point to yield a better approximation (*dashed*).

**Fig. 2.6** Sampling abstraction is concerned with selecting informative points of an unknown but computable function. Input and output represent variables of a collective, e.g. *production* to *costs*

(i.e. a piecewise linear function) can be used at a higher level.[8] We revisit plants $a$ and $b$ with production spaces $\langle[0,0],[2,5]\rangle$ and $\langle[0,0],[8,15]\rangle$, respectively. We know that $\{a,b\}$ may only produce in $\langle[0,0],[2,5],[8,20]\rangle$. Now we basically ask "What is the cheapest way to configure $a$ and $b$ such that their joint contribution is $x$?". A sequence of optimisation problems is consequently solved for various input values of $x$, e.g. $\{0,3,14\}$ to have one point for every interval, and the respective output is used to form sampled input-output pairs.

Using these sampled points, a piecewise linear function approximates the true underlying function $f$. However, the choice of useful sampling point inputs is not straightforward. When just equidistantly sampling the function's domain, we might "miss" important (i.e. "informative") points. For example, in Fig. 2.6a the optima were captured *worse* with 8 (hence, more) equidistantly selected points than with 6.[9] If these points happen to be critical, bad coarse choices made by the superordinate intermediary cannot be compensated well. Such effects were observed empirically in [21] where offering *more* sampling points actually led to *less precise* approximations with worse overall schedules.

In [24], we therefore presented a machine learning-guided approach to sampling point selection to mitigate these effects. The algorithm trains a probabilistic regression model (i.e. for an unknown input $x$ it yields both mean $\mu$ and variance $\sigma^2$ of the predicted output $y$) with a set of already sampled points. It then proceeds by asking for function values at locations where the regression model is *most uncertain* (see Fig. 2.6b). Possible regressors include Gaussian Processes or Decision Forests. The choice has to be made in accordance with the universe of possible functions a regressor can model (smooth functions, linear functions with jumps etc.). For

---

[8]Piecewise linear approximations offer to formulate problems as mixed integer linear programs which have a rich and efficient algorithmic support.

[9]Supposedly, more points were expected to provide higher accuracy.

our considered cost and inertia functions, Decisions Forests with linear leaf models turned out to be more effective than Gaussian Processes due to the presence of discontinuities and jumps [26, 27]. With this improved selection strategy, offering more sampling points indeed led almost monotonically to better results (in contrast to an equidistant strategy) and reduced the overhead costs compared to optimal solutions from 1.7 % to 0.9 % [24].

### 2.3.3  Preference Specification

The scheduling constraints imposed by physics are hard restrictions on the sets of feasible trajectories. However, not all schedules are perceived equally good, especially by different agents. Instead, some schedule properties might just be specified as optional, yet desirable. For instance, consider that an operator could restrict the rate of change between two time steps to avoid damaging the power plant. Classical constraint problems only include hard constraints that must hold in any solution. Certainly, one could attempt to model preferences as additional hard constraints but that process is likely to result in an over-constrained model, i.e. one that admits no solution. Especially if the actual problem instances emerge at runtime in an autonomous system, one should not expect to satisfy all constraints but rather design for flexibility.

Therefore, the constraint framework has been extended to *soft constraints* to allow for satisfaction degrees such as weights or probabilities [28]. Besides formulating optimisation problems, soft constraints can also be employed to order states in the corridor of correct behaviour, leading to a notion more graded than the bi-level distinction in acceptance and target space in [4]. In most soft constraint approaches, the image of the objective function is an algebraic structure that includes multiplication to combine several valuations (a so-called decomposable objective function) as well as addition to calculate suprema of partially ordered elements (in the case of c-semirings [29]) or directly use an ordering (in the case of valuation structures [30, 31]). Based on these structures, reusable optimisation algorithms including branch-and-bound, soft constraint propagation, or bucket elimination have been proposed [28].

However, there is limited use of these formalisms for open self-organising systems. Clearly, various agents may show potentially opposing preferences over the possible outcomes, e.g. schedules. If we simply applied some quantitative scheme (violation of constraint $c_1$ "costs" penalty 10), agents could outbid each other in an open system by arbitrarily increasing the penalties of "their" own soft constraints, making a weighted approach useless. Instead, we want agents to only issue *qualitative* (ordinal) preferences over constraints. In [32], we introduced *constraint relationships* to specify preferences over constraints as a directed graph (digraph) with an edge $c_1 \rightarrow c_2$ indicating that $c_2$ is *more important* than $c_1$. To indicate *how* much more important $c_1$ is, we proposed several dominance properties in [32]. It turns out that for constraint relationships, neither a total ordering is mandatory

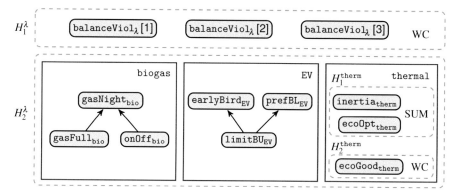

**Fig. 2.7** Case study depicting the composition of preference structures for an AVPP $\lambda$ and 3 time steps. Each *dashed, rounded rectangle* indicates a PVS. Lexicographic products are shown by vertical, direct products by horizontal alignment. Directed graphs represent constraint relationships; sets of constraints are aggregated by either worst-case (WC) or summed (SUM) error (adapted from [34])

(rendering valuation structures inappropriate) nor suprema have to exist (making c-semirings not directly applicable) [33]. Instead, we relied on the recently introduced notion of a partially ordered valuation structure (PVS) [31] that properly generalises the two former structures.

To capture the compositional nature of our system, we investigated algebraic products of PVS. Interestingly, PVS are closed under lexicographic products as long as some little restrictive conditions hold – in contrast to c-semirings [31]. Also, a direct product can be defined in the usual way and effectively leads to a Pareto-ordering of the individual agents' preferences. With both products at hand, we can map organisational structures in a hierarchical (lexicographic) or egalitarian (direct) sense. An example modified from [34] illustrates this principle, as shown in Fig. 2.7. We describe how larger PVS are composed of smaller ones.

Assume an AVPP composed of three prosumers *biogas*, *EV* (an electric vehicle), and *thermal*. For simplicity, the *overall* goal is to meet the demand. This is represented by constraints `balanceViol`$_\lambda[t]$ for each time step $t$. Each constraint maps to a PVS by taking the absolute error between summed supply and demand. The PVS for $H_1^\lambda$ is thus composed of the carrier set $\mathbb{R}^+$, the natural ordering $\geq_\mathbb{R}$ (0 is best) as well as a suitable combination. Assume that we compare solutions by the *worst* violation, $x \cdot y = \max\{x, y\}$, with $x, y \in \mathbb{R}$.[10] This PVS is the primary filter of optimal solutions. A schedule with a worst case violation of 6 should be less desirable than one with 5 – no matter how the other soft constraints rate it. We capture this using the lexicographic product. The second layer of this product is itself a *direct* product of three individual PVSs. The prosumers *biogas* and *EV* specify PVSs in terms of constraint relationships over desirable properties. For

---

[10]Note that this operator leads to so-called *collapsing elements* [31] that need further attention [34].

instance, *biogas* aims to have gas available at night to sell at high prices due to the lack of photovoltaic energy. Similarly, the electric vehicle *EV* wants to be charged sufficiently in the morning, and specifies preferred battery levels. Finally, a generic thermal unit reuses the idea of constraint hierarchies [35] that can be modelled using lexicographic products internally. It puts constraints regarding reduced rates of change and desirable production ranges into layers. We obtain as PVS for the overall problem (shown in Fig. 2.7):

$$P_{\lambda_1} \ltimes (P_{biogas} \times P_{EV} \times (P^1_{thermal} \ltimes P^2_{thermal})) \tag{2.6}$$

where $P_a$ represents the PVS of agent $a$. Since our language is mathematically positioned in existing abstract formalisms, we can instantiate generic optimisation algorithms. Moreover, the semantics of constraint relationships give rise to interesting variable and value ordering heuristics that can significantly reduce the size of the search trees to be explored. For instance, exploring variables involved in important constraints first led to significant runtime savings [33]. Additional exploitable properties are subject to further research.

## 2.4   Trust as Enabler for Robust Resource Allocation

A major challenge of the resource allocation problem (RAP) defined in Sect. 2.2 is to hold the balance between supply and demand despite uncertainties in the form of possible deviations from the predicted demand or the scheduled supply. For the system's stable and efficient operation, the agents have to quantify and anticipate these uncertainties and to incorporate this information into their scheduling decisions. In our approach, this is achieved by enabling the intermediaries to create models about the trustworthiness of their subordinates. When creating schedules, intermediaries use these models to derive an *expected* demand or supply from the possibly erroneous predictions or promises.[11]

As for uncertain demand, we proposed to use our concept of *Trust-Based Scenario Trees* (TBSTs) [36] to obtain *robust solutions* [37] in the sense that the system can efficiently and effectively achieve its goals despite disturbances. TBSTs serve as predictive models in which each scenario represents an expected development of the demand based on previously observed deviations from demand predictions. Creating schedules for multiple scenarios, together with the ability to choose the most suitable scenario at runtime, avoids situations in which deviations

---

[11]We opted for anticipating prediction errors, i.e. deviations, instead of the agents' behaviour because some agents make better prediction about their future behaviour than others and anticipating the agents' actual behaviour without incorporating their prediction requires additional information which makes the task of creating an adequate probabilistic model much more difficult.

between supply and demand are higher than (technically) allowed, or where their compensation is either very costly or not feasible due to the agents' inert behaviour.

In Sect. 2.4.1, we sketch the concept of TBSTs as a means to quantify and anticipate uncertainties in demand predictions. In Sect. 2.4.2, we borrow and adapt techniques from the field of *online stochastic optimisation* [38] to create TBST-based schedules that enable the system to deal with different possible developments of the demand. In Sect. 2.4.3, we outline a regionalised auction-based mechanism for scalable schedule creation in large-scale systems. It not only considers uncertain demand by means of TBSTs but also implements a trust-based risk avoidance strategy that mitigates uncertainties originating from schedule violations.

## *2.4.1 Trust-Based Scenarios*

As explained in Sect. 2.2, inertia requires the intermediaries to allocate resources proactively on the basis of demand predictions requested from their subordinate non-dispatchable agents. However, these predictions might turn out to be wrong, resulting in a deviation between the predicted and the actual demand (see Fig. 2.8). If prior prediction errors are indicative of future deviations, agents can use their observations to deduce a probabilistic model of their environment or interaction partners. In PMSs, such deviations stem from inaccurate or outdated standard load profiles, the prosumers' geographic location that influences local weather conditions, or imprecise sensor data used to make predictions, among others. Given a demand prediction of one or a group of its subordinate agents, an intermediary can use such a model to anticipate future deviations which – combined with the *prediction* – yield an *expected* demand for a series of future time steps (see Fig. 2.8). To create a meaningful probabilistic model of an agent or the environment, we have to meet three major challenges [36]: (C1) the agents' or the environment's

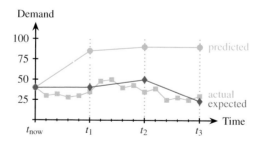

**Fig. 2.8** Uncertainties manifest as deviations between the predicted and the actual demand, which corresponds to the residual load in the power management case study. Relying on expectations instead of predictions can significantly reduce observed deviations (note that the curve "expected" is closer to "actual" than the curve "predicted"). The *dotted vertical lines* indicate the time steps $t_i$ for which predictions and expectations are used to create schedules

behaviour can change over time (e.g. due to temporary environmental influences, such as snow); (C2) only few assumptions about the behaviour can be made (e.g. weather conditions influence consumers and producers in different ways); (C3) the behaviour might be time-dependent in the sense that an inaccurate prediction for time step $t$ is likely to be followed by an inaccurate prediction for time step $t + 1$. Due to challenges (C2) and (C3), a simple trust value reflecting the mean deviation – maybe even in combination with the variance of deviations – is often not sufficient to obtain an informative probabilistic model. On the other hand, due to challenge (C1), a precise offline model of the stochastic process is either not accurate enough for momentary situations or computationally not feasible for fast reactions.

In the domain of operations research and PMSs, scenarios and scenario trees are proven concepts to describe a stochastic process (see, e.g. [39, 40]). Each scenario represents a possible behaviour over a series of future time steps and has a probability of occurrence. Due to the computational complexity of creating adequate scenarios and scenario trees, many approaches make assumptions that do not comply with the challenges of open systems, though. As a consequence, scenarios and their probabilities are often predetermined and generated offline or cannot mirror time-dependent behaviour [40]. Other methods predefine the tree's structure, the number of scenarios, or the underlying probability distribution (cf. [41]). An approach for open self-organising systems must not make such assumptions and derive scenarios from up-to-date data at runtime, which is why computationally efficient solutions are needed. Other predictive models, such as *Hidden Markov Models* [42], often lack the ability to reflect time-dependent behaviour for multiple time steps (due to the Markov property) or cannot provide agents with different (possibly related) scenarios.

In [36], we introduced the concept of *Trust-Based Scenario Trees* (TBSTs) that meets the challenges listed above. By classifying (i.e. discretising) sequences of deviations by means of bins (i.e. intervals) of a predefined size, an agent obtains an individual empirical probability mass function specifying a discrete probability distribution over multiple time steps. Each observed sequence of bins represents a *Trust-Based Scenario* (TBS), which, in turn, stands for a possible sequence of deviations. The presumed probability that a TBS occurs depends on how often the corresponding sequence was observed relative to the occurrence of the other sequences. In combination, the TBSs yield a TBST whose transitions are annotated with conditional probabilities that the expected deviation changes from one value to another. Figure 2.9 illustrates the process of creating a TBST from an agent's observed deviations in detail. For the sake of clarity, we call such a tree and its scenarios a *deviation tree* and *deviation scenarios* in the following.

With respect to the hierarchical system structure, each intermediary employs the concept of TBSTs to measure the accuracy of its local demand predictions and to deduce expected deviations. As schedules are created for the next $N$ time steps, the experiences used for the generation of deviation trees encompass $N$ deviations each. Every time schedules are created, intermediaries update their deviation trees with their latest experiences. In our case study, each AVPP creates a deviation tree to anticipate prediction errors of its local residual load that comprises its

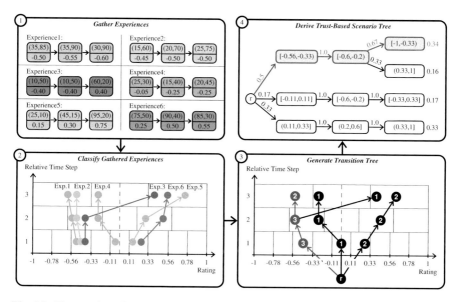

**Fig. 2.9** The creation of a *Trust-Based Scenario Tree* (TBST) is reminiscent of the creation of a histogram in which time dependencies are taken into account: A TBST is based on a set of experiences, each of which captures a sequence of deviations between the actual and the predicted demand (cf. step 1). Each deviation is normalised to an interval between $-1$ and 1 (here we use a normalisation factor of 100). Regarding Experience 1 in step 1, for instance, the deviation of $35 - 85 = -50$ between actual and predicted demand is normalised to $-0.5$. Each normalised experience is then classified by means of a grid of bins (cf. step 2). Classifying *sequences* of deviations allows the agents to record time-dependent behaviour. A set of classified experiences that results in the same sequence of bins constitutes a *Trust-Based Scenario*, as is the case with Experiences 1 and 2 (cf. step 2). In step 3, we regard the set of TBSs as a tree whose branches result from common prefixes of the sequences of bins (each path from the root $r$ to a leaf represents a TBS). The numbers in the tree's nodes indicate how often a bin is reached from another bin. By using the relative frequency of these numbers, we obtain a node-specific frequency distribution of its child. The result is a TBST with conditional probabilities as shown at the TBST's transitions in step 4. A TBS's probability of occurrence is equal to that of the corresponding leaf. With regard to a specific TBS, the series of the bins' mean values embodies an expected sequence of deviations. For example, the uppermost TBS $\langle[-0.56, -0.33), [-0.6, -0.2), [-1, -0.33)\rangle$ in step 4 represents an expected sequence of deviations of $\langle -44.5, -40.0, -66.5\rangle$ of probability 0.34 (the bins' mean values were multiplied by the normalisation factor of 100). The grid's granularity not only influences the number of TBS, the shape of the TBST, and the conditional probabilities, but also the quality of derived expectations. If the quality of long-term predictions is less important than those of short-term predictions, one can decrease the bins' granularity with the relative time step as shown in steps 2 and 3

subordinate non-dispatchable power plants and, in case of the top-level AVPP, also the consumers. Apart from the top-level AVPP, the AVPPs' local residual load is thus most likely negative.

## 2.4.2   Robust Resource Allocation on the Basis of Scenario Trees

To create schedules on the basis of the expected instead of the predicted demand, each intermediary uses a so-called *demand tree* consisting of *demand scenarios*. It is derived from the intermediary's deviation tree, reflecting the uncertainties of its local demand, by adding the predicted demand to each deviation scenario. For instance, adding the deviation scenario $\langle -44.5, -40.0, -66.5 \rangle$ given in the caption of Fig. 2.9 to the demand prediction $\langle 85, 90, 90 \rangle$ depicted in Fig. 2.8 yields the demand scenario $\langle 40.5, 50, 23.5 \rangle$, labelled "expected" in Fig. 2.8.

If intermediaries created schedules for a single demand scenario, they would have to decide for a specific TBS. Since this decision can turn out to be wrong, *stochastic programming* [43] proposes to consider multiple scenarios when solving an optimisation problem under uncertainty. By taking the scenarios' probabilities into account, intermediaries create schedules that minimise the *expected* violation of the demand [44]. This yields *robust solutions* [37] as the effect of changes in the environment or the decision variables is less severe than in a situation in which only a single scenario is regarded (see Fig. 2.10).

In our case, each intermediary creates schedules for the entire demand tree and thus solves a so-called *multi-stage stochastic program*. Due to their computational complexity [45], most of the scenario-based approaches that can be found in the literature (e.g. [46, 47]) use a *two-stage stochastic program* as approximation. A solution to a two-stage problem is composed of a first- and a second-stage decision: The first-stage decision states how many resources the agents should

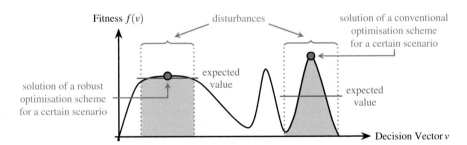

**Fig. 2.10** A fitness landscape illustrating the idea of robust solutions (according to [37]): A conventional optimisation scheme searches for the optimal solution that might only be feasible for a specific scenario (e.g. it finds the least expensive schedules for a residual load of 10 MW). In case of disturbances, the solution's actual fitness might turn out to be much lower, though (e.g. assume that the actual residual load is 12 MW so that a costly peaking power plant has to be ramped up to satisfy the additional demand). A robust optimisation scheme incorporates uncertainties in the form of multiple scenarios. Robustness is achieved by, e.g. searching for a plateau of good fitness values that yields a higher expected fitness than the solution of the conventional optimisation scheme (e.g. as a residual load of either 10 MW or 12 MW is expected, it schedules the power plants in such a way that both scenarios get by with inexpensive power plants)

provide independently of the realisation of the uncertain demand that has to be met in $t_{now} + \Delta\tau$ (recall that we defined $\Delta\tau$ as a schedule's resolution in Sect. 2.2). The second-stage decision serves as a scenario-specific corrective, i.e. a *recourse action*, that is carried out to balance supply and demand as soon as its realisation is known. A typical example would be to take the risk of buying resources at a higher price once the actual demand is known instead of pre-ordering them due to storage costs and the possibility of a surplus. The concept of recourse actions (which is also used in multi-stage problems) is, however, not applicable to our RAP because inertia is likely to prevent the agents from performing the action as scheduled (e.g. because of their limited rate of change). As opposed to this, our agents have to monitor the development of the demand at runtime and to make continuous reactive supply adjustments in order to maintain the balance as well as possible [48]. Apart from inertia, continuous reactive adjustments are necessary because of the following three reasons: (1) The scheduling problem's complexity and the uncertainties involved call for rather coarse-grained schedules, which is why we create them for a time pattern of multiples of $\Delta\tau$. Still, the demand has to be satisfied in a fine-grained time pattern of $\Delta t \leq \Delta\tau$ (see Sect. 2.2). (2) Some agents might contribute according to the wrong scenario. Such a mistake is caused by a false expectation of how the demand will develop, e.g. from $t_{now}$ until $t_{now} + \Delta\tau$. Our approach allows the agents to self-improve their flexibility in dealing with expected uncertainties as they can choose the most appropriate schedule at runtime [48]. In [44], we demonstrate that the ability to switch to the most suitable scenario at runtime reduces the prediction error by 75.03 % (standard deviation $\sigma = 0.36\,\%$) on average, compared to 59.67 % ($\sigma = 2.04\,\%$) when sticking to the TBSTs' most probable development. (3) The system must be able to deal with unforeseen developments of the demand, i.e. even those that are not captured by any demand scenario.

In the context of continuous adjustments, considering a multi-stage instead of a two-stage problem is advantageous because scenarios are treated as a tree instead of a fan of unrelated scenarios. By taking account of the demand tree's structure (this means that we schedule contributions for nodes, which might be part of multiple scenarios), we ensure that the agents cannot only provide the scheduled output in $t_{now} + \Delta\tau$ but also in subsequent time steps (note that there might be a branch following $t_{now} + \Delta\tau$). This characteristic allows the agents to delay their decision which demand scenario to choose, i.e. their assumption in which direction the demand develops, until the time step before a branch in the tree has to be taken.

Since each schedule has the same shape as the intermediary's demand tree, scenario-based schedules proactively guide the agents' decisions of how much resources to provide in which situation. In other words, the schedules encode strategies for possibly necessary contribution adjustments or, in terms of stochastic programming, schedules provide the agents with a decision rule [43]. An example illustrating this principle is shown in Fig. 2.11 where the combined scheduled output of a base load and a peaking power plant has to meet different residual load scenarios. The power plants use their schedule as a source of information about adequate reactive output adjustments that comply with the actual residual load. As

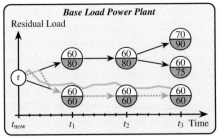 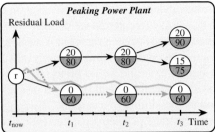

**Fig. 2.11** The power plants use TBST-based schedules as a blueprint for how much power to provide in which situation. For each node, the sum of scheduled output (upper half of the nodes) of the base load and peaking power plant matches the corresponding expected residual load (lower half of the nodes). While the base load power plant should provide an output that is more or less constant and independent of changes in the residual load, the peaking power plant – whose maximum output is 20 MW – should make adjustments in accordance with residual load changes. The *dotted line* symbolises the development of the selection of the most suitable scenario, i.e. the scenario the power plants identified as closest to the actual residual load, which is indicated by the *light curve*. Between $t_{now}$ and $t_1$, the power plants reactively switch from one scenario to another after they noticed that the demand tends to be closer to 60 MW instead of 80 MW

we showed in [48], this procedure allows the system to improve its efficiency and stability.

### 2.4.3  Auction- and Trust-Based Resource Allocation

The decision to underpin the system's robustness by creating schedules for several demand scenarios complicates the search for optimal solutions in large-scale systems. As stated in Sect. 2.2, the environment's dynamic and uncertain nature requires to revise the schedules over time. It is therefore more beneficial to be able to update schedules frequently with a fast but possibly sub-optimal method than spending much time on calculating *optimal* schedules for a problem whose conditions might change during calculation. In other words, sparing no effort in finding an optimal solution would be out of proportion to the benefit. This not only justifies our approach to decompose the scheduling problem by means of a self-organising hierarchical system structure as shown in Sect. 2.5, but also the application of heuristics for solving the scheduling problem within each organisation (i.e. AVPP).

In [49], we presented an auction-based algorithm, called TruCAOS, that solves the scheduling problem in a cooperative and regionalised manner. As the provision and consumption of resources, such as electricity, are already subject to rewards and costs in real systems, a market-based approach is a natural choice. TruCAOS deals with an uncertain provision of scheduled resources by means of trust values and with uncertain demand by means of TBSTs. Furthermore, it can schedule the provision of reserves, that is, it can proactively increase the agents' available degrees of freedom [50]. This measure promotes the agents' ability to adapt their supply to unforeseen situations. In the following, we give a brief overview of TruCAOS's functionality. For more details, we refer the interested reader to [49, 50].

Similarly to the regio-central approach sketched in Sect. 2.2, TruCAOS determines schedules in a top-down manner: The schedule creation is triggered by the top-level intermediary and subordinate intermediaries are responsible for recursively distributing their fraction of the overall demand. In contrast to the regio-central approach, which *assigns* schedules, TruCAOS does not accumulate the complexity of solving the scheduling problem in the intermediaries, though. To decrease complexity, each intermediary's subordinate dispatchable agents become an active part in the scheduling process by enabling them to sell or buy resources according to the demand (tree) it has to distribute. This is done in an iterative and incremental process that, in its basic form, is reminiscent of an iteratively performed first-price sealed-bid auction (see, e.g. [51]).

In each iteration, the subordinate dispatchable agents $\mathscr{D}_\lambda$ of an intermediary $\lambda$ can bid for a part of the *remaining demand* it has to distribute. A corresponding *proposal*, i.e. a *proposed schedule*, includes a promised contribution along with the costs, i.e. a remuneration, for providing the contribution. Having gathered the proposals of all bidders in a set $\mathscr{P}$, the intermediary completes the bidding iteration by identifying and accepting one or more suitable winner proposals $\mathscr{P}_w \subseteq \mathscr{P}$. For the selection of $\mathscr{P}_w$, we opted for a compromise between the number of bidding iterations and resulting monetary costs. Clearly, accepting only the proposal with the best *price-performance ratio* (defined as the ratio between the expected total contribution and the expected remuneration) that improves the demand's satisfaction leads to low-priced allocations. Yet, we allow intermediaries to accept a combination of proposals to decrease the number of bidding iterations and to take advantage of synergy effects (these are especially beneficial in the context of multi-objective optimisation). This requires solving the combinatorial auction problem in which the intermediary chooses $\mathscr{P}_w$ in such a way that there is no other combination that yields a greater expected gain in satisfaction of the remaining demand. As the secondary goal is to minimise the expected costs, these objectives as well as their lexicographical order correspond to those defined in Sect. 2.2. Because there might be less expensive yet suitable proposals in the next bidding iteration, intermediaries filter out, i.e. reject, proposals with a price-performance ratio worse than a historical average (calculated as a moving average over a number of previous schedule creations) before determining $\mathscr{P}_w$. While this procedure does not yield minimal costs, it ensures that the average costs do not increase. If there is no proposal whose price-performance ratio is better or equal to the historical average, only the proposals with the best price-performance ratio pass the filtering stage. As filtered proposals are rejected, the complexity of the combinatorial optimisation problem that is solved to determine $\mathscr{P}_w$ is reduced. The *most recently* accepted proposal of a dispatchable agent $a$ defines its schedule, which is a contract between $a$ and its intermediary for all time steps in the regarded scheduling window $\mathscr{W}$: $a$ has to comply with its schedule in exchange for payment.

In TruCAOS, the dispatchable agents create their proposals by solving an optimisation problem that is very similar to the one solved by the regio-central scheduling approach introduced in Sect. 2.2. An agent creates its proposals according to its control model including a cost function and may involve individual preferences that should be considered as much as possible (see Sect. 2.3.3). However, since each dispatchable agent now only has to determine the scheduled contribution for itself, TruCAOS mitigates the scalability issues discussed in Sect. 2.2. Instead of $O\left(2^{|\mathscr{D}_\lambda|\cdot N}\right)$, the complexity of solving the RAP for a subsystem $\mathscr{A}_\lambda$ with dispatchable agents $\mathscr{D}_\lambda$ is only $O\left(j_{\text{total}} \cdot \left(|\mathscr{D}_\lambda| \cdot 2^N + 2^{|\mathscr{D}_\lambda|}\right)\right)$, with $\mathscr{D}_\lambda = \mathscr{P}$, $j_{\text{total}}$ the total number of iterations needed to solve the RAP, and $O\left(2^{|\mathscr{D}_\lambda|}\right)$ the complexity of selecting winner proposals $\mathscr{P}_w$ from $\mathscr{P}$. Note that we still benefit from a hierarchical approach due to the complexity of proposal selection.[12] Because of the top-down creation of schedules, intermediaries submit bids before their subordinates. Therefore, they have to be aware of the capabilities of their collective to avoid infeasible schedules that would have to be corrected. Since intermediaries do not impose schedules on subordinates in TruCAOS, they can use the abstracted control model of their collective to create their own proposals in $O\left(2^N\right)$ instead of $O\left(2^{|\mathscr{D}_\lambda|\cdot N}\right)$ (see Sect. 2.3.2).

The iterative process of distributing the remaining demand terminates either if it is sufficiently satisfied (i.e. if its absolute values are below a predefined threshold), if $\lambda$ did not receive any proposals (i.e. $\mathscr{P} = \emptyset$), if there is no proposal that increases the demand's satisfaction, or if a maximum number of bidding iterations is exceeded. The information about termination originates from the top-level intermediary and propagates downwards in the hierarchy.

To cope with uncertain supply, each intermediary assesses the behaviour of each of its subordinate dispatchable agents by means of two trust values: The first trust value records a dispatchable agent's *mean* deviation from its scheduled supply and thus captures systematic misbehaviour. The second trust value is used to mirror a dispatchable agent's *predictability*. It represents the risk that the goal of balancing supply and demand is not achieved because the agent does not provide resources as stipulated or expected. An agent's predictability decreases with the *variance* of its deviations (this criterion is part of the *confidence metric* we defined in [52]). Both trust values are assessed as a function of an agent's scheduled supply. Intermediaries incorporate these trust values when selecting winner proposals to anticipate uncertainties and incentivise benevolent behaviour: Instead of relying on a proposed contribution, intermediaries use a dispatchable agent's first trust value to determine its expected contribution.[13] The concept of predictability is used to put

---

[12]Bear in mind that model abstraction requires additional computational effort (see Sect. 2.3.2).

[13]Note that we do not use TBSTs to reflect uncertainties in the *dispatchable* agents' supply. If we used TBSTs, we would be faced with the problem that changing the contribution of a proposer $a_i$ in response to the TBST of a proposer $a_j$ could cause a change in $a_i$'s TBST, whereupon $a_j$ would have to change its contribution and so on and so forth. It is not guaranteed that there is a fixed point, i.e. a steady state.

the dispatchable agents into states of less uncertainty. This is obtained by decreasing the price-performance ratio of agents of low predictability. As a consequence, trustworthy agents can charge higher prices for a contribution than untrustworthy agents (cf. *price premiums* and *price discounts* in [53]). In conjunction with a payment function that distributes rewards according to the agents' actual instead of their scheduled supply and that penalises schedule deviations, these measures incentivise benevolent behaviour. This corresponds to the idea of *mechanism design* [54]. A more detailed explanation of the trust-based techniques, accompanied by an evaluation, can be found in [55].

Our evaluations confirm that these characteristics allow TruCAOS to create high-quality schedules in much shorter time than a central or even the regio-central approach at marginally higher costs. While both the regio-central approach and TruCAOS profit from the creation of hierarchical system structures in general, we observed that the shape of an adequate structure can differ substantially. Because TruCAOS can deal with much larger subsystems, the overall structure can be kept flatter, which prevents the introduction of unnecessary abstraction errors (see Sect. 2.3.2). Comprehensive empirical evaluations concerning TruCAOS's performance in terms of runtime and the schedules' quality as well as a comparison to the regio-central approach can be found in [49, 50]. Compared to other agent-based resource allocation mechanisms, TruCAOS is unique in the way it combines ideas from the field of mechanism design and online stochastic optimisation in a market-based approach that creates schedules for multiple future time steps. Other approaches for resource allocation either do not regard uncertainties at all (e.g. [56–58]) or are specialised to specific types (e.g. [59–62]).

## 2.5 Self-Organised Formation of System Structures Promoting Robustness

In numerous multi-agent systems (MAS), the task is to solve an optimisation problem whose complexity is subject to the number of participating agents. A well-known representative is the scheduling problem considered in this chapter. To achieve scalability in large-scale systems, a crucial step is to establish an organisational structure that supports the agents' and the system's objectives [63]. If the regarded optimisation problem can be reasonably decomposed in a hierarchical manner, hierarchical system structures come into play. In this section, we describe how such hierarchies can evolve in a self-organising manner and show that they allow a system to come to a compromise between solution quality and performance in terms of runtime. Essentially, hierarchies are obtained by recursively partitioning a set of agents into disjoint subsystems represented by intermediaries. These are then arranged in a tree. If the system has to deal with uncertainties originating from participants that can or should not be excluded from the system, the characteristics of the created partitionings become a major concern: A single subsystem not being able to cope with its uncertainties endangers the stability of the overall system.

We define the partitioning problem that aims at creating scalable system structures that promote the system's robustness in Sect. 2.5.1. In Sect. 2.5.2, we present a self-organisation algorithm that solves these partitioning problems in a decentralised manner. The formation of hierarchies is regulated by a control loop presented in Sect. 2.5.3.

## 2.5.1   The Homogeneous Partitioning Problem

Many agent organisations are based on structures that can be described as a *partitioning*. In the *partitioning problem* (PP) [64], a set $\mathfrak{A} = \{a_1, \ldots, a_n\}$ of $n > 1$ agents $a_i$ is partitioned into non-empty and pairwise disjoint subsets, called *partitions*, that together constitute a partitioning at minimal cost. Finding the optimal partitioning for non-trivial cost functions is NP-hard [65]. We presume that feasible partitions are only constrained in terms of a minimum $s_{min}$ and maximum $s_{max}$ size. In the unbounded case, the number of feasible partitions $m$ grows exponentially with $n$. In this situation, the size of the search space, i.e. the number of possible partitionings, is given by the $n$-th *Bell number* $\mathscr{B}_n$ (e.g. $\mathscr{B}_{50} \approx 1.86 \cdot 10^{47}$) [66]. In contrast to the well-known *set partitioning problem* (SPP) (cf. [65]), we assume that the mere number of feasible partitions prevents us from pre-calculating all of them in advance. To allow for more flexible objective functions, we further do not assume that the costs of having a feasible partition included are additive and predefined. Instead, we only presume an application-specific metric that evaluates if a partitioning, i.e. a combination of partitions, is fit for purpose. If the metric defines how well agents can work together on a common task, the PP is equivalent to *coalition structure generation* (cf. [67]). If it specifies to group similar or dissimilar agents, the PP is equivalent to *strict partitioning clustering (with outliers[14])* or *anticlustering* (cf. [68, 69]), respectively.

Another form of partitionings, called *homogeneous partitioning* [64], is of particular interest for a certain class of open systems: Some of these systems suffer from agents that, on the one hand, introduce uncertainties and thus jeopardise its stability but, on the other hand, cannot or should not be excluded. This is the case, e.g. if the system depends on their resources or if they can provide them in a particularly cost-efficient way. For instance, although the output of solar power plants is difficult to predict, they might be needed to satisfy the load at on-peak hours and should not be turned off due to their low-cost generation. If, in such a situation, scalability requires the agents to self-organise into subsystems, the system's stability and efficiency hinges on the way agents are grouped according to their trustworthiness (i.e. predictability). Homogeneous partitioning aims at the

---

[14]Supported by a separate partition that holds all outliers.

creation of organisations that are, with respect to certain (possibly aggregated) criteria, as similar as possible. Examples of such criteria are partitions with a similar number of dispatchable power plants or a similar average costs per kWh. This idea is based on the assumption that a centralised system imposes an upper bound on the ratio between trustworthy and untrustworthy agents: The global knowledge about possible uncertainties and the centralised control over the trustworthy agents allow the system to fulfil its task as well as possible. If each organisation now exhibits similar characteristics, such as a similar ratio between controllability and uncertainty, they approximate the corresponding ratio of the centralised system.[15] Consequently, they also inherit its positive properties.

Another important attribute of homogeneous partitions is that the resulting subsystems are loosely coupled, meaning that the underlying optimisation problem (that is, the scheduling problem) is decomposed into independent sub-problems: Since each organisation has a similar ratio between controllability and uncertainty, the trustworthy agents' degrees of freedom can be used to compensate for the uncertainties stemming from untrustworthy agents internally. This avoids affecting other organisations or involving them into the decision-making process.

In the class of open systems regarded in this chapter, homogeneous partitioning increases the system's robustness and efficiency, and should be preferred to other types of organisations, e.g. those consisting of homogeneous agents. With respect to the power management case study, this is achieved by forming partitions with a similar ratio between the sum of the typical prediction errors of the weather-dependent power plants and the sum of the rate of change of dispatchable power plants. Recall that the information about typical prediction errors is captured in the power plants' trust models.

Note that many instances of homogeneous partitioning are not supported by the original SPP due to its restriction to additive and predefined costs of partitions. In [70], we demonstrated that homogeneous partitionings are far more robust against environmental changes than organisations consisting of homogeneous agents. When partitions are formed on the basis of aggregated criteria, robustness further increases when creating larger partitions. This characteristic highlights the advantage of employing efficient scheduling mechanism like TruCAOS from another perspective (see Sect. 2.4.3).

To guide the self-organised problem decomposition, we proposed in [64] to allow the user or the system itself to specify suitable *ranges* for the number and the size of partitions, i.e. the minimum $n_{min}$ and the maximum $n_{max}$ number of partitions *as well as* their minimum $s_{min}$ and maximum $s_{max}$ size. The parametrisation of the *partitioning constraints* defines the shape of the hierarchy. In a hierarchical system,

---

[15]If the objective is to have similar mean values, *optimal* anticlusterings also yield partitions whose mean values correspond to the mean of all elements in the system. However, the anticlustering metric still implies another order on candidate solutions than homogeneous partitioning. As the large search space prevents us from taking optimal results for granted, anticlustering is not of use here. Homogeneous partitioning is further not limited to establishing similar mean values. This is shown by the example of forming partitions with a similar number of agents of a specific type.

the ranges for the number and the size of partitions stipulate how many subsystems or agents should be controlled by an intermediary. Note that both aspects have an influence on the hierarchy's height and can therefore be used to make a trade-off between solution quality and performance in terms of runtime. Using ranges instead of fixed values provides the system with degrees of freedom needed to optimise the partitionings' composition according to application-specific formation criteria. In the example of creating AVPPs, it is required that each AVPP's size is not less than two and below a certain threshold restricting the maximum time needed for schedule creation, including the time needed for model abstraction.

## 2.5.2  Self-Organisation Algorithms for the Partitioning Problem

Algorithms for the solution of the PP in MAS have a broad area of application, e.g. in sensor networks [71], power management systems [60], manufacturing systems [72], communication systems [73], or e-commerce [74]. The large size of the PP's search space calls for efficient solutions. For this reason, approaches solving instances of the PP propose to exploit properties of the objective function, such as additivity, to represent the search space in a way that allows for a systematic search for high-quality solutions [75], distribute the search space among the agents or try to exclude specific solutions in advance [67], trade optimality for efficiency by relying on metaheuristics (such as genetic algorithms [65] or particle swarm optimisers [76]), or try to handle complexity by solving the PP in a completely decentralised fashion on the basis of local knowledge [77]. Because of the PP's complexity, they are often designed as anytime algorithms (cf. [64, 67, 75]). Usually, algorithms solving the PP either (1) are specialised to a particular problem in a certain domain (cf. the examples listed above), (2) depend on the properties of a specific objective function, or (3) are very restrictive with regard to the possibility to specify mandatory characteristics of the resulting partitioning's structure in the form of the number and the size of partitions. These attributes limit the algorithms' applicability, in particular with regard to self-organised problem decomposition in large-scale MAS. As for point (2), many algorithms – for instance, those addressing the original SPP (e.g. [65]) or coalition structure generation [75] – are specialised to certain objective functions, e.g. those in which the quality of partitions is additive and can thus be assessed independently of each other. Another example is the well-known k-means algorithm [78], its variants (e.g. [79]), and different implementations (e.g. [76]). With respect to point (3), most algorithms either do not allow to characterise valid partitionings at all (cf. [77]) or the user or the agents have to be very specific, such as in [78] or [67]. While the x-means algorithm [80] automatically finds a suitable number of partitions for a given data set, it is not possible to specify appropriate ranges for the size and the number of partitions. An exception to the rule is the discrete particle swarm optimiser *PSOPP* [64]. Due to its centralised optimisation scheme, PSOPP struggles with very large numbers of participating agents in the context of multi-objective optimisation, though.

In this chapter, we present a substantially revised version of SPADA [81], the *Set Partitioning Algorithm for Distributed Agents*. As opposed to the afore-mentioned approaches, SPADA (1) implements a decentralised optimisation scheme, (2) solves the PP in a general manner, and (3) allows to specify suitable ranges for the number as well as the size of partitions. Similar to [77], the agents to be partitioned $\mathfrak{A} \subseteq \mathscr{A}$ solve the PP by themselves. To comply with large search spaces, SPADA applies a regionalised optimisation technique in which the agents decompose the overall PP into multiple sub-problems, i.e. regional partitionings. The decomposition is obtained on the basis of an overlay network, called *acquaintances graph*, which represents the current partitioning (SPADA is an anytime algorithm) and acquaintances between agents. Compared to a fully localised optimisation as shown in [77, 81], the regionalised optimisation scheme allows SPADA to benefit from synergy effects, which is of particular interest in multi-objective optimisation problems. In SPADA, the PP is solved in an iterative manner. We refer to iterations as *optimisation cycles*. In each of these cycles, every agent performs an *optimisation step* in which it tries to increase the fitness of its regional partitioning. Since regional partitionings are likely to change from one step to another, the overall solution results from an iterative refinement of overlapping partial solutions that is carried out from different perspectives. Its regionalised principle further allows SPADA to make selective changes with respect to the composition of an existing partitioning, which is beneficial in case of a reorganisation.

Due to these characteristics, SPADA can be applied to many different applications in which solving the PP is relevant. In conjunction with the control loop presented in Sect. 2.5.3, it can be used to establish self-organised problem decomposition by means of self-organising hierarchical system structures. In the following, we give an overview of the most important properties of the acquaintance graph before we summarise SPADA's basic functionality and characteristics.

*The Acquaintances Graph.* In order to lower complexity when solving the PP in large-scale MAS, SPADA operates on an overlay network generated for the purpose of constraining communication and direct interactions between agents. This overlay network is a simple directed graph, hereinafter called *acquaintances graph* [81]. All operations the agents apply to establish a suitable partitioning can therefore be mapped to graph operations. The nodes of the acquaintances graph are the agents participating in the PP. Directed edges symbolise acquaintance relationships between agents. In SPADA, a partitioning of $\mathfrak{A}$ is a division of the acquaintances graph into several subgraphs with a pairwise disjoint set of nodes. Each of these subgraphs stands for a partition. To specify a partitioning, edges can be marked with a partition-specific flag. A *marked edge* $(a, b)$ between two agents $a, b$ states that $a$ is acquainted with $b$ and, additionally, that $a$ and $b$ are members of the same partition. For the sake of clarity, we call edges without such a mark *unmarked edges*. Partitions are thus defined by the transitive-reflexive closure of the binary relation induced by the marked edges.

Each partition has a designated leader that is responsible for optimising the composition of a part of the overall partitioning according to application-specific formation criteria. This part is restricted to the leader's own as well as its acquainted partitions (i.e. those containing acquaintances of the leader's partition members). Limiting a leader's changes to a part of the entire partitioning restricts the size of its (regional) search space and thereby reduces its computational cost of finding suitable modifications. That way, SPADA uses the acquaintances graph to decompose the overall PP into multiple sub-problems.

Although every agent is capable of being a leader, there is only one leader per partition to avoid inconsistencies in the course of the formation process. Consequently, non-leaders show a rather passive behaviour until they become leaders themselves. Because partitions located in separated subgraphs cannot exchange agents, SPADA is initialised with a weakly connected acquaintances graph (i.e. the graph's undirected counterpart is connected). SPADA's graph operations ensure that modifying partitions and acquaintances does not break the weakly connectivity. This prevents SPADA from not being able to reach specific positions in the search space. An example of such an acquaintances graph is depicted in Fig. 2.12.

*SPADA's Basic Procedure.*   Once a reorganisation is triggered, SPADA starts with the initialisation of the acquaintances graph for the agents $\mathfrak{A}$ participating in the PP. This encompasses (1) the creation of the graphs of marked edges representing the partitions, i.e. the (sub)systems, of the partitioning that has to be reorganised as well as (2) the randomised yet guided generation of unmarked edges. The latter ensures the acquaintances graph's weakly connectivity. In case SPADA is used to create an initial partitioning, it is initialised with a randomly generated partitioning. We assume that SPADA is always initialised with a partitioning satisfying the partitioning constraints introduced in Sect. 2.5.1.

Subsequent to the initialisation, each agent performs an optimisation step in each optimisation cycle. As mentioned before, non-leaders exhibit a passive behaviour and thus finish their optimisation step without performing any action. Figure 2.13 shows the main activities each leader's optimisation step comprises

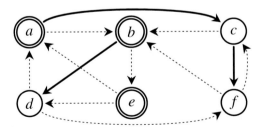

**Fig. 2.12** An exemplary acquaintances graph for a system consisting of six agents: agents are represented as nodes and acquaintances as directed edges, e.g. $d$ is acquainted with $a$ and $f$. Marked edges (symbolised as *solid arcs*) indicate that their tail and head belong to the same partition. In this example, there are three partitions $\{a, c, f\}, \{b, d\}, \{e\}$ with leaders $a, b, e$ (represented by *double-bordered nodes*)

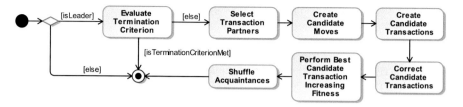

**Fig. 2.13** Actions leaders perform during their optimisation step in each optimisation cycle

in order to improve the partitioning's fitness: If the chosen termination criterion is not met, the regarded leader first determines a regional partitioning to optimise by choosing a set of transaction partners from its set of acquainted partitions. Afterwards, it creates candidate moves, i.e. possible modifications, for its regional partitioning to optimise. Several candidate moves are then combined to candidate transactions. The concept of candidate transactions allows SPADA to profit from synergy effects originating from changing the affiliation of two or more agents at once. While candidate transactions are created in a target-oriented manner such that their application would increase the region's fitness, the procedure does not guarantee that the resulting partitioning would satisfy the partitioning constraints. The sacrifice of creating feasible candidate transactions reduces complexity and fosters SPADA's exploratory behaviour. However, since the partitioning ultimately has to comply with the partitioning constraints, the leader corrects the candidate transactions after their creation. Apart from the first correction needed to abide by the global number-of-partitions constraints, all corrections can be made locally. Having repaired all candidate transactions, the leader applies the best candidate transaction that increases the region's fitness to the acquaintances graph. This means that the changes stipulated in the candidate transaction are transferred to the underlying graph structure representing the current partitioning. To localise the global minimum- and maximum-number-of-partitions constraints, each leader holds upper bounds for creating and resolving partitions that are updated in accordance with the applied candidate transaction. Finally, the leader shuffles the acquaintances of its partition members so that regional partitionings change from one optimisation step to another. This allows regional solutions to evolve over time and to spread out across wider parts of the overall partitioning. The overall solution is thus the result of an iterative refinement of overlapping partial solutions that is carried out from different perspectives.

SPADA provides several termination criteria, such as a maximal runtime or a minimal fitness value. The algorithm expects that the termination criterion is formulated as a conjunction of hard constraints. Other application-specific termination criteria that are in line with the corridor of correct and preferred behaviour can therefore be easily integrated into the algorithm. With regard to the power management case study, the objective is to establish a homogeneous partitioning (i.e. similar AVPPs) with respect to the ratio between the sum of the typical prediction errors of non-dispatchable power plants and the sum of the rate of change of dispatchable power plants, among others (see Sect. 2.5.1). The runtime of a reorganisation is limited as AVPPs must have sufficient time to recalculate the schedules without exceeding their date of expiry. If a centralised perspective is necessary to decide whether to terminate or not, a dedicated leader checks if the termination criterion is satisfied at the beginning of each optimisation cycle. In case the number of partitions is restricted, the same leader also takes care of the one-time centralised correction with respect to the global number-of-partitions constraints. If this correction has not yet been performed, the dedicated leader repairs the overall partitioning before returning it as solution. Due to that and because the satisfaction of the partition-size constraints is ensured during the entire optimisation process, SPADA always returns a feasible solution. However, since SPADA is a heuristic, it is not complete in a general sense. Basically, this can be ascribed to its decentralised regional optimisation scheme. While SPADA is complete if feasible solutions are only restricted by the partitioning constraints, it cannot guarantee to find solutions exhibiting other mandatory properties, such as solutions of predefined quality.

An in-depth empirical evaluation of SPADA and PSOPP demonstrating SPADA's advantages in multi-objective optimisation is provided in [82].

## 2.5.3  Self-Organising Hierarchies

Self-organising hierarchies are obtained by a hierarchical control loop [83] that runs on each intermediary. To ensure that the hierarchy is created with respect to the application-specific formation criteria, the control loop makes use of a partitioning algorithm, such as SPADA or PSOPP [64]. The hierarchical control loop's main purpose is to monitor the intermediary it runs on and to react to the violation of three basic constraints. In essence, it constitutes a partitioning control. One of these constraints, the so-called *composition constraint*, targets maintaining suitable partitionings within the hierarchy. It is evaluated in the context of the partitioning the intermediary's children belong to. A violation indicates that this partitioning features an unwanted composition. It is optimised by means of a reorganisation (see left subtree in Fig. 2.14a, b). The set of affected agents is called the interme- diary's *neighbourhood* which consists of its children and nephews. The two other constraints address the system's performance in terms of runtime. For this purpose, each intermediary observes the time it needs to create schedules. If the runtime of solving the scheduling problem exceeds a given threshold, the so-called *introduction constraint* is violated. In this case, the intermediary triggers the introduction of new intermediaries that requires partitioning its children into subsystems (see right subtree in Fig. 2.14a, b). Consequently, the degree of decomposition is increased. If the runtime falls below another threshold, a violation of the *dissolution constraint* is registered. Because a violation indicates that the degree of decomposition is too high, the intermediary adds its children to its parent and, subsequently, dissolves itself. Since the purpose of these three control actions is to restore these constraints, the approach complies with the Restore Invariant Approach [2] (see Sect. 2.1). With

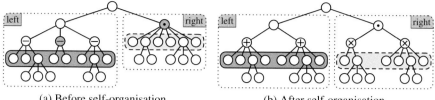

|  (a) Before self-organisation.  |  (b) After self-organisation.  |

**Fig. 2.14** The left subtrees in (**a** and **b**) depict a re-partitioning of an intermediary's neighbourhood (indicated by the *solid rectangle*). The nodes "⊖", representing the initiating intermediary (marked in *gray*) and its siblings, are replaced by the new intermediaries "⊕". The right subtrees in (**a** and **b**) illustrate the introduction of new intermediaries, which is accomplished by solving the partitioning problem for the children (marked by the *dashed rectangle*) of the initiating intermediary "⊙". Each created partition is represented by a new intermediary "⊗"

regard to our case study, the control loop runs on each AVPP, which results in a self-organising hierarchy as depicted in Fig. 2.4.

An evaluation showing that the ability to form adequate hierarchical system structures at runtime lowers overall scheduling times can be found in [82].

## 2.6  Conclusion and Future Work

Open self-organising systems composed of heterogeneous participants need high quality solutions to cope with uncertainties and (un)intentional misbehaviour of the agents. In this chapter, we outlined several building blocks that, put together, allow for self-organised and robust resource allocation in large-scale open technical systems. Based on the idea of a hierarchical system structure, abstraction of control models (see Sect. 2.3) allows for scalable resource allocation that incorporates trust-based probabilistic models (see Sect. 2.4) to deal with uncertainties. By designing the formation of hierarchical system structures as a self-organising process (see Sect. 2.5), the system autonomously comes to a compromise between solution quality and runtime performance. The presented techniques are applicable to a broad class of systems, including other supply systems (e.g. gas pipeline, water supply, or district heating system), or desktop computing grids [84].

With respect to our power management case study, we anticipate a challenging road ahead in the transition of our prototype from laboratory to productive usage that will stipulate further research. But until then, we believe that our developed techniques are useful even at smaller scale. For instance, a single plant owner might organise her power plants into a hierarchy of virtual power plants and benefit in terms of robustness and scalability. This direction could confirm the industrial importance of self-organisation practices.

En route to a broader practical adoption of the proposed techniques, there remain various open questions addressing how to systematically assure the quality of self-organising solutions. Various interconnected optimisation problems in a highly dynamic environment need tools beyond the corridor of correct behaviour [2]. Analysis and testing activities have to cater the needs of self-organising systems [85] such that they truly excel at outperforming conventional systems in a reliable fashion.

**Acknowledgements** This research is partly sponsored by the research unit *OC-Trust* (FOR 1085) of the German Research Foundation.

# References

1. Müller-Schloer, C., Schmeck, H., Ungerer, T.: Organic Computing – A Paradigm Shift for Complex Systems. Springer, Basel (2011)
2. Nafz, F., Seebach, H., Steghöfer, J.-P., Anders, G., Reif, W.: Constraining self-organisation through corridors of correct behaviour: the restore invariant approach. In: Müller-Schloer, C., Schmeck, H., Ungerer, T. (eds.) Organic Computing – A Paradigm Shift for Complex Systems, vol. 1, pp. 79–93. Springer, Basel (2011). ISBN:978-3-0348-0129-4
3. Güdemann, M., Nafz, F., Ortmeier, F., Seebach, H., Reif, W.: A specification and construction paradigm for organic computing systems. In: Second IEEE International Conference on Self-Adaptive and Self-Organizing Systems (SASO '08), Venice, pp. 233–242 (2008)
4. Schmeck, H., Müller-Schloer, C., Çakar, E., Mnif, M., Richter, U.: Adaptivity and self-organization in organic computing systems. ACM Trans. Auton. Adapt. Syst. **5**, 10:1–10:32 (2010)
5. Anders, G., Seebach, H., Steghöfer, J.-P., Reif, W., André, E., Hähner, J., Müller-Schloer, C., Ungerer, T.: The social concept of trust as enabler for robustness in open self-organising systems. In: Reif, W., Anders, G., Seebach, H., Steghöfer, J.-P., André, E., Hähner, J., Müller-Schloer, C., Ungerer, T. (eds.) Autonomic Systems, vol. 7, pp. 1–16 (2016)
6. Steghöfer, J.-P., Seebach, H., Eberhardinger, B., Reif, W.: PosoMAS: an extensible, modular SE process for open self-organising systems. In: Dam, H., Pitt, J., Xu, Y., Governatori, G., Ito, T. (eds.) PRIMA 2014: Principles and Practice of Multi-Agent Systems, vol. 8861, pp. 1–17. Springer (2014). ISBN:978-3-319-13190-0
7. Dötsch, F., Denzinger, J., Kasinger, H., Bauer, B.: Decentralized real-time control of water distribution networks using self-organizing multi-agent systems. In: Proceedings of the 4th International Conference on Self-Adaptive and Self-Organizing Systems (SASO'10), Budapest, pp. 223–232 (2010)
8. Mora, T., Sesay, A.B., Denzinger, J., Golshan, H., Poissant, G., Konecnik, C.: Cooperative search for optimizing pipeline operations. In: Proceedings of the 7th International Joint Conference on Autonomous Agents and Multiagent Systems: Industrial Track, Portugal, pp. 115–122. International Foundation for Autonomous Agents and Multiagent Systems (2008)
9. Benonysson, A., Bøhm, B., Ravn, H.F.: Operational optimization in a district heating system. Energy Convers. Manag. **36**, 297–314 (1995)
10. UCTE: UCTE operation handbook – policy 1: load-frequency control and performance. Technical report UCTE OH P1. Union for the Co-ordination of Transmission of Electricity (2009)
11. Van Zandt, T.: Hierarchical computation of the resource allocation problem. Eur. Econ. Rev. **39**, 700–708 (1995)
12. Rani, L., Mam, M., Kumar, S.: Economic load dispatch in thermal power plant taking real time efficiency as an additional constraints. Int. J. Eng. Res. Technol. (IJERT) **2**. ISSN:2278-0181 (2013)
13. Padhy, N.: Unit commitment – a bibliographical survey. IEEE Trans. Power Syst. **19**, 1196–1205. ISSN:0885-8950 (2004)

14. Kwon, W.H., Han, S.H.: Receding Horizon Control: Model Predictive Control for State Models. Springer, Dordrecht (2006)
15. Bar-Noy, A., Bar-Yehuda, R., Freund, A., Naor, J., Schieber, B.: A unified approach to approximating resource allocation and scheduling. J. ACM (JACM) **48**, 1069–1090 (2001)
16. Ramchurn, S.D., Vytelingum, P., Rogers, A., Jennings, N.R.: Putting the "Smarts" into the smart grid: a grand challenge for artificial intelligence. Commun. ACM **55**, 86–97 (2012)
17. Steghöfer, J.-P., Anders, G., Siefert, F., Reif, W.: A system of systems approach to the evolutionary transformation of power management systems. In: Proceedings of INFORMATIK 2013 – Workshop on "Smart Grids", vol. P-220. Bonner Köllen Verlag, Bonn (2013)
18. Abouelela, M., El-Darieby, M.: Multidomain hierarchical resource allocation for grid applications. J. Electr. Comput. Eng. **2012** (2012). ISSN:2090-0147
19. Boudjadar, A., David, A., Kim, J., Larsen, K., Mikučionis, M., Nyman, U., Skou, A.: Hierarchical scheduling framework based on compositional analysis using Uppaal (English). In: Fiadeiro, J. L., Liu, Z., Xue, J. (eds.) Formal Aspects of Component Software, vol. 8348, pp. 61–78. Springer, Springer International Publishing, Cham (2014). ISBN:978-3-319-07601-0
20. Hooker, J.N.: Integrated Methods for Optimization. International Series in Operations Research & Management Science. Springer (2012)
21. Schiendorfer, A., Anders, G., Steghöfer, J.-P., Reif, W.: Abstraction of heterogeneous supplier models in hierarchical resource allocation (English). In: Nguyen, N.T., Kowalczyk, R., Duval, B., van den Herik, J., Loiseau, S., Filipe, J. (eds.) Transactions on Computational Collective Intelligence XX. Lecture Notes in Computer Science, vol. 9420, pp. 23–53 (2015)
22. Van Hentenryck, P.: The OPL Optimization Programming Language. MIT Press, Cambridge (1999). ISBN:0-262-72030-2
23. Schiendorfer, A., Steghöfer, J.-P., Reif, W.: Synthesis and abstraction of constraint models for hierarchical resource allocation problems. In: Proceedings of the 6th International Conference on Agents and Artificial Intelligence (ICAART'14), vol. 2, pp. 15–27. SciTePress, Angers, France (2014)
24. Schiendorfer, A., Lassner, C., Anders, G., Lienhart, R., Reif, W.: Active learning for efficient sampling of control models of collectives. In: 2015 IEEE 9th International Conference on Self-Adaptive and Self-Organizing Systems (SASO), Cambridge, pp. 51–60 (2015)
25. Yingvivatanapong, C., Lee, W.-J., Liu, E.: Multi-area power generation dispatch in competitive markets. IEEE Trans. Power Syst. **23**, 196–203 (2008)
26. Criminisi, A., Shotton, J., Konukoglu, E.: Decision forests for classification, regression, density estimation, manifold learning and semi-supervised learning. Technical report MSR-TR-2011-114. Microsoft Research (2011)
27. Lassner, C., Lienhart, R.: The fertilized forests decision forest library. In: Proceedings of the International Conference on ACM Multimedia (ACMMM'15), Brisbane (2015)
28. Meseguer, P., Rossi, F., Schiex, T.: Soft constraints. In: Rossi, F., van Beek, P., Walsh, T. (eds.) Handbook of Constraint Programming, vol. 2, pp. 281–328. Elsevier, Amsterdam/Boston (2006)
29. Bistarelli, S., Montanari, U., Rossi, F.: Semiring-based constraint satisfaction and optimization. J. ACM (JACM) **44**, 201–236 (1997)
30. Schiex, T., Fargier, H., Verfaillie, G.: Valued constraint satisfaction problems: hard and easy problems. In: Proceedings of the 14th International Joint Conference on Artificial Intelligence (IJCAI'95), Montréal, vol. 1, pp. 631–639. Morgan Kaufmann (1995)
31. Gadducci, F., Hölzl, M., Monreale, G., Wirsing, M.: Soft constraints for lexicographic orders (English). In: Castro, F., Gelbukh, A., González, M. (eds.) Advances in Artificial Intelligence and Its Applications, vol. 8265, pp. 68–79. Springer, Berlin/Heidelberg (2013). ISBN:978-3-642-45113-3
32. Schiendorfer, A., Steghöfer, J.-P., Knapp, A., Nafz, F., Reif, W.: Constraint relationships for soft constraints (English). In: Bramer, M., Petridis, M. (eds.) Research and Development in Intelligent Systems XXX, pp. 241–255. Springer (2013). ISBN:978-3-319-02620-6

33. Knapp, A., Schiendorfer, A., Reif, W.: Quality over quantity in soft constraints. In: Proceedings of the 26th International Conference on Tools with Artificial Intelligence (ICTAI'2014), Limassol, pp. 453–460 (2014)
34. Schiendorfer, A., Knapp, A., Steghöfer, J.-P., Anders, G., Siefert, F., Reif, W.: Partial valuation structures for qualitative soft constraints (English). In: Nicola, R.D., Hennicker, R. (eds.) Software, Services, and Systems, vol. 8950, pp. 115–133. Springer, Cham (2015)
35. Borning, A., Freeman-Benson, B., Wilson, M.: Constraint hierarchies. LISP Symb. Comput. **5**, 223–270 (1992). ISSN:0892-4635
36. Anders, G., Siefert, F., Steghöfer, J.-P., Reif, W.: Trust-based scenarios – predicting future agent behavior in open self-organizing systems (English). In: Elmenreich, W., Dressler, F., Loreto, V. (eds.) Self-Organizing Systems, vol. 8221, pp. 90–102. Springer, Berlin/Heidelberg (2014). ISBN:978-3-642-54139-1
37. Branke, J.: Evolutionary Optimization in Dynamic Environments. Kluwer Academic, Norwell (2001)
38. Hentenryck, P.V., Bent, R.: Online Stochastic Combinatorial Optimization. MIT Press (2009) ISBN:978-0262513470
39. Hochreiter, R., Pflug, G.: Financial scenario generation for stochastic multi-stage decision processes as facility location problems. Ann. Oper. Res. **152**, 257–272 (2007)
40. Zhang, B., Luh, P., Litvinov, E., Zheng, T., Zhao, F., Zhao, J., Wang, C.: Electricity auctions with intermittent wind generation. In: Power and Energy Society General Meeting, Detroit, pp. 1–8 (2011)
41. Bouffard, F., Galiana, F.: Stochastic security for operations planning with significant wind power generation. In: Power and Energy Society General Meeting-Conversion and Delivery of Electrical Energy in the 21st Century, Pittsburgh, pp. 1–11 (2008)
42. Bishop, C.M.: Pattern Recognition and Machine Learning. Springer, New York (2006)
43. Shapiro, A., Dentcheva, D., Ruszczyński, A.: Lectures on Stochastic Programming: Modeling and Theory. Society for Industrial and Applied Mathematics (SIAM), Philadelphia (2014)
44. Anders, G., Schiendorfer, A., Steghöfer, J.-P., Reif, W.: Robust scheduling in a self-organizing hierarchy of autonomous virtual power plants. In: 2014 27th International Conference on Architecture of Computing Systems (ARCS), Lübeck, pp. 1–8 (2014)
45. Shapiro, A.: On complexity of multistage stochastic programs. Oper. Res. Lett. **34**, 1–8 (2006). ISSN:0167-6377
46. Scott, P., Thiébaux, S., van den Briel, M., Van Hentenryck, P.: Residential demand response under uncertainty English. In: Schulte, C. (ed.) Principles and Practice of Constraint Programming, vol. 8124, pp. 645–660. Springer, Berlin/Heidelberg (2013). ISBN:978-3-642-40626-3
47. Ruiz, P., Philbrick, C., Zak, E., Cheung, K., Sauer, P.: Uncertainty management in the unit commitment problem. IEEE Trans. Power Syst. **24**, 642–651 (2009). ISSN:0885-8950
48. Anders, G., Siefert, F., Mair, M., Reif, W.: Proactive guidance for dynamic and cooperative resource allocation under uncertainties. In: 2014 IEEE Eighth International Conference on Self-Adaptive and Self-Organizing Systems (SASO), London, pp. 21–30 (2014)
49. Anders, G., Schiendorfer, A., Siefert, F., Steghöfer, J.-P., Reif, W.: Cooperative resource allocation in open systems of systems. ACM Trans. Auton. Adapt. Syst. **10**, 11:1–11:44. ISSN:1556-4665 (2015)
50. Kosak, O., Anders, G., Siefert, F., Reif, W.: An approach to robust resource allocation in large-scale systems of systems. In: 2015 IEEE 9th International Conference on Self-Adaptive and Self-Organizing Systems (SASO), Cambridge, pp. 1–10 (2015)
51. Klemperer, P.: What really matters in auction design. J. Econ. Perspect. **16**, 169–189 (2002)
52. Kiefhaber, R., Anders, G., Siefert, F., Ungerer, T., Reif, W.: Confidence as a means to assess the accuracy of trust values. In: 2012 IEEE 11th International Conference on Trust, Security and Privacy in Computing and Communications (TrustCom), Liverpool, pp. 690–697 (2012)
53. Ba, S., Pavlou, P.: Evidence of the effect of trust building technology in electronic markets: price premiums and buyer behavior. MIS Q. **26**, 243–268 (2002)
54. Dash, R.K., Jennings, N.R., Parkes, D.C.: Computational-mechanism design: a call to arms. IEEE Intell. Syst. **18**, 40–47 (2003)

55. Anders, G., Steghöfer, J.-P., Siefert, F., Reif, W.: A trust- and cooperation-based solution of a dynamic resource allocation problem. In: 2013 IEEE 7th International Conference on Self-Adaptive and Self-Organizing Systems (SASO), Philadelphia, pp. 1–10 (2013)
56. Wedde, H.F.: DEZENT – a cyber-physical approach for providing affordable regenerative electric energy in the near future. In: 38th EUROMICRO Conference on Software Engineering and Advanced Applications (SEAA'12), Cesme, pp. 241–249 (2012)
57. Kok, K., Warmer, C., Kamphuis, R.: PowerMatcher: Multiagent control in the electricity infrastructure. In: Proceedings of the 4th International Joint Conference on Autonomous Agents and Multiagent Systems, pp. 75–82. ACM, New York (2005). ISBN:1-59593-093-0
58. Li, J., Poulton, G., James, G.: Coordination of distributed energy resource agents. Appl. Artif. Intell. **24**, 351–380 (2010)
59. Ströhle, P., Gerding, E.H., de Weerdt, M.M., Stein, S., Robu, V.: Online mechanism design for scheduling non-preemptive jobs under uncertain supply and demand. In: Proceedings of the 13th International Conference on Autonomous Agents and Multiagent Systems, pp. 437–444. International Foundation for Autonomous Agents and Multiagent Systems, Richland (2014). ISBN:978-1-4503-2738-1
60. Chalkiadakis, G., Robu, V., Kota, R., Rogers, A., Jennings, N.R.: Cooperatives of distributed energy resources for efficient virtual power plants. In: Proceedings of the 10th International Conference on Autonomous Agents and Multiagent Systems, vol. 2, pp. 787–794. International Foundation for Autonomous Agents and Multiagent Systems, Taipei (2011). ISBN:0-9826571-6-1, 978-0-9826571-6-4
61. Vytelingum, P., Ramchurn, S.D., Voice, T.D., Rogers, A., Jennings, N.R.: Trading agents for the smart electricity grid. In: Proceedings of the 9th International Conference on Autonomous Agents and Multiagent Systems, vol. 1, pp. 897–904. International Foundation for Autonomous Agents and Multiagent Systems, Toronto (2010). ISBN:978-0-9826571-1-9
62. Dash, R., Vytelingum, P., Rogers, A., David, E., Jennings, N.: Market-based task allocation mechanisms for limited-capacity suppliers. Syst. Man Cybern. Part A IEEE Trans. Syst. Hum. **37**, 391–405 (2007)
63. Horling, B., Lesser, V.: A survey of multi-agent organizational paradigms. Knowl. Eng. Rev. **19**, 281–316 (2004)
64. Anders, G., Siefert, F., Reif, W.: A heuristic for constrained set partitioning in the light of heterogeneous objectives (English). In: Duval, B., van den Herik, J., Loiseau, S., Filipe, J. (eds.) Agents and Artificial Intelligence, vol. 9494, pp. 223–244. Springer (2015). ISBN:978-3-319-27946-6
65. Chu, P., Beasley, J.: Constraint handling in genetic algorithms: the set partitioning problem (English). J. Heuristics **4**, 323–357 (1998). ISSN:1381-1231
66. Bender, C., Brody, D., Meister, B.: Quantum field theory of partitions. J. Math. Phys. **40**, 3239 (1999)
67. Shehory, O., Kraus, S.: Methods for task allocation via agent coalition formation. Artif. Intell. **101**, 165–200 (1998)
68. Valev, V.: Set partition principles revisited. In: Amin, A., Dori, D., Pudil, P., Freeman, H. (eds.) Advances in Pattern Recognition, vol. 1451, pp. 875–881. Springer, Berlin/Heidelberg (1998). ISBN:978-3-540-64858-1
69. Späth, H.: Anticlustering: maximizing the variance criterion. Control Cybern. **15**, 213–218 (1986)
70. Eberhardinger, B., Anders, G., Seebach, H., Siefert, F., Reif, W.: A research overview and evaluation of performance metrics for self-organization algorithms. In: 2015 IEEE International Conference on Self-Adaptive and Self-Organizing Systems Workshops (SASOW), Cambridge, pp. 122–127 (2015)
71. Younis, O., Fahmy, S.: HEED: a hybrid, energy-efficient, distributed clustering approach for ad hoc sensor networks. IEEE Trans. Mobile Comput. **3**, 366–379 (2004). ISSN:1536-1233

72. Anders, G., Seebach, H., Nafz, F., Steghöfer, J.-P., Reif, W.: Decentralized reconfiguration for self-organizing resource-flow systems based on local knowledge. In: 2011 8th IEEE International Conference and Workshops on Engineering of Autonomic and Autonomous Systems (EASe), Las Vegas, pp. 20–31 (2011)
73. Al Faruque, M.A., Krist, R., Henkel, J.: ADAM: run-time agent-based distributed application mapping for on-chip communication. In: Proceedings of the 45th ACM/IEEE Design Automation Conference, pp. 760–765. ACM, Anaheim (2008). ISBN:978-1-60558-115-6
74. Buccafurri, F., Rosaci, D., Sarnè, G., Ursino, D.: An agent-based hierarchical clustering approach for E-commerce environments. In: Bauknecht, K., Tjoa, A, Quirchmayr, G. (eds.) E-Commerce and Web Technologies, vol. 2455, pp. 109–118. Springer, Berlin/New York (2002). ISBN:978-3-540-44137-3
75. Rahwan, T., Ramchurn, S.D., Jennings, N.R., Giovannucci, A.: An anytime algorithm for optimal coalition structure generation. J. Artif. Intell. Res. **34**, 521–567 (2009)
76. Alam, S., Dobbie, G., Riddle, P.: An evolutionary particle Swarm optimization algorithm for data clustering. In: IEEE Swarm Intelligence Symposium, St. Louis, pp. 1–6 (2008)
77. Ogston, E., Overeinder, B., Steen, M.V., Brazier, F.: A method for decentralized clustering in large multi-agent systems. In: Proceedings of the 2nd International Joint Conference on Autonomous Agents and Multiagent Systems, Melbourne, pp. 789–796 (2003)
78. MacQueen, J.: Some methods for classification and analysis of multivariate observations. In: Proceedings of the Fifth Berkeley Symposium on Mathematical Statistics and Probability Volume 1: Statistics, pp. 281–297. University of California Press, Berkeley (1967)
79. Kaufman, L., Rousseeuw, P.: Clustering by Means of Medoids, pp. 405–416. North-Holland, Amsterdam, Netherlands (1987)
80. Ishioka, T.: An expansion of X-means for automatically determining the optimal number of clusters. In: Proceedings of the International Conference on Computational Intelligence, Calgary, Canada, pp. 91–96 (2005)
81. Anders, G., Siefert, F., Steghöfer, J.-P., Reif, W.: A decentralized multi-agent algorithm for the set partitioning problem (English). In: Rahwan, I., Wobcke, W., Sen, S., Sugawara, T. (eds.) PRIMA 2012: Principles and Practice of Multi-agent Systems, vol. 7455, pp. 107–121. Springer, Berlin/Heidelberg (2012). ISBN:978-3-642-32728-5
82. Anders, G.: Self-organized robust optimization in open technical systems. PhD thesis, University of Augsburg (2016)
83. Steghöfer, J.-P., Behrmann, P., Anders, G., Siefert, F., Reif, W.: HiSPADA: self-organising hierarchies for large-scale multi-agent systems. In: Proceedings of the Ninth International Conference on Autonomic and Autonomous Systems (ICAS) (IARIA 2013), pp. 71–76. ISBN:978-1-61208-257-8
84. Klejnowski, L.: Trusted community: a novel multiagent organisation for open distributed systems. PhD thesis, Leibniz Universität Hannover (2014)
85. Eberhardinger, B., Seebach, H., Knapp, A., Reif, W.: Towards testing self-organizing, adaptive systems (English). In: Merayo, M., de Oca, E. (eds.) Testing Software and Systems, vol. 8763, pp. 180–185. Springer, Berlin/Heidelberg (2014). ISBN:978-3-662-44856-4

# Chapter 3
# A User Trust Model for Automatic Decision-Making in Ubiquitous and Self-Adaptive Environments

Stephan Hammer, Michael Wißner, and Elisabeth André

**Abstract** Ubiquitous Environments are able to support users during their daily life by intelligently self-adapting to changed contexts. Examples include home automation systems which can support energy saving by switching off unused devices or public displays which enable users to present and interact with data, but maintain the users' privacy by hiding sensible data if others pass by. However, such proactive adaptations could also cause frustration and thus harm the users' acceptance and trust towards a system if they do not match the users' preferences or are not self-explanatory. In the worst case, wrong or incomprehensible decisions by the system even could make the users abandon the system. To address this concern, we propose a generic trust-based model, called User Trust Model (UTM), which facilitates automatic decision-making in ubiquitous and self-adaptive environments. It is supposed to monitor users' trust in the system and to select context-aware system actions that maintain, restore, or even foster user trust. In this chapter, the construction of the generic model as well as its integration into two case studies will be presented. We will provide a detailed description of how to customise the UTM for the respective scenarios and share results and experiences from various studies conducted with the developed systems.

**Keywords** User trust • Affective trust • Trust modelling • Decision-making • Ubiquitous systems • Adaptive environments

S. Hammer (✉) • M. Wißner
Human-Centered Multimedia, University of Augsburg, Augsburg, Germany
e-mail: hammer@hcm-lab.de; wissner@hcm-lab.de

E. André
Human-Centered Multimedia, University of Augsburg, Augsburg, Germany
e-mail: andre@hcm-lab.de

© Springer International Publishing Switzerland 2016                                              55
W. Reif et al. (eds.), *Trustworthy Open Self-Organising Systems*,
Autonomic Systems, DOI 10.1007/978-3-319-29201-4_3

## 3.1  Introduction

Ubiquitous environments, such as public display environments or home automation systems, are able to monitor the current states of people (e.g. presence, attention, movement) and devices (e.g. displays, lights), as well as their surroundings (e.g. social context, ambient noise, brightness). Using this data, these systems can automatically adapt the provided information or services to the current situation. Furthermore, users are also able to interact with these environments through various means. Examples include manipulating or sharing data via a multitude of devices, such as (semi-)public displays, or mobile, private devices such as smartphones. As a consequence, such environments are no longer static and simple, but open, highly dynamic, and complex and have to cope with a number of issues.

An environment could, for example, be manipulated to expose users' private data. However, even if it can be assumed that an environment in general has the ability and intention to act trustworthy, the actual system behaviour could be undesirable because it was negatively affected by the high dynamics (e.g. a multitude of continuously approaching or leaving people) or error-prone parts of the system (e.g. cheap or damaged sensors). Most of the contributions in this book focus on trust between entities and agents in a system to increase its reliability, robustness, or safety; criteria that were also considered by most work in the area of computational trust models to assess a system's trustworthiness.

However, even if a system is robust and secure, it might be used by very heterogeneous user groups (different age groups, different technical backgrounds, different preferences etc.). Thus, some of them may not understand the rationale behind sudden adaptations, such as changes of the presented information, the utilised modality, or switched-off devices, or might not consider them as plausible given the current situation. As a consequence, they could lose their trust in the system's truth and worth [1, 2]. In the worst case, they even might no longer use it.

There are further factors that could influence users' trust towards a system, such as the system's perceived controllability, the protection of users' private data (see for example [3]) or a certain degree of comfort while interacting with the system.

All these factors influence how users perceive a system while interacting with it. And they influence the users' perceived trust towards the system. Therefore, in this chapter we will focus on "trust" following Castelfranchi's and Falcone's [4] terminology of "affective" forms of trust that are based on the user's appraisal mechanisms.

Since it is impossible to develop a once-and-for-all solution to cope with all the issues related to users' perceived trust, ubiquitous and self-adaptive environments require the functionality for a sophisticated trust management to maintain or maybe even foster users' acceptance and trust. Therefore, this chapter presents a generic decision-theoretic approach to a trust management system, called User Trust Model (UTM). The UTM is based on Bayesian networks and assesses the user's affective trust in a system, monitors it during the interaction and applies appropriate measures to maintain trust in critical situations [5].

In the following chapter, we will first discuss prior work on which the development of the generic UTM was based. This includes work in modelling trust in agent-based societies, social media, and adaptive and personalised systems. This chapter's main contribution is a detailed description of the generic UTM's construction (Sect. 3.3), as well as its exemplary integration and its evaluation within two case studies (Sects. 3.4 and 3.5). To facilitate the development of other ubiquitous and self-adaptive environments, we will provide detailed insights into the experiences and lessons learnt during the development and evaluation of the two systems. Finally, Sect. 3.6 will give a conclusion and an outlook on future work.

## 3.2 Related Work

While research on computational models of trust has become very popular in the areas of agent-based societies and user modelling, approaches that model trust as a user experience and focus on the affective dimension of trust are rare. This is unsurprising because the psychological aspects of trust are hard to measure directly. In this section, we will first give an overview of computational models starting from approaches that have been presented for agent-based societies, social networks, recommender systems, and interactions with virtual characters. After that, we discuss how the concept of trust has been treated in ubiquitous environments.

### 3.2.1 Computational Models of Trust

Much of the original research on trust comes from the social sciences. Psychologists and sociologists have tried for a very long time to get a grasp of the inner workings of trust in interpersonal and interorganisational relationships. Other fields, such as economics and computer science, relied on their findings to come up with dedicated models of trust that are adapted to the specific requirements of their domains and the context they are applied to. Since trust is a social phenomenon, it seems to be a promising approach to exploit models that have been developed to characterise trust in human societies as a basis for computational models of trust.

Especially in the area of multi-agent systems, computational models for trust-based decision support have been researched thoroughly. Pioneering work in this area has been conducted by Marsh [6] who modelled trust between distributed software agents as a basis for the agents' cooperation behaviour. Computational mechanisms that have been proposed for trust management in agent-based societies include Bayesian networks [7], Dempster-Shafer theory [8], hidden Markov models [9], belief models [10], fuzzy models [4], game-theoretic approaches [11], or decision trees [12]. [13] describe a trust-enabled middleware which uses a combination of trust, reputation and confidence to enhance a system's self-x properties. All in all, there is empirical evidence that the performance of agent-based societies may be improved by incorporating trust models.

In contrast to the approaches above, work in the area of social media aims to model trust between human users, see [14] or [15] for a survey investigating trust in social networks. Using algorithmic approaches or machine learning techniques, trust between users is derived from objective observations, such as behaviour patterns in social networks. For example, Adali et al. [16] assess trust between two users based on the amount of conversation and the propagation of messages within Twitter. Other approaches derive trust that is given to users from community-based reputation or social feedback, e.g. Ivanov et al. [17].

In the area of recommender systems, computational models related to trust have also been explored. Apparently, it does not suffice to generate recommendations solely based on the users' profile and preferences: The trustworthiness of people, organisations, and services involved in the recommendation process also have to be taken into account. There is empirical evidence that computational models of trust may help improve the recommendation accuracy of traditional collaborative filtering approaches, see, for example, [18]

Computational models that assess trust felt by a user while interacting with a system are rare. One notable exception is the work by Bickmore and Cassell [19] in which they describe a model of social dialogue that a virtual character can employ to build trust with a human interlocutor through conversational strategies that increase familiarity and solidarity between the character and the user.

Finally, there is a large amount of work that aims to identify factors that impact user trust. For example, Glass et al. [20] research trust-enhancing factors for adaptive and personalised applications. However, they do not implement a model of the user's trust into an adaptive and personalised system based on these factors. Starting from the observation that people respond to technology socially, Lee and See [21] discuss psychological factors of trust (such as the visual appearance of the interface) that influence to what extent people rely on technology. Yan et al. [5] model captures the trust which users experience when interacting with mobile applications. In order to present users with recommendations that help increase their trust, they identified various behaviours that can be monitored by a mobile device in addition to external factors such as brand impact. The benefits of this approach have been shown by means of simulations. However, the approach has not been embedded in an adaptive and personalised mobile application to control the selection of system actions during an interaction with the user.

### 3.2.2 Trust in Ubiquitous Environments

In the area of ubiquitous computing, the topic of trust has attracted a significant amount of interest. This comes as no surprise since the high dynamics and openness of ubiquitous environments come not only with great benefits, but also a number of trust-threatening issues in the areas of security, privacy, predictability and transparency.

Due to the large variety of smart objects and devices that can exchange information, the underlying infrastructure is heavily imperilled by manipulations. Typically users interact with such environments on a short-term basis without having the possibility to verify the security of the underlying infrastructure. Vice versa access control in open environments which people can enter and leave at any time is a challenging task. To solve these issues, a number of research projects have investigated how to apply trust mechanisms from the area of network security to pervasive computing. A common approach is to explicitly model trust relationships between physical devices and exploit this information to choose appropriate devices for cooperatively solving a task (e.g. [22]). The approach by Arimura et al. [23] takes a different direction by using physical social trust relationships between users for authentication purposes. First, actual physical vicinity between users is confirmed by the authentication system. Then, whenever one of the users needs to be authenticated, the other user is asked by the system to confirm the former's identity. Only in cases where this kind of authentication was not successful, the system would ask for additional information, such as passwords.

At the same time, a significant amount of private data is collected silently using sensors worn on the user's body as well as external sensors smoothly integrated into the user's environment. On the one hand, the comprehensive collection of user data contributes to a better personalisation of information and services. On the other hand, excessive data collection may be considered as a threat to privacy. To mitigate this threat, a variety of mechanisms has been presented to preserve the user's privacy and hide confidential information from others, such as preventing the tracking of tagged consumer items or displaying private information on the user's personal device. Cao et al. [24] proposed an approach that enabled users to access personalised information in public places through their mobile devices while ensuring their anonymity. The basic idea was to publicly present all information on a display, but to indicate to individual users only which part of the information is relevant to them by sending personal crossmodal cues (such as vibrations) to their mobile devices. In other words, the approach tried to enhance the users' privacy by obscuring the access to personal information to the public. Initial evaluations of the approach focused on usability issues, but not on the question of whether crossmodal cues appropriately address the users' privacy concerns.

Another factor that may affect the users' trust is the high uncertainty and unpredictability of ubiquitous environments. Despite the large number of sensors that are employed to capture user and context information, the analysis and interpretation of the sensor data might be error-prone which in turn could lead to unpredictable behaviour. But since it could be difficult for a user to tell whether the current behaviour of the system is the result of an error or not, this could lead to trust issues. To counter these issues and give the user an insight into the system's reasoning process, a number of researchers propose to display confidence values (see, for example, the work by Antifakos et al. [25]).

Finally, due to the high complexity and dynamics at which the interaction with a ubiquitous environment might take place, a user may no longer be able to comprehend the rationale behind the system's decisions which may negatively affect the formation of user trust. Lim et al. [26] present a toolkit for generating eight different kinds of explanations automatically (such as what-if, why, how-to etc.), in order to increase the transparency of context-aware systems. Even though the connection to user trust is emphasised in their paper, they do not provide a mechanism to computationally model user trust. Cheverst et al. [27] investigate techniques to increase the transparency of a system and to give users a higher level of control in a smart office environment. Their work is similar to ours since it investigates the tension between proactive system behaviour and user control and aims at improving the transparency of system behaviour. Even though the topics they address have a tight relationship to user trust, they do not explicitly model user trust itself to decide on appropriate system behaviours. Hochleitner et al. [28] describe the Trust Feedback Toolkit which allows users to view detailed information on outgoing and incoming connections for any device in an Internet of Things application, thus building trust by providing additional transparency in security-critical situations.

## 3.3  The User Trust Model

The main idea underlying our approach to model the users' trust in a computer system is to derive the trust from a set of intermediate dimensions, the so-called trust dimensions. These trust dimensions describe relevant properties of the system in question. Their definition is based on an earlier literature survey [29] where we elaborated on the determinants of trust in highly dynamic computing systems and a summary can be found in the introductory chapter of this book [13].

However, for the construction of our UTM we were specifically interested in the trust factors that are relevant for a user's experience during the interaction with a system. Therefore, we performed a series of interviews with 20 computer science students in which they were asked to indicate factors of trust that they felt contributed to their assessment of the trustworthiness of a user interface [30]. The most frequently mentioned factors fell into the following categories that formed the basis of our User Trust Model (typical statements given by participants are indicated in parentheses):

- Comfort of Use ("The system should be easy to handle")
- Transparency ("I need to understand what the system is doing")
- Controllability ("I want to be in control of the system's actions")
- Privacy ("The system should neither ask for nor reveal private information")
- Reliability ("The system should run in a stable manner")
- Security ("The system should safely transfer data")
- Credibility ("The system should have been recommended by others")
- Seriousness ("The system should have a professional appearance")

Now that we have selected this set of trust dimensions as the basis for our computational trust model, the next step is to identify a suitable representation. Such a representation should be able to account for the following characteristics of trust:

**Trust as a subjective concept**: There is a consensus that trust is highly subjective. A person who is generally confiding is also more likely to trust a piece of software. Furthermore, users respond individually to one and the same event. While some users might find it critical if a software asks for personal information, others might not care. We aim at a computational model that is able to represent the subjective nature of trust.

**Trust as a non-deterministic concept**: The connection between events and trust is inherently non-deterministic. We cannot always be absolutely sure that the user notices a critical event or actually considers such an event as critical. As a consequence, it does not make sense to formulate rules that predict in a deterministic manner which level of trust a user has in a particular situation. A computational model of trust should be able to cope with trust as a non-deterministic concept.

**Trust as a multifaceted concept**: As shown above, trust is a multi-faceted concept. Computational models should be able to explicitly represent the relative contribution of the trust dimensions to the assessment of trust. In particular, the model should help us predict the user's level of trust based on dimensions, such as the perceived transparency and controllability of a user interface. Furthermore, it should be easy to alter the model by adding or removing trust dimensions based on new experimental findings or if a certain dimension is not applicable in a given system.

**Trust as a dynamic concept**: Trust depends on experience and changes over time. Following Lumsden [31], we distinguish between *Initial Trust* and *Interaction-Based Trust*. Both contribute to the user's overall trust in the system. Initial trust dimensions, such as seriousness, come into effect as soon as a user gets in touch with the system while interaction-based trust dimensions, such as transparency of system behaviour, influence the users' experience of trust during the interaction.

We have chosen to model the users' feelings of trust by means of Bayesian networks. A Bayesian network (BN) is a directed acyclic graph in which the nodes represent random variables while the links connecting nodes describe the direct influence in terms of conditional probabilities. Observations, or evidence, can be entered into nodes in the network and the probability of other nodes can then be inferred [32]. An often used example for the application of a BN are diseases and symptoms: The observation of symptoms is entered as evidence, and the possible presence of certain diseases can be inferred.

Bayesian networks meet the requirements listed above very well: First, we can represent the model's uncertain belief about a user's trust by a probability distribution over different levels of trust (subjective nature of trust). Second, a BN allows us to make predictions based on conditional probabilities that model how likely the value of the child variable is, given the value of the parent variables. For example, we may model how likely it is that the user has a moderate level of trust if the system's behaviour is moderately transparent. This allows for a much more flexible approach than, for example, rigid rules that exactly predict how a certain event or situation changes the user's trust (non-deterministic nature of trust). Third, with a BN we are able to model the relationship between trust and its dimensions in a rather intuitive manner. For example, it is rather straightforward to model that reduced transparency leads to a decrease of user trust. In a BN, each trust dimension can represented by a specific node (multifaceted nature of trust). In a similar manner, a BN also allows us to model initial and interaction-based trust as two different concepts, each influenced through different trust dimensions, but both contributing to the overall user trust (dynamic nature of trust).

As a next step, the BN can be constructed, based on the trust dimensions and requirements identified above. Figure 3.1 shows the result for a generic UTM, i.e. one that is not yet tailored to any specific application. We started with a node for *User Trust* and followed Lumsden's [31] distinction between *Interaction-Based Trust* and *Initial Trust*. Both depend on the users' *Trust Disposition* which

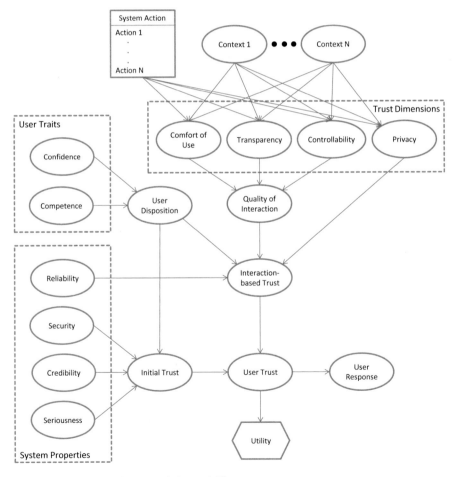

**Fig. 3.1** Generic Bayesian network for modelling trust

is characterised by their *Competence* and general *Confidence* towards technical systems.

Next, we introduce a specific node for each trust dimension. Those in the lower left part of the network (*System Properties*) represent the factors influencing the establishment of *Initial Trust* that arises when a user gets a first impression of a system: *Security*, could be, for example, conveyed by the use of certificates. A system's *Seriousness* is reflected, for example, by its look-and-feel. *Credibility* could be supported by additional information, such as a company profile. In this context, we would like to emphasise that trust dimensions may only affect the user's trust if the user is aware of them. For example, high security standards will only have an impact on user trust if the user knows that they exist. For the sake of simplicity, we assume that initial trust dimensions do not change over time. That is, we do not consider the fact that a user might notice references to security certificates only after working with a system over a longer period of time.

To describe the determinants of *Interaction-Based Trust*, we further distinguish between *Quality of Interaction* and the trust dimensions *Reliability* and *Privacy*. Finally, the *Quality of Interaction* is characterised by *Transparency*, *Controllability* and *Comfort of Use*. Since the four trust dimensions *Security*, *Seriousness*, *Credibility* and *Reliability* are more contributing to a system's trustworthiness as a whole and not as much to specific interactions, we decided to focus further refinements of the model on the other four dimensions.

Each of these four trust dimensions is treated as a hidden variable that cannot be observed directly, but may be inferred from observable variables. In our case these observable variables take the form of the user's *Context* and the system's chosen *System Action*. In other words: Any specific situation can be modelled as a certain combination of observable (i.e. known) contexts, and then the BN can be used to estimate the impact that certain system actions will have on the different trust dimensions and consequently on the overall user trust. As an early example from the case study described in Sect. 3.4, the context nodes could specify that the user is alone and is viewing data that is considered private. No system action is necessary in this situation. Then, another person might arrive, triggering a change in context to describe the new situation, and now a possible system action to protect the user's privacy could be to hide private data.

We also decided to add a node *User Response*, representing the user's trust-induced reaction to the system's decision. The idea is that this node could be used to enter evidence of the user's observable behaviour into the BN, allowing to derive user trust by means of diagnostic inference.

Now that the structure of the BN is complete, the last step is to initialise the conditional probabilities for each node combination (except for the ones that are application-specific, i.e. the influence of *System Action* and *Context* on the four trust dimensions). For this, we were again able to use data from our previous work: a second study presented in [30] which provided insight into (1) the relationship between the trust dimensions and user trust and (2) the relationship between the user's trust disposition and user trust. However, data for other user groups can be easily integrated into the BN by replacing the corresponding distributions.

Finally, in order to use the BN for decision-making, we extended it to an influence diagram: We changed *System Action* into a so-called decision node and added a *Utility* node that is directly influenced by *User Trust*. Thus, the more positively a certain system action influences the trust dimensions in any given contextual situation, the higher the resulting user trust and consequently the utility of that system action will become. With this change, the decision-making algorithm can select the best system action (i.e. the one that helps to maintain the user trust the most in a certain situation) by choosing the one with the highest utility.

The general idea and process of using the UTM in an application is as follows: There is one UTM per user, but it is not user-specific. Every time a user's context changes, that change is entered as evidence into the BN. Then the decision-making algorithm is invoked, iterating through all possible system actions and selecting the most appropriate one, as described above. Depending on the situation, the most appropriate system action could actually be to do nothing at all. The chosen system action is then performed by the application. The BN itself (both structure and conditional probabilities) is not altered during runtime (i.e. there is no learning).

The case studies in the next two sections will illustrate how the generic UTM can be made application-specific by selecting appropriate system actions, contexts and conditional probabilities.

## 3.4   Case Study 1: Public Display Environments

Recent years have brought about a large variety of interactive displays that are installed in many public places, such as coffee bars or airports. Apart from simply providing information (e.g. news or weather), public displays make it possible for passing individuals to view, edit, and exchange specific data between each other. Mobile phones represent a popular interaction device for interacting with these displays since they have been widely adopted by people as an everyday companion and can be customised to individual interaction preferences.

In this case study we report on our experience of adapting the UTM for four prototype applications for public displays which also include a user's mobile phone into the interaction process. All four applications require sophisticated mechanisms to adapt to various trust-critical events: Some may disclose private information about users and thus should be able to intelligently adapt to the surrounding social context in order to avoid possible privacy threats. Others might allow multiple users to interact simultaneously and thus should open space for new users as they approach.

In the following, we describe how we customised the generic UTM presented in the last section for these applications by gathering empirical data from two different studies and how we validated the resulting application-specific UTMs. Note that some details were omitted for the sake of brevity, see [33] for a more detailed overview of this work.

## 3.4.1   Customising the Generic UTM

Customising the generic UTM was split into two parts: Determining system actions and contexts and modelling the conditional probabilities of how they influenced the different trust dimensions.

### 3.4.1.1   System Actions and Contexts

Our goal was to find a common set of system actions and contexts that could be used to describe each scenario occurring in the four applications. Figure 3.2 gives an idea of the nature of each of the four prototypes: Friend Finder (FF), represents a public display supporting social networking [34]. Once a user comes closer, the large display shows the user's social network overlaid over a local map, depicting the status and locations of friends. By selecting individual friends via their mobile phone, users are able to display a route to the selected friend.

Media Wall (MW), supports media exchange within a community [34]. It displays a gallery of private media items (pictures or videos) when users approach. Then the users can browse or rank the items via their mobile phone.

Travel Planner (TP), helps students arrange low-budget trips around Europe. By browsing the map on the large display map via their mobile phone, users can retrieve information on the cities and the estimated cost of a visit. Apart from this neutral information, the application is also able to consider private budget-related data and shows whether the estimated costs are affordable.

Shopping Mall Display (SMD), aims at supporting customers of a shopping mall in finding products of their interests and the corresponding shops by displaying personalised information when a user approaches.

All four applications require mechanisms for deciding how to respond to trust-critical events, such as a passer-by approaching the display. Since all applications may disclose private information, such as a user's social network (FF), personal preferences (MW and SMD), or budget limitations (TP), they should be able to appropriately adapt to the surrounding social context in order to avoid potential privacy threats. Whether displaying private data might be considered untrustworthy might also depend on who else is present (if at all), and their relationship to the user. Potential protection mechanisms include the migration of personal data from

**Fig. 3.2** Prototype applications, f.l.t.r.: Friend Finder, Media Wall, Travel Planner, Shopping Mall Display

the public display to the user's mobile device, the hiding or masking of personal information as well as offering these actions to the users via their mobile phones. The corresponding scenarios in which users interact with a display while others pass or join will be in the following summarised under the common term "Spectator Scenario".

Besides people quickly passing the public display without taking notice of its content and people that may stop and watch, people may even engage in an interaction as well. In this case, the system does not only have to protect private information against unwanted disclosure, it should also account for strategies to handle the data and input originating from multiple users [35]. For example, several users may interact with the Shopping Mall display in parallel to explore product information ("Space Scenario"). To accommodate the needs of multiple users, the size of the space allocated to particular users may be dynamically adapted. Alternatively, data may migrate to the user's mobile device. On the one hand, these strategies enable the simultaneous exploitation of a public display by multiple users. On the other hand, users might get irritated by the unsolicited customisation. As a consequence, the system has to carefully balance the benefits and drawbacks of each action in order to come up with an optimised solution.

In addition, three of the applications (FF, MW, and SMD) utilise additional sensors, such as cameras, to also offer proxemic interaction [35]. The corresponding scenarios for these applications will in the following be summarised under the term "Proximity Scenario". Whenever a user approaches the display, information relevant to him or her could be proactively presented on the screen. As soon as the user leaves the display, this information could be immediately removed again. On the one hand, this feature offers great comfort. On the other hand, it limits the user's control over the system and might also be considered as opaque. Therefore, whenever a user approaches or leaves, the system could ask the user for confirmation via the user's mobile phone. Again, this is a situation in which a system has to find a trade-off between comfort of use, transparency, and controllability to maximise the user's trust. The high dynamics in public places make this task even more difficult.

Given these potential scenarios, we decided to include context nodes for the user's activity (arriving, leaving), their social context (alone, or in presence of a friend, acquaintance or total stranger), and the privacy of the content shown (private, not private). The system actions can be divided into three categories: *Do Nothing*, *Act Autonomously*, and *Ask For Conformation*. While the first should be self-explanatory, the second category comprises the various means to handle data (show it, hide it, mask critical parts), and the third asks the user for confirmation on their mobile device, offering a choice between all the previous options. Figure 3.3 shows the relevant part of the UTM with these nodes.

Before we describe how we determined the conditional probabilities, let us first consider an example of how the constructed UTM might make decisions: Let us assume a user wishes to display data on a public display while other people are present. Such a situation could be described by the values of the BN's context nodes *Social* (e.g. set to "'Stranger'") and *Privacy of Content* (e.g. set to "'Private'"). These have been determined by sensors or application data and are thus known by

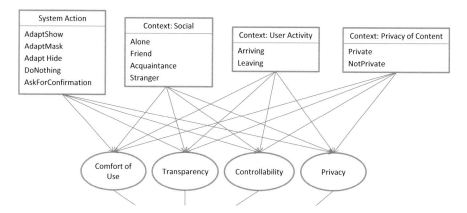

**Fig. 3.3** System actions and contexts in a Bayesian network for modelling trust in public display environments

the system. The system may now consider three options to cope with the user's request: (1) transferring all data to the public display no matter whether they are private or not, (2) show only the information marked as non-private or (3) asking the user for a confirmation of one of these actions. Considering the example, option (1) may result in serious privacy concerns, option (2) may confuse the users if there is no plausible explanation for the adaptation, and option (3) could be less comfortable to use in a dynamic setting but gives the full control to the user. On the other hand, if the system decides in favour of option (1) or (2), the users might perceive the system as less controllable.

### 3.4.1.2   Conditional Probabilities

Now that the structure of the application-specific UTM was complete, we needed data which described the conditional probabilities between the newly introduced contexts and system actions and the trust dimensions. We decided to collect this data through experiments conducted with potential users: The users were confronted with scenarios illustrating different contextual combinations (situations) and possible adaptive reactions of the displays in these situations that differed in the degree of transparency, user control, privacy, and comfort of use. To discover which of the system reactions succeeded in maintaining the users' trust and which did not, they had to reflect on their perception of the reactions in the specific situation and had to give insights into their feelings of trust and the related trust dimensions.

The data collection was arranged in two steps: First, an online survey targeting as many users as possible was conducted. But since an online survey might not convey the experience of a real interaction and thus affect the ratings of the users, we also performed a live study. The live study only included two of the four applications but was otherwise designed identically to the online survey (except that it of course involved real user interactions).

All in all, the online survey was aimed at gathering as much data as possible, involving online users. The live study was aimed to complement the online survey, supporting the results collected online by the evaluations of users during a real interaction.

Online Survey

The online survey was aimed at capturing the users' subjective assessment of display reactions in various situations. To this end, participants were shown videos clips of the four prototypes. For each prototype, we recorded several short videos demonstrating scenarios in which a specific situation was given, the context changed, and the display conducted a possible reaction. For example, the "Spectator Scenario" of Friend Finder first showed a single user interacting with the display in a public area, see Fig. 3.4 top. Then, the display recognised the arrival of an unknown person (change in social context) and masked the user's social network automatically (reaction), see Fig. 3.4 case A. Another video first illustrated the same situation and context change, but then a different display reaction: Instead of masking the data automatically, the data was removed entirely and the user was presented with various options on their mobile phone, see Fig. 3.4 case B.

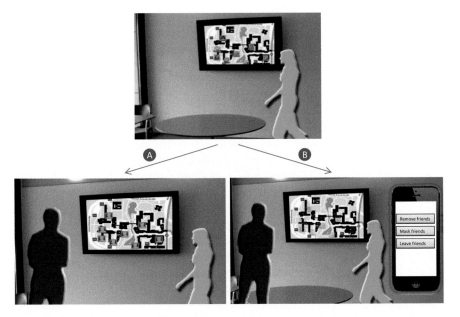

**Fig. 3.4** Screenshots of video "Friend Finder – Approaching Stranger": *Top*: single user interacting with private data on public display; Case A: display reaction: mask private data; Case B: display reaction: remove private data and present possible actions on the user's mobile phone

**Table 3.1** Scenarios illustrated by videos: possible display reactions in different contextual combinations (situations)

Proximity scenario

| User context | Data context | Social context | Display reaction |
|---|---|---|---|
| User approaching (FF, MW, SMD) | (a) Private data | (a) User alone | (a) Show user data automatically |
| | (b) Neutral data | (b) User not alone | (b) Ask for confirmation |
| | | | (c) Do nothing |
| User leaving (FF, MW) | (a) Private data | (a) User alone | (a) Remove user data automatically |
| | (b) Neutral data | (b) User not alone | (b) Ask for confirmation |
| | | | (c) Do nothing |

Spectator scenario

| User context | Data context | Social context | Display reaction |
|---|---|---|---|
| User interacts alone (FF, MW) | (a) Private data | A person comes: | (a) Hide private data |
| | (b) Neutral data | (a) Friend | (b) Mask private data |
| | | (b) Acquaintance | (c) Ask via mobile device |
| | | (c) Stranger | (d) Do nothing |
| User logged in (TP) | (a) Private data | (a) User alone | (a) Show data on public display |
| | (b) Neutral data | (b) User not alone | (b) Show data on mobile device |

Space scenario

| User context | Devices context | Social context | Display reaction |
|---|---|---|---|
| User A interacts with the display (SMD) | (a) Mobile available | User B approaches the display: | (a) Provide space for B, shrink data of A |
| | (b) Not available | (a) B is female | (b) Provide space for B, move data of A to mobile |
| | | (b) B is male | (c) Do nothing. B will wait |

Table 3.1 summarises the recorded scenarios including possible situations which were represented by different settings of contextual variables, such as the social context and the privacy of the displayed content, and possible display reactions. Some scenarios were illustrated by different applications, in order to compare how people perceive the same adaptations applied to different content. The applications illustrating the scenarios are indicated by the capital letters in the "User Context" column.

All in all, four to six situations for each scenario, see Table 3.1 column 1–3, and 22 situations in total were investigated. Considering two to four possible display reactions per situation, see Table 3.1 column 4, this resulted in a total number of 68 recorded short videos. In order to reduce the time of the survey completion to about 10 min, we grouped the videos into six online surveys. Each survey contained about 8–12 videos. After an introductory page, the surveys provided a description of the used applications. Then, the user was confronted with the first scenario. The corresponding video illustrated the first situation and the first display reaction to the context change. After watching a video, the user had to fill in a questionnaire. The questions aimed at capturing the participants' perception of the shown display reaction in terms of transparency, controllability, comfort of use, privacy, and trust.

The questions represented statements which had to be ranked on a Likert scale from 1 ("absolutely disagree") to 5 ("absolutely agree"):

- Q1: I understood why the system was reacting in this way.
- Q2: I had control over the system.
- Q3: I found the system comfortable to use.
- Q4: The system protected my privacy in an appropriate way.
- Q5: I found the system trustworthy.

After presenting all possible display reactions for a particular situation, the users were asked to rank their preferences for it. The preferences also had to be estimated as statements of a 5-point Likert scale. The statements emphasised the context of the given scenario, such as the presence of others or the privacy of data. For instance, a statement for the scenario of Friend Finder where the user was interacting with the display in a public area looked liked this:
"When I am watching my social network alone and a stranger approaches the display..."

- P1: I prefer to hide my data.
- P2: I prefer to mask my data.
- P3: I prefer no reaction from the display.
- P4: I prefer to be asked by my mobile phone.

Questions Q1–Q4 were aimed to collect empirical data to initialise the BN. Question Q5 was required to validate the network by checking whether the generated decisions matched the system action that created the highest user trust. Questions P1–P4 reflected subjective user preferences. In particular, we wanted to find out whether user preferences were in accord with the highest trust ratings and decisions generated by the BN. All in all, we collected evaluations of 85 online users and each video was seen by at least seven participants (Mean: 14). Supplying gender and age was not mandatory. The 73 users that provided demographic data included 24 women and 49 men. They were aged between 23 and 62 years, with an average age of 33.3 years.

Live Study

For the live study we picked two prototypes from the online surveys that could be easily installed and tested and that covered all scenarios related to privacy issues: Friend Finder and Travel Planner. The experiments were conducted individually in front of large displays that were installed in a university public area with a moderate circulation of researchers, students, and visitors. That is, the study participants were not just watching a video, but actively experiencing an application by interacting with it. In each application, the users were confronted with a variety of trust-critical situations, such as another person approaching, while they were viewing private information. As in the online survey, the users had to assess potential system reactions to these events. Hence, the procedure and the questions used in the live study reproduced the web-based survey as closely as possible to control for any unintended side effects. Both prototypes were tested between groups: Every participant evaluated either Friend Finder or Travel Planner. Altogether, 36 people took part in the live experiments (FF: 16; TP: 20). Among them there were 16 female and 20 male persons, aged from 20 to 36 (mean 28.3).

The results of the live study generally matched the results obtained in the online survey. Both experiments yielded similar distributions of user rankings for transparency, controllability, comfort of use, privacy, and reliability. Moreover, we found similar distributions of trust and user preferences. Interestingly, the participants gave higher trust ratings in the live condition than in the online condition. A two-tailed t-test showed that the differences were significant with mean values of 3.66 (standard deviation = 1.50) and 3.08 (STD = 1.27) in FF ($t(238) = 2.46, p < 0.02$) and mean values of 3.98 (STD=0.84) and 3.14 (STD = 1.40) in TP ($t(248) = 5.86, p < 0.001$). Apparently, the fact that the participants had the chance to interact with the system had influenced their ratings positively.

However, the important result for us was to see that apart from a few exceptions the ranking of system reactions in the online survey was in line with that obtained in the live study. Independently of whether users had to evaluate the online or the live setting, participants preferred the same system reaction. Overall, the results indicate that the online survey provides realistic input for the initialisation of the BN despite a few discrepancies.

Finally, the quantitative data obtained in the studies enabled us to derive distributions for each trust dimension related to each contextual combination. For each trust dimension, we modelled the probability distribution for all combinations of context and display reaction in the BN after the data taken from both studies.

## 3.4.2 Validation of the UTM

With our customised UTM finally complete, we were interested in how well it was suited to create trustworthy decisions.

Although we also asked for the users' preferred display reaction for each context combination as well as their trust in the display reaction presented for each such combination, it should be noted that this information was not used to model the UTM. As mentioned above, we only used the users' rankings of the different trust dimensions for each combination of context and display reaction. Instead, the data on user trust ratings and user preferences was used as a ground truth to validate the decisions generated by the UTM. In this vein, we were able to check to what extent the relationship between trust and trust dimensions was application-independent. For the validation of the UTM we generated decisions for all contextual combinations. These decisions were compared to the results from the user studies. In particular, we compared the decision obtained from the UTM with the user's ratings of system actions and their own trust.

The contextual combinations were set by entering appropriate evidence into the matching context nodes. For example, for a specific situation in the Proximity scenario, the evidence would be set to "Privacy of Content → Private", "User Activity → Arriving" and "Social → Alone". We only used "hard" evidence at this point, i.e. the corresponding values were set to 100 %. For each of these combinations, the display reaction with the highest utility rating (which was directly based on the computed value of user trust) was chosen as the system's decision.

First, we compared these generated reactions with those preferred by the participants in the studies: For each context combination, we selected the display reaction that received the highest average score in the experiments. When comparing the display reactions preferred by the users with those generated by the UTM, we found that they matched in 21 out of the 22 situations (95.45 %). Second, we compared the generated reactions with those that received the highest trust in the studies. They matched in all 22 situations.

These results show that the BN delivers good accuracy in the generated decisions. As an example from the results, let us take a look at the first Spectator scenario (the third row in Table 3.1), one of its situations and the one mismatch mentioned above: In case of the data shown being private and a friend present, the reaction to present the different options via mobile phone received the highest trust from the participants. This was also the reaction that the UTM deemed the most trustworthy. However, the *preferred* reaction for this situation was "Hide private data". In other words, the participants' trust ratings were in line with those determined by the UTM while their favoured reaction was not.

However, this form of validation only validated our model within the same population and also the generated decisions were compared to average and not individual preferences. Thus we were also interested in how its generated decisions matched with the preferences of "new" and individual users. Therefore we also performed a leave-one-person-out cross-validation: For each scenario, we performed n validations, where n is the number of users that participated in the respective experiment for that scenario. In each of the n validations, the UTM was initialised with the data from $(n-1)$ users and then validated with the missing user. The final result for each scenario was the average of all n validations. The comparison of user preferences with the adaptations generated now resulted in 15.84 out of 22 matching situations (72.00 %). The comparison with the highest-trust adaptations now matched in 17.26 out of 22 (78.45 %). These results are in line with the percentages of participants who individually preferred the system reaction which received the highest average score, 78.80 % for preference and 82.58 % for trust.

### 3.4.3 Discussion of Results

Using empirical data collected in online and live experiments, we demonstrated how the UTM was initialised and cross-validated. The evaluation revealed that the approach succeeded in determining system actions that obtained the highest value for trustworthiness from users. An interesting result obtained by the empirical validation of the Bayesian network was the mismatch between the system reactions users *preferred* most and the system reactions resulting in the highest amount of user *trust*. From the comments of the live study participants, we found that the feeling of trust often depends on the person's ability to explain the system reaction and agree with it. For example, when a person comes closer to the display, it seems logical and expected that the display does not show any reaction. We learn this behaviour from everyday life: Fixtures, even electronic ones, usually do not react. Apparently, the option "Do nothing" therefore received highest trust rankings. However, the most understandable reaction might not be the most preferred or the most convenient one. Here, the more creative (but less predictable) reactions were favoured. For example, the users found it smart and convenient that the display noticed them and proposed via a mobile device to show their data on the large screen. Thus, the "Ask via mobile device" option was chosen as a preference.

Future work should aim at gaining a deeper insight into this question, investigating which factor – trust or subjective preference – drives the user's ultimate choice of a system reaction. One limitation of our live studies is the homogeneity of the participants, since most of them were rather young students of computer science. Also, while we already reached a larger demographic variety with our online studies, future work should also extend the live studies in a similar fashion.

## 3.5 Case Study 2: Energy-Aware Device Management Systems

Energy-aware device management systems, such as home automation systems, could support users in saving energy either by switching off devices proactively if they are not needed, or by providing personalised advice respectively, asking the users for confirmation before executing an action. However, autonomously performed actions not only contribute to the users' convenience, they also limit the users' control over the system. Furthermore, it may confuse if the system, for example, switches off a device automatically without any information or explanation. On the other hand, asking the users for confirmation via a message, e.g. on a display or a mobile device, would offer more control and transparency, but might disturb the users. Alternatively, the system could also decide to do nothing. This certainly would leave the user undisturbed and in control, but might not be the proper reaction one expects from a smart and adaptive system that is intended to act proactively. As a consequence, each of the possible system actions could be the most suitable in one situation, but might impair the users' trust in another situation. Hence, smart device management systems are another example for systems that could benefit from using the UTM.

In this section, we will describe how the UTM was customised for and integrated into a smart office environment and present important findings that could influence the development of similar systems. These findings (in contrast to the first case study where we only validated the application-specific UTM) also include the results of a live study in which participants actually interacted with the system whose decisions were driven by the UTM.

### 3.5.1  Customising the UTM for a Smart Office System

In this case study, the device management system should be used in an application that is able to control the employees' displays and the room's light in an office occupied by several people. Therefore, for each device, a specific model was constructed from the generic UTM described in Sect. 3.3. This represents a difference to the previous case study, where only a single UTM was needed for each application. Also, this case study focused on a slightly different set of trust dimensions: Even though privacy issues could not be completely excluded, we assumed that they were less of a concern in the investigated scenario and focused on the tension between transparency, controllability, comfort of use, and trust.

#### 3.5.1.1  System Actions and Contexts

To customise the UTM for the given scenario, first the available system actions and the considered context information had to be defined. We found three general reactions that the intended system could execute for both devices given a specific situation. They fall into the same broad categories as the ones in the previous case study:

1. *Do nothing*: If there was no reason to react in the current situation or if it was more important to not disturb the user than to change a device's state, the system could decide to do nothing although this could result in wasted energy.
2. *Act autonomously*: If the system decided that a device should be switched off or on to adapt the environment to a changed situation and if it was not necessary to disturb the user by asking for confirmation, the system was enabled to change the device's state automatically.
3. *Ask for confirmation*: If the current situation required a change in a device's state and if it was assumed that the user would be better asked for confirmation, the system sent a message to one of the user's devices. For the light control this message could be sent either to the user's *mobile device* or his or her *display*. Since the display should only be switched off, if the user was not using it, the later option was not implemented for the display control.

Whether the room's light should be on or off mainly depended on the *luminance outside* and the presence of people in the room. The presence of people was further divided into the *presence of the user* and the *presence of the user's colleagues or co-workers (social context)*. The only context that affected the need for a switched-on

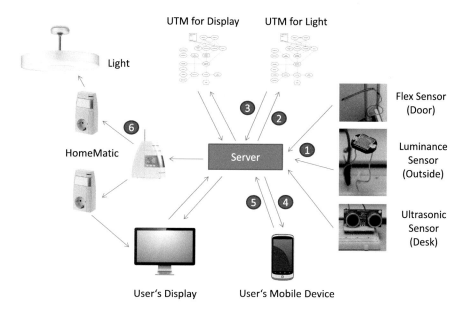

**Fig. 3.5** Architecture of the smart office system

display was the user's current *state*. However, for this context a more fine-grained representation of the user's current activity was needed to distinguish, e.g. whether the user was *working with the PC (respectively display)* or *engaged in another activity*, such as reading a book, or whether the user *was away from the desk*.

### 3.5.1.2   Architecture

Figure 3.5 shows the overall architecture of the Smart Office System. It runs on a central server which also stored the UTMs for the devices and was enabled to send messages to the users' displays as well as their mobile devices. To gather the required context data, several Arduino-Sensors[1] were distributed in the office: The outdoor luminance was measured by light sensors. The presence of persons at the desks was detected by ultrasonic sensors. Furthermore, based on the assumption that the door would be closed if nobody is in the office, a flex sensor was attached to the door to determine whether the office was abandoned. To control the displays and the light, a HomeMatic[2] system and remote controlled plugs were used.

A typical scenario concerning the light could be the following, see circled numbers in Fig. 3.5: The user is working alone in the office in the morning. Since it is still dark outside, the light is on. The system is aware of all devices' states

---

[1] http://arduino.cc/

[2] http://www.homematic.com/

and regularly polls the sensors for the most recent context data (1). As long as the context does not change, nothing needs to be done. However, for example, as soon as it is getting bright outside, the system becomes active. In order to decide which reaction may be the best in the current situation, the system enters the current context information into the appropriate BN (2) and the system actions' impact on the different trust dimensions as well as the resulting user trust and the action's utility are calculated. Finally, the best action is chosen and communicated back to the server (3). Let us assume that the system decides to send a request for confirmation to the user's mobile device (4). The user chooses "yes", the answer is sent back to the server (5) which then switches off the light via the HomeMatic (6).

### 3.5.1.3 Conditional Probabilities

To derive the probability distributions for each trust dimension for all combinations of contexts and system actions, two online surveys (one for each device) were conducted. The goal was once again to discover how the system actions would affect the trust dimensions and the users' trust in typical situations during daily office routines. To this end, we employed a procedure similar to the online survey in the previous case study. However, this time we decided to use textual descriptions instead of videos to outline the different situations, since the contexts and system actions were easier to describe. Again, participants were asked to rate the various system actions by answering the following statements on a 5-point Likert scale:

- Q1: I understood why the system was reacting in this way.
- Q2: I had control over the system.
- Q3: I found the system comfortable to use.
- Q4: I found the system to be trustworthy.

Table 3.2 summarises the possible system reactions per device and the investigated situations represented by different settings of contextual variables.

In total, seven women and nine men evaluated the situations and actions for the light and nine women and twelve men rated the situations and actions for the display. They were aged between 24 and 51 years (mean: 28).

## 3.5.2 Live Study in the Lab

To investigate whether the developed system would be able to predict users' trust and preferences in a live setting, a live study was conducted. In this study, the decisions taken by the UTM were evaluated along the lines of the validation in the first case study: (1) Would the chosen actions affect the users' trust in a positive way? (2) Would the chosen actions match the actions favoured by the users?

**Table 3.2** Possible system reactions in different contextual combinations

| Device | Situation | | | System reaction |
| | User state | Social context | Luminance outside | |
|---|---|---|---|---|
| Display | (1) Working at PC | – | – | (a) Switch display automatically |
| | (2) Idle at PC | – | – | (b) Ask for confirmation via mobile |
| | (3) Away from desk | – | – | (c) Do nothing |
| | (4) Out of room | – | – | |
| Light | (1) Arriving | (1) Co-worker present | (1) Dark | (a) Switch light automatically |
| | (2) Present | (2) Co-worker away | (2) Bright | (b) Ask for confirmation via mobile |
| | (3) Leaving | | | (c) Ask for confirmation via display |
| | | | | (d) Do nothing |

### 3.5.2.1 Procedure

First, the participants had to provide general demographic information and information about their experience with home automation systems. Furthermore, the participants were asked whether they considered themselves to have a trusting nature and whether they trust computer systems in general.

After a short introduction to the setting and the scenario, the participants had to run through several tasks and situations, all of which simulated the daily routine in an office occupied by several people. In each situation, the system performed the actions that were selected by the UTM and the participants had to rate them by filling in a short questionnaire that included the questions Q1–Q4 as shown above. Furthermore, the users were asked to choose their preferred system action. For instance, the statement concerning the display and the first task was: "When I enter my office and sit at my desk, I prefer ...

- P1: ... no reaction from the display."
- P2: ... to switch the display on automatically."
- P3: ... to be asked via mobile phone for permission to switch on the device."

All tasks and situations, as well as the system reactions selected by the UTM are summarised in Table 3.3. To ensure that all participants conducted the study under the same realistic conditions, the tasks were embedded in a coherent story. Furthermore, the room was darkened and changes in the outdoor luminance were simulated by a lamp. Changes in the participant's and the co-worker's state were triggered by the participants themselves and by one of the experimenters who played the role of the co-worker.

**Table 3.3** Tasks, situations, and system actions selected by the UTM

| | Situation | | | System action | |
|---|---|---|---|---|---|
| Task | User state | Social context | Outside luminance | Light | Display |
| 1. Enter the office | Arriving | Co-worker away | Dark | Phone | |
| 2. Sit down at PC | Working at PC | | | | Auto |
| It is getting light | | | | | |
| 3. Check slides for mistakes | | | Bright | Display | |
| The participant's colleague enters the room and sits down at the desk | | | | | |
| 4. Take book X off the shelf | Away from Desk | Co-worker present | | | Nothing |
| 5. Come back and read chapter Y | Idle at PC | | | | Auto |
| 6. It is getting dark | | | | | |
| | | | Dark | Phone | |
| The participant's colleague leaves the room | | | | | |
| 7. Finish work and leave | Leaving | Co-worker away | | Phone | |
| 8. Close the door | Out of room | | | | Auto |

Abbreviations: *Nothing* do nothing; *Auto* switch automatically; *Phone* ask via mobile phone; *Display* ask via display

After rating all tasks, the participants had to state what they liked and disliked about the system and to rate statements related to their attitude towards the system.

### 3.5.2.2 Results

All statements in the questionnaires could be rated on a 5-point Likert scale. Ratings lower than 3 were interpreted as disagreement, ratings higher than 3 as agreement with a statement, and a rating of 3 as a neutral attitude.

Overall 6 women and 18 men (mean age: 26) took part in the study. Five of them were well experienced with home automation technology, such as automatic timers. By contrast, 75 % of the participants had only little or no experience at all. One participant reported a mediocre experience. As for their disposition to trust, 63 % of all participants agreed that they act based on the saying "Trust, but verify". Only one participant disagreed with this statement and 33 % had a neutral attitude. Concerning the statements "I am overly trusting" and "On most systems, you can be assured that they will do what they should", one third each agreed, disagreed, or rated neutrally.

The adaptations the system had chosen for the light achieved consistently high ratings for all trust dimensions, and the *User Trust*, see Fig. 3.6. However, some participants felt that trust was impaired because of missing feedback when the light was switched off after leaving the office. Furthermore, despite the action "Ask for confirmation via the user's mobile phone" received high ratings, most of the participants instead would have preferred messages on their displays and

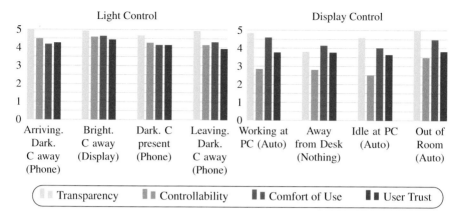

**Fig. 3.6** Results of the live study: user ratings for the trust dimensions and the perceived trust related to the selected system reaction (Abbreviations: Co-worker: *C*; Do Nothing: *Nothing*; Switch Automatically: *Auto*; Ask via Mobile Phone: *Phone*; Ask via Display: *Display*)

especially automatic system actions. Several users stated that using a phone in an office scenario is inconvenient in many situations – either because it is not within reach or because they have to interrupt their work to read the message on the phone.

By contrast, the executed actions concerning the display matched the preferences of most of the participants in all situations. The participants clearly favoured a system that acts autonomously. However, some people missed a confirmation that the display was switched off when they left the room, an authentication mechanism after switching on the display, and functionality to set or disable the automatic control of the display. This affected to some extent the ratings for the *User Trust*, but especially the ratings for the *Controllability*, see Fig. 3.6.

### 3.5.3  Further Investigations

The live study showed that high user ratings for the trust dimensions and the user trust not necessarily also meant that the system's decisions matched the users' preferences and vice versa. The results indicated that the users weighted the trust dimensions differently. For example, it seemed like most of the participants preferred system actions with a higher comfort of use to actions that kept them in control over the system. To further investigate these findings, an additional survey was conducted under similar conditions as the live study.

#### 3.5.3.1  Procedure of the Live Survey

The live survey, similar to the online survey in the first case study, was aimed to acquire ratings for all combinations of situations and possible system reactions, but under realistic conditions. The experimental setting was adopted from the live study, see Sect. 3.5.2. However, instead of running the system and presenting only the actions selected by the UTM, all available actions were shown to the participants in each situation. Furthermore, the participants had to rate the statement "I would prefer the system action..." for each action on a 5-point Likert scale (from 1 = "not at all" to 5 = "in any case") in order to enable a more detailed comparison of the users' preferences.

### 3.5.3.2 Results

In total, eight men and two women (mean age: 28) took part in the live survey.

Similar to the live study, we compared the chosen system action of the UTM for each situation with the one the users found the most preferable or the most trustworthy. The results confirmed the findings of the live study. For the display, most of the participants preferred the actions chosen by the UTM (73 %) and provided the highest trust ratings for them (80 %). However, the actions selected for the light were much less in line with the preferences of the users. Only 18 % of them expressed the highest preference for the selected system actions. Nevertheless, 80 % of the participants rated their trust towards these actions the highest. These results confirmed that the UTM was able to make trustworthy decisions. Trust was of course not the only factor, but there was a significant relationship between the users' trust and their preferences (Pearson correlation coefficient: $r = 0.481$, $p(one\text{-}tailed) < 0.01$).

A detailed analysis of the ratings provided for the specific trust dimensions showed that the *Controllability* did not significantly influence the users' preferences ($r = 0.117$, $p = 0.139$). Although autonomous decisions were rated as less controllable, see Fig. 3.7, they were preferred by most of the participants, see Fig. 3.8.

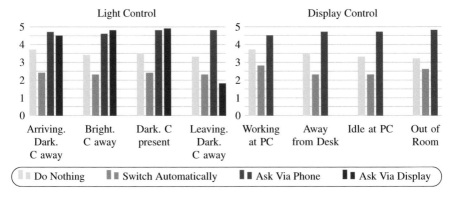

**Fig. 3.7** Investigated trust dimension: controllability (*left*: actions concerning the light, *right*: actions concerning the display)

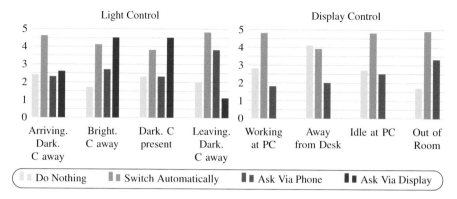

**Fig. 3.8** Investigated: preferences (*left*: actions concerning the light, *right*: actions concerning the display)

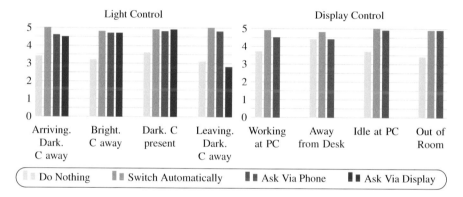

**Fig. 3.9** Investigated trust dimension: transparency (*left*: actions concerning the light, *right*: actions concerning the display)

Concerning the perceived *Transparency*, the users' ratings showed a significant correlation with the preferences ($r = 0.489$, $p < 0.01$). However, except for the action "Do nothing", all system actions were rated as very transparent in most of the situations, see Fig. 3.9. Thus, it is difficult to infer why the participants preferred some system actions over others.

In contrast, automatic system actions that were preferred by most of the users were rated as most comfortable, whereas "Do Nothing" and especially the action "Ask the user for confirmation via her or his mobile phone" scored significantly worse, see Fig. 3.10. This could be emphasised by the fact that the perceived *Comfort of Use* was significantly correlated with the users' preferences ($p < 0.01$). A Pearson correlation coefficient of 0.744 even showed that the perceived *Comfort of Use* was the most decisive factor that influenced the users' preferences.

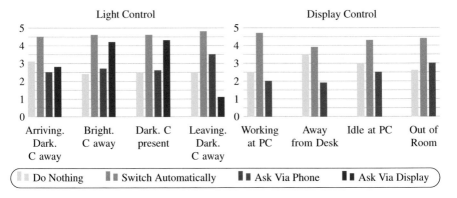

**Fig. 3.10** Investigated trust dimension: comfort of Use (*left*: actions concerning the light, *right*: actions concerning the display)

### 3.5.4  Discussion of Results

Overall, the results in the live study as well as in the live survey revealed that users had a high amount of trust in the system actions that were chosen by the UTM. However, they also showed that the participants preferred more comfortable system actions over more controllable actions, even if this resulted in less trusted system actions. The participants liked the idea of being asked in some situations. However, they considered a message on their mobile phone only reasonable when they entered or left the office. When they were seated at their desk, they preferred autonomous decisions by the system or messages that were shown on their displays instead of their phone that often is not within reach and would require the participants to interrupt their work every time the phone received a message.

In future work, it should be investigated whether giving more weight to a trust dimension (in this case the *Comfort of Use*) when selecting a system action could increase the UTMs accuracy concerning users' trust as well as preferences.

The results in this case study also showed that users seem to weight trust dimensions differently depending on whether they are confronted with a realistic setting or just a verbal description of it. In the first case study, see Sect. 3.4, this mismatch between online and live data was less pronounced. One reason could be that in case study 1, the users' choice between different system actions was mainly based on privacy concerns both in the online and the live setting. We assume that privacy issues are apparent even if they are not experienced in a live scenario. By comparison, the trust dimension that mainly influenced the users' ratings and decisions in the smart office scenario was the perceived comfort of use. While actually experienced interruptions through messages via the mobile phone obviously affected the users' experience and thus also their ratings, the participants in the online survey lacked this experience. Another option to explore would be to collect a sufficient amount of live data by recruiting a larger number of users as a basis for the training of the BNs.

Furthermore, future data collection efforts should concentrate on longer scenarios with a larger number of tasks presented in randomised order. In this case study the sequence of tasks was not randomised, but determined by the story line representing a working day in the life of the user. While this approach helped us create a plausible scenario for users, it might have led to an overfitting of the BNs.

## 3.6 Conclusion

The ability of smart environments to dynamically adapt to changing contexts comes with a lot of benefits, such as protected privacy or increased convenience. At the same time, if an automatically executed system action does not match the users' assessment of the situation, it also raises issues with the users' trust. In this chapter, a decision-theoretic mechanism to trust management, called User Trust Model, was delineated that utilises Bayesian networks to assess user trust through trust dimensions, monitor it during the interaction, and choose appropriate measures to ensure user trust in critical situations. The two different case studies presented in this chapter showed how the UTM could be customised for different applications. Since both case studies showed that the UTM's decisions resulted in a highly trustworthy system behaviour, it seems promising to integrate it in other smart and self-adaptive environments, too.

However, since we focused on the challenge of modelling experience-based user trust, the findings from the case studies also showed two important facts that have to be considered when utilising the UTM: Whilst online surveys bear the advantage that a lot of data can be collected within a short period of time, in some scenarios they might not convey the experience of a real interaction and thus affect the users' ratings. Although the first case study seemed to indicate that it is possible to train BNs from online data and employ them in live scenarios, for the energy-aware device management system the reliance on the online data was only possible to a limited extent. In such cases, it might be essential to collect a sufficient amount of live data for the BN's initialisation. Furthermore, depending on the intended system, it might be necessary to weight the trust dimensions influence on the users' trust differently. While *privacy* was an important factor for the users in public display scenarios, *comfort of use* played an significant role in the users' assessment of the device management system's decisions.

For future work, we plan extensions that might further increase the UTM's quality and flexibility and be necessary especially in complex scenarios that require the consideration of additional trust indicators.

First of all, we aim to derive user trust not only from its causes, i.e. system properties, but also from its effects, i.e. observable user behaviours. In earlier work [36], we investigated various physiological patterns as an indicator of trust felt by a user when viewing web pages. As a next step, we will concentrate on the identification of behavioural factors from which experience-based user trust might be derived in smart and self-adaptive environments, such as the time spent in front of a public display or the extent to which users are willing to relinquish control to the system. These factors correspond to reliance as a behaviour [21] as opposed to trust as an attitude that we focused on so far.

The detection of behavioural patterns also could be used for more objective measurements when evaluating a system's ability to select actions that maximise user trust. So far we only asked participants' to rate the perceived trustworthiness of individual actions.

As another future step, we intend to enable the UTM to consider how user trust felt at a particular point in time depends on user trust experienced at an earlier point in time. Therefore, we will extend the Bayesian network to a dynamic Bayesian network. A topology of such a network was already presented in [37], but so far it has not been grounded and evaluated by user data.

Finally, the BNs in both case studies were initialised with data from several individuals. Consequently, the BNs rather reflected the attitude of a variety of users as opposed to an individual user. Due to the subjectiveness of trust, users might, depending on their trust disposition, favour different system reactions. For example, users that tend to distrust technical systems in general might give more importance to a high level of control than to a high level of comfort. In our future work, we will investigate how to improve the accuracy of the user trust model by incorporating knowledge about user-specific attitudes. A promising approach might be to distinguish between different categories of users based on multiple dimensions [38]. Following Westin's privacy indices [39], examples for such categories might be privacy fundamentalists, pragmatists and unconcerned users. In case study 2, the questionnaire for the live survey already contained questions about participants' opinions and habits concerning sustainability and their trust towards other people and technical systems in general. Such data could be included in the UTM in the future. In order to achieve an even higher degree of personalisation, the UTM could also be trained with data from individual users. In the ideal case, the UTM should not require extensive training before it can be used, but dynamically adapt to people's preferences by learning from their behaviour during the interaction with the smart environment.

**Acknowledgements** This research is partly sponsored by the research unit *OC-Trust* (FOR 1085) of the German Research Foundation.

The authors would like to thank Karin Bee and Ekaterina Kurdyukova for their contributions to the work presented in this chapter.

The core of our implementation is based on the SMILE reasoning engine and the networks shown in this chapter were created using the GeNIe modelling environment. Both SMILE and GeNIe are developed and contributed to the community by the Decision Systems Laboratory, University of Pittsburgh and available at http://genie.sis.pitt.edu/.

# References

1. Rothrock, L., Koubek, R., Fuchs, F., Haas, M., Salvendy, G.: Review and reappraisal of adaptive interfaces: toward biologically inspired paradigms. Theor. Issues Ergon. Sci. **3**, 47–84 (2002)
2. Yan, Z., Zhang, P., Vasilakos, A.V.: A survey on trust management for internet of things. J. Netw. Comput. Appl. **42**, 120–134 (2014)
3. Röcker, C., Hinske, S., Magerkurth, C.: Intelligent privacy support for large public displays. In: Stephanidis, C. (ed.) Universal Access in HCI, Part II, HCII 2007, LNCS 4555. Proceedings of the 12th International Conference on Human-Computer Interaction (HCI International), 22–27 July 2007, Beijing International Conference Center, Beijing, pp. 198–207. Springer, Heidelberg (2007)
4. Castelfranchi, C., Falcone, R.: Trust Theory: A Socio-Cognitive and Computational Model. Wiley, Hoboken (2010)
5. Yan, Z., Holtmanns, S.: Computer Security, Privacy and Politics: Current Issues, Challenges and Solutions, pp. 290–323. IGI Global, Hershey (2008)
6. Marsh, S.: Trust in distributed artificial intelligence. In: 4th European Workshop on Modelling Autonomous Agents in a Multi-agent World, Artificial Social Systems, pp. 94–112. Springer, Berlin/Heidelberg (1992)
7. Wang, Y., Vassileva, J.: Bayesian network trust model in peer-to-peer networks. In: 2nd International Workshop on Agents and Peer-to-Peer Computing, pp. 23–34. Springer, Berlin/Heidelberg (2003)
8. Yu, B., Singh, M.P.: An evidential model of distributed reputation management. In: Proceedings of the 1st International Joint Conference on Autonomous Agents and Multiagent Systems, pp. 294–301. ACM, New York (2002)
9. Vogiatzis, G., MacGillivray, I., Chli, M.: A probabilistic model for trust and reputation. In: 9th International Conference on Autonomous Agents and Multiagent Systems, pp. 225–232. IFAA-MAS, Richland (2010)
10. Jøsang, A., Hayward, R., Pope, S.: Trust network analysis with subjective logic. In: 29th Australasian Computer Science Conference, vol. 48, pp. 85–94. Australian Computer Society, Darlinghurst (2006)
11. Sankaranarayanan, V., Chandrasekaran, M., Upadhyaya, S.J.: Towards modeling trust based decisions: a game theoretic approach. In: Proceedings of the 12th European Symposium on Research in Computer Security, pp. 485–500. Springer, Berlin/Heidelberg (2007)
12. Burnett, C., Norman, T.J., Sycara, K.: Trust decision-making in multi-agent systems. In: Proceedings of the 22nd International Joint Conference on Artificial Intelligence (IJCAI/AAAI), Barcelona, pp.115–120 (2011)
13. Msadek, N., Ungerer, T.: Trust as important factor for building robust self-x systems. In: Reif, W., Anders, G., Seebach, H., Steghöfer, J.-P., André, E., Hähner, J., Müller-Schloer, C., Ungerer, T. (eds.) Autonomic Systems, vol. 7, pp. 151–181. Springer, Cham (2016)
14. Sherchan, W., Nepal, S., Paris, C.: A survey of trust in social networks. ACM Comput. Surv. **45**, 47:1–47:33 (2013)
15. Bhuiyan, T., Xu, Y., Jøsang, A.: A review of trust in online social networks to explore new research Agenda. In: Proceedings of the 2010 International Conference on Internet Computing, pp. 123–128. CSREA Press, Las Vegas (2010)
16. Adali, S., Escriva, R., Goldberg, M.K., Hayvanovych, M., Magdon-Ismail, M., Szymanski, B.K., Wallace, W.A., Williams, G.T.: Measuring behavioral trust in social networks. In: IEEE International Conference on Intelligence and Security Informatics, pp. 150–152. IEEE, Piscataway (2010)
17. Ivanov, I., Vajda, P., Korshunov, P., Ebrahimi, T.: Comparative study of trust modeling for automatic landmark tagging. IEEE Trans. Inf. Forensics Secur. **8**, 911–923 (2013)
18. O'Donovan, J., Smyth, B.: Trust in recommender systems. In: Proceedings of the 10th International Conference on Intelligent User Interfaces, pp. 167–174. ACM, New York (2005)

19. Bickmore, T., Cassell, J.: Relational agents: a model and implementation of building user trust. In: Proceedings of the SIGCHI Conference on Human Factors in Computing Systems, pp. 396–403. ACM, New York (2001)
20. Glass, A., McGuinness, D.L., Wolverton, M.: Toward establishing trust in adaptive agents. In: Proceedings of the 13th International Conference on Intelligent User Interfaces, pp. 227–236. ACM, New York (2008)
21. Lee, J.D., See, K.A.: Trust in automation: designing for appropriate reliance. J. Hum. Factors Ergon. Soc. **46**, 50–80 (2004)
22. Denko, M.K., Sun, T., Woungang, I.: Trust management in ubiquitous computing: a Bayesian approach. Comput. Commun. **34**, 398–406 (2011)
23. Arimura, S., Fujita, M., Kobayashi, S., Kani, J., Nishigaki, M., Shiba, A.: i/k-Contact: a context-aware user authentication using physical social trust. In: 12th International Conference on Privacy, Security and Trust, Toronto, pp. 407–413 (2014)
24. Cao, H., Olivier, P., Jackson, D.: Enhancing privacy in public spaces through cross-modal displays. Soc. Sci. Comput. Rev. **26**, 87–102 (2008)
25. Antifakos, S., Kern, N., Schiele, B., Schwaninger, A.: Towards improving trust in context-aware systems by displaying system confidence. In: Proceedings of the 7th International Conference on Human Computer Interaction with Mobile Devices & Services, pp. 9–14. ACM, Salzburg (2005)
26. Lim, B.Y., Dey, A.K.: Toolkit to support intelligibility in context-aware applications. In: Proceedings of the 12th International Conference on Ubiquitous Computing, Copenhagen, pp. 13–22. ACM (2010)
27. Cheverst, K., Byun, H., Fitton, D., Sas, C., Kray, C., Villar, N.: Exploring issues of user model transparency and proactive behaviour in an office environment control system. User Model. User-Adapt. Interact. **15**, 235–273 (2005)
28. Hochleitner, C., Graf, C., Unger, D., Tscheligi, M.: Making devices trustworthy: security and trust feedback in the Internet of things. In: 4th International Workshop on 'Security and Privacy in Spontaneous Interaction and Mobile Phone Use' at Pervasive'12, Newcastle (2012)
29. Steghöfer, J.-P., Kiefhaber, R., Leichtenstern, K., Bernard, Y., Klejnowski, L., Reif, W., Ungerer, T., André, E., Hähner, J., Müller-Schloer, C.: Trustworthy organic computing systems: challenges and perspectives. In: Autonomic and Trusted Computing, pp. 62–76. Springer, Berlin/Heidelberg (2010)
30. Bee, K., Hammer, S., Pratsch, C., André, E.: The automatic trust management of self-adaptive multi-display environments. In: Khalil, I., Mantoro, T. (eds.) Trustworthy Ubiquitous Computing, vol. 6, pp. 3–20. Atlantis Press, Amsterdam (2012)
31. Lumsden, J.: Triggering trust: to what extent does the question influence the answer when evaluating the perceived importance of trust triggers? In: Proceedings of the 2009 British Computer Society Conference on Human-Computer Interaction, pp. 214–223. British Computer Society, Swinton (2009)
32. Russell, S.J., Norvig, P.: Artificial Intelligence: A Modern Approach 2nd International. Prentice Hall, Upper Saddle River (2003)
33. Wißner, M., Hammer, S., Kurdyukova, E., André, E.: Trust-based decision-making for the adaptation of public displays in changing social contexts. Journal of Trust Management. **1**, 1–23 (2014)
34. Kurdyukova, E., Bee, K., André, E.: Friend or Foe? Relationship-based adaptation on public displays. In: Proceedings of the 2nd International Conference on Ambient Intelligence, pp. 228–237. Springer, Berlin/Heidelberg (2011)
35. Greenberg, S., Marquardt, N., Ballendat, T., Diaz-Marino, R., Wang, M.: Proxemic interactions: the new Ubicomp? ACM Interact. **18**, 42–50 (2011)
36. Leichtenstern, K., Bee, N., André, E., Berkmüller, U., Wagner, J.: Physiological measurement of trust-related behavior in trust-neutral and trust-critical situations. In Proceedings of the 5th IFIP International Conference on Trust Management, pp. 165–172. Springer, Berlin/Heidelberg (2011)

37. Kurdyukova, E., André, E., Leichtenstern, K.: Trust management of ubiquitous multi-display environments. In: Krueger, A., Kuflik, T. (eds.) Ubiquitous Display Environments, pp. 177–193. Springer, Berlin/Heidelberg (2012)
38. Knijnenburg, B.P., Kobsa, A., Jin, H.: Dimensionality of information disclosure behavior. Int. J. Hum.-Comput. Stud. **71**, 1144–1162 (2013)
39. Kumaraguru, P., Cranor, L.F.: Privacy indexes: a survey of Westin's studies. Technical report, CMU-ISRI-5-138. Institute for Software Research International, Carnegie Mellon University (2005)

# Chapter 4
# Normative Control: Controlling Open Distributed Systems with Autonomous Entities

Jan Kantert, Sarah Edenhofer, Sven Tomforde, Jörg Hähner, and Christian Müller-Schloer

**Abstract** Open distributed systems consisting of a potentially large set of autonomous entities might not be controllable directly. More precisely, standard control interventions, such as altering parameters and behaviour, are not possible due to the entity's autonomy. However, indirect control using socio-inspired mechanisms can be applied to guide the system's behaviour and influence the distributed entities using sanctions and incentives. The demanded behaviour as well as the corresponding sanctions and incentives are coded as norms and generated in response to perceived environmental and internal conditions. Such a norm is issued by centralised authorities. Norm violation is monitored using a higher-level observer in a distributed manner. After an introduction and motivation for using social mechanisms in technical systems, we present a novel normative control loop establishing the afore-described concept within a Trusted Desktop Grid scenario. The evaluation demonstrates the potential benefit in terms of an increased system robustness and fast recovery from attack states.

**Keywords** Organic computing • Agent organisation • Norms • Normative control • Open distributed systems • Desktop grid

---

J. Kantert (✉)
Institute of Systems Engineering, Leibniz Universität Hannover, Hannover, Germany
e-mail: kantert@sra.uni-hannover.de

S. Edenhofer • S. Tomforde
Organic Computing Group, University of Augsburg, Augsburg, Germany
e-mail: sarah.edenhofer@informatik.uni-augsburg.de;
sven.tomforde@informatik.uni-augsburg.de

J. Hähner
Organic Computing Group, University of Augsburg, Augsburg, Germany
e-mail: jorg.hahner@informatik.uni-augsburg.de

C. Müller-Schloer
Institute of Systems Engineering, University of Hannover, Hannover, Germany
e-mail: cms@sra.uni-hannover.de

© Springer International Publishing Switzerland 2016
W. Reif et al. (eds.), *Trustworthy Open Self-Organising Systems*,
Autonomic Systems, DOI 10.1007/978-3-319-29201-4_4

## 4.1  Introduction

The development of Information and Communication Technology (ICT) has faced a rapid increase of complexity that has its roots in non-trivial and partly indirect interactions, mutual influences, and an increasing interweaving of former isolated systems[1] (see e.g. [2]). One particular challenge within this observable trend is the rise of open agent ecosystems (see [3, 4]). More precisely, we have to cope with systems that allow for a continuous joining and leaving of agents at runtime, a cooperation of heterogeneous agents, and a typically selfish behaviour of participating agents without the possibility to consider their individual motivation.

Openness, heterogeneity, and dynamics, however, present severe challenges to providing stable and efficient system behaviour, since this allows, by design, unpredictable, exploiting, or even malicious behaviour of participating entities. Therefore, we present a concept for guided self-organised behaviour to counter negative emergent effects within this chapter. Consider a Desktop Computing Grid (DCG) as particular instance of this aforementioned problem class. In such a DCG, agents cooperate by sharing computing resources. The basic idea is to ask other agents to process computational tasks in order to achieve a better performance compared to processing these tasks individually. Obviously, these systems depend on reciprocity: The system will only be successful if agents continuously contribute their resources. In order to motivate agents to do so and to further provide fairness and efficiency, the introduction of computational trust relationships among agents has been shown to achieve promising results – resulting in a Trusted Desktop Grid (TDG) [5]. Distributed rendering of films is an exemplary application running on top of the TDG which is also presented in the evaluation chapter. The same mechanism can also be applied to the domain of Low Power Sensor Networks[3].

Unfortunately, trust itself comes with major drawbacks – for instance, decisions based on trust relationships might result in negative emergent behaviour. The "trust breakdown" [6] serves as illustration for such an effect: Here, a large set of malicious and colluding agents joins the system simultaneously which results in numerous bad trust ratings. As a consequence, a massive drop of the average reputation among agents can be observed, meaning that agents stop cooperating. This effect is caused by the large numbers of bad ratings. As a consequence, the benefit for all participants decreases significantly and the system itself becomes dysfunctional to a certain degree. To counteract such events and to further guide the self-organised behaviour, this chapter introduces a concept working at system-level without interfering with the agents' autonomy: A higher-level observation and control loop following the general Observer/Controller pattern [7] of Organic Computing is proposed and applied to the TDG. This loop derives an appropriate situation description in the first place that covers abstract information about work and trust relationships among

---

[1] We will refer to these individual systems as "agents" throughout the chapter, since we assume technical solutions that act on behalf of a user in an automated manner. This term goes back to the domain of multi-agent systems, see [1].

agents, augmented by figures reflecting detected patterns (e.g. quantifying negative emergent behaviour). Afterwards, a control mechanism decides about interventions that make use of sanctioning and incentive techniques to motivate the agents to adapt their behaviour. Such a concept based on sanctions and incentives to guide self-organised system behaviour implements a version of "normative control" [8].

The remainder of this chapter is organised as follows: Based on a brief introduction to rational agent behaviour, Sect. 4.2 outlines which insights from (human) social organisations and game theory can be utilised to improve open agent organisations consisting of heterogeneous and distributed entities. Section 4.3 provides a discussion of the overall goal to be achieved by normative control concepts – the application of self-organisation and adaptivity in combination with social-inspired techniques serves the idea to establish *more robust and scalable* solutions. Section 4.4 aligns the presented work in the context of the state-of-the-art and highlights relevant contributions from this research domain. Section 4.5 describes the novel approach to establish a system-wide observation and control loop to guide the individual behaviour of the participating agents while still considering them as black-boxes. The presented approach is evaluated in Sect. 4.6 using simulations of the TDG as application scenario. Finally, Sect. 4.7 summarises the chapter and gives an outlook to future work.

## 4.2 Social Mechanisms in Technical Systems

The general assumption for normative control of large-scale distributed and open systems is the underlying rationality of the participating agents. Apart from the possibility to exploit or even damage the system, individuals have an inherent motivation to join since there is an individual benefit expected from participation. In the following section, we discuss this rationality in more detail by deriving fundamental concepts from social behaviour in human organisations that are applicable to technical systems.

### 4.2.1 Rational Agents

In economics, game theory, decision theory, and artificial intelligence, agents have been modelled as so called *rational* agents [9]. A rational agent has clear goals and preferences, it will always try to optimise the outcome (or, in game-theoretical terms: the utility) for itself. E.g. the main objective of an eBay bidding agent is to win the auction. In addition, it models uncertainty with probabilities and expectation values and always chooses to perform the action that most likely results in the optimal outcome for itself or its owner from among all feasible actions. In the example of the eBay bidding agent, the optimal outcome of the agent is to win the auction paying the lowest price possible.

In general, we can measure the outcome of an action as *utility* meaning that we map the outcome of an action (or more generally, the profile of all agents' chosen actions) to a number. In the example of the eBay bidding agent, the utility value of the current bidding is high if the offered amount of money is low. Vice versa, the utility value is the smaller the higher the offered price is. However, we have to distinguish between personal utility and system utility. The personal utility is the utility assigned to each single agent, and the system utility is the total utility resulting from the actions of a group of agents. Personal and system utilities are not necessarily the same: Consider a team game played repeatedly where all players of a group must win the rounds with a threshold frequency to reach the next level. If one player was able to win all rounds this would be optimal for its personal utility value. However, the team would not step up necessarily in the next level if the other players did not perform equally well. In addition, personal and system utility can be opposite: Chimpanzees behave cooperatively and share their food with other chimpanzees. This decreases the personal utility but it increases the system utility of the chimpanzee colony [10].

As mentioned above, a rational agent tries to optimise its own outcome which means it tries to maximise its personal utility. Hence, rational agents behave egoistically. But in the scope of Organic Computing, we have to deal with many rational agents which have to cooperate. Therefore, the question arises if egoistic behaviour of agents is useful from the overall system point-of-view. The example of the Prisoner's Dilemma [11] demonstrates that "rational" behaviour may even lead to both, a low personal utility and a low system utility: Let us assume two persons $i$ and $j$ are accused of having committed a crime. Both of them are in prison and they are kept separately so that they can not talk to each other. The maximum (individual) penalty is 5 years in prison. Each prisoner is given two options: He can confess (C) or defect (D). If both $i$ and $j$ decide to deny the crime, each of them gets 3 years in prison. If both of them decide to confess, each of them gets 2 years in prison because they cooperate with the prosecutor. But if only one of them confesses while the other defects the first one gets 5 years in prison and the second one 0 years.

This situation can be modelled by a utility matrix. It shows the two possible decisions for each agent (C, D). Therefore this "game" has four possible outcomes. The values in the matrix show the payoff for each outcome (see Fig. 4.1a). Since in the classical prisoner's dilemma the payoff is "years in prison", which is the opposite of a utility, let us transform the matrix into a real utility matrix by defining:

$$\text{utility} := 5 - \text{"years in prison"} \qquad (4.1)$$

The resulting matrix is shown in Fig. 4.1b. Now each prisoner – being a rational agent – will order the four possible outcomes according to his own objective (to maximise the utility):

$$\text{Prisoner}_i : DC > CC > DD > CD$$

$$\text{Prisoner}_j : CD > CC > DD > DC$$

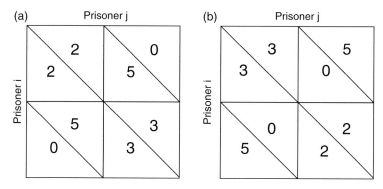

**Fig. 4.1** Number of years in prison/utility per prisoner. (**a**) Matrix describing the years in prison dependent on the prisoners' decisions. (**b**) Utility matrix according to Equation (4.1)

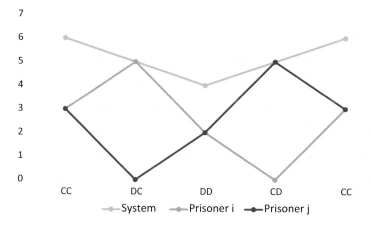

**Fig. 4.2** Penalties for the Prisoner's Dilemma: $C$ = Confess crime, $D$ = Deny to confess crime

Each prisoner will conclude from this ranking that, no matter what his opponent does (C or D), for himself D is better. The result is a (D, D) decision with a payoff of 2 for each prisoner. In Game Theory, the outcome (D, D) is called a *Nash equilibrium* in strictly dominant strategies [12]: Neither agent has an incentive to deviate from (D, D) because the utility can only drop by changing the decision.

This looks fine so far. Why then is it a dilemma? First because each prisoner has to make a difficult decision. But there is a second problem. Let us have a look at the system utility (Fig. 4.2), i.e. the total of the two agents' utilities. The *Nash equilibrium* and the rational decisions of the agents lead to the lowest possible system utility of four (D, D). Apparently both prisoners would be better off with (C, C)! What would be necessary to reach a higher system utility (and, in this case, also a higher individual utility) are two things: (1) Communicate, and (2) trust each other!

It has been discussed extensively if this analysis means that the Prisoner's Dilemma is invalid. The reason for this discussion is the feeling that our society apparently works quite well and that after all altruism and cooperation have developed by evolution. So there must be a fitness benefit in such social behaviours. Binmore [13] argues that there is nothing wrong with the Prisoner's Dilemma except that it is not the correct model for our social behaviour. We usually do not play one-shot games, i.e. as members of a stable society we are subject to repeated games with the same partners. This introduces the idea of reciprocity and of empathetic preferences. Putting oneself in the position of another makes all the difference. The so-called original position asks a member of a society to envisage the social contract to which they would agree if their eventual roles in this society were concealed from them behind a "veil of ignorance". Social rules putting some members of the society at a gross disadvantage are not acceptable any more as soon as I can possibly be in exactly that miserable position. This "original position" is perfectly rational if we change the model assumptions of the Prisoner's Dilemma. We play the game repeatedly; as a matter of fact, we play it permanently, probably hundreds of times every day. We communicate extensively with and without words. And we have developed effective mechanisms of gauging the trustworthiness of our interaction partners.

Binmore [13] argues convincingly how such social behaviour can have developed through evolution. And this means that it must have an evolutionary advantage over less cooperative or purely selfish behaviours. In the light of this discussion it must be asked why economists call the Prisoner's Dilemma behaviour "rational". The "invisible hand" alone cannot account for all the interactions necessary to construct a successful society. Hence, we should refrain from calling this behaviour "rational". It is much more rational to follow the idea of an "extended selfishness", which motivates altruism by a long-term reciprocal well-being of the altruist.

### 4.2.2   Social Awareness

But let us return to the discussion of the prerequisites for a functional and efficient society of *technical agents*. In order to overcome the limitations of the Prisoner's Dilemma, we have to allow our agents to communicate, and we must introduce the equivalent of trust and the notion of binding commitments. Since it will be difficult to implant a kind of "moral responsibility" into the agents, we need different mechanisms to enforce socially acceptable behaviour. As we will see in the following, we can again copy from human societies. The mechanism we are using is social pressure. And one of its varieties is reputation. (Just as another aside: It can be guessed that even human agents are not altruistic just for reasons of a higher moral. As Binmore[13] points out: Justice and fairness are just concepts and will as such not be effective. They require power for their enforcement. Social pressure represents such a power.)

The Prisoner's Dilemma can be illustrated looking at the scenario of the *Tragedy of the Commons* [14]: Let us assume there is a piece of land (the Commons) and several peasants (agents) who may use it. Because of their local (and rational) view each of them will use as much land as possible to plant his wheat. This seems like a good idea for each of them because it increases the personal utility in the short-term view. But in the long-term, the land is overused which results in less lucrative harvests and thus leads to both low personal and low system utilities. This could be improved if the peasants would cooperate limiting their individual usage of the common good or using techniques such as crop rotation.

Again this example shows that rational behaviour of agents may lead to low utilities. We motivated the effects by examples inspired by nature but they are the same looking at technical systems. Therefore, it might be a good idea to introduce social awareness into technical systems in order to mitigate the effects of the agents' classical rational behaviour. However, this will introduce overhead in terms of communication, memory and computation. Therefore, we have to design socially aware technical systems in a way that optimising the personal and system utilities pays off even with regard to the introduced overhead.

### 4.2.3  Why Social Awareness and/or Self-Awareness Matters

The conclusion from the last section is that, if we extend the agent's view[2] by social awareness, then there is a way out of the tragedy. Social awareness requires interaction and thus communication between the agents. In addition, we have to introduce a notion of trust between the agents which enables them to estimate the reliability of each other. In other words, if an agents trusts that another agent will perform an action this means that the first agent expects that the second agent will perform the action with a high probability. Also, if a group of agents assumes that another agent performs an action but this agent fails to perform the action, the other agents can decide to punish the agent. However, the question is how the values of trust are to be computed and which sanctions are to be imposed in case of failures or abnormal behaviour? The answer is that we need a social framework which defines the rules and norms of interaction, communication, and trust between agents. The agents need to evaluate their actions (a priori and a posteriori) according to a kind of ethics, i.e. a set of rules (or norms), which are able to influence the decisions of the agents.

When we introduce such a norm, we have to decide if this is a hard (or mandatory) norm, which the agent must obey, or a soft norm, which might be violated. In the latter case, we need also a sanctioning mechanism. Agents that are sanctioned will change their behaviour in the future. Moreover, we need a mechanism to invent and adopt norms and to change the severity of sanctions. This constitutes a closed control loop used to create, adapt and even delete norms and rules.

---

[2]The view can be extended not only locally (aware of the environment and other agents) but also on the time axis. History-aware agents can predict future developments more accurately.

Looking once more over the fence we find that such a social framework of norms, which is able to overcome the Tragedy of the Commons (TtC), has already been defined in the context of economics. Elinor Ostrom [15] has stated eight principles of Enduring Institutions. An institution is a body of agents with a common set of objectives and rules. "Enduring" refers to a long-term sustainability, even in the presence of limited common resources. Here, Harvey's Commons have been generalised to the so-called Common Pool Resources problem (CPR). Ostrom's eight principles constitute conditions for overcoming the tragedy. The principles are as follows (see [8] for details):

1. *Clearly defined boundaries: Those who have rights or entitlement to appropriate resources from the CPR are clearly defined, as are its boundaries.* An example of this principle regarding the TtC is that the part of land belonging to each peasant must be clearly defined. The same is true for the peasants eligible to use it.
2. *Congruence between appropriation and provision rules and the state of the prevailing local environment:* The rules must prevent overuse or degradation of the common goods.
3. *Collective choice arrangements: In particular, those affected by the operational rules participate in the selection and modification of those rules.* Regarding the TtC example this means that the peasants farming the land also administer the rules defining the farming. This principle prevents third parties imposing their interests.
4. *Monitoring, of both state conditions and appropriator behaviour, is by appointed agencies, who are either accountable to the resource appropriators or are appropriators themselves.* This principle means that only such people may monitor the CPR who are involved in the CPR themselves. This prevents corruption and manipulated monitoring.
5. *A flexible scale of graduated sanctions for resource appropriators who violate communal rules.* In the TtC example this principle defines in which way a peasant violating the rules of farming can be sanctioned.
6. *Access to fast, cheap conflict resolution mechanisms.* A result of this principle is that the reaction to conflicts can occur fast, by e.g. changing the rules of farming or sanctioning a peasant.
7. *Existence of and control over their own institutions is not challenged by external authorities.* This rule states that the Enduring Institution must be self-ruling. External authorities overriding the rules might endanger the stability of the system.
8. *Systems of systems: CPRs can be layered or encapsulated.* This principle means that hierarchies of CPRs are possible in order to save communication overhead or to simplify decision-making processes.

When considering open distributed systems, we aim to implement organisations which follow those principles as shown in the next section.

## 4.2.4  Trust Communities as Self-Organised Social Infrastructures

We are interested in complex technical systems consisting of autonomous agents. Here, an agent is a hardware/software subsystem with some kind of sensory (or at least communication) equipment. If this sensory equipment adds information pertaining to other agents and to certain higher-level entities, this agent becomes socially aware. Also it must be able to take decisions and to act accordingly. Our research question is if and how Ostrom's principles are applicable and advantageous for our technical system.

We call our approach Trust Communities (TCs). A TC comprises a set of agents with a mutual trust relationship. It is characterised by a set of rules (norms), which agents who want to be TC members must adhere to. TCs can be implicitly or explicitly managed. In the latter case, there is a (possibly distributed) management entity taking care of admission and exclusion of agents, norm adaptation, and the TC life-cycle [16].

But in any case, TCs are *self-organised*. TC membership is beneficial for an agent: The advantage of simplified interaction with other agents (no assessment about trust has to be performed for agents within the TC), access to community resources, and reciprocal treatment (priority over outside agents) must outweigh the overhead usually associated with each form organisation (additional communication and an elected manager). So far TCs are not full Enduring Institutions in Ostrom's sense.

Let us explain the TC concept and its benefits using the Desktop Grid Computing (DGC) System as a concrete application example. A DGC system allows for the distribution of computing tasks, so-called work units (WUs), within a network of personal computers. The idea is that computers with a temporary overload can transfer WUs to presently idling ones. As long as all PCs are benevolent, they should all be willing to accept WUs. In an open system, however, there might be agents trying to exploit others, i.e. they distribute their WUs but do not adequately treat WUs from others. As a consequence, the agents will replicate WUs in order to increase the likelihood of success. But, from the overall system point of view, this introduces unnecessary overhead. Therefore, we would like to impose a rule of conduct with an incentive to accept WUs. For this we use the reputation of the agents. Any time an agent performs a WU calculation satisfactorily, the client will rate its success positively. If this is done by many agents, the client will build a high reputation. And this, in turn, increases the likelihood to be able to off-load WUs. This constitutes a control loop rewarding a behaviour which is beneficial for the community. After a while, all agents who act socially responsibly in the above sense will form a group of high-reputation agents: a Trust Community. TC members will co-operate preferably within the TC, and doing this will increase their efficiency since they can get rid of expensive checking procedures and WU replication.

There are more scenarios where the TC concept could be useful. Robots exploring and mapping an unknown terrain can be led to share their findings with other explorers. Sensors in an open Wireless Sensor Network (WSN) are guided to supply correct information to others even at the expense of their own battery lifetime. And an open network of smart surveillance cameras can self-organise as a TC in order to isolate the less reliable ones.

## 4.3 Robustness

Before we discuss the state-of-the-art followed by our approach in more detail, we want to state the overall objective of our system research more clearly. It is the ultimate goal of OC systems to become more resilient against disturbances and attacks from outside. We call this property "robustness".

It should be noted that the goal of building OC systems is not primarily the construction of adaptive or self-organising systems. Self-organisation and self-adaptation are just means to make technical systems resistant against external or internal disturbances. It is also a misconception to assume that OC systems achieve a higher performance than conventional systems. OC systems are not per se faster than conventional systems but they *return* faster to a certain target performance in the presence of disturbances. In the following, we want to define the robustness of systems under attack of disturbances more clearly and quantitatively.

### 4.3.1 Passive and Active Robustness

We assume a system in an undisturbed state to show a certain target performance. More generally, we rate a system by a utility measure $U$, which can take the form of a performance or a throughput (in case of a computing system), a speed (in case of car), or any other application-specific metric. The system reacts to a disturbance by deviating from its target utility $U_{target}$ by $\Delta U$.

*Passively* robust systems like e.g. a flexible post or tower under wind pressure react to the disturbance by a deflection $\Delta U = \Delta x$. This deflection remains constant as long as the disturbance remains. *Active* robustness mechanisms (such as self-organisation effected by an observer/controller) counteract the deviation and guide the system back to the undisturbed state with $\Delta U = 0$ or $U \geq U_{target}$. If we want to quantify robustness (for comparison between different systems) we have to take into account the following observables:

1. The strength of the disturbance, $\delta$
2. The drop of the system utility from the acceptable utility $U_{acc}$, $\Delta U$, and
3. The duration of the deviation (the recovery time $t_{rec}$).

**Fig. 4.3** System behaviour in state space under a disturbance $\delta$

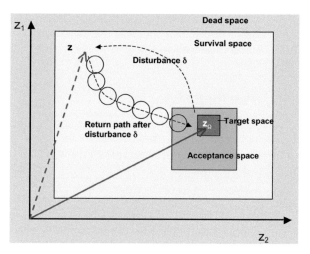

## 4.3.2 Robustness in State Space

In [17], we have explained this behaviour in a state space model as follows (Fig. 4.3):

Let a system $S$ be characterised by a state vector in $n$-dimensional state space. We assign a utility $U$ to each state by the evaluation function $\eta : U = \eta(z)$. The set of acceptable states (the acceptance space) corresponds to a minimal acceptable utility $S_{\mathrm{acc}} = \{z \in S \mid \eta(z) \geq U_{\mathrm{acc}}\}$.

## 4.3.3 Utility Degradation over Time

In the time domain, the deviation and the recovery will happen in two phases:

- **Phase I (passive robustness):** A disturbance of strength $\delta$ is applied to the system, which changes its state to $z_{\mathrm{disturbed}}$ and its utility to $U_{\mathrm{disturbed}} < U_{\mathrm{acce}}$. The deviation begins when the state vector leaves the acceptance space. This occurs at time $t_\delta$ (and not necessarily when the disturbance occurs). A disturbance taking effect at time $t_\delta$. The drop occurs within $t_{\mathrm{drop}}$. In the passive robustness (or drop) phase a control mechanism is not yet active. The system utility drops by $\Delta U$. The drop $\Delta U$ and the time $t_{\mathrm{drop}}$ are a function (1) of the strength of the disturbance, $\delta$, and (2) of the structural stability (robustness) of the system. In our experimental observations, $t_{\mathrm{drop}}$ was usually very short, the drop occurs "instantaneously" in many cases.
- **Phase II (active robustness):** A control mechanism (which in the case of an adaptive self-organising system is part of the system itself) actively guides the system back into the acceptance space (recovery). The time needed for this recovery is $t_{\mathrm{rec}}$. Given an effective control mechanism the system will return to $U \geq U_{\mathrm{acc}}$ within time $t_{\mathrm{rec}}$.

Phases I and II together are called the deviation phase. In practical cases it might be difficult to discriminate between the two phases, they might overlap since the active recovery mechanism will start working already at or shortly after $t_\delta$.

### 4.3.4   Passive Robustness

Passive Robustness $R_{\text{passive}}$ is measured by the sensitivity of $U$ against $\delta$, i.e. $\frac{dU}{d\delta} = \frac{1}{R_{\text{passive}}}$. Thereby, $R_{\text{passive}}$ is a measure of the structural stability of a system in the presence of a disturbance $\delta$.

- **Example 1:** A very stable concrete tower, which does not move ($\Delta U = 0$) under a storm of strength $\delta$, is structurally infinitely stable.
- **Example 2:** A communication link with an error correcting code, which corrects errors up to 3 bits, is structurally infinitely stable under a disturbance of strength $\delta = 1$ bit.

If $\delta$ has no effect on a system ($\Delta U = 0$) its passive robustness is $R_{\text{passive}} = \inf$. More generally $R_{\text{passive}}$ is defined as:

$$R_{\text{passive}} = \frac{1}{\frac{dU}{d\delta}}$$

### 4.3.5   Recovery by Active Robustness

Active robustness $R_{\text{active}}$ is defined as the (averaged) recovery speed of the system, i.e. $R_{\text{active}} = \frac{dU}{dt}$ or $R_{\text{active}} = \frac{\Delta U}{t_{\text{rec}}}$ in case of a full recovery. With $t_{\text{rec}} = \frac{\Delta U}{R_{\text{active}}}$ and $\Delta U = \frac{\delta}{R_{\text{passive}}}$ we get:

$$t_{\text{rec}} = \frac{\delta}{R_{\text{passive}} \cdot R_{\text{active}}}$$

$R_{\text{active}}$ is a property of the Observer/Controller (O/C) mechanism. Without an O/C the system stays at $U_{\text{disturbed}}$ at least as long as the disturbance remains. The recovery time $t_{\text{rec}}$ depends on the initial utility drop $\Delta U$ determined by the passive system resistance against the disturbance as well as the active recovery mechanism.

### 4.3.6   Effective Utility Degradation

As discussed above the robustness of a system under a given disturbance of strength $\delta$ is characterised by the triple ($\delta$, $\Delta U$, $t_{\text{rec}}$) or ($\delta$, $R_{\text{passive}}$, $R_{\text{active}}$). In order to gauge

**Fig. 4.4**  Utility degradation over time

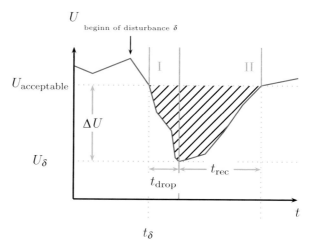

the total effect of the disturbance on the system we use the area $A$ of the utility deviation from $U_{\text{acceptable}}$ until full recovery back to $U_{\text{acceptable}}$ (see Fig. 4.4): We define the effective utility degradation as $A = \Delta U \cdot \left(t_{\text{drop}} + t_{\text{rec}}\right) - \int_{t_\delta + t_{\text{rec}}}^{t} U(t)dt$ where $A$ is a cost $\times$ time product. To achieve a minimal degradation we have to minimise $t_{\text{rec}}$ and hence $A$. For simplification, we assume that the drop occurs very fast: $t_{\text{drop}} = 0$. Also, we assume for simplification a linear utility increase, which renders the utility degradation triangular. Then $A \approx \Delta U \cdot \frac{t_{\text{rec}}}{2} = \frac{1}{2} \frac{\delta}{R_{\text{passive}}} \cdot \frac{\delta}{R_{\text{passive}} \cdot R_{\text{active}}}$. Hence, the effective utility degradation is:

$$A = \frac{1}{2} \frac{\delta^2}{R_{\text{passive}}^2 \cdot R_{\text{active}}} \tag{4.2}$$

It follows from Equation (4.2) that an increase of $R_{\text{passive}}$ decreases $A$ more effectively than an $R_{\text{active}}$ increase. The reason is that $R_{\text{passive}}$ influences $\Delta U$ as well as $t_{\text{rec}}$. We also note that there is a trade-off possible between $R_{\text{passive}}$ and $R_{\text{active}}$ depending on the cost incurred for passive and active robustness measures, respectively.

### 4.3.7  Interpretation by Mechanical Analogy

We can understand the terms $R_{\text{passive}}$ and $R_{\text{active}}$ by using a physical analogy: The system under disturbance is interpreted as a linear-elastic body modelled as a mechanical spring, which is extended from an undisturbed position $\Delta U = 0$ under a "stress" $\delta$ to a disturbed position, or "strain", $\Delta U$. $R_{\text{passive}}$ is, by comparison with Hook's law, the stiffness of the system. The inverse $\frac{1}{R_{\text{passive}}}$ can be interpreted as the sensitivity of the system under a strain $\delta$.

The active correction mechanism (i.e. the self-organised O/C structures) builds up an increasing counterforce, which eventually completely sets off the effects of the disturbance. If we want the disturbance $\delta$ to be counteracted within time $t_{rec}$, then we need a recovery speed $R_{active} = \frac{\delta}{R_{passive} \cdot t_{rec}}$.

This formula can be interpreted also slightly differently: $R_{active} \cdot R_{passive} = \frac{\delta}{t_{rec}}$. The recovery effort $\frac{\delta}{t_{rec}}$ can be made by a combination of passive and active measures: $R_{active} \cdot R_{passive}$. Higher structural robustness $R_{passive}$ allows for a lower active robustness $R_{active}$ and vice versa.

### 4.3.8 Example

The following is an example of Trust Community experiments with three experimental recovery behaviours. We use the average speedup as the utility metric $U$. Figure 4.5 shows the undisturbed utility over time as well as the utility drops for

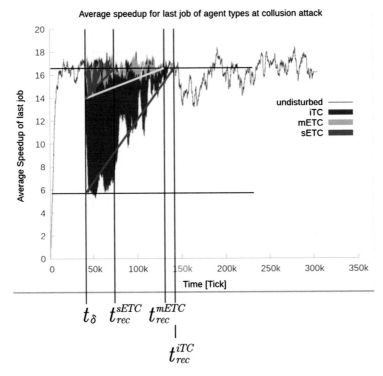

**Fig. 4.5** Trust Community experiments with three alternative O/C mechanisms result in different recovery behaviours. iTC (*red* effective utility degradation) shows the lowest active robustness, sETC (*blue area*) guides the system more quickly back into acceptance space. The *blue, yellow,* and *red lines* indicate the linearised recovery behaviours for iTC, mETC, and sETC, respectively

**Table 4.1** Results of
Robustness Experiments

|      | $\Delta U$ | $t_{\text{rec}}$ | $A[x10^3]$ | $R_{\text{passive}}$ | $R_{\text{active}}$ | $\delta$ |
|------|------------|------------------|------------|----------------------|---------------------|----------|
| iTc  | 11         | 140,000          | 770        | 4.5                  | $8 \cdot 10^{-5}$   | 50       |
| mTc  | 3          | 130,000          | 195        | 17                   | $2.3 \cdot 10^{-5}$ | 50       |
| sTc  | 3          | 70,000           | 105        | 17                   | $4.3 \cdot 10^{-5}$ | 50       |

the Trust Community variants iTC, mETC, and sETC (see Chapter 5). As metric for the disturbance $\delta$ we used the number of attacking agents, which was identical for all three experiments ($\delta = 50$). The O/C solutions mETC and sETC counteract the attack so fast, that $\Delta U$ is reduced as well. The coloured areas under the drop curves show the effective utility degradations. An approximate evaluation of these curves results in comparison values for $t_{\text{rec}}$, $A$, $R_{\text{passive}}$, and $R_{\text{active}}$ according to Table 4.1. The usage of the robustness metric as defined above can be difficult in practical cases due to the noisy character of many experiments. Nevertheless, it is useful as a concept for the understanding of passive and active robustness mechanisms in OC systems.

## 4.4 State-of-the-Art

Our application scenario is a Trusted Desktop Grid System which is an Open Distributed Systems consisting of an unknown number of autonomous entities that are heterogeneous with respect to goals, capabilities, preferences, and behaviours [18]. These systems are used to share resources between multiple administrative authorities [19]. Additionally, there is no central control [20]. The ShareGrid Project in Northern Italy is an example for a peer-to-peer-based system [21]. A second approach is the Organic Grid which is peer-to-peer-based with decentralised scheduling [22]. Contrary to our system, these approaches assume that there are no malicious parties involved and each node behaves well. Another implementation with a central tracker is the Berkeley Open Infrastructure for Network Computing project (BOINC) [23].

All those systems solve a distributed resource allocation problem. Since work units can be computed faster when agents cooperate, they reward and, thus, maximise cooperation. Additionally, a high fairness value ensures equal resource distribution (cf. [24–26]). Agents can form Trust-based multiagent organisations [16, 27, 28].

We model our grid nodes as agents. Agents follow a local goal which might differ from the global system goal [29]. We consider agents as black boxes which means that we cannot observe their internal state. Thus, their future actions and behaviour is unknown [30]. Our Trusted Desktop Grid supports Bag-of-Tasks applications [31].

A classification of Desktop Grid Systems can be found in [32]. A taxonomy can be found in [33]. It is emphasised there that there has to be some mechanism to detect failures and malicious behaviour in large-scale systems. Nodes cannot be expected to be unselfish and well-behaving.

In contrast to other state-of-the-art works, we do not assume the benevolence of the agents [34]. To cope with this information uncertainty, we introduced a trust metric. A general overview about trust in Multi-Agent Systems can be found in [6]. Another implementation of trust in a Desktop Grid System was evaluated in [35].

### 4.4.1   Norms

Explicit norms are similar to laws and can be expressed in deontic logic and argumentation. Individuals can reason based on these norms. Since there are multiple actions available, they may use additional factors or preferences [36]. Other approaches use defeasible logic (DL) to efficiently model [37] and reason [38] about norms. They separate facts and rules, which can be strict rules, defeasible rules, and exceptions from defeasible rules (called defeaters). To resolve conflicts between two rules reasoning about the same action, priorities can be specified [39]. All reasoning can be performed in linear time and is stable even when norms are not consistent [40].

We base our norm format on [41]. The authors developed a model for representing norms using context-aware policies with sanctions. They consider reputation when making decisions based on norms. We use a conditional norm structure as described in [42]. Most of our norms can be characterised as "prescriptions" based on [43], because they regulate actions. Our norms are generated by a centrally elected component representing all agents which classifies them as an "r-norm" according to [44]. By using norms, our agents can reach agreements and express commitments [44]. However, the agents can still violate such commitments and risk a sanction. Thereby, the agents stay autonomous. In [45], the authors present a norm life-cycle including norm creation, enforcement, and adaptation.

### 4.4.2   Normative Multi-Agent Systems

This work is part of wider research in the area of norms in multi-agent systems. However, we focus more on improving system performance by using norms than researching the characteristics of norms [46]. Our scenario is similar to management of common pool resources. According to game theory, this leads to a "tragedy of the commons" [14]. However, Ostrom [15] observed cases where this did not happen. She presented eight design principles for successful self-management of decentralised institutions. Pitt et al. [8] adapted these to Normative Multi-Agent Systems (see Sect. 4.2.3 above in this chapter).

Normative Multi-Agent Systems are used in multiple fields: e.g. in [47] they focus on so-called policy-based intentions in the domain of business process design. Agents plan consecutive actions based on obligations, intentions, beliefs, and desires. Based on DL, social agents reason about norms and intentions.

In [48], the authors present a generic approach to form organisations using norms. They assign a role to agents in a normative system. This system defines a goal, a process to reach the goal, required skills, and policies constraining the process. Agents directly or indirectly commit to certain actions using a predefined protocol. Agents may join or form an organisation with additional rules.

The normchange definition describes attributes, which are required for Normative Multi-Agent Systems [49]. Ten guidelines for implementation of norms to MAS are given. We follow those rules in our system. When norms are involved, agents need to make decisions based on these norms. Rosaria et al. [50] argue that agents have to be able to violate norms to maintain autonomy. However, the utility of certain actions may be lower due to sanctions.

According to [51], Normative Multi-Agent Systems can be divided into five categories: norm creation, norm identification, norm spreading, norm enforcement, and network topology. We use a leadership mechanism for norm creation and norm spreading. For norm identification, we use data mining and machine learning. For norm enforcement, we use sanctioning and reputation. Related approaches use Normative Multi-Agent Systems for governance or task delegation in distributed systems [52].

To detect the system state, we use social network analysis. All algorithms used for this purpose can be found in [53]. A survey of different analysed social networks was done by [54].

### 4.4.3   Robustness

Robustness has been defined in the literature mostly informally, e.g. in [55] as: "...a robust system can be defined as a system that functions correctly within a broad range of operational conditions." There exist also formal definitions: The FePIA procedure [56] defines a tolerance region of some system parameter which must not be violated by an external perturbation. The difference between the nominal value of the perturbation values which map onto the upper and lower limit of the tolerance region, respectively, is called robustness diameter ($2\times$ the robustness radius). England et al. [57] propose a statistical approach based on the difference of two cumulative distribution functions, one with and one without the perturbation. These ideas, however, do not consider the time behaviour of the system which is subject to the disturbance and which has to react, either by passive resistance or by active countermeasures. The formalism we have presented above takes the timing behaviour into account and proposes metrics for a quantitative assessment of the system recovery.

## 4.5    Normative Control Loop

In our Trusted Desktop Grid (TDG), different attacks by malevolent agents can
occur (for instance, the aforementioned "trust breakdown"). We implemented
various counter and security measures to maintain a good utility for well-behaving
agents. However, most of these measures appear with some attached costs. Although
we do not benefit from those mechanisms under normal conditions, they are
essential under attack or at least lead to a significantly faster recovery from attacks.
Additionally, we can configure our reputation system and change the effect of
ratings. This may increase or decrease robustness but it also influences how fast
new agents are integrated into the system. Offering larger incentives leads to a faster
system start-up and a better speedup when well-behaving agents join the system.
However, it also gets easier to exploit the system for malevolent agents.

In the TDG, a variety of different parameters exist which influence the system
behaviour. They must be set before system start. For example, they enable or disable
security measures or change the influence of a rating to the reputation system. Some
settings result in a better speedup when no attacks occur, but lead to a higher impact
on the performance in case of the system being under attack. There is no global
optimal value for most of these scenarios. The ideal value or setting depends on the
current situation.

To obtain the best overall performance, we need to change these parameters
and settings during runtime according to the current situation. However, we cannot
detect global system states such as the "trust breakdown" or overload situations,
from the local viewpoint of an agent. It is also not possible to influence agents
directly since they are autonomous. There needs to be a higher-level instance which
can detect the current system state and consequently guide the agent's behaviour
through indirect influences. The assessment of the current system situation is
presented in the remainder. Active guidance of the agents is realised by norm-based
control, which is briefly outlined in the following.

### 4.5.1    Norms and Sanctions

A norm is a rule with a sanction (such as laws in a society) or an incentive if certain
conditions are met or violated. We formalise a norm as a three-tuple:

$$\text{Norm} := \langle \text{Evaluator, Action}, (\text{Policy}_1 \ldots \text{Policy}_n) \rangle$$

$$\text{Policy} := \langle \text{Context, Sanction} \rangle$$

The *Evaluator* is either the worker or submitter part of an agent. Both have
different *Actions* they can perform. The following list names examples for both
components.

1. Worker

   (a) AcceptJob($A_w, A_s$): Agent $A_w$ accepts a job from agent $A_s$
   (b) RejectJob($A_w, A_s$): Agent $A_w$ rejects a job from agent $A_s$
   (c) ReturnJob($A_w, A_s$): $A_w$ returns the correct calculation for job to $A_s$
   (d) CancelJob($A_w, A_s$): $A_w$ cancels job of $A_s$

2. Submitter

   (a) AskForDeadline($A_s, A_w$): $A_s$ asks worker $A_w$ for the deadline for a job
   (b) GiveJobTo($A_s, A_w$): $A_s$ asks worker $A_w$ to do a job
   (c) CancelJob($A_s, A_w$): $A_s$ cancels a job $A_w$ is working on
   (d) ReplicateJob(*copies*): Copies a job multiple times and uses GiveJobTo() on
       them

A norm may contain multiple *Policies* that consist of a *Context* and a *Sanction*,
which can also be an incentive (implemented as negative Sanction). The *Context*
contains one or multiple conditions which must be true to trigger a certain *Sanction*.
Since all agents want to achieve a maximal speedup, it is not possible to give a direct
reward to an agent and we can only increase or decrease the speedup indirectly by
varying the reputation of an agent. The *Sanction* may also influence more indirect
parameters, which in turn can influence the success of an agent. The following list
summarises the possible interventions in terms of sanctions and incentives:

1. *Incentive*

   (a) Reputation is increased
   (b) Monetary incentives

2. *Sanction*

   (a) Reputation is decreased
   (b) Loss of monetary incentives

Figure 4.6 shows an exemplary norm which is used in the TDG in extended OCL
format [58]. In this example, the norm formulates that a *Worker* should always finish
a job and will receive an incentive which is stronger when the requester has a low
reputation. Otherwise, the working agent will receive a sanction (see [59] for more
details).

  Agents in the TDG need to be able to understand the currently valid norms, which
enables them to trade-off sanctions and incentives in their decision making. This
allows them to follow short- or long-term strategies based on these norms. Since
the agents are autonomous and free to obey or ignore these norms, the system still
needs to enforce the sanctions and give incentives to agents [41].

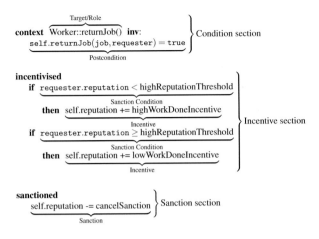

**Fig. 4.6** Norm used in the evaluation. It sanctions cancelling work and rewards the completion of work. In addition, working for submitters with lower reputation generates a stronger reward

## 4.5.2 Higher-level Norm Manager

In Fig. 4.7, we present our concept of the Norm Manager (NM), which uses the common Observer-Controller pattern [7]. The complete control loop implemented by the Observer-Controller component helps to mitigate effects of attacks to the TDG and allows a better fulfilment of the system goals. Thereby, it defines an intelligent control mechanism working at system-level. However, if the additional NM fails, the system itself is still operational and can continue to run (this refers to the desired OC characteristic of *non-critical complexity* [60]). When the NM is recovered, it can start to optimise the system again.

## 4.5.3 System Observation

To detect the current system state, the observer in the NM monitors work relations of all agents. Based on the observations, the controller in the NM creates a directed *work graph* with agents as nodes and edges between agents which have cooperated in the monitored period. The intensity of the cooperation between two agents determines the weight of the edge connecting them. In this context, the intensity is determined according to the number of shared work packages. Additionally, the controller creates a directed *trust graph* with agents as nodes and trust relations as edges. Trust relations $T(a, b)$ between two agents $a$ and $b$ can be obtained from the reputation system and define how trustworthy agents estimates each other within an interval between 0 (not trustworthy at all) and 1 (fully trustworthy). Agents fully trust themselves and, therefore, $T(a, a)$ is always 1 (self-trust).

Since we cannot see the internal implementations of agents, we need to observe them from the outside. We could monitor all interactions between agents, but this may lead to a bottleneck in larger systems. However, it is easy to monitor the actions

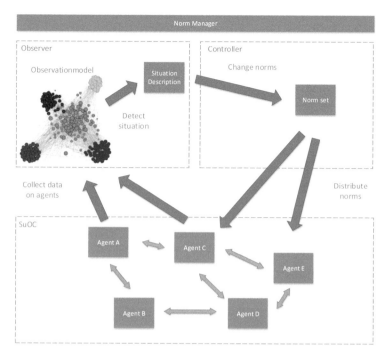

**Fig. 4.7** System Overview of the Norm Manager consisting of an Observer and a Controller which control the System under Observation and Control (SuOC) using norms

indirectly: We can observe the reputation system and use the ratings which agents give to their partners after every interaction. When we collect those ratings, we can build a trust-graph. Multiple ratings will be merged using an arithmetic mean.

Afterwards, the NM calculates certain common graph metrics for every node and the global system state is determined. Based on this metrics, our algorithm forms clusters and finds groups of similar agents. By further classifying these groups, the Observer achieves an even better understanding about potentially happening attacks which allows it to detect attacks happening in the future faster. In the end, it is able to classify whether the system is under attack, categorise the type of the attack, and rank attacks according to their severity. This is accompanied by an estimation of how accurate this information is.

From a methodical point of view, the observer works as follows: First, it builds graphs for trust and work relations between agents. In a second step, it applies graph metrics to be able to identify groups or clusters of similar agents. Afterwards, it runs statistics on every cluster found and compares them to historic or threshold values. Clusters are tracked over time to detect tendencies and predict future values. We presented this method in [61, 62] and visualised it in [63].

### 4.5.4  System Control Using Norms

The controller is responsible for guiding the overall system behaviour by applying norms. Such a norm contains a rule and a sanction or an incentive [41]. Agents are still autonomous and can violate norms with the risk of being sanctioned.

Based on the information obtained by the observer, the controller decides whether the system norms need to be changed. As discussed above, norms can not directly influence agents but modify their actions. To be more specific, norms can impose sanctions or offer incentives to actions. To defend against attacks, we can increase sanctions for certain actions. Under certain conditions we can allow agents to perform security measures, which would lead to sanctions otherwise [42]. We show results for one group of attackers in Sect. 4.6.3.1. Additionally, we published other possible norm changes in [64].

## 4.6  Implementation and Evaluation

The following section analyses the benefit of the previously introduced normative control loop for open distributed systems. First, we describe the experimental setup and the application scenario. Afterwards, we evaluate three basic characteristics: (a) how the overall system's robustness can be increased by reliably detecting malicious agents, (b) how disturbances can be handled using normative control, and (c) how the approach outperforms comparable solutions from the state-of-the-art within a specific application case.

### 4.6.1  Experimental Setup

As an application scenario, we investigate open grid computing systems, which can host numerous distributable workloads, e.g. distributed rendering of films. The system is considered open since there is no central controlling entity, all communication is performed peer-to-peer, and agents are free to join. Worker nodes belong to different administrative domains, thus, benevolent behaviour cannot be assumed. Nodes participate voluntarily to submit work into the system and, thereby, achieve a speedup of their jobs. However, a successful system relies on reciprocity: Agents also have to compute work units for other submitters [16].

To analyse such systems, we model nodes as agents and run a multi-agent system in simulation. Every agent works on behalf of a user and periodically receives a job, which contains multiple parallelisable work units. It aims to accomplish all work units as fast as possible by asking other agents to work for it. Since we are interested in an open system, agents behave autonomously, and can join or leave at any time.

The system performance is measured by the speedup $\sigma$. In Equation (4.3), $\tau_{self}$ is the time it would require an agent to compute a job containing multiple work units without cooperation. $\tau_{distributed}$ represents the time it takes to compute all work units of one job with cooperation of other workers including all communication times. Since all work requests are sent at the same time $\tau_{distributed}$ depends only on the sum of computation time $t_{computation,p}$ and communication time $t_{communication,p}$ of the slowest worker (Equation (4.4)). As a consequence, speedup can only be determined after the result of the last work unit has been returned (simplified version of the speedup definition in Chapter 5).

$$\sigma := \frac{\tau_{self}}{\tau_{distributed}} \quad (4.3)$$

$$\tau_{distributed} := \max_{p \in \text{Partners}} \left\{ t_{communication,p} + t_{computation,p} \right\} \quad (4.4)$$

If no cooperation partners can be found, agents need to compute their own work units and achieve a speedup value equal to one (i.e. no speedup at all). In general, agents behave selfishly and only cooperate if they can expect an advantage. They have to decide which agent they give their work to and for which agents they work themselves. In an open system, it is not possible to control the agent implementation, so agents might behave uncooperatively or even maliciously.

We consider the following stereotype agent behaviours in our system:

1. *Adaptive Agents* – These agents are cooperative. They work for other agents who earned high reputation in the system. How high the reputation value has to be generally depends on the estimated current system load and how much the input queue of the agent is filled up. We refer to this group as well-behaving (WB) agents.
2. *Freeriders* – Such agents do not work for other agents and reject all work requests. However, they ask other agents to work for them. This increases the overall system load and decreases the utility for well-behaving agents.
3. *Egoists* – These agents only pretend to work for other agents. They accept all work requests but return fake results, which wastes the time of other agents. If results are not validated, this may lead to errors. In any case it lowers the utility of the system.
4. *Cunning Agents* – These agents behave well in the beginning but may change their behaviour later. Periodically, randomly, or under certain conditions they behave like *Freeriders* or *Egoists*. This is hard to detect and may lower the overall system utility.

See Chapter 5 for more details.

## *4.6.2 Robustness Increase*

In this section, we show how to counter permanent threats by changing norms during runtime. To evaluate the outcome, we measure the utility and calculate the robustness.

### 4.6.2.1  Detecting and Isolating Cunning Agents

We have shown [16] that Freeriders and Egoists can be effectively isolated using self-organising Trust Communities (see Chapter 5). *Cunning Agents*, however, cannot be easily detected and isolated locally in a distributed system. Therefore, they pose a permanent threat to the TDG. In the following, we discuss how a higher-level NM can detect them and then change norms to isolate them.

To detect *Cunning Agents* in the NM, we cluster groups using the MCL [65] and the BIRCH [66] algorithm on the *trust graph* and classify them using a decision matrix. For the purpose of this chapter the matrix can only identify groups of *Cunning Agents*. The methods used for that purpose were presented in [62]. In particular, we use the metrics of *Authorities* and *DegreeCentrality* to detect groups of *Cunning Agents*.

Once the NM detects groups of *Cunning Agents* it has to isolate them. Unfortunately, it cannot influence agents directly but it can do this using norms. Therefore, it introduces a new norm which allows agents to refuse work from *Cunning Agents*. We propose to detect them based on their inconsistent behaviour as will be explained below.

### 4.6.2.2  Inconsistent Behaviour

In a trust-based distributed system such as the TDG, we condense a series of $k$ trust ratings $R$ into a single reputation value $\tau$ (see Equation (4.5)). However, this does not take into account how consistent those ratings are. Normally, agents make their decisions based on the aggregated value $\tau$.

$$r \in [-1, 1] \Rightarrow R \in [-1, 1]^k$$

$$\tau := \frac{\sum_{r \in R} r}{\sum_{r \in R} |r|} \tag{4.5}$$

However, *Cunning Agents* behave strategically regarding their reputation value: They behave well until they reach a certain threshold $\tau_{upper}$ and then stop to cooperate with other agents until they fall below a threshold $\tau_{lower}$. Therefore, their reputation $\tau$ is between those two values most of the time. Moreover, they adjust their $\tau_{upper}$ and $\tau_{lower}$ to be considered as well-behaving by other agents based on the reputation (see Equation (4.6)).

$$\tau_{\text{wb}} \leq \tau_{\text{lower}} \leq \tau \leq \tau_{\text{upper}} \tag{4.6}$$

Since those agents intentionally exploit the trust metric they cannot get detected and isolated using the reputation value. However, they receive very inconsistent ratings $r$ because of their changing behaviour. We can leverage that to detect them. Therefore, we define the consistency $\kappa$ based on the standard deviation:

$$\kappa := 1 - \frac{\sum_{r\in R, r>0} r}{\sum_{r\in R} |r|} \cdot (\tau - 1)^2 + \frac{\sum_{r\in R, r<0} r}{\sum_{r\in R} |r|} \cdot (\tau + 1)^2$$

We expect a very low $\kappa$ value for *Cunning Agents* and a value close to one for *Adaptive Agents*. Other agents such as *Freeriders* or *Egoists* also should get a $\kappa$ value of approximately one since they behave consistently maliciously.

#### 4.6.2.3  Incentivising Consistent Behaviour

The NM cannot directly influence agents or force them to perform any actions. However, it can change norms and, thereby, change incentives and sanctions for certain actions. To cope with *Cunning Agents* while maintaining the autonomy of all agents, we chose to allow them to reject jobs from inconsistently behaving agents. Therefore, agents can decide on their own if they want to work for *Cunning Agents* since they will still receive an incentive for that.

In Fig. 4.8, we show the changed norm. The threshold $\omega$ for the reputation $\tau$ is smaller than $\tau_{\text{lower}}$ and threshold $\gamma$ for consistency is 0.8 in our experiment. `requester.reputation` is calculated using the trust metric $\tau$ and `requester.consistency` is determined by $\kappa$. The sanction results in a rating $r$ for the working agent.

**Fig. 4.8** Changed norm used in the evaluation to isolate *Cunning Agents*. It allows agents to reject jobs from inconsistently behaving agents

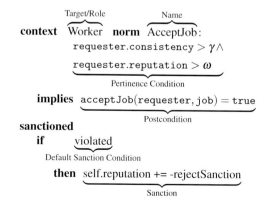

#### 4.6.2.4 Results

The setup in the evaluation comprises 100 *Adaptive Agents* and additional 50 *Cunning Agents* for all experiments with attackers. Each experiment ran for 300,000 ticks and was repeated 100 times. We performed three series of experiments: (E1) without attacker; (E2) with attackers; (E3) with attackers and our norm changes.

In this experiment, we measure the average speedup as defined in Equation (4.3) for the attacking *Cunning Agents* and the well-behaving *Adaptive Agents*. The detection of *Cunning Agents* in (E2) by the NM can be observed between tick 15,000 and 50,000 (compare Fig. 4.9) and was successful in all experiments. On average, the NM detected the attackers at tick 24,920 with a standard deviation of 15,301. Normally, the NM can introduce the norm at this point. However, to make the impact of the norm change more comparable, we set the time $t_{change}$ to 100,000 for the subsequent experiment in (E3). We measured the consistency values $\kappa$ for *Adaptive Agents* and *Cunning Agents* in (E2) at the end of the experiment. Both $\kappa$ values turned out to be as expected: *Adaptive Agents* have a value of $0.99 \pm 0.00053$. In contrast, *Cunning Agents* have a value of $0.06 \pm 0.013$ which is next to zero.

We measure the influence of the norm change using the speedup $\sigma$ for *Adaptive Agents* and *Cunning Agents* in experiments (E1), (E2) and (E3) (see Fig. 4.10). In Fig. 4.9, we show one single experiment of (E3) as an example with speedup over time. In the beginning *Adaptive Agents* and *Cunning Agents* achieve a similar but varying speedup. The oscillating character in the beginning is due to the periodic behaviour of the cunning agents. After the NM introduced the norm change at tick 100,000 the speedup for *Cunning Agents* falls below one. Those agents no longer gain any advantage from participating in the system. In contrast, *Adaptive Agents* gain a stable high speedup again.

In the undisturbed experiment (E1), we measured that *Adaptive Agents* can achieve a speedup of $11.75 \pm 0.73$ when there is no attack. When a heavy attack

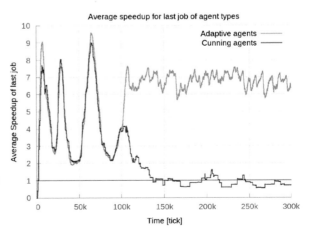

**Fig. 4.9** Exemplary simulation run of experiment E3 with *Adaptive Agents* and *Cunning Agents*. In the beginning *Cunning Agents* change their behaviour periodically and the speedup oscillates between values of two and ten. At tick 100,000 the norm is introduced. *Cunning Agents* get isolated and reach a speedup of less than one meaning that they no longer have an advantage from participating in the system

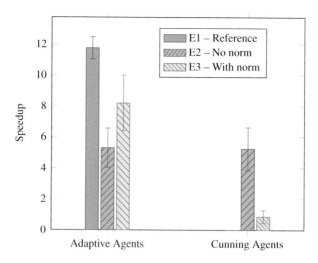

**Fig. 4.10** Speedup for *Adaptive Agents* and *Cunning Agents* for every experiment series with 100 Experiments each. Experiment E1 uses only *Adaptive Agents* without any attackers. In E2 we introduced attackers but no countermeasures. In E3 the norm was introduced to counter the attack at tick 100,000. All experiments lasted 300,000 ticks

**Table 4.2** Speedup for *Adaptive Agents* and *Cunning Agents* for every experiment series with 100 Experiments each. In E3 the norm was introduced at tick 100,000. All experiments lasted 300,000 ticks

| Speedup | E1 – Reference | E2 – No norm | E3 – With norm |
|---|---|---|---|
| Adaptive agents | 11.75±0.73 | 5.29±1.26 | 8.19±1.79 |
| Cunning agents | 0±0 | 5.23±1.38 | 0.86±0.41 |

of *Cunning Agents* is added in (E2) the speedup decreases to $5.29 \pm 1.26$. With norm change by the NM the speedup increases again to $8.19 \pm 1.79$ in (E3).

*Cunning Agents* achieve a speedup of $5.23 \pm 1.38$ when they exploit the system in (E2). At the same time they work significantly less than *Adaptive Agents*. However, when the NM changes the norm the speedup of *Cunning Agents* decreases to $0.86 \pm 0.41$.

In the reference experiment the $R_{\text{active}}$ and $R_{\text{passive}}$ are 0 because the system does not recover at all. To calculate the robustness when using our norm we introduce $t_{\text{detection}}$ which is the time after $t_{\text{drop}}$ until the attack is detected and before the recovery starts. In this experiment $t_{\text{detection}}$ is set to tick 100,000 to allow better comparison of the recovery phases. Based on the data from Table 4.2, $t_{\text{recovery}}$ is 7,931 ticks in average. In the norm change case we can calculate: $R_{\text{passive}} = \frac{1}{\frac{11.74-5.29}{100}} = 15.50$ and $R_{\text{active}} = \frac{8.19-5.29}{7.931} = 3.66 \cdot 10^{-4}$.

#### 4.6.2.5  Summary

We implemented an approach which allows well-behaving agents to react to *Cunning Agents* in a distributed manner. The Norm Manager triggers a norm change when it detects an attack. Afterwards, *Adaptive Agents* recover from the attack and *Cunning Agents* get isolated.

### 4.6.3   Counteracting Disturbance

In this section, we focus on the controller component. The controller is responsible for guiding the overall system behaviour by applying norms. Such a norm contains a rule and a sanction [41]. Agents are still autonomous and can violate norms at the risk of sanctioning.

Based on the information obtained by the observer, the controller decides whether the system norms need to be changed. Norms cannot directly influence agents but modify their actions. To be more specific, norms can impose sanctions or offer incentives to actions. To defend against attacks, we can increase sanctions for certain actions under some conditions or we can allow agents to perform security measures, which lead to sanctioning otherwise [42]. Certainly, changed sanctions or incentives take effect only on actions which will be taken after the change.

#### 4.6.3.1  Reducing the Effect of Disturbances

To counter attacks of malicious agents the controller utilises various counter measures: change or create norms; issue incentives or add sanctions. In Fig. 4.6, the default norms of our TDG are shown. Agents get positive reputation when they finish the work for other agents. If they reject work they get a bad rating, unless the reputation of the requesting agent $A_s$ is below $\alpha$.

When an agent enters the system it gets an initial reputation $\rho$. To facilitate integration into the system, $\rho$ is greater 0. However, malicious agents can use this initial trust to exploit other agents. Especially in sybil attacks [67], where agents have multiple identities, this becomes a big issue. Unfortunately, $\rho > 0$ is also needed to efficiently integrate well-behaving agents. Fortunately, the observer can detect such attacks, so the controller can react based on that knowledge. In our approach, the controller changes $\alpha$ in Norm 1 to a value $\alpha > \rho$ (see Fig. 4.8).

As a result we expect a decrease in the impact of attacks by *Freeriders* and *Egoists* since they will no longer be able to cause a *Trust Breakdown* with their initial reputation. This effect can be measured by the time between attack start and the point where all attackers are isolated. We want to minimise this duration until isolation. As our approach also affects well-behaving agents, we also measure the increase of duration to integrate them into the system.

### 4.6.3.2 Results

We consider attacks by *Freeriders* and *Egoists* and evaluate both attacks by adding 100 attacker agents each to a system of 200 *Adaptive Agents*. To measure the effect on well-behaving agents we repeat the experiment with 100 *Adaptive Agents* entering the system. The described norm change is performed at the beginning of the attack. Additionally, we run a reference experiment without norm change for all agent types. Since isolation and integration of agents is slower during low load situations, we added this as a scenario. Every experiment was repeated one-thousand times – resulting in 12,000 experiments.

After the attack starts at $t_{\text{start}}$, we periodically calculate the speedup $\sigma$ (defined in Equation (4.3)) for the attacking agents. $t_{\text{isolation}}$ is defined to be the smallest value with $t_{\text{end}} > t_{\text{start}} \wedge \sigma \leq 1$ (Equation (4.7)). The duration until isolation $\Delta t_{\text{isolation}}$ is then determined as the difference of $t_{\text{end}}$ and $t_{\text{start}}$ (Equation (4.8)).

$$t_{\text{isolation}} := \min\{t : t > t_{\text{start}} \wedge \sigma_t \leq 1\} \tag{4.7}$$

$$\Delta t_{\text{isolation}} := t_{\text{isolation}} - t_{\text{start}} \tag{4.8}$$

For *Adaptive Agents*, we similarly calculate the duration until integration $\Delta t_{\text{integration}}$ (Equation (4.10)). In a reference experiment without norm change, we determine the final speedup after integration $\sigma_{\text{ref}}$. $t_{\text{integration}}$ is then defined to be the first time after a group of agents joins where $\sigma \geq \sigma_{\text{ref}}$ (Equation (4.9)).

$$t_{\text{integration}} := \min\{t : t > t_{\text{start}} \wedge \sigma_t \geq \sigma_{\text{ref}}\} \tag{4.9}$$

$$\Delta t_{\text{integration}} := t_{\text{integration}} - t_{\text{start}} \tag{4.10}$$

In Fig. 4.11, we present our results for three agent types. For *Freeriders* and *Egoists*, the graph shows $\Delta t_{\text{isolation}}$. In contrast, for *Adaptive Agents*, it illustrates $\Delta t_{\text{integration}}$. Full results with standard deviation are listed in Table 4.3.

The results show that isolation of malicious agents greatly improves when norms are changed, especially, in low load situations. For *Freeriders* the duration decreases by 78 % under normal load. Under low load, *Freeriders* are not fully isolated without our norm change. However, this changes with our approach: The system does properly isolate the attackers in all experiments. Since isolation does not work in the reference case, we limited the length of that experiment. Therefore, the value for low load without norms in Table 4.3 has no variance at all and the relative gain cannot be calculated.

### 4.6.3.3 Discussion

Our normative control approach is very effective when dealing with *Egoists*. With changed norms during attack they get isolated after calculating their first job

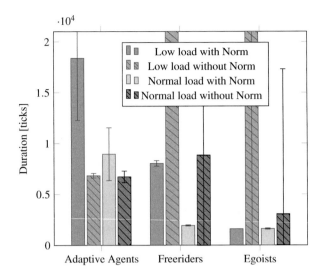

**Fig. 4.11** Duration until integration for *Adaptive Agents* and the duration until isolation for attackers. Shorter is better for both. With our norms the duration until isolation decreases significantly. However, the duration until integration increases slightly for *Adaptive Agents*

**Table 4.3** Duration until isolation/integration per agent group

| Agent | Low load without norm | Normal load without norm | Low load with norm | Normal load with norm |
|---|---|---|---|---|
| Adaptive agents | $6,837.1 \pm 228.06$ | $6,722.1 \pm 568.06$ | $18,375.3 \pm 6,098.97$ | $8,945.7 \pm 2,585.81$ |
| Freerider | $145,000 \pm 0$ | $8,841.6 \pm 17,597.08$ | $8,037.9 \pm 275.77$ | $1,930.8 \pm 57.37$ |
| Egoists | $41,178.4 \pm 64,102.20$ | $3,034.1 \pm 14,268.11$ | $1,600 \pm 0$ | $1,609.3 \pm 62.47$ |

(duration of a job is 1,600 ticks). Without the change they did not get isolated in most cases under low load and it took about twice as long under normal load.

However, well-behaving agents are also affected by the norm change: *Adaptive Agents* need 33 % longer under normal load and 169 % longer under low load. Integration still worked in all experiments and can be considered stable.

Our results show that changing norms reduces the impact of attacks by *Freeriders* and *Egoists*. However, this change cannot become the default because it also affects the integration of well-behaving agents. Nevertheless, by using our NM we can change norms in critical situations, i.e. when the observer detects an attack by *Freeriders* or *Egoists*.

Critical to the success of this method is fast detection of such attacks. After isolation of the attackers the norm changes can be reversed since isolation of those two groups is permanent. Isolation is performed using trust and reputation mechanism of the TDG. We chose this approach to keep maximal autonomy for the agents.

## 4.6.4   Open Rendering Farm

As a third experiment, we apply our techniques to a volunteer-based distributed rendering application. Rendering cinematic films typically requires very long calculations and, therefore, most productions are rendered in parallel using a high number of computers. Films can easily be partitioned into frames, which then can be calculated in parallel without any data dependencies. However, in a volunteer-based system users may produce invalid results and, therefore, work has to be replicated. Our TDG supports dynamic replication factors. We compare our approach with a static replication factor of 2 used by Big and Ugly Rendering Project (BURP) which is based on BOINC [23].

### 4.6.4.1   Comparing TDG with BOINC/BURP

In BURP every work unit is given to two workers. When both return the same result, the work is accepted. Otherwise, all results are thrown away and the unit is replicated until, eventually, two workers return the same results. This approach is very simple and works in practice. However, it generates at least 50 % overhead if all workers compute everything correctly.

When using the TDG as application platform for distributed rendering, we also replicate work units multiple times. However, we choose the replication factor based on the reputation of the worker in the system. Initially, all workers are untrusted and we start with a replication factor of 5. As soon as all results are collected, we check if we find a quorum of equal results (i.e. in this case three equal results). All workers with the supposedly correct result receive a good rating and gain reputation. All other workers receive a bad rating and loose reputation.

Based on the reputation of every worker, we calculate the minimal replication factor when using the worker. To reduce the overall amount of replication, we group workers by minimal replication factor and try to always select from within one group. Additionally, if possible, we add at least one trustworthy worker (with high reputation) to a replication set containing untrusted workers. For trustworthy workers, we only do probabilistic replication in one out of ten cases resulting in an average replication factor of 1.1 (e.g. 10 work units result in 11 computations).

### 4.6.4.2   Results

To compare the approaches, we measure replication factor, throughput and correctness. We did experiments for independent and colluding attackers. The results of independent attackers are distinguishable when calculating a quorum. However, colluding attackers communicate and return the same faked results which may result in a quorum for the incorrect result when comparing. Every experiment is repeated ten times and consist of 100 workers which compute 30,000 work units.

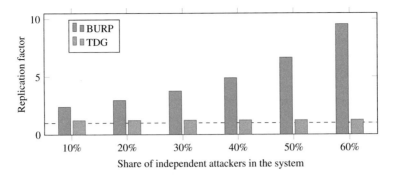

**Fig. 4.12** Average replication factor with increasing share of independent attackers. The replication factor of BURP starts at two with no attackers and increases to nearly 10 when adding 60 % of attackers. In contrast, the replication factor of the TDG stays near one and only increases very slightly

**Table 4.4** Throughput (jobs per second) with no attackers, 20 % independent attackers and 20 % colluding attackers

| Throughput | No attackers | 20 % colluding attackers | 20 % independent attackers |
|---|---|---|---|
| BOINC | 39.88 ± 0.03 | 26.65 ± 0.078 | 27.92 ± 0.097 |
| TDG | 72.23 ± 0.054 | 56.80 ± 0.097 | 56.43 ± 0.25 |

In Fig. 4.12, we show the results for different shares of independent attackers. Since two results of independent attackers can always be distinguished the correctness is 100 % in all experiments. However, the replication factor increases when the share of attackers increases. For BURP it starts at a value of 2.42 with 10 % attackers and increases to 9.55 for 60 % attackers which generates nearly 90 % overhead. For the TDG the replication factor only increases very slightly from a value of 1.23 to 1.27. In Table 4.4, we show throughput values for TDG which are in all cases roughly twice as large as those of BOINC.

Similarly, as shown in Fig. 4.13, we performed experiments with colluding attackers with increasing shares of attackers. When we consider colluding attackers, replication can also lead to incorrect results. Therefore, we also show the correctness in Fig. 4.14. Compared to Fig. 4.12, BURP has a lower replication factor and TDG shows a higher replication factor. However, the correctness decreases with increasing share of attackers. For BURP it starts at a correctness of 99.1 % and decreases to 41 % with 60 % of attackers. The TDG reaches 100 % correctness for 10–40 %. Unfortunately, when attackers start to become the majority of the system at 50 % and more, the correctness degrades. For 20 % colluding attackers the TDG-based approach shows about twice the throughput of BURP because of the smaller replication factor. At the same time it produced 100 % correct results in our experiments.

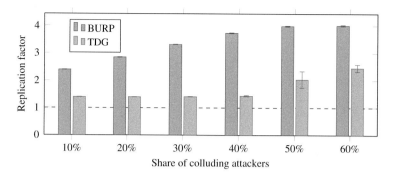

**Fig. 4.13** Average replication factor with increasing share of colluding attackers. The replication factor of BURP starts at two with no attackers and increases to about 4 when adding 60 % of attackers. In contrast, the replication factor of the TDG starts near one and only increases to about 2.5

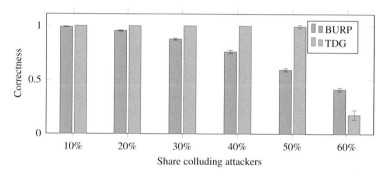

**Fig. 4.14** Average correctness factor with increasing share of colluding attackers. The correctness of the TDG is 100 % for up to 40 % of attackers. With 50 % it drops minimally. For 60 % it is less than 20 % because attackers have the majority. The correctness of BURP starts at 100 % without attackers and drops as soon as attackers join. It is worse than the TDG as long as the attacker are not the majority

### 4.6.4.3 Summary

We demonstrated that our approach is applicable to real world applications by implementing it in a distributed volunteer-based rendering application and comparing it to BURP. The TDG shows better performance by using less replication and generating less overhead. Additionally, when dealing with colluding attackers it generates a higher correctness (100 % in our experiments) when dealing with less than 50 % attackers in the system. However, our approach performs worse than the base line as soon as attackers become the majority of the system.

## 4.7  Conclusion and Outlook

This chapter presented a system-wide control loop to guide self-organised behaviour in distributed systems. Therefore, we introduced a norm-based solution and illustrated the success within simulations of a Desktop Grid Computing system as application scenario. As motivation, we outlined that open systems (i.e. agent societies) allowing autonomous and heterogeneous participants to join freely suffer due to uncooperative or even malicious behaviour. A successful concept to counter these challenges posed by openness and heterogeneity is establishing computational trust relationships among agents. However, negative emergent behaviour can appear in some cases when dealing with computational trust – with disturbed system operation as result (i.e. in terms of efficiency and fairness). Since we assume autonomous and self-motivated agents, a direct intervention is hardly possible.

As a reaction to the observed challenges, we proposed a concept that resembles Organic Computing's observer/controller pattern at system-level. This loop derives a situation description from externally observable information, such as trust and cooperation relationships, and guides the self-organised behaviour of participating agents by issuing norms as response to the currently observed conditions. For the observation part, we introduced a graph-based method that can be utilised to identify agents or groups of agents with malicious intentions by applying e.g. clustering techniques. The controller part follows a rule-based approach by issuing norms in response to the previously defined situation descriptions.

The evaluation has been performed as simulation of a Trusted Desktop Grid in which several classes of stereotype agent behaviour have been considered. The results highlight three basic insights: First, we demonstrate the success of identifying malicious agents or groups of malicious agents without the need of internal agent information. Secondly, we showed the increase of robustness in terms of a faster recovery and a decreased drop of performance in the presence of varying disturbances. And finally, we compared the developed concept to the most successful solution in the Grid Computing domain: *BOINC*. Here, we have shown that our concept is able to significantly reduce redundant work packet calculation while simultaneously improving the speedup compared to individual calculation. As a result, we demonstrated that the system can recover significantly faster from emergent situations, such as the "trust breakdown", compared to other solutions.

Current and future work focus on the improvement of a set of minor issues concerning the scalability and performance of the concept. First, we are working on the question how the partly centralised solution as investigated in this chapter can be combined with completely distributed mechanisms. The idea is to offload responsibilities (i.e. surveillance of norm compliance, identification of best solutions to be established as norms, or notification about conflicting goals defined by active norms) to the agents without decreasing the security level. This is accompanied by the question which more sophisticated threats may appear that have been neglected so far – and how counter measures have to be designed to be incorporated in the proposed process. In addition, a self-stabilisation process that makes use of accusations can further introduce social-inspired capabilities that help to maintain the overall system utility. Finally, we are interested in a more generic evaluation of the developed concepts by evaluating the developed approach in other application scenarios, e.g. from the wireless sensor network domains.

**Acknowledgements** This research is partly sponsored by the research unit *OC-Trust* (FOR 1085) of the German Research Foundation.

# References

1. Wooldridge, M.J.: Agent technology: foundations, applications, and markets. Springer, Berlin/Heidelberg/New York (1998). ISBN:3-540-63591-2
2. Tomforde, S., Hähner, J., Seebach, H., Reif, W., Sick, B., Wacker, A., Scholtes, I.: Engineering and mastering interwoven systems. In: ARCS 2014 – 27th International Conference on Architecture of Computing Systems, Workshop Proceedings, Luebeck, University of Luebeck, Institute of Computer Engineering, 25–28 Feb 2014, pp. 1–8 (2014). http://ieeexplore.ieee.org/xpl/articleDetails.jsp?arnumber=6775093
3. Kantert, J., Wildemann, S., von Zengen, G., Edenhofer, S., Tomforde, S., Wolf, L., Hähner, J., Müller-Schloer, C.: Improving reliability and endurance using end-to-end trust in distributed low-power sensor networks. In: Pinho, L., Karl, W., Cohen, A., Brinkschulte, U. (eds.) Proceedings of the 28th International Conference on Architecture of Computing Systems (ARCS 2015), vol. 9017, pp. 135–145. Springer (2015). ISBN:978-3-319-16085-6
4. Kantert, J., Edenhofer, S., Tomforde, S., Müller-Schloer, C.: Distributed rendering in an open self-organised trusted desktop grid. In: ICAC 2015, pp. 267–272. IEEE, Grenobles (2015)
5. Bernard, Y., Klejnowski, L., Hähner, J., Müller-Schloer, C.: Towards trust in desktop grid systems. In: Proceedings of CCGrid 2010, Melbourne, pp. 637–642 (2010)
6. Castelfranchi, C., Falcone, R.: Trust Theory: A Socio-Cognitive and Computational Model. Wiley, Chichester (2010). ISBN:0470028750, 9780470028759
7. Tomforde, S., Prothmann, H., Branke, J., Hähner, J., Mnif, M., Müller-Schloer, C., Richter, U., Schmeck, H.: Observation and control of organic systems. In: Müller-Schloer, C., Schmeck, H., Ungerer, T. (eds.) Organic Computing – A Paradigm Shift for Complex Systems, pp. 325–338. Birkhäuser, Basel (2011)
8. Pitt, J., Schaumeier, J., Artikis, A.: The axiomatisation of socio-economic principles for self-organising systems. In: 2011 Fifth IEEE International Conference on Self-Adaptive and Self-Organizing Systems (SASO), pp. 138–147. IEEE, Michigan (2011)
9. Russell, S., Norvig, P., Intelligence, A.: Artificial Intelligence: A Modern Approach, vol. 25. Prentice-Hall, Egnlewood Cliffs (1995)
10. Dawkin, R.: The Selfish Gene. Oxford University Press, New York (1976)
11. Osborne, M.J.: An Introduction to Game Theory. Oxford University Press (2003). ISBN:0195128958
12. Nash, J.F.: Non-cooperative games. PhD thesis, Princeton University (1950)
13. Binmore, K.: The Origins of Fair Play. Max Planck Institute of Economics, Evolutionary Economics Group (2006)
14. Hardin, G.: The tragedy of the commons. Science **162**, 1243–1248 (1968)
15. Ostrom, E.: Governing the Commons: The Evolution of Institutions for Collective Action. Cambridge University Press, Cambridge (1990)
16. Klejnowski, L.: Trusted community: a novel multiagent organisation for open distributed systems. PhD thesis, Leibniz Universität Hannover (2014). http://edok01.tib.uni-hannover.de/edoks/e01dh11/668667427.pdf

17. Schmeck, H., Müller-Schloer, C., Çakar, E., Mnif, M., Richter, U.: Adaptivity and self-organization in organic computing systems. ACM Trans. Auton. Adapt. Syst. (TAAS) **5**, 1–32 (2010). ISSN:1556-4665
18. Centeno, R., Billhardt, H.: Using incentive mechanisms for an adaptive regulation of open multi-agent systems. In: Proceedings of the Twenty-Second International Joint Conference on Artificial Intelligence, vol. 1, pp. 139–145 Barcelona (2011)
19. Hermoso, R., Billhardt, H., Ossowski, S.: Role evolution in open multi-agent systems as an information source for trust. In: Proceedings of the 9th International Conference on Autonomous Agents and Multiagent Systems, vol. 1, pp. 217–224 Toronto (2010)
20. Centeno, R., Billhardt, H., Hermoso, R.: An adaptive sanctioning mechanism for open multi-agent systems regulated by norms. In: 2011 23rd IEEE International Conference on Tools with Artificial Intelligence (ICTAI), Boca Raton, pp. 523–530 (2011)
21. Anglano, C., Canonico, M., Guazzone, M., Botta, M., Rabellino, S., Arena, S., Girardi, G.: Peer-to-peer desktop grids in the real world: the ShareGrid project. In: Proceedings of CC-Grid 2008, vol. 8(4), pp. 609–614 Lyon (2008)
22. Chakravarti, A.J., Baumgartner, G., Lauria, M.: Application-specific scheduling for the organic grid. In: Proceedings of GRID 2004 Workshops, pp. 146–155. IEEE, Washington, DC (2004). ISBN:0-7695-2256-4
23. Anderson, D.P., Fedak, G.: The computational and storage potential of volunteer computing. In: Proceedings of CCGRID 2006, pp. 73–80. IEEE, Singapore (2006). ISBN:0-7695-2585-7
24. Jain, R., Babic, G., Nagendra, B., Lam, C.-C.: Fairness, call establishment latency and other performance metrics. ATM-Forum **96**, 1–6 (1996)
25. Demers, A., Keshav, S., Shenker, S.: Analysis and simulation of a fair queueing algorithm. In: Symposium Proceedings on Communications Architectures & Protocols, pp. 1–12. ACM, New York (1989)
26. Bennett, J.C., Zhang, H.: WF2Q: worst-case fair weighted fair queueing. In: INFOCOM '96. Fifteenth Annual Joint Conference of the IEEE Computer Societies. Networking the Next Generation. Proceedings IEEE, vol. 1, pp. 120–128. IEEE, San Francisco (1996)
27. Horling, B., Lesser, V.: A survey of multi-agent organizational paradigms. Knowl. Eng. Rev. **19**, 281–316 (2004)
28. Oussalah, M., Griffiths, N.: Cooperative clans. Kybernetes **34**, 1384–1403 (2005)
29. Rosenschein, J.S., Zlotkin, G.: Rules of Encounter: Designing Conventions for Automated Negotiation Among Computers. MIT, Cambridge (1994). ISBN:0-262-18159-2
30. Hewitt, C.: Open information systems semantics for distributed artificial intelligence. Artif. Intell. **47**, 79–106 (1991)
31. Anglano, C., Brevik, J., Canonico, M., Nurmi, D., Wolski, R.: Fault-aware scheduling for bag-of-tasks applications on desktop grids. In: Proceedings of GRID 2006, pp. 56–63. IEEE, Singapore (2006). ISBN:1-4244-0343-X
32. Choi, S., Kim, H., Byun, E., Baik, M., Kim, S., Park, C., Hwang, C.: Characterizing and classifying desktop grid. In: Proceedings of CCGRID 2007, pp. 743–748. IEEE, Rio de Janeiro (2007)
33. Choi, S., Buyya, R., Kim, H., Byun, E.: A taxonomy of desktop grids and its mapping to state of the art systems. Technical report, Grid Computing and Distributed Systems Laboratory, The University of Melbourne, pp. 1–61 (2008)
34. Wang, Y., Vassileva, J.: Trust-based community formation in peer-to-peer file sharing networks. In: Proceedings on Web Intelligence, pp. 341–348. IEEE, Beijing (2004)
35. Domingues, P., Sousa, B., Moura Silva, L.: Sabotage-tolerance and trustmanagement in desktop grid computing. Future Generat. Comput. Syst. **23**, 904–912 (2007)
36. Sartor, G.: Legal Reasoning: A Cognitive Approach to Law. Springer, Berlin/Heidelberg (2005)
37. Nute, D.: Defeasible logic. Handb. Log. Artif. Intell. Log. Program. **3**, 353–395 (1994)
38. Nute, D.: Defeasible reasoning: a philosophical analysis in prolog. In: Aspects of Artificial Intelligence, pp. 251–288. Springer, Berlin/Heidelberg (1988)
39. Nute, D.: Defeasible logic. In: Proceedings of the Applications of Prolog 14th International Conference on Web Knowledge Management and Decision Support, pp. 151–169. Springer, Berlin/Heidelberg (2003). ISBN:3-540-00680-X

40. Billington, D.: Defeasible logic is stable. J. Log. Comput. **3**, 379–400 (1993)
41. Urzicaă, A., Gratie, C.: Policy-based instantiation of norms in MAS. In: Fortino, G., Badica, C., Malgeri, M., Unland, R. (eds.) Intelligent Distributed Computing VI, vol. 446, pp. 287–296. Springer, Calabria (2013)
42. Balke, T., da Costa Pereira, C., Dignum, F., Lorini, E., Rotolo, A., Vasconcelos, W., Villata, S.: Norms in MAS: definitions and related concepts. In: Normative Multi-Agent Systems, vol. 4, pp. 1–31. Schloss Dagstuhl–Leibniz-Zentrum fuer Informatik, Dagstuhl (2013). ISBN:978-3-939897-51-4
43. Von Wright, G.H.: Norms and Action: A Logical Enquiry. Routledge & Kegan Paul, London (1963)
44. Tuomela, R., Bonnevier-Tuomela, M.: Norms and agreements. Eur. J. Law Philos. Comput. Sci. **5**, 41–46 (1995)
45. Hollander, C.D., Wu, A.S.: The current state of normative agent-based systems. J. Artif. Soc. Soc. Simul. **14**, 6 (2011). ISSN:1460-7425
46. Singh, M.P.: An ontology for commitments in multiagent systems. Artif. Intell. Law **7**, 97–113 (1999)
47. Governatori, G., Rotolo, A.: BIO logical agents: norms, beliefs, intentions in defeasible logic. Auton. Agents Multi-Agent Syst. **17**, 36–69 (2008). ISSN:1387-2532
48. Artikis, A., Pitt, J.: Specifying open agent systems: a survey. In: Artikis, A., Picard, G., Vercouter, L. (eds.) Engineering Societies in the Agents World IX, vol. 5485, pp. 29–45. Springer, Saint-Etienne (2009). ISBN:978-3-642-02561-7
49. Boella, G., Pigozzi, G., van der Torre, L.: Normative systems in computer science – ten guidelines for normative multiagent systems. In: Boella, G., Noriega, P., Pigozzi, G., Verhagen, H. (eds.) Normative Multi-Agent Systems, pp. 1–21. Schloss Dagstuhl – Leibniz-Zentrum fuer Informatik, Dagstuhl (2009)
50. Conte, R., Castelfranchi, C., Dignum, F.: Autonomous norm acceptance. In: Müller, J., Rao, A., Singh, M. (eds.) Intelligent Agents V: Agents Theories, Architectures, and Languages, vol. 1555, pp. 99–112. Springer, Paris (1999). ISBN:978-3-540-65713-2
51. Savarimuthu, B.T.R., Cranefield, S.: Norm creation, spreading and emergence: a survey of simulation models of norms in multi-agent systems. Multiagent Grid Syst. **7**, 21–54 (2011)
52. Singh, M.P., et al.: The uses of norms. In: Normative Multi-Agent Systems, vol. 4, pp. 191–229. Schloss Dagstuhl–Leibniz-Zentrum fuer Informatik, Dagstuhl (2013). ISBN:978-3-939897-51-4
53. Wasserman, S.: Social Network Analysis: Methods and Applications. Cambridge University Press, Cambridge (1994)
54. Newman, M.E.J.: The structure and function of complex networks. SIAM Rev. **45**, 167–256 (2003)
55. Waldschmidt, K., Damm, M.: Robustness in soc design. In: 9th EUROMICRO Conference on Digital System Design: Architectures, Methods and Tools (DSD 2006), Dubrovnik, pp. 27–36 (2006)
56. Shestak, V., Siegel, H.J., Maciejewski, A.A., Ali, S.: The robustness of resource allocations in parallel and distributed computing systems. In: Architecture of Computing Systems-ARCS 2006, pp. 17–30. Springer, Berlin/Heidelberg (2006)
57. England, D., Weissman, J., Sadagopan, J.: A new metric for robustness with application to job scheduling. In: Proceedings of 14th IEEE International Symposium on High Performance Distributed Computing (HPDC-14 2005), Research Triangle Park, pp. 135–143 (2005)
58. Warmer, J., Kleppe, A.: The Object Constraint Language: Precise Modeling with UML. Addison-Wesley Longman, Boston (1999). ISBN:0-201-37940-6
59. Steghöfer, J.-P., Anders, G., Reif, W., Kantert, J., Müller-Schloer, C.: An effective implementation of norms in trust-aware open self-organising systems. In: 2014 IEEE Eighth International Conference on Self-Adaptive and Self-Organizing Systems Workshops (SASOW), pp. 76–77. IEEE, London (2014)

60. Schmeck, H., Müller-Schloer, C., Çakar, E., Mnif, M., Richter, U.: Adaptivity and self-organization in organic computing systems. ACM Trans. Auton. Adapt. Syst. **5**, 10:1–10:32 (2010). ISSN:1556-4665
61. Kantert, J., Klejnowski, L., Bernard, Y., Müller-Schloer, C.: Influence of norms on decision making in trusted desktop grid systems: making norms explicit. In: Proceedings of the 6th International Conference on Agents and Artificial Intelligence, vol. 2, pp. 278–283. SciTePress, Angers (2014)
62. Kantert, J., Scharf, H., Edenhofer, S., Tomforde, S., Hähner, J., Müller-Schloer, C.: A graph analysis approach to detect attacks in multi-agent-systems at runtime. In: 2014 IEEE Eighth International Conference on Self-Adaptive and Self-Organizing Systems, pp. 80–89. IEEE, London (2014)
63. Kantert, J., Bödelt, S., Edenhofer, S., Tomforde, S., Hähner, J., Müller-Schloer, C.: Interactive simulation of an open trusted desktop grid system with visualisation in 3D. In: 2014 IEEE Eighth International Conference on Self-Adaptive and Self-Organizing Systems (SASO), pp. 191–192. IEEE, London (2014)
64. Kantert, J., Edenhofer, S., Tomforde, S., Hähner, J., Müller-Schloer, C.: Defending autonomous agents against attacks in multi-agent systems using norms. In: Proceedings of the 7th International Conference on Agents and Artificial Intelligence. SciTePress, Lisbon, pp. 149–156 (2015)
65. Van Dongen, S.M.: Graph clustering by flow simulation. PhD thesis, Utrecht University (2001). http://dspace.library.uu.nl/bitstream/handle/1874/848/full.pdf
66. Zhang, T., Ramakrishnan, R., Livny, M.: BIRCH: an efficient data clustering method for very large databases. In: ACM SIGMOD Record, vol. 25, pp. 103–114. ACM, Montreal (1996)
67. Fraga, D., Banković, Z., Moya, J.M.: A taxonomy of trust and reputation system attacks. In: 2012 IEEE 11th International Conference on Trust, Security and Privacy in Computing and Communications (TrustCom), Liverpool, pp. 41–50 (2012)

# Chapter 5
# Trust Communities: An Open, Self-Organised Social Infrastructure of Autonomous Agents

Sarah Edenhofer, Sven Tomforde, Jan Kantert, Lukas Klejnowski,
Yvonne Bernard, Jörg Hähner, and Christian Müller-Schloer

**Abstract** Future technical systems will be increasingly characterised by openness and heterogeneity of participating elements. Based on exemplary application
scenarios such as Desktop Computing Grids, Smart Power Grids, and Networked
Camera Systems, this chapter develops a solution perspective to handle anomalies,
disturbances, and malicious behaviour by making use of trust and reliability
measures in self-organised systems. The overall goal is to increase the robustness
of open distributed systems with low overhead. Therefore, a novel self-organised
multi-agent organisation—the Trust Community—is introduced in two variants:
as implicit and as explicit self-structuring society of autonomous agents. For the
explicit variant, a life-cycle and management routines are described. For evaluation
purposes, we simulate a Trusted Desktop Computing Grid and introduce different
types of stereo-type agent behaviour, ranging from altruistic to egoistic and to
cunning behaviour. In order to support efficiency and stabilise the process, we
show the benefits of explicit Trust Communities, which results in significantly lower
overhead and more reliable relations among agents compared to other forms of agent
societies.

S. Edenhofer (✉) • S. Tomforde
Organic Computing Group, Augsburg University, Augsburg, Germany
e-mail: sarah.edenhofer@informatik.uni-augsburg.de;
sven.tomforde@informatik.uni-augsburg.de

J. Kantert • L. Klejnowski • Y. Bernard
Institute of Systems Engineering, Leibniz Universität Hannover, Hannover, Germany
e-mail: kantert@sra.uni-hannover.de; klejnowski@sra.uni-hannover.de;
bernard@sra.uni-hannover.de

J. Hähner
Organic Computing Group, University of Augsburg, Augsburg, Germany
e-mail: joerg.haehner@informatik.uni-augsburg.de

C. Müller-Schloer
Institute of Systems Engineering, University of Hannover, Hannover, Germany
e-mail: cms@sra.uni-hannover.de

© Springer International Publishing Switzerland 2016
W. Reif et al. (eds.), *Trustworthy Open Self-Organising Systems*,
Autonomic Systems, DOI 10.1007/978-3-319-29201-4_5

127

**Keywords** Trust communities • Multi-agent systems • Autonomous agents • Self-organisation • Trusted desktop grid

## 5.1 Introduction

Self-organised systems such as Vehicular Traffic Control [1] and Intrusion Detection [2] are facing challenges regarding controllability and administrability due to severe complexity and interaction [3]. Typically, such a system consists of a potentially large set of autonomous agents that act on behalf of a user and try to achieve an intrinsic goal, potentially resulting in selfish behaviour. This is accompanied by general characteristics of the self-organising system, such as heterogeneity (in terms of participating agents), openness (i.e. there is no authorisation and participation control mechanism), or geographic distribution. As a consequence of these properties, we face challenges in terms of identifying reliable and trustworthy interaction partners within such systems.

Establishing *computational trust* as basis for decisions about interaction partners has been shown to be beneficial [4]. Thereby, the term *trust* comprises several facets that all contribute to the prediction of the counterpart's behaviour for an upcoming interaction, e.g. reliability, predictability, compliance, or availability. In general, trust is an individual experience—which can be combined with aggregated community-based measures such as *reputation*. If taking trust experiences and reputation values into account during selection of interaction partners, an agent can decrease the fraction of unsatisfying experiences [5].

In this chapter, we utilise the concept of computational trust and improve its impact within *self-organising systems*. In order to be able to decrease safety measures and simultaneously increase efficiency and robustness, we propose a novel multi-agent organisation called *Trust Community* (TC).[1] Such a TC is formed by individual agents that have strong mutual trust relationships and it is maintained as long as there is a benefit of participation. We describe the entire TC life-cycle with all constituting elements in the remainder of this chapter.

To illustrate the developed concept, we consider a *Desktop (Computing) Grid* (DG, see [6]) as one particular instance of the aforementioned problem class. The goal of participating in a DG is to utilise resources provided by other agents in a reciprocal manner (i.e. each agent contributes a fair share of its resources to keep the system running). In such a system, agents can join and leave at any time, and there is no mechanism to control their participation strategy. More precisely, each agent can (and probably will) behave selfishly, and malicious elements may become part of the system as well. In this chapter, we apply the TC concept to an exemplary DG system and demonstrate that such malicious agents are isolated fast and efficiently. We also show that becoming a TC member has significant benefits in terms of speedup of the

---

[1] In earlier publications referred to as *Trusted Communities*.

*work units (WUs)* to be processed. In addition, we compare the developed concept with the *Clans* [7] concept that is a successful representative from the state-of-the-art.

The remainder of this chapter is organised as follows: Sect. 5.2 gives a brief overview of the state-of-the-art with respect to trust and reputation, multi-agent systems, and our application scenario. Afterwards, Sect. 5.3 presents the application scenario—the *Trusted Desktop (Computing) Grid* (TDG)—in more detail, including the considered agent behaviour, the individual agent's goal, and the overall system goal. Section 5.4 introduces the concept of *Self-organising TCs*—a novel multi-agent organisation to improve robustness and efficiency in open, distributed systems. The approach is evaluated in Sect. 5.5 using simulations of the TDG. Finally, Sect. 5.6 summarises the chapter and gives an outlook to future work.

## 5.2  Related Work

*Trust* is a concept well studied in fields such as philosophy [8], psychology [9], or sociology [10, 11]. In human societies, every person is first of all concerned with his or her individual interests, but we have learned to expect certain behaviours of our fellow members of society and rely on them. "Trust is a belief an agent has that the other party will do what it says it will (being honest and reliable) or reciprocate (being reciprocative for the common good of both), given an opportunity to defect to get higher payoffs" [4]. Many sociologists see trust as the fundamental basis for a well functioning and stable society [12]. "Without trust, the (human) society would cease to exist" [13]. The term *Reputation* is usually used as the combined trust value of several agents towards a single agent [11, 14].

We can distinguish four possible sources of trust in computing systems [15]: *Direct experiences* can be gained by direct interaction between two agents, or from observation of an interaction between two other agents. *Witness Information* (or: Indirect Information) is communicated by other agents of the system. Therefore, it is far more abundant than direct experience and it is important in order to get an accurate estimation of a member with whom an agent has not interacted with yet. At the same time, it poses security threats as other members can also spread wrong information. *Sociological information* is gained by taking social relationships into account. An example is an employee's position within a company, it has to be added to the system manually. *Prejudice* is estimated by observing signs which identify members of a community. The last two sources of information can rarely be found in current technical systems, so only the first two sources are considered.

Traditional *trust models* are widely used as sources of inspiration for the improvement of the efficiency of computing systems. In this case, "reputation systems should not be designed to emulate the sometimes irrational behaviour of humans. Instead, they should improve the ability of users[i.e. agents—author's note] to evaluate opinions and to come to the most beneficial decision" [16]. In this chapter, the prime example are *multi-agent systems* [17]. These are distributed systems consisting of several interconnected, autonomous, and self-interested nodes referred to as *agents* [4]. The agents can, for example, be computers controlled by users (as in an e-commerce setting) or computers connected into a DG (cf. [18]). We assume trust as "a subjective expectation an agent has about another's future behavior based on the history of their encounters" [19].

Our application scenario described in Sect. 5.3 is such a DG System. The grid nodes, implemented as agents, work on behalf of the user (corresponding to the concepts prompted by the domain of multi-agent systems). Therefore, we do not consider user interactions. Agents can be seen as *blackboxes*, i.e. they are autonomous and their internal state cannot be observed by other agents in the system (*no full disclosure*). A classification and taxonomy of DG Systems can be found in [20].

DGs are used to share the resources between multiple administrative authorities. One example for a peer-to-peer based system is the ShareGrid Project [21]. A second approach is the Organic Grid, a peer-to-peer based approach with decentralised scheduling [22]. The before-mentioned systems assume *benevolence* [23], i.e. that there are no malfunctioning, malicious, or misbehaving agents participating. Otherwise, not assuming benevolence means that there are misbehaving agents which are only downloading files while not offering them for others. At the same time, there can be malicious agents which damage the system on purpose by lying, offering corrupted or infected files in content sharing networks, or do not fulfil their part of a mutual agreement in an e-commerce systems (like not sending a bought item) [13].

Other approaches are, on the one hand, the open source *Berkeley Open Infrastructure for Network Computing Project* (BOINC) [24] and *XtremWeb* [25] on the other hand, which aim at setting up a Global Computing application and "harvest[ing] the idle time of Internet-connected computers which may be widely distributed across the world, to run a very large and distributed application" with an ad-hoc verification process for participating computers. BOINC has at least 50 % overhead, since it replicates every WU at least once (for more details see [26]). A panoramic view on computational trust in multi-agent systems can be found in [27] or [15]. Sabotage-tolerance and distributed trust management in DGs are evaluated in [28], where mechanisms for sabotage detection are presented, but proposed for a paradigm of volunteer-based computing.

The concept of *clans* [7] describes a multi-agent system organisation based on the idea of congregations [29] and trust management. Clans are used as reference solution for our evaluation in Sect. 5.5. They are formed by the agents if one of the thresholds, for either the number of missed opportunities for cooperation, the lack of scalability, lack of information, or a high failure rate, is exceeded. In this case, one agent starts to form a clan and invites other agents based on their trustworthiness (i.e. with focus on reliability) and the agents' capability. Inside a clan, agents' benefits derive primarily from the *kinship motivation*. In contrast to TCs which are semi-closed systems with central structures of power (e.g. TC Manager, described in Sect. 5.4.3), clans are purely decentralised. Each clan member can invite other agents into the clan. This makes clans vulnerable to concerted attacks, for instance.

## 5.3  Application Scenario: Trusted Desktop (Computing) Grid

For illustration purpose, we use the open *Trusted Desktop (Computing) Grid* (TDG) as application scenario. Due to the openness of the grid, the autonomous agents can join (or leave) voluntarily at any time. In the TDG, various autonomous agents can distribute their work among the other agents (as submitter) as well as process work of others (as worker, cf. Sect. 5.3.3)—following the concept of reciprocity. We call this work *jobs*, which can be split into atomic WUs. Consider as example the rendering of a cinematic film [26].

Rendering cinematic films (of about 100 min length) requires long calculations [30]. In consequence, most productions are rendered in parallel on several computers, i.e. different agents, since rendering is by far the most expensive task during the movie production process. Films can be partitioned into so-called frames, i.e. WUs, without data dependencies. Here, the theoretical maximum rendering speed ($max(v_{rend})$) is determined by the number of frames in the film, i.e. the duration of the film multiplied by frames per second (fps, cf. Equation (5.1)).

$$v_{rend} \leq |frames| = duration \cdot fps \qquad (5.1)$$

Considering a 100 min film at 30 fps, we get $\sigma_{rend} \leq 100 \cdot 60 \cdot 30 = 180,000$. The actual value for $\sigma_{rend}$ is lower in practice, because the time to render a frame is not constant. After the parallel rendering, all frames are merged into one film and encoded for the target container. Usually, these finishing steps are done without parallelisation, since they can be processed efficiently on modern computers.

Uncompressed films can be very big. To estimate the required network bandwidth for the above-mentioned distributed rendering, we analyse the short film *Big Buck Bunny* [31] of about 10 min length. This film has been developed by the Blender Foundation and is publicly available. It has a frame rate of 60 frames per second due to stereoscopic 3D and consists of 79,781 frames, each raw frame has a size of 10–20 MB and has to be transmitted to the participants of the network. Furthermore, the participants need some rendering environment. Each scene may have a different rendering equipment. *Big Buck Bunny* is divided into 120 scenes, each compressed scene's rendering environment has a size between 1 and 60 MB, but the submitter can restrict the worker to only render frames from one scene, so the required bandwidth can be kept small compared to the computational requirements. The latter are ranging "from a few hours to several weeks of CPU time" per frame [31]. For the film *Cars2*, 12,500 CPU cores were required, a single frame took 11.5 h to render [32].

This rendering example shows, how important it can be to split up work and calculate it distributedly. In this section, we want to give further details about the TDG needed for the distributed processing. First, we will introduce different agent stereotypes in Sect. 5.3.1, agent components are presented in Sect. 5.3.2. Afterwards, in Sect. 5.3.3 the agent goal is defined, the worker and submitter components are explained, and the global (system) goal is introduced.

### 5.3.1  Agent Stereotypes

The TDG is open and freely accessible for all different kinds of agents. Therefore, we waived the assumption of benevolence in the system, which typically serves as basis [23]. This allows for various types of agents: *malicious, uncooperative*, or *malfunctioning* agents. Consequently, we can distinguish between well-behaving (WB) and bad-behaving agents (BB) in open systems. In the following, we discuss different types of agents, which can possibly join the TDG:

**Adaptive Agents (ADA)**   are cooperative agents. They work for other agents, taking into account several aspects, for example their reputation in the system and how much their WU-queue is saturated to capacity (in this case, the agent may reject another WU).

**Altruistic Agents (ALT)**   accept every WU. They do not take into account their own status, the environmental conditions, or experiences with cooperation partners.

**Freeriding Agents (FRE)**   are not willing to work for other agents and, therefore, reject all work requests but keep asking others to work for them. This behaviour increases the overall system load and can decrease the benefit for well-behaving agents.

**Egoistic Agents (EGO)**   accept most WUs but only pretend to work for other agents. They often return fake results instead of processing the WU correctly. This wastes the time of other agents. Result validation can be a counter measure, but this decreases the global speedup (see Sect. 5.3.3).

**Cunning Agents (CUN)**   show an oscillating behaviour. In the beginning, they act cooperatively, which increases their reputation value. Later, they change their behaviour (periodically, randomly, or under certain conditions, e.g. if this reputation is high enough) and behave like FRE or EGO. Such a behaviour is hard to detect and lowers the overall system performance [33].

**Sloppy Agents (SLA)**   are cooperative but do only accept a certain percentage of all WUs, which are offered to them [34]. This percentage is expressed by the acceptance rate $\alpha$.

**Defecting Agents (DFA)**   are a behavioural stereotype that can be imposed on other agent types. It models the threat of false results for non-validating DG applications by adding a probability (0.2) of returning a wrong WU result to the submitter (cf. Sect. 5.3.3).

ADA can be classified as WB agents, ALT are not fully WB, since they work for BB agents—this lowers the fairness of the whole system. FRE and EGO are BB. CUN cannot clearly be classified due to their oscillating behaviour; the same holds for SLA. A big problem can be observed, if several BB agents join the system simultaneously and try to exploit, respectively attack the system. In order to intercept this behaviour, the agents can form Trust Communities (TC), which will be discussed in Sect. 5.4.

## 5.3.2   Agent Components

In this section, the ADA is presented in more detail. It is well-suited for the TDG, since it takes trust and reputation into account when making decisions. Basic characteristics of the agent are described in the following. *Autonomy*—to a certain degree—is granted to the agents since we have an open system. We consider all agents as *blackboxes*, i.e. other agents have no knowledge about the internal state of their respective cooperation partners. *Interactions* between the agents are based on a commonly understandable communication protocol. This helps to encourage *cooperation*, which is—besides the shared environment (promoting stigmergy) and external entities such as users—an important source of information. Due to the distributedness of the system, the agents have a strictly *local view*.

An ADA implements the Observer/Controller design pattern [35] and relies on agent models in the literature, where software agents act on behalf of a user and/or a programme (cf. [17]).

In Fig. 5.1 (in accordance with [36]), the basic structure of such an agent model is depicted: The **user** $U^x$ sets up an **agent** $A^x$ to control its **production engine**, a client software that allows participating in the hosting system and defines a performance measure. This production engine is monitored by the **Observer** (O), based on an **observation model**. This observation model specifies which sensor information is gathered at which resolution and augmented with predictions or emergence detection. Together with knowledge gained from monitoring the environment (also done by the observer), a situation description is created and passed on to the **Controller** (C). Based on this situation description, the Controller can alter the behaviour of the production engine and/or change the observation model. Therefore, the Controller decides—based on observed **input information** ($O^x$, $i \in$

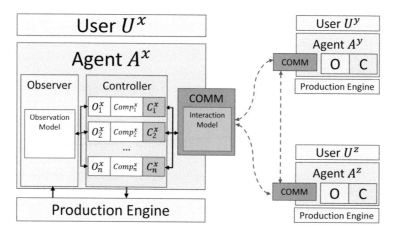

**Fig. 5.1** Organic Computing-based ADA component with Observer/Controller design pattern. A communication component COMM helps to communicate with other agents. The agents control the production engine on behalf of the user

[1..*n*]—which **components** ($Comp^x = \{Comp^x_1, \ldots, Comp^x_n\}$) are triggered. Their encapsulated decision-making determines the **interactions** ($C^x_i, i \in [1..n]$). This can also influence the **interaction model** (sum of interactions provided to other agents) of the **communication interface** (COMM). The COMM interface allows for communication with the other agents, e.g. $A^y$ and $A^z$.

### 5.3.3 Agent Goal, Worker/Submitter Component, and Global Goal

**Agent Goal.** The benefit of an agent can be measured by its *speedup* $\sigma$, informally speaking its benefit of having its work processed distributively over having to process all work on its own (in accordance with [36]). A job $J$ is a set of WUs, which is released in time step $t^{rel}_J$ and completed in $t^{compl}_J$, when the last WU is finished.

The speedup $\sigma$ in Equation (5.2) is a metric known from multi-core systems. It is based on the assumption that parallelisation helps to process a task (i.e. a job) faster than processing it on a single core. $\sigma$ is the ratio of the time the agent would have needed to process all WUs on its own to the real time it took to calculate $J$ distributedly in the system. This is why the speedup can only be determined after the last result has been returned to the submitter.

$$\sigma = \frac{\sum_J (t^{compl}_{self} - t^{rel}_{self})}{\sum_J (t^{compl}_{dist} - t^{rel}_{dist})} \tag{5.2}$$

In short, we can write $\sigma := \frac{t_{self}}{t_{dist}}$ with $t_{self}$ being the time it would require an agent to process all WUs of a job without cooperation, i.e. sequentially. $t_{dist}$ is the time it takes until all WUs are computed distributedly and the last result is returned to the submitting agent. If no cooperation partners can be found, agents need to calculate their own WUs. This results in a speedup value equal to one. In general, we assume that agents behave selfishly and only cooperate if they can expect an advantage, i.e. $\sigma > 1$, which corresponds to the agent type ADA.

**Worker and Submitter Component.** Each agent is free do decide which agent it wants to give its WUs to and for which agents it wants to work for. Therefore, every agent has a *submitter* and a *worker* component.

The *submitter component* is the scheduler of the agent and responsible for distributing WUs. If an agent receives a job $J$ from the user consisting of multiple WUs, it creates a list of suited workers, i.e. workers it trusts. It then asks workers from this list to cooperate and calculate WUs, until either no more WU or no more workers are left. If all workers were asked and still unprocessed WUs remain, the agent calculates them on its own.

The *worker component* decides whether an agent wants to work for a certain submitter. When the agent receives a request to process a WU, it calculates its expected reward for accepting and rejecting the WU. If the reward of accepting the WU prevails, the agent takes the WU, puts it in its own working queue, where the WU remains until the agent starts to process it, i.e. until the other WU in the queue were processed. Afterwards, it transfers the result back to the submitter where the result is validated [36]. A job is completed, if all WUs were returned to the submitter.

**Global Goal.** The global goal—also referred to as the system goal—is to enable and encourage agents to cooperate and thereby achieve the best possible *average speedup*. The systems' focus is *coordination*, i.e. shaping the environment in a way that allows for cooperation and, thereby, leads to optimising the global goal.

## 5.4   Self-Organising Trust Communities

The problem with the before-mentioned distributed processing of WUs, e.g. the rendering of different scenes of a film, is that there can be agents in the system that are trying to exploit it in different ways. This happens due to the fact that agents can join the system at any time, and that their internal state is unknown. As a countermeasure against exploiting agents, e.g. EGO or CUN, we introduce *Trust Communities* (TCs). In this section, we first explain the role of computational trust in Computing Grids in Sect. 5.4.1. Then we introduce explicit TC (eTCs) (Sect. 5.4.2) and their typical life-cycle (Sect. 5.4.3), including different strategies to form and control the eTC, as well as different surveillance strategies as additional counter measure against malicious agents (Sect. 5.4.4).

### 5.4.1   Computational Trust in Computing Grids

In Computing Grids, trust is mainly used to help the agents find suitable cooperation partners for processing each others' work. This increases the performance and robustness of the system [37]. Furthermore, we need trust to identify malicious, uncooperative, or malfunctioning agents. Malfunctioning and uncooperative agents mostly follow certain behaviour patterns. Therefore, they are relatively easy to identify. Malicious agents, however, are willingly trying to harm the Computing Grid or exploit other agents, such as the ADA. Thereby, they actively avoid being detected. This affects the average speedup negatively and can even lead to a breakdown of the whole system, e.g. in case they attack coordinately.

A first step towards the avoidance of these negative emergent effects inside the TDG is that agents form *implicit Trust Communities* (iTC) [38]: If agents have good experiences with each other, their mutual trust values increase over time. In consequence, these agents are more likely to distribute their work to and accept work from the other agents in this group. Thus, agents they had bad experiences with get marginalised.

With this measure, certain solely negatively acting agents can easily be isolated. Problems arise, if several malicious agents plan coordinated joint attacks on the system (*collusion attacks*). A solution for such attacks is to make the implicit TCs *explicit*.

## 5.4.2 Explicit Trust Communities

The key concept of the TC approach is to provide an environment in which the agents can interact, share information and cooperate like in a *closed* system—without applying safety measures, such as replication or surveillance. Since there are no explicit safety measures in an iTC, there is still a need for replication and the iTC does not stand a chance against colluding attacks.

Therefore, we introduce the concept of eTCs [37]. An eTC is a semi-closed system within the open system with several benefits for the agents: Inside the eTC, no replication is necessary. Furthermore, the agents in the eTC are obliged to accept any work from other eTC members and to share their current status, e.g. their queue-length. A disadvantage of an eTC is that significantly more overhead effort is required compared to the iTC, e.g. for maintenance issues. This is why the agents in the system are constantly weighing the benefits of being in an eTC against the disadvantages, since they are free to leave the eTC at any time.

An eTC $i$ at time $t$ is defined by the tuple shown in Equation (5.3):

$$eTC_i(t) := \langle M_i(t), \text{TCM}_i(t), \Psi_i(t) \rangle \tag{5.3}$$

$M_i(t)$ are all members of $eTC_i$. i.e. selected from all agents. Subsequently, $M(t)$ are all members in all eTCs at time $t$.

The membership in an eTC is disjoint, i.e. each agent can only be in one eTC at each time. $\text{TCM}_i(t)$ is the elected *Trust Community Manager* (short: TCM), which will be described in detail in Sect. 5.4.3, and $\Psi_i(t)$ is a set of roles that can be assigned to agents in $M_i$ by the TCM.

The assignment of roles is a necessity in an eTC to reduce the TCM's administration overhead. An example for such a role is the active search for potential new members at runtime (basic active TC expansion strategy, cf. Sect. 5.4.3). This delegation of tasks is required, since the TCM is a self-interested agent: if it performs all obligations by itself, this would reduce the utility it gains by being member of an eTC considerably. As a consequence, the agent would leave the eTC.

In Fig. 5.2, an eTC is shown. Inside the **open system**, there are several agents, which may have **trust-based interactions**. The **unassociated members** (containing the **misconducting agents**) are outside the **eTC**, but may have **outbound inter-**

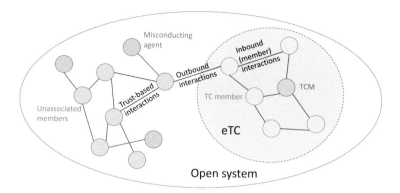

**Fig. 5.2** An eTC in an open system. All members are either unassociated (and maybe misconducting) or eTC members (with one of them being the TCM). Some members are connected by a *line* which shows trust-based interactions

**actions** with **TC members**. The **TC members** (containing the **TCM**) may have **inbound (member)** interactions.

## 5.4.3  Life-Cycle of an eTC

The formation of an eTC follows a certain order. The whole life-cycle of an eTC can be seen in Fig. 5.3. The life-cycle starts with the **pre-organisation phase**. At the beginning, all system members are unassociated and the whole system is unstructured. Furthermore, no trust-relationships exist and the agents have to distribute their work randomly and apply sub-optimal interactions. Based on the trust metric of the TDG, the agents rate other agents with a value representing the amount of trust earned through this interaction. Each rating is between −1 (e.g. the agent rejects the work request) and 1 (e.g. the WU is calculated correctly and returned in time). For more details see [39]. During this self-organising process, uncertainty is reduced and trust-relationships are established among the agents. If a critical number of agents with strong mutual trust-relationships is exceeded, these agents can decide to form an eTC from this group. The agents have to decide, whether they would benefit from a potential membership in an eTC. Next, the eTC gets into the **TC formation phase**. This phase is dominated by negotiations of all potential future eTC members. We need this mechanism to give each agent the chance to weigh its decision, since not all agents have the same interaction partners and the same knowledge. The phase ends, if there are still enough potential members left, with the election of the *Trust Community Manager* (TCM). The TCM takes over the role to organise and maintain the eTC. The election process can take different criteria into account, e.g. trust, reputation, or availability. In general, we make use of *leader election* algorithms from the domain of distributed systems [40].

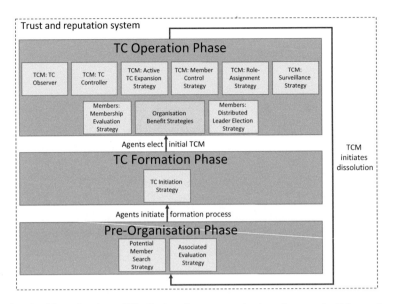

**Fig. 5.3** The life-cycle of an eTC: During the pre-organisation phase, potential members are searched. Then, the eTC is formed (TC formation phase). Afterwards, a TCM is elected and the eTC is in the TC operation phase, where the TCM and the members use strategies, e.g. to observe the environment and control the eTC

In each phase, the agents can follow certain strategies [36]. During the pre-organisation phase and the eTC formation phase, these are:

- *Potential Member Search Strategy*: Each agent decides: which are, in its opinion, the most trustworthy agents?
- *Associated Evaluation Strategy*: With this strategy, agents decide whether to form a new eTC, join the forming eTC, follow an invitation for a eTC, or remain unassociated.
- *TC Initiation Strategy*: Here, criteria are defined for the eTC formation, respecting the group of the initiating agents.

After all these preparations, the newly formed eTC enters the main phase, the **TC operation phase**. During this phase, the TCM can assign roles to other members in order to distribute the effort of administrating the eTC, it establishes norms to determine the behaviour of all agents inside the eTC, and accepts agents to join or excludes members from the eTC [26]. Members inside the eTC can compare their own *predicted utility* to the *(actual) utility* periodically. In the TDG, the utility refers to the speedup $\sigma$. If the agents discover, that the utility did not improve (enough), they leave the eTC. If a critical number of agents does so and the number of eTC members falls below a certain threshold, the TCM dissolves the eTC. During the TC operation phase, the following strategies are applied by the members:

- *Membership Evaluation Strategy*: eTC members determine their utility and whether it has improved in order to decide about staying in or leaving the eTC.
- *Organisation Benefit Strategies*: All strategies to increase the utility of each agent, including efficient interactions, cooperation among the members, and sharing information about the current status.
- *Distributed Leader Election Strategy*: To elect the TCM, this strategy includes criteria for TCM qualification and distributed leader election algorithms.

When being elected as TCM, this agents needs the following strategies:

- *TC Observer*: The observer part of the Observer/Controller-loop, including observation criteria and approaches.
- *TC Controller*: The controller part of the Observer/Controller-loop of the TCM which regulates the operation of the eTC based on the observations (cf. the description of the observer and controller in Sect. 5.3.2).
- *Active TC Expansion Strategy*: In order to quickly adapt to environmental changes, this strategy helps to extend the composition of the eTC.
- *Member Control Strategy*: This strategy aims at controlling the members inside an eTC by providing feedback to their actions and possibly even punishing them (at worst, with exclusion from the eTC).
- *Role-Assignment Strategy*: Management tasks can be distributed by the TCM with this strategy by assigning roles to other agents in the eTC.
- *Surveillance Strategy*: This strategy helps the TCM to decide whom to monitor if it only has a limited surveillance budget.

With the help of all these strategies, the eTC can be self-organised and deal with the above-mentioned negative aspects of the openness of the system. Independently from what is happening inside the eTC, the unassociated members in the system continue interacting with each other, as well as with the eTC members. If an unassociated agents considers the membership in an eTC and is acceptable from the eTC's point of view, it can join the eTC later, since we have a dynamic system.

## 5.4.4  eTC Surveillance Strategies

As described above, the TCM has the ability to monitor the eTC members with different surveillance strategies. But total surveillance is neither desirable nor possible in an open, distributed system with autonomous agents. It should further be noted that the knowledge acquisition involves computational and communication costs. Therefore, the TCM can only monitor a certain percentage of all eTC members at each time, expressed by the *surveillance rate* $\mathscr{S} \in [0, 1]$. It can use different *surveillance strategies* to choose this fraction $\mathscr{S}$ of agents, which we refer to as the *chosen* agents. These surveillance strategies are presented in the following:

- *Accusation-Based Strategy*: Agents can accuse other agents in case of an incident, for example if they return no result for a given WU. The more accusations an agent has, the more likely it is among the observed agents [34].
- *Reputation-Based Strategy*: Here, an agent is more likely to be monitored if its reputation is low compared to the other eTC members' reputation. This concept can be realised by using a roulette-wheel approach that considers the available reputation values [41].
- *Round-Robin-Based Strategy*: For this strategy, we consider all eTC members as elements in a sorted list, illustrated in Fig. 5.4a: The chosen agents (dark grey) are the first fraction $\mathscr{S}$ of elements in the first time step $t_1$, in our example $a_1, a_2$, and $a_3$. In the second time step $t_2$, the chosen agents are the next $\mathscr{S}$ of all elements, shifted by (in this example) *step-width* $= 2$: $a_3, a_4$ and $a_5$.
- *Random-Based Strategy*: The agents to be observed are chosen randomly. Each agent has the same probability of being selected.
- *Lottery-Based Strategy*: The agents to be observed are randomly chosen in each time step—but no repetition is allowed until all agents have been observed, see Fig. 5.4b: In $t_1$, agents $a_1, a_4$ and $a_{10}$ are selected (dark grey). In $t_2$, these agents cannot be chosen again (striped), instead $a_2, a_3$ and $a_8$ are chosen randomly from the remaining agents.

The accusation-based and reputation-based strategies use additional knowledge about the agents (i.e. their previous incidents, and their reputation-value). Therefore, we call these strategies *quality-based*. We call the other three strategies *quantity-based*, since their success highly depends on the parameter assignment of $\mathscr{S}$, distinctly more so than the quality-based strategies.

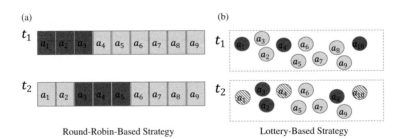

Round-Robin-Based Strategy                                    Lottery-Based Strategy

**Fig. 5.4** The Round-Robin-Based Strategy (**a**) with *step-width* $= 2$ and $\mathscr{S} = 0.3$, i.e. 3 of 9 agents are chosen (represented by *dark grey*), these agents are shifted by *step-width* 2 each time step, and the Lottery-Based Strategy (**b**) with $\mathscr{S} = 0.3$. At each timestep, 3 out of 10 agents are chosen (*dark grey*) as a set disjoint to the agents chosen before (*striped*) until every agent has been chosen once

## 5.5  Evaluation

In this section, we evaluate the performance of the agents in the TDG. Therefore, we will start with the detailed description of clans in Sect. 5.5.1. Afterwards, we describe the experimental setup in Sect. 5.5.2, then we compare clans to iTC as well as eTC in Sect. 5.5.3. The robustness of iTC, Clan, and eTC in the case of a collusion attack is evaluated in Sect. 5.5.4. We conclude with Sect. 5.5.5, where we have a closer look at the surveillance strategies which were already described in Sect. 5.4.4.

### 5.5.1  Clans as Reference Solution

In Sect. 5.2, we already introduced the concept of clans [7] and emphasised its relevance as related work for our concept of TC. Therefore, we use clans as reference solution for our evaluations, which we do under identical system conditions for both agent organisations. To begin with, we will outline what clans are and differentiate them from eTCs.

The formation of clans is based on a check of criteria against certain thresholds, such as missed opportunities for cooperation, lack of scalability, lack of information, or high failure rate. A situation where agent $a$ rejects a request from agent $b$, but at the same time $a$ requested $b$ to work for him and got rejected, for instance, qualifies as a missed opportunities. If such a criterion is met, the agent decides to form a clan and starts to invite appropriate agents. These agents are determined by their *trustworthiness*, and their number—the preferred clan size—is determined by the initiator of the clan formation based on the number of agents it needs for its current plan (expressed by the average number of WUs of one job) and an additional redundancy. The invited agents make their decision to join depending on the trustworthiness of the initiator and the promised benefits.

The kinship motivation, i.e. the motivation to cooperate if requested by another member of the clan, is one of the most important influences on the cooperation decision. In the TDG, it is interpreted as a situation-aware probability (cf. Table 5.1). These probabilities are not final. They can be changed, if situations occur that encourage a higher motivation for cooperation, e.g. if the agent itself has a job to distribute.

Clans are purely decentralised organisations. Every member of a clan can invite other agents, which makes this organisation susceptible to attacks and exploitation. In other words, in a clan there is no authority which helps in managing and

**Table 5.1**  Values for the kinship motivation

|                            | No jobs | Unprocessed jobs |
|----------------------------|---------|------------------|
| Worker decision negative   | 0.5     | 0.8              |
| Worker decision positive   | 1.0     | 1.0              |

regulating the organisation, respectively which copes with undesired emergent system states. Contrary to an eTC, where the TCM has some authoritative powers, e.g. inviting agents, or excluding agents.

## 5.5.2  Experimental Setup

For the evaluation, we use the agent types described in Sect. 5.3.1. For all experiments, the agent society consists of different agent types. The DG applications used are non-validating, a job is generated in average after 4,500 ticks and has an average of 11 WU. As a result, a single WU is processed in 70–175 ticks. The preferred clan size, resulting from the maximum WU number 15 plus a redundancy of 10, is 25 agents. The initial reputation of each agent is 0.05—whereas the reputation value is $\in [-1, 1]$.

$$accuracy = \frac{number\ of\ correctly\ accepted\ WU\ results}{total\ number\ of\ accepted\ WU\ results} \qquad (5.4)$$

Metrics we use are the speedup $\sigma$ (cf. Equation (5.2)) and the accuracy (cf. Equation 5.4), which measures the relative amount of correctly accepted results. Furthermore, we use the number of operating organisations (i.e. eTCs) as metric, as well as the organisation utility, which is the speedup gain of all agents in an eTC, calculated by their current utility minus their utility when entering the eTC. For all metrics, we provide means and standard deviations ($s_{N-1}$).

## 5.5.3  Performance Comparison of iTCs, eTCs, and Clans

The first experiment is set up to find out about the improvement of the basic performance of eTC—in comparison to iTC and clans. The agent societies consists of 250 agents: 10 % FRE, 10 % EGO and 80 % ADA. Under various conditions we performed 100 runs each, one run lasted 500,000 ticks. The aim of the experiment is to show the ability of the eTC to optimise themselves and to quantify the difference towards other agent societies. The results of our experiment are shown in Table 5.2. 20 % CUN for example means that, additionally to the original setting of 250 agents, $250 \cdot 0.2 = 50$ CUN are added.

In the undisturbed experiments, there are no malicious agents (apart from the initial 10 % FRE and 10 % EGO). eTCs are taking advantage of the organisation benefit strategies while clans profited from the corresponding kinship motivation. The average speedup is best for eTCs with a mean value of 8.491 (compared to 7.223 for clans and 5.411 for iTC) and an average organisation utility of 2.827 (compared to 1.770 for clans). If we change the agent society and have 20 % or 30 % DFA, we are able to measure the risk of transparent WU validation. Replication

**Table 5.2** Comparison of the performance—under various conditions—of different agent societies according to the three approaches iTC, clan, and eTC. The best results are written bold font

| Conditions | Metrics ($s_{N-1}$) | iTC | clan | eTC |
|---|---|---|---|---|
| Undisturbed | Avg. speedup | 5.411 (0.222) | 7.223 (0.373) | **8.491** (0.623) |
| | Accuracy | 1.0 (0.0) | 1.0 (0.0) | 1.0 (0.0) |
| | Avg. org. utility | – | 1.770 (0.461) | **2.827** (0.494) |
| | Avg. operating org. | – | 5.280 (0.877) | 3.730 (1.100) |
| 20 % DFA | Avg. speedup | 5.327 (0.203) | 7.066 (0.309) | **7.108** (0.353) |
| | Accuracy | 0.994 (0.001) | **0.998** (0.001) | 0.996 (0.001) |
| | Avg. org. utility | – | 1.667 (0.332) | **2.284** (0.406) |
| | Avg. operating org. | – | 4.880 (1.387) | 3.360 (0.746) |
| 30 % DFA | Avg. speedup | 5.316 (0.207) | **6.936** (0.309) | 6.702 (0.234) |
| | Accuracy | 0.987 (0.002) | **0.995** (0.002) | 0.991 (0.002) |
| | Avg. org. utility | – | 1.567 (0.458) | **1.920** (0.178) |
| | Avg. operating org. | – | 4.350 (1.794) | 3.820 (0.626) |
| 20 % CUN | Avg. speedup | 4.962 (0.195) | 6.785 (0.209) | **8.102** (0.418) |
| | Accuracy | 1.0 (0.0) | 1.0 (0.0) | 1.0 (0.0) |
| | Avg. org. utility | – | 2.042 (0.254) | **3.530** (0.387) |
| | Avg. operating org. | – | 4.980 (0.284) | 2.500 (0.659) |
| 30 % CUN | Avg. speedup | 4.686 (0.184) | 6.393 (0.202) | **7.346** (0.366) |
| | Accuracy | 1.0 (0.0) | 1.0 (0.0) | 1.0 (0.0) |
| | Avg. org. utility | – | 2.158 (0.196) | **3.517** (0.369) |
| | Avg. operating org. | – | 4.650 (0.479) | 2.470 (0.540) |

as safety measure are abandoned and the agents are able to collude to produce wrong WU results, resulting in the possibility to overcome majority votings. This is especially quantified by the accuracy metric, which is better for the explicit agent societies. Clans and eTCs reach a comparable speedup and outperform iTCs. Yet, the average speedup for eTCs drops to 83.71 % for 20 % DFA, respectively 78.93 % for 30 % DFA.

By adding 20 % or 30 % CUN, we evaluate the susceptibility of the three approaches towards malicious agents, which are trying to exploit the system with their oscillating behaviour: This agent type acts as a FRE until its reputation dropped below 0.1, then acts cooperatively until it reaches the threshold 0.5, where it begins to act like a FRE again. As we can see in Table 5.2, iTCs achieve 91.70 %, Clans 96.03 %, and eTCs 95.42 % of the undisturbed speedup with 20 % CUN-agents, and 86.60 % (iTC), 88.51 % (Clans), and 86.52 % (eTCs) of the speedup with 30 % CUN-agents in the system. eTCs outperform clans and iTC with an average speedup of 8.102, respectively 7.346. Furthermore, we see that explicit approaches perform significantly better than the implicit approach. In Fig. 5.5, an exemplary run from this experiment, with 20 % CUN, is depicted. For the three agent organisations the respective average speedup is shown for the different agent types. We can see that for eTCs, the exploiting behaviour is punished and results in a higher speedup for

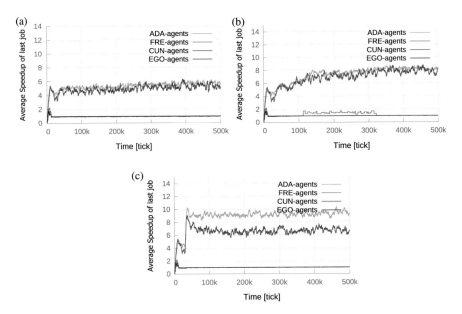

**Fig. 5.5** The average speedup of the last job of different agent types in iTC, clan, and eTC with 20 % CUN in the system. While in the iTC- and Clan- approaches the CUN-agents are allowed to have a high speedup, eTCs punish this behaviour, which results in a lower speedup. Furthermore, this helps to increase the overall speedup and results in a higher speedup for cooperative agents. (**a**) iTC. (**b**) Clan. (**c**) eTC

cooperative ADA and lower speedup for CUN. Bad-behaving agent types (EGO and FRE) with a simple behaviour pattern (compared to CUN) do not achieve good speedup values in all three approaches.

## 5.5.4   Robustness

In the second experiment, we examine the behaviour of the three approaches, especially the eTC approach, in case of a colluding attack of varying intensity. A major goal of the development of eTCs is the increase in robustness compared to former approaches. We perform 25 runs of 250,000 ticks length with each configuration, the mean results are shown in Table 5.3. ds $\in [0, 1]$ (normalised strength of disturbance $\delta$) shows the intensity of the disturbance, i.e. the amount of attackers compared to the number of agents. With an agent society of 250, $ds = 0.1$ means a simultaneous entry of 25 malicious agents into the system in tick 100,000. Metrics are the recovery duration, i.e. the time it takes the system to reach approximately the speedup level it had before the disturbance, as well as the intensity of the speedup collapse. For both metrics holds: the lower, the better. The $ds$ is varied from 0.1 to 1.0.

**Table 5.3** Robustness evaluation of the eTC approach for different disturbance sizes

| Cond. | Metrics ($s_{N-1}$) | iTC | Clan | eTC |
|---|---|---|---|---|
| ds. 0.1 | Recovery duration | 5,755 (1,321) | 28,476 (47,837) | **5,318** (1,082) |
| | Speedup collapse | 0.057 (0.046) | 0.122 (0.113) | **0.026** (0.031) |
| ds. 0.2 | Recovery duration | 11,096 (3,848) | 25,377 (40,097) | **5,640** (1,046) |
| | Speedup collapse | 0.166 (0.064) | 0.205 (0.099) | **0.047** (0.037) |
| ds. 0.3 | Recovery duration | 16,918 (3,895) | 24,412 (37,948) | **6,300** (1,520) |
| | Speedup collapse | 0.284 (0.080) | 0.287 (0.094) | **0.061** (0.040) |
| ds. 0.4 | Recovery duration | 20,730 (6,943) | 15,367 (4,695) | **8,353** (4,942) |
| | Speedup collapse | 0.392 (0.139) | 0.395 (0.129) | **0.080** (0.053) |
| ds. 0.5 | Recovery duration | 27,923 (10,091) | 18,724 (10,402) | **12,536** (7,367) |
| | Speedup collapse | 0.505 (0.166) | 0.451 (0.139) | **0.094** (0.055) |
| ds. 0.6 | Recovery duration | 32,176 (9,214) | 29,147 (30,796) | **14,526** (10,528) |
| | Speedup collapse | 0.611 (0.159) | 0.538 (0.130) | **0.111** (0.060) |
| ds. 0.7 | Recovery duration | 38,619 (8,861) | 31,093 (27,556) | **14,501** (11,731) |
| | Speedup collapse | 0.692 (0.130) | 0.627 (0.105) | **0.101** (0.065) |
| ds. 0.8 | Recovery duration | 39,075 (7,835) | 34,731 (26,865) | **19,616** (11,392) |
| | Speedup collapse | 0.728 (0.123) | 0.660 (0.083) | **0.137** (0.061) |
| ds. 0.9 | Recovery duration | 44,534 (7,137) | 37,878 (34,825) | **20,418** (13,043) |
| | Speedup collapse | 0.773 (0.074) | 0.687 (0.078) | **0.132** (0.060) |
| ds. 1.0 | Recovery duration | 44,113 (5,298) | 35,139 (26,976) | **20,028** (11,764) |
| | Speedup collapse | 0.799 (0.030) | 0.692 (0.075) | **0.133** (0.066) |

The results show that eTCs outperform clans as well as iTCs in all cases we examined. For example, the recovery time of eTCs does not exceed 20,028, though we have a $ds$ of 1.0, i.e. 250 agents attacking. This is more than half the recovery time for iTCs (44,113) and less than 60 % of the recovery time for clans (35,139). The mean relative recovery costs are 0.095 in the maximum, compared to 0.426 (iTC) and 0.375 (clans). This means about 400 % savings of recovery costs. The speedup collapse emphasises these results with a maximum of 0.137 for eTCs, compared to 0.773 for iTCs and 0.687 for clans. In Fig. 5.6, we see an exemplary run with $ds = 0.6$. The reputation for each agent type is shown over time. We can see that the time until recovery is reached is about 25,000 ticks.

For the data shown in Fig. 5.7, which shows the average speedup for iTC, clan and eTC with ds = 0.6, we calculate the values for passive robustness ($R_{passive}$), active robustness ($R_{active}$) and the effective utility degradation ($A$, cf. Table 5.4). $R_{passive}$ is a measure of the structural stability of a system, while $R_{active}$ is the averaged recovery speed of the system. $A$ depicts the area of the utility deviation, effectively representing the total cost of the disturbance. For further details, see [26].

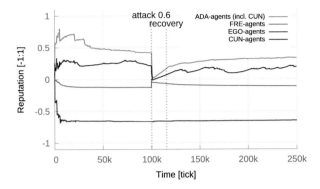

**Fig. 5.6** Reputation values for all agent types during one run with an attack ($ds = 0.6$) at tick 100,000. From top to bottom: reputation values for ADA, CUN, FRE, and EGO

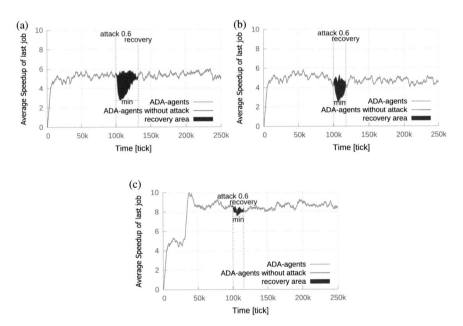

**Fig. 5.7** Average speedup for the last job for iTC, clans and eTC for agent type ADA. Results are shown for one run with an attack of $ds = 0.6$ at tick 100,000. The speedup of ADA drops for all agent organisation forms, but the recovery time and speedup collapse are way better, i.e. lower, for eTC compared to clans and especially compared to the iTC-approach. (**a**) iTC. (**b**) Clan. (**c**) eTC

**Table 5.4** Robustness evaluation of the three organisation approaches. $\Delta U$ is the change in speedup, $t_{drop}$ is the time it takes until the lowest speedup during the disturbance is reached, and $t_{rec}$ is the time it takes until the speedup from before the attack is achieved again. $ds$ represents the strength of disturbance

| Organisation | $\Delta U$ | $t_{drop}$ | $t_{rec}$ | A | $R_{passive}$ | $R_{active}$ | $ds$ |
|---|---|---|---|---|---|---|---|
| iTC | 2.8 | 5,000 | 27,000 | 46,770 | 21 | $1.0\times10^{-4}$ | 0.6 |
| Clan | 2.0 | 5,000 | 13,000 | 10,967 | 30 | $1.5\times10^{-4}$ | 0.6 |
| eTC | 0.9 | 6,000 | 10,000 | 7,142 | 67 | $0.9\times10^{-4}$ | 0.6 |

For $A$, we do not assume $t_{drop} = 0$, but we follow the assumption of linear utility change, resulting in Equation (5.5).

$$A = \frac{\delta}{2 \cdot R_{passive}} \left( t_{drop} + \frac{\delta}{R_{passive} \cdot R_{active}} \right) \tag{5.5}$$

The data shows that eTCs have the best structural stability with $R_{passive} = 67$. Though eTCs show a lower $R_{active}$ than clans, their $A$ is still better. Both, clans as well as eTC, show superior $A$ compared to iTC.

## 5.5.5  Surveillance Strategies

In the third experiment, we compared the performance of different surveillance strategies (cf. Sect. 5.4.4). Therefore, we used two performance metrics: the *number of exclusions* and the *average residence time* ($\varnothing t^{res}$). $t^{res}$ is the time an agent spends in an eTC, i.e. the time from becoming a member of an existing eTC (or the respective eTC enters the TC Operation Phase with this agent as initial member), until the exclusion due to misbehaviour (or due to the dissolution of the eTC). A lower $t^{res}$ for malicious agents indicates that the used surveillance strategy identifies these agents faster.

The agent population for these experiments consists of 100 agents (70 ALT and 30 SLA with $\alpha = 0.8$). The experiments compare a surveillance rate $\mathscr{S}$ of 0.05 to 0.25. The results show the average of 100 runs, whereby one run lasts 250,000 ticks. The agents are excluded, if a third incident is monitored (expressed in the variable $ibe = 2$, *incidents before exclusion*) in a certain period of time. This is expressed in the *forgiveness* of 10,000 ticks—all of an agent's incidents are forgiven, if it commits no further incident for 10,000 ticks. We only show the results for the random-based strategy as representative of the quantity-based strategies, since the three quantity-based strategies (random-based, round-robin-based, and lottery-based strategy, see Sect. 5.4.4) show very similar results.

In Fig. 5.8, the results for the random-based (a), accusation-based (b), and reputation-based (c) strategies are depicted. Most importantly, we observe that quality-based strategies perform better than quantity-based strategies on low $\mathscr{S}$-

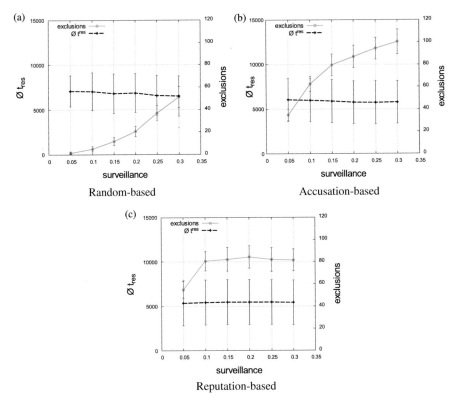

**Fig. 5.8** Results of the evaluation of the surveillance strategies. For each strategy, the number of exclusions and the average residence time $t^{res}$ are shown for different surveillance levels $\mathscr{S}$. The quality-based strategies (accusation-based (**b**) and reputation-based (**c**)) outperform the quantity-based strategy (random-based (**a**)) in both metrics

levels. This is due to the quality-based strategies are more likely to choose the "right" agents to observe, because they use additional knowledge. $t^{res}$ is continuously better (i.e. lower) for quality-based strategies, expressing that misbehaving agents are identified earlier and stay in the eTC for a shorter period of time. The number of exclusions for the random-based strategy is slightly increasing with higher $\mathscr{S}$, yet it stays distinctly lower than for the accusation-based and reputation-based strategies. The two quality-based strategies perform quite similar, both show good results even for a low $\mathscr{S}$.

## 5.6 Conclusion

In this chapter, we introduced a new form of agent societies in distributed, open, heterogeneous multi-agent systems with (technical) trust: the *explicit Trust Community (eTC)*.

Initially, we introduced our application scenario, the *Trusted Desktop Grid* (TDG). In this TDG, we can find several different autonomous agent types, some are bad-behaving agents, some are well-behaving, some are in-between, but they all have in common that they see each other as blackboxes. This means, they cannot observe the internal behaviour of other agents in the system. The agent components of the *Adaptive Agent* (ADA) were described in detail afterwards and implement the Organic Computing-pattern of Observer and Controller. The agent's goal is to maximise its own speedup by having its work computed distributedly by the workers, whereas itself acts as submitter. The deduced global goal is to maximise the global speedup in the system.

After the introduction of the TDG, we had a closer look at the before-mentioned eTC as an improvement of *implicit Trust Communities* (iTC). eTCs are formed according to their life-cycle—consisting of pre-organisation phase, formation-phase, and operation phase—if several agents in the system have formed strong mutual trust-relationships over time. The behaviour of eTC members and the *Trust Community Manager* (TCM) is following certain rules, or strategies.

In the following, we did experiments to shown the effectiveness of eTCs with performance and robustness as major criteria, since these are of great importance in self-organising systems. We compared eTCs not only to iTCs, but also to the concept of *clans* as reference solution. Results showed that eTCs outperform both, iTCs and clans, significantly in nearly all cases. They were proven to be especially robust towards colluding attacks of malicious agents.

For future work, we plan to further improve our concept of eTCs. Since we reach for full distribution, the TCM as central element inside the eTCs, and in consequence the central reputation-database inside the eTC, will be replaced by a more distributed solution. This will be done by using *digital pheromones*, that stick to each agent and represent its trust-values, i.e. the trust rating the agent gets from other agents. To avoid abuse of these ratings by malicious agents, the trust ratings will be encrypted by the giving agent.

Another research area is the concept of the *goal-oriented holonic agent*. Holonic architectures go back to Koestler's concept of so-called holons and Simon's pioneering work in complex systems [42, 43]: Holons are entities that are wholes and parts at the same time. This idea has been used in the context of technical systems in the form of "holonic agents" organised in "holarchies". Such systems are characterised by four properties [44]: (1) Sufficient autonomy of the agents, (2) recursive structure, (3) layered structure, and (4) dynamic reconfiguration at runtime. The holonic concept has been applied e.g. for the smart grid [44], manufacturing systems [45], street lighting control [46], and wireless sensor networks [47].

So far the emphasis in holonic systems research was put on their recursive structure, which allows for relative autonomy of the holons and dynamic reconfiguration following the blackbox principle. Possible conflicts between agents were solved, e.g. with a contract net approach. In open heterogeneous systems this is not sufficient because agents are unknown and neither benevolent nor reliable. Each agent is semi-autonomous, i.e. it can follow its own goals while it is still subject to goals from other entities. Such external goals can be soft (i.e. wishes from peer agents) or hard (e.g. strict commands from higher-level agents). The latter type of goals can be expressed as a norm and enforced with sanctions. In order to accommodate this behaviour we need an extended observer/controller architecture, which (1) makes goals explicit, (2) provides for a goal reconciliation mechanism, and (3) implements an iterative escalation scheme in case of non-compliance of goal-receiving agents. First ideas for such a "goal-oriented holonic agent architecture" have been presented in [48, 49]. We intend to refine these approaches in the future and use them for computing grid or smart grid applications.

**Acknowledgements** This research is partly sponsored by the research unit *OC-Trust* (FOR 1085) of the German Research Foundation. Further, we want to thank Christopher Stifter for his work.

# References

1. Prothmann, H., Branke, J., Schmeck, H., Tomforde, S., Rochner, F., Hähner, J., Müller-Schloer, C.: Organic traffic light control for urban road networks. Int. J. Auton. Adapt. Commun. Syst. **2**, 203–225 (2009). ISSN:1754-8632
2. Fisch, D., Kastl, F., Sick, B.: Novelty-aware attack recognition—intrusion detection with organic computing techniques. In: Distributed, Parallel and Biologically Inspired Systems—7th IFIP TC 10 Working Conference, DIPES 2010 and 3rd IFIP TC 10 International Conference, BICC 2010, Held as Part of WCC 2010, Brisbane, 20–23 Sept 2010. Proceedings (2010), pp. 242–253
3. Müller-Schloer, C.: Organic computing—on the feasibility of controlled emergence. In: 2nd International Conference on Hardware/Software Codesign and System Synthesis CODES + ISSS 2004, pp. 2–5 (2004)
4. Ramchurn, S.D., Huynh, D., Jennings, N.R.: Trust in multi-agent systems. Knowl. Eng. Rev. **19**, 1–25 (2004)
5. Klejnowski, L., Niemann, S., Bernard, Y., Müller-Schloer, C.: Using trusted communities to improve the speedup of agents in a desktop grid system. English. In: Zavoral, F., Jung, J.J., Badica, C. (eds.) Intelligent Distributed Computing VII, vol. 511, pp. 189–198. Springer (2014). ISBN:978-3-319-01570-5
6. Foster, I.: The grid: computing without bounds. Sci. Am. **288**, 78–85 (2003)
7. Griffiths, N.: Cooperative clans. Kybernetes **34**, 1384–1403 (2005)
8. Karlins, M., Abelson, H.: Persuasion: How Opinions and Attitudes are Changed. Springer, New York (1959)
9. Hume, D.: A Treatise of Human Nature. Oxford University Press, New York (1739)
10. Buskens, V.: The social structure of trust. Soc. Netw. **20**, 265–289 (1998). ISSN:0378-8733
11. Mui, L.: Computational models of trust and reputation: agents, evolutionary games, and social networks. PhD thesis, Massachusetts Institute of Technology (2002)
12. Luhmann, N.: Trust and Power. Wiley, Chichester (1979)

13. Hung, L.V.: High quality P2P service provisioning via decentralized trust management. PhD thesis, École Polytechnique Fédérale de Lausanne (2010)
14. Aberer, K., Despotovic, Z., Galuba, W., Kellerer, W.: The complex facets of reputation and trust. In: Computational Intelligence, Theory and Applications, pp. 281–294. Springer, Berlin/Heidelberg (2006)
15. Sabater, J., Sierra, C.: Review on computational trust and reputation models. Artif. Intell. Rev. **24**, 33–60 (2005). ISSN:0269-2821
16. Gutscher, A.: A trust model for an open, decentralized reputation system. In: Trust Management, pp. 285–300. Springer, Boston (2007)
17. Wooldridge, M.: An Introduction to MultiAgent Systems, 2nd edn. Wiley, Chichester (2009)
18. Casanova, H.: Distributed computing research issues in grid computing. SIGACT News **33**, 50–70 (2002)
19. Mui, L., Mohtashemi, M., Halberstadt, A.: A computational model of trust and reputation. In: Proceedings of 35th Hawaii International Conference on System Sciences (HICSS 2002), pp. 2431–2439 (2002)
20. Choi, S., Kim, H., Byun, E., Baik, M., Kim, S., Park, C., Hwang, C.: Characterizing and classifying desktop grid. In: 7th IEEE/ACM International Symposium on Cluster, Cloud and Grid Computing (CCGrid 2007), pp. 743–748 (2007)
21. Anglano, C., Canonico, M., Guazzone, M., Botta, M., Rabellino, S., Arena, S., Girardi, G.: Peer-to-peer desktop grids in the real world: the ShareGrid project. In: 8th IEEE International Symposium on Cluster Computing and the Grid (CCGrid 2008), pp. 609–614 (2008)
22. Chakravarti, A.J., Baumgartner, G., Lauria, M.: Application-specific scheduling for the organic grid. In: Proceedings of GRID 2004 Workshops, pp. 146–155. IEEE, Washington, DC (2004). ISBN:0-7695-2256-4
23. Wang, Y., Vassileva, J.: Trust-based community formation in peer-to-peer file sharing networks. In: IEEE/WIC/ACM International Conference on Web Intelligence (WI 2004), pp. 341–348 (2004)
24. Anderson, D., Fedak, G.: The computational and storage potential of volunteer computing. In: Proceedings of CCGRID 2006, pp. 73–80. IEEE (2006). ISBN:0-7695-2585-7
25. Fedak, G., Germain, C., Neri, V., Cappello, F.: XtremWeb: a generic global computing system. In: 1st IEEE/ACM International Symposium on Cluster, Cloud and Grid Computing (CCGrid 2001), pp. 582–587 (2001)
26. Kantert, J. Edenhofer, S., Tomforde, S., Hähner, J., Müller-Schloer, C.: Normative control— controlling open distributed systems with autonomous entities. In: Reif, W., Anders, G., Seebach, H., Steghöfer, J.-P., André, E., Hähner, J., Müller-Schloer, C., Ungerer, T. (eds.) Autonomic Systems, vol. 7, pp. 87–123. Springer, Cham (2016)
27. Castelfranchi, C., Falcone, R.: Trust Theory: A Socio-Cognitive and Computational Model. Wiley (2010). ISBN:0470028750, 9780470028759
28. Domingues, P., Sousa, B., Moura Silva, L.: Sabotage-tolerance and trustmanagement in desktop grid computing. In: Future Gener. Comput. Syst. **23**(7), 904–912 (2007)
29. Brooks, C.H., Durfee, E.H.: Congregation formation in multiagent systems. English. Auton. Agents Multi-Agent Syst. **7**, 145–170 (2003). ISSN:1387-2532
30. Kantert, J., Spiegelberg, H., Tomforde, S., Hahner, J., Müller-Schloer, C.: Distributed rendering in an open self-organised trusted desktop grid. In: 12th IEEE International Conference on Autonomic Computing (ICAC 2015), pp. 267–272 (2015)
31. Goedegebure, S.: Big Buck Bunny. https://peach.blender.org/the-team/ (2007). Online; Accessed 03 Sept 2015
32. Terdiman, D.: New Technology Revs up Pixar's 'Cars 2'. http://www.cnet.com/news/new-technology-revs-up-pixars-cars-2/ (2011). Online; Accessed 24 Sept 2015
33. Edenhofer, S., Kantert, J., Klejnowski, L., Tomforde, S., Hähner, J., Müller-Schloer, C.: Advanced attacks to trusted communities in multi-agent systems. In: 8th IEEE International Conference on Self-Adaptive and Self-Organizing Systems (SASO 2014), pp. 186–191 (2014)

34. Edenhofer, S., Stifter, C., Jänen, U., Kantert, J., Tomforde, S., Hähner, J., Müller-Schloer, C.:
    An accusation-based strategy to handle undesirable behaviour in multi-agent Systems. In: 8th
    IEEE International Conference on Autonomic Computing (ICAC 2015), (2015)
35. Tomforde, S., Prothmann, H., Branke, J., Hähner, J., Mnif, M., Müller-Schloer, C., Richter,
    U., Schmeck, H.: Observation and control of organic systems. In: Organic Computing—A
    Paradigm Shift for Complex Systems, pp. 325–338. Birkhäuser, Basel (2011)
36. Klejnowski, L.: Trusted community: a novel multiagent organisation for open distributed
    systems. PhD thesis, Leibniz Universität Hannover (2014)
37. Klejnowski, L., Bernard, Y., Anders, G., Müller-Schloer, C., Reif, W.: Trusted community—
    a trust-based multi-agent organisation for open systems. In: Filipe, J., Fred, A.L.N. (eds.)
    5th International Conference on Agents and Artificial Intelligence (ICAART 2013) (1),
    pp. 312–317 (2013)
38. Steghöfer, J.-P., Nafz, F., Reif, W., Bernard, Y., Klejnowski, L., Hähner, J., Müller-Schloer,
    C.: Formal specification and analysis of trusted communities. In: 4th IEEE International
    Conference on Self-Adaptive and Self-Organizing Systems (SASO 2010), pp. 190–195 (2010)
39. Kantert, J., Edenhofer, S., Tomforde, S., Müller-Schloer, C.: Representation of trust and
    reputation in self-managed computing systems. In: IEEE 13th International Conference on
    Dependable, Autonomic and Secure Computing, DASC 2015, pp. 1827–1834. IEEE, Liverpool
    (2015)
40. Lynch, N.A.: Distributed Algorithms. Morgan Kaufmann, San Francisco (1996).
    ISBN:1558603484
41. Jadaan, O.A., Rajamani, L., Rao, C.R.: Improved selection operator for GA. J. Theor. Appl.
    Inf. Technol. (JATIT) (2008)
42. Koestler, A.: The Ghost in the Machine. Penguin Group, Hutchinson/Macmillan (1967)
43. Simon, H.A.: The architecture of complexity. Proc. Am. Philos. Soc. **106**, 467–482 (1962).
    ISSN:0003049X
44. Negeri, E., Baken, N., Popov, M.: Holonic architecture of the smart grid. Smart Grid Renew.
    Energy **4**, 202–212 (2013)
45. Van Brussel, H., Wyns, J., Valckenaers, P., Bongaerts, L., Peeters, P.: Reference architecture
    for holonic manufacturing systems: {PROSA}. Comput. Ind. **37**, 255–274 (1998). ISSN:0166-
    3615
46. Moghadam, M., Mozayani, N.: A street lighting control system based on holonic structures
    and traffic system. In: 3rd International Conference on Computer Research and Development
    (ICCRD 2011), vol. 1, pp. 92–96 (2011)
47. Ye, Y., Hilaire, V., Koukam, A., Wandong, C.: A holonic model in wireless sensor networks.
    In: 4th International Conference on Intelligent Information Hiding and Multimedia Signal
    Processing (IIHMSP 2008), pp. 491–495 (2008)
48. Diaconescu, A., Pitt, J.: Holonic institutions for multi-scale polycentric self-governance.
    English. In: Ghose, A., Oren, N., Telang, P., Thangarajah, J. (eds.) Coordination, Organizations,
    Institutions, and Norms in Agent Systems X, vol. 9372, pp. 19–35. Springer (2015). ISBN:978-
    3-319-25419-7
49. Müller-Schloer, C.: The holonic agent—a building block for systems of systems. In: Keynote
    in Workshop on Self-Improving System Integration (SISSY), ICAC, Grenoble (2015)

# Chapter 6
# Trust as Important Factor for Building Robust Self-x Systems

Nizar Msadek and Theo Ungerer

**Abstract** Open self-x systems of a very large scale – interconnecting several thousand of autonomous and heterogeneous entities – become increasingly complex in their organisational structures. This is due to the fact that such systems are typically restricted to a local view in the sense that they have no global instance, which can be responsible for controlling or managing the whole system. Therefore, new ways have to be found to develop and manage them. An essential aspect that has recently gained much attention in this kind of systems is the social concept of trust. Using appropriate trust mechanisms, entities in the system can have a clue about which entities to cooperate with. This is very important to improve the robustness of self-x systems, which depends on a cooperation of autonomous entities. The contributions of this chapter are trustworthy concepts and generic self-x algorithms with the ability to self-configure, self-optimise, and self-heal that work in a distributed manner and with no central control to ensure robustness. Some experimental results of our algorithms are reported to show the improvement that can be obtained compared with the baseline measurements.

**Keywords** Self-x systems • Self-adaptive systems • Autonomic computing • Organic computing • Trust • Self-Organisation

## 6.1 Introduction

The proliferation of self-x systems capable of acting autonomously to achieve the overall system goal is already happening. Examples of such systems are Autonomic and Organic Computing systems [1, 2]. These are typically based on decentralised autonomous cooperation of system's entities and make use of a number of desirable self-x properties, e.g. the ability to self-configure, self-optimise, self-heal and

N. Msadek (✉)
Systems and Networking Group, University of Augsburg, Augsburg, Germany
e-mail: msadek@informatik.uni-augsburg.de

T. Ungerer
Systems and Networking Group, University of Augsburg, Augsburg, Germany
e-mail: ungerer@informatik.uni-augsburg.de

© Springer International Publishing Switzerland 2016
W. Reif et al. (eds.), *Trustworthy Open Self-Organising Systems*,
Autonomic Systems, DOI 10.1007/978-3-319-29201-4_6

153

self-protect in order to be manageable. The quality of their autonomy mostly depends on their ability to adapt their behaviour in response to changes in their environment. At runtime, they should be able to trustworthy deal with situations not anticipated at design-time. One way to tackle trustworthiness issues is to enable humans to supervise the system and perform all trustworthy operations. However, this solution solves the problem only partially because the transfer of control to humans would also drastically decrease the system's autonomy, especially in the context of reactive environments. Therefore, new ways have to be found to ensure the trustworthiness of modern self-x systems by regarding different facets of trustworthiness. Such facets may concern, for example, reliability, credibility, availability, functional correctness and safety [3].

In this chapter, we describe our efforts to develop a generic architecture that supports the trustworthy design of modern self-x systems. The baseline self-x system examined in this work is OC$\mu$ [4], an Organic Computing middleware implemented in Java and based on a peer-to-peer network. All of its self-x properties were developed without trust involvement. We propose to incorporate a trustworthy self-x layer into the middleware to allow network entities to decide how far to cooperate with other entities. This information is used to maintain a trustworthy and robust configuration of the self-x properties in the face of untrustworthy entities.

The remainder of this chapter unfolds as follows. In Sect. 6.2, we highlight relevant self-x middlewares originated from the field of Organic and Autonomic Computing. Section 6.3 describes the baseline self-x middleware we use as reference for our main results and also addresses the benevolence limitation that hinders the baseline system to perform well in hostile environments. Section 6.4 introduces the novel developed Trust-Enabling Middleware (TEM) we designed to host the trust-aware self-x properties. Then, Sect. 6.5 introduces the application case studies implemented based on TEM. Finally, Sect. 6.6 concludes the chapter.

## 6.2 Related Work

This section presents relevant service-oriented self-x middlewares originated from the field of Organic and Autonomic Computing.

Lund et al. [5] introduce an organic middleware called Artificial Hormone System (AHS) – providing self-x properties – to autonomously assign tasks to heterogeneous processing elements. The middleware makes use of different artificial hormones to find the best suitable processing element (PE) taking into account constraints such as the current PE workload and the task relationships. The following type of hormones exist: *eager value*, *suppressor* and *accelerators*. The eager hormone aims to determine the suitability of a PE to execute a specific task. The other hormones are responsible for reducing or increasing the eager value and thus by applying suppressor and accelerator respectively. Through the use of hormones, the AHS middleware implements the self-x properties: self-configuration in terms of finding an initial allocation of tasks by exchanging hormones, self-optimisation by task migration when hormone levels change, and self-healing by autonomous task reassignment due to task or resource failure. Compared to our middleware, the AHS assumes the trustworthiness of PEs to perform well, i.e. all PEs are considered to be trustworthy to further the system goal.

CARISMA [6] is a service-oriented middleware for hard real-time environments. It realises self-configuration and self-optimisation with the focus on real-time system capabilities. The services have real-time constraints, meaning that their correctness does not only depend on their computational results, but also on the time at which the results are delivered. For allocating services, CARISMA makes use of an auction mechanism based on the Contract Net Protocol [7] to decide whether a service can be contracted and which quality can be achieved. Afterwards, the whole system is optimised by re-contracting the services to other nodes with better resource availability. In contrast to CARISMA, our middleware focuses on the general applicability of system's service that are not restricted by real-time constraints. Additionally, CARISMA does not provide a differentiation between the importance levels of services. This differentiation is necessary to allocate the most important services only on trustworthy nodes and thus to increase the robustness of the system.

FraSCAti [8] is a service-oriented middleware supporting Autonomic Computing principles. It exhibits self-x properties to add new services at runtime or to remove existing ones. The self-x properties are obtained by applying the MAPE (monitoring, analysis, planning, and execution) control loop of Autonomic Computing. The monitoring phase is responsible for collecting, aggregating and filtering the information collected from the services and the middleware itself. The gathered information is examined in the analysis phase. If the examination reveals a need to adapt the placement of services, a new plan is created which is then realised in the execution phase. In contrast to our middleware which supports trust in the development of the self-x properties, FraSCAti expects the benevolence of device nodes limiting its usefulness in open environments.

An organic middleware for building self-organising smart camera systems is presented in [9, 10] and has been extended in [11] to provide support for cloud services. The middleware consists of a number of cameras which are able to collaborate together to detect intruders in non-public areas. At runtime, each camera can adapt its position view while keeping other cameras' positions. The self-healing property is used to maintain the whole tracking system stable even under failure of a single camera or a loss of connectivity. The overall result afterwards is achieved by merging the sub-results of each camera. The general assumption here is that cameras always voluntarily cooperate to realise the common goal. This assumption hinders the middleware to be used in hostile environments, in contrast to our work.

## 6.3   The Baseline OC$\mu$ Architecture

The baseline self-x system considered in this work is OC$\mu$ [4], a middleware
for Organic Computing systems. The OC$\mu$ middleware was developed in the
German Research Foundation (DFG) priority program "Organic Computing" at
the University of Augsburg and is comparable to other state-of-the-art distributed,
service-oriented middleware architectures. But it has the advantage that it implements several self-x properties and thus has the ability to be slightly extended
to provide the desired trustworthy self-x layer. The OC$\mu$ middleware consists
of a collection of heterogeneous devices – called nodes for short – with diverse
capabilities of computing power, memory space and energy supply. These devices
interact with each other using message passing. An overview of a single OC$\mu$ node
is illustrated in Fig. 6.1. It is composed of five main parts: the transport connector,
the message dispatcher, the service proxy, the service interface, and the services
which are explained in the following.

- **Transport Connector:** The communication system used in the middleware is
  modelled similar to [12]. Each OC$\mu$ node $p$ has a buffered transport connector
  enabling it to connect fast and reliably with other OC$\mu$ nodes. In the baseline
  implementation, the two following communication primitives are used:

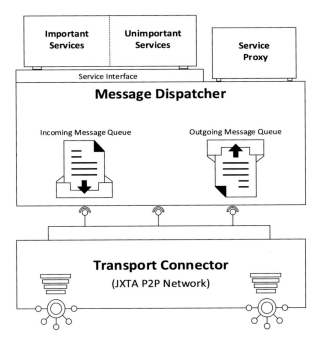

**Fig. 6.1** Structure of the baseline OC$\mu$ node depicting its most relevant parts: the transport
connector, the message dispatcher, the service proxy, the service interface and the services

- **Receive**: removes existing messages from $p$'s buffer and delivers the messages to the message dispatcher of $p$.
- **Send**$(m, q)$: Sends a message $m$ over $p$'s transport connector and places it in the buffer of $q$.

The protocol used for the current implementation of the transport connector is JXTA.[1] This can be replaced or extended with any other communication protocol, since it is transparent to the rest of the middleware.

- **Message Dispatcher:** The message dispatcher handles the message delivery between the services in the middleware. It offers the services the functionality to send messages and register themselves as listener for specified types of messages. With this functionality it is also possible for a service to register itself for different types of messages. In such a case, the service will be informed whenever a message with one of the registered types is received.
- **Service Proxy:** A service proxy is used to forward messages for a service that was recently moved to another node. During the service transfer, the service proxy stores the incoming messages, it then forwards them as soon as the service becomes available at the new position node. The life span of a service proxy is predefined at runtime by its corresponding service, such that it dies after that time.
- **Service Interface:** The service interface is the connector between the middleware and a service. Each service has to implement this logical interface to bind itself to the middleware. The interface provides all required methods to send and receive messages via the message dispatcher to the services.
- **Services:** The considered middleware is based on the assumption that applications are composed of services. These services are distributed to the nodes of the network. We distinguish two kinds of services, namely important services and unimportant services. Important services are those which are necessary for the functionality of the entire system. However, unimportant services are those which only have a low negative effect on the entire system if they fail.

A crucial part of the OC$\mu$ middleware is to investigate decentralised solutions to self-configuration, self-optimisation and self-healing [13]. These self-x properties were developed independently without trust guidance. In the following, a general description of their functional parts is given:

- **Self-configuration [14]:** The regarded applications produce a set of services that are independent of each other. These services are initially distributed to available nodes in the network through the self-configuration process. If, for example, a new node joins the system, it will configure itself autonomously in the middleware such that the overall resource utilisation is as good as possible.

---

[1]JXTA: Open source peer-to-peer protocol specification begun by Sun Microsystems in 2001 – [Accessed: December 16, 2015] – http://jxta.kenai.com.

- **Self-optimisation [15]:** The self-optimisation process enables the system to autonomously reach an optimised state. This optimisation might concern the runtime allocation of services on nodes to ensure a uniform distribution of load.
- **Self-healing [16]:** The self-healing aims to ensure a valid state of the system even in the presence of failure. If, for instance, a node fails, the system must be able to detect its failure using a runtime monitoring approach [17] and then to restart all of its services on other available nodes.

The baseline middleware introduced so far does not consider the trust behaviour of the system during runtime. It is based on the benevolence assumption that all participating nodes want to help each other whenever possible to further the system goal. Because of this assumption, nodes were considered to be always trustworthy and the self-x properties were developed without regarding the node's trustworthiness. However, in open and heterogeneous systems where nodes can enter and leave the system at any point in time, this benevolence assumption has to be dropped, since nodes might behave untrustworthy and try to exploit the system. This introduces a level of uncertainty in the middleware that has been largely neglected so far.

## 6.4 The Trust-Enabling Middleware TEM

The integration of trust to deal with uncertainty gives OC$\mu$ the ability to better adapt to changes in the environment. The approaches and techniques proposed in this section are technological and based on the notion of trust to enable the creation of more robust self-x properties.

### 6.4.1 General Overview

The extension of the OC$\mu$ proposed in this section aims to incorporate trust into the basic self-x properties. For this, the distributed Observer/Controller architecture suggested by Richter et al. in [18] is used and refined by providing trust guidance. Figure 6.2 gives an overview of the proposed TEM concept.

The baseline OC$\mu$ node is enhanced by a trustworthy self-x layer providing a feedback control loop to observe and control the behaviour of OC$\mu$. It includes an observer component, the functional element responsible for monitoring the trust behaviour of the baseline system. This is performed by using trust metrics enabling the generation of data about the trustworthiness of the system's entities. The collected data is used by the controller as indicator to make decisions that will influence the future course of the self-x properties. The following section describes the functional parts of the observer and controller components.

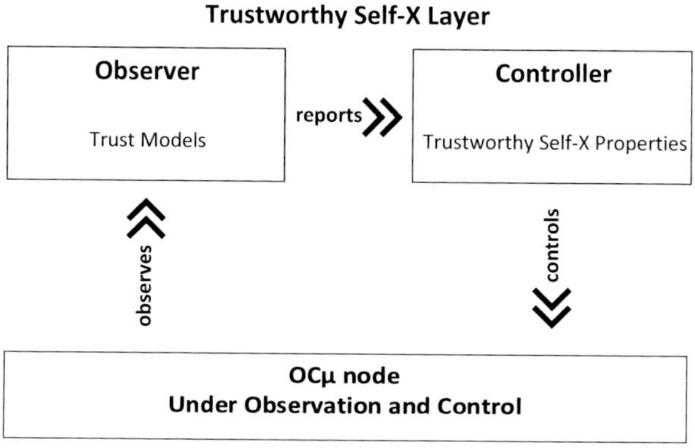

**Trustworthy Self-X Layer**

Fig. 6.2 The generic Observer/Controller architecture used for the establishment of the trustworthy self-x layer. The observer incorporates trust models and the controller is composed of trust-aware self-x properties. Communication between observer and controller is based on the feedback control loop that OC$\mu$ nodes provide

## 6.4.2   The Trust Observer

The main objective of the observer is to monitor the current behaviour of nodes in the system and to calculate trust data from this information. This trust data is used by the controller to guide the overall system goal in a trustworthy way by applying the self-x properties. The observation process mainly consists of the following three steps: monitoring, transformation, and trust interpretation, as shown in Fig. 6.3.

In the monitoring step, a distributed strategy is needed to allow nodes to autonomously determine who is monitoring whom. In order to do this and to be at least scalable, we make use of our former developed self-monitoring approach [19] as basis for enhancing nodes with the ability to collect raw data in the system. These raw data represent experiences that nodes have made with their interaction partners in a specific context and per trust facet. They contain all relevant information about the interaction partner such as message delays and loss as well as its ability to perform services at the right time. The raw data are stored in a distributed log file for every loop of observation. Then, they are transformed into a valid format that makes them easily accessible to the interpreter. Finally, the interpreter uses these transformed data to estimate the trustworthiness of a node. The metrics used by the interpreter to calculate trust data are named *trust metrics* [20]. These metrics have been developed during the two first phases of the OC-Trust project and integrated in TEM. The metrics consist of the following presented aspects.

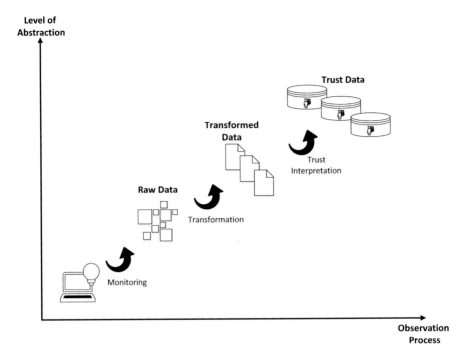

**Fig. 6.3** Illustration showing the different levels of abstraction of the observation process starting from monitoring, to transformation, to the final interpretation of the trust data. Please note that only the most interesting parts of the process are presented, due to space limitations

#### 6.4.2.1 Direct Trust

The algorithm used by the observer to calculate the direct trust of a node is called the *Delayed-Ack* [21]. The Delayed-Ack algorithm covers the reliability aspect of trust as a facet and measures trust by observing the message flow between nodes. More precisely, it requires that each sent message is being acknowledged. Thus the lost of each message is determined, resulting in a negative experience (represented by 0) for lost messages and a positive experience (represented by 1) for acknowledged messages. All these experiences are stored for each participating node. The output is a direct trust value $t_{dt}(n_i, n_j)$ within [0, 1] calculated by taking the mean or weighted mean of past experiences. $t_{dt}(n_i, n_j) = 0$ means $n_i$ does not directly trust $n_j$ at all while a value of 1 stands for a whole trust.

#### 6.4.2.2 Confidence

In addition, a metric is used to evaluate the confidence of the own direct trust value of a node. This is called the *confidence metric* [22] and aims at describing how

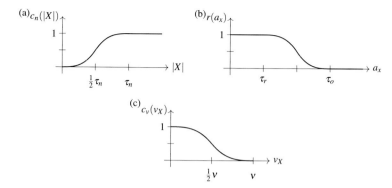

**Fig. 6.4** The three parts of the confidence value. (**a**) Illustration of the number confidence function $c_n(X)$ assuming that a certain number of experiences $\tau_n$ is sufficient to derive an accurate trust value. The more experiences with an interaction partner were made, the more confidence in the trust value. (**b**) The age confidence function $r(a_x)$ aims at calculating a low rating value for a quite outdated experience and high rating value for a quite recent experience. (**c**) The variance function $c_v(v_X)$ is used to indicate the behavioural changes of a node. A confidence of 1 equals 0 variance. Vice versa, a confidence of 0 equals 1 variance

reliable the direct trust value is. The higher the confidence is, the more certain one can be that the trust value matches the actual behaviour of an interaction partner. The confidence value is split in three parts:

- **Number Confidence:** The more experiences exist, the higher is the confidence, up to a threshold $\tau_n$. Figure 6.4a shows details of this function. If the number of experiences $|X|$ is greater or equal to $\tau_n$ then the *number confidence* $c_n(|X|)$ is 1.
- **Age Confidence:** Every experience $x$ is rated regarding its actuality $a_x$. The resulting rating $r(a_x)$ describes how recent or outdated the experience is (see Fig. 6.4b). The *age confidence* is higher if the experiences were made more recently. Two thresholds, $\tau_o$ and $\tau_r$, are defined for this rating function: An experience older than $\tau_o$ counts as outdated and its age rating is set to 0. If an experience is newer than the threshold $\tau_r$, then it counts as a recent experience and its age rating is therefore set to 1. From $\tau_r$ to $\tau_o$, the age rating is gradually decreasing. The total age confidence $c_a(X)$ is the mean of all ratings (see Equation (6.1)).

$$c_a(X) = \frac{\sum_{x \in X} r(a_x)}{|X|} \tag{6.1}$$

- **Variance Confidence:** It evaluates the variance of the experience values $v_X$. The more the values fluctuate, the lower is the *variance confidence* $c_v(v_X)$. If the experiences have 0 variance, i.e. the experiences are rated exactly the same, the variance confidence is 1. It decreases with increasing variance (see Fig. 6.4c).

**Confidence Value:** The total confidence $c(X)$ is then calculated by a weighted mean of the three parts, as seen in Equation (6.2). $w_n$ denotes the weight for the number confidence, $w_a$ the weight for the age confidence and $w_v$ the weight for the variance confidence. We assume $w_n, w_a, w_v \geq 0$ and $w_n + w_a + w_v > 0$.

$$c(X) = \frac{w_n \cdot c_n(|X|) + w_a \cdot c_a(X) + w_v \cdot c_v(v_X)}{w_n + w_a + w_v} \tag{6.2}$$

### 6.4.2.3  Reputation

As reputation metric the *neighbour-trust metric* introduced in [23] is used. The metric is based upon a weighted mean value of the direct trust values of all other nodes that had direct interactions with the node, the so-called *neighbours*. The weights represent the truthfulness of neighbours regarding their reputation data. A high weight indicates a neighbour whose reputation data correlates with direct experiences of oneself, whereas a low weight stands for a neighbour whose reputation data differs a lot from the own experiences. To achieve this, two thresholds are defined for the reputation metric: $\tau$ defines the positive area, where reputation and direct trust are similar enough to increase the weight, the larger $\tau^*(\tau^* \geq \tau)$ denotes the negative area, where reputation and direct trust are too far apart which will reduce the weight. If the difference between reputation and direct weight is greater than $\tau^*$, then the weight is decreased by a maximum of $\theta$. Similarly, the weight is increased by a maximum of $\theta$. Therefore, upcoming reputation information from a neighbour will be rated up or down depending on the information the neighbour gave so far. A node will then only listen to other neighbours whose experiences are similar to its own. Since the weight gets adjusted per interaction, the reputation has to start with an initial value, which is defined as $r_s$. Figure 6.5 depicts the function to calculate the weight adjustment after each interaction. $t_{ac}$ denotes the direct trust a node $a$ has about another node $c$ and $t_{bc}$ the reputation information of node $b$ about node $c$. In the figure the weight $a$ has about $b$ would be reduced, because both values differ by more than $\tau$.

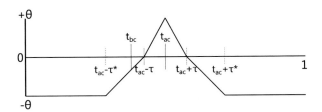

**Fig. 6.5** A graphic representation of the neighbour-trust metric. $t_{ac}$ denotes the direct trust a node $a$ has about another node $c$ and $t_{bc}$ the reputation information of node $b$ about node $c$. In this example, the weight $a$ has about $b$ would be reduced, because both values differ by more than $\tau$

### 6.4.2.4   Aggregation

When all the aforementioned values are obtained, a total trust value $t_{total}$ based on direct trust $t_{dt}$ and reputation $t_r$ values can be calculated using confidence $w_c(c(X))$ to weigh both parts against each other. This $t_{total}$ value is calculated with Equation (6.3).

$$t_{total} = w_c(c(X)) \cdot t_{dt} + (1 - w_c(c(X))) \cdot t_r \qquad (6.3)$$

The higher the confidence, the higher is $w_c(c(X))$ and therefore the weight of the direct trust data in total. The formula to calculate $w_c(c(X))$ is based on the function depicted in Fig. 6.6. This function is enclosed in two thresholds $\tau_{cl}$ and $\tau_{ch}$. Outside these thresholds, the function is constant with extreme values; in between them monotonically increasing with near linear slope in the middle at $\frac{\tau_{ch}-\tau_{cl}}{2}$. Near the thresholds the slope is low. This function is based on the consideration that a small step over a threshold should only result in a small change in value. The domain is restricted to $[0, 1]$, because valid confidence values must be in this interval. The result of the function, i.e. the co-domain, is also $[0, 1]$ representing the weight $w_c(c(X))$ for the aggregation function by means of Equation (6.4).

$$w_c(c(X)) = \begin{cases} 0 & \text{if } c(X) < \tau_{cl} \\ 4\left(\frac{c(X)-\tau_{cl}}{\tau_{ch}-\tau_{cl}}\right)^3 & \text{if } \tau_{cl} \le c(X) \le \tau_{cl} + \frac{1}{2}(\tau_{ch} - \tau_{cl}) \\ 4\left(\frac{c(X)-\tau_{ch}}{\tau_{ch}-\tau_{cl}}\right)^3 + 1 & \text{if } \tau_{cl} + \frac{1}{2}(\tau_{ch} - \tau_{cl}) < c(X) \le \tau_{ch} \\ 1 & \text{if } \tau_{ch} < c(X) \end{cases} \qquad (6.4)$$

Figure 6.7 summarises the main hypothesised trust metrics used for the calculation of total trust. Experiments in [24] attest that integrating such metrics into our middleware results in a better estimation of the real hidden trust value of an interaction node with increasing number of its interactions. For more information about the implementation details, please refer to [25].

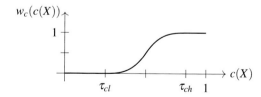

**Fig. 6.6** A graphic representation of the function $w_c(c(X))$. The higher the confidence, the higher $w_c(c(X))$ and therefore the higher the influence direct trust has over reputation

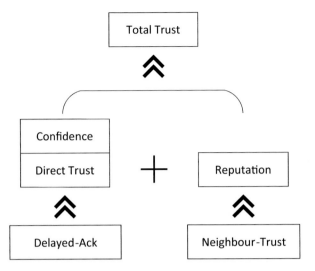

**Fig. 6.7** Illustration showing how direct trust, reputation and confidence are aggregated to form the total trust

## 6.4.3   The Trust-Enhanced Self-x Controller

The aim of the controller is to guide and control the self-organisation process between nodes. To make trustworthy control decisions, it uses the trust data received from the observer and affects the global system by influencing the execution rules of self-x properties. The current implementation suffers from the drawback that the self-x properties are not designed to incorporate trust decisions in their actual executions. They assume the benevolence assumption of nodes at all time and thus cannot be applied for open systems. Details on this assumption were given in Sect. 6.3. In this work, we abandon this benevolence assumption and instead provide a new trustworthy design of the baseline self-x properties allowing them to operate robustly even in open and hostile environments.

### 6.4.3.1   The Trust-Aware Self-Configuration

The capability of self-configuration in open distributed environments comprises the abilities (1) to perform an initial and trust-based distribution of services on nodes, (2) to cope with the problem of scalability, and (3) to allow a reconfiguration of the system during runtime due to self-optimisation or self-healing demands.

   Regarding (1): There are many sophisticated approaches to deal with the initial distribution of services on nodes, either to achieve good load balancing or to minimise energy consumption. An approach that has become a standard by FIPA[2] is the Contract Net Protocol [7]. It consists of finding an agent that is the most suitable to provide a service. This approach is often adapted and applied in many application domains, for example, manufacturing systems [26], resource allocation in grids and sensor web environments [27, 28], as well as in hospitals [29], electronic marketplaces [30] or power distribution network restoration [31]. It is a generic protocol [32] and thus provides an excellent basis for developing self-configuring systems. However, it is limited in some issues and has some shortcomings if the setting for service assignment is more complicated. For example trust limitation in the service assignment – some of nodes are more trustworthy to do important services while others are less trustworthy and should focus only on the processing of unimportant services. Helping to develop these trust enhancements was the aim of our self-configuration research. The outcome of this investigation is an approach [33] based on the Contract Net Protocol which aims on the one hand to equally distribute the load of services on nodes as in a typical load balancing scenario and on the other hand to assign services with different importance levels to nodes so that the more important services are assigned to more trustworthy nodes. Similar to [7], nodes in our system can act as a manager or contractor. A *manager* is responsible for assigning services. A *contractor* is responsible for the actual execution of the service. Figure 6.8 depicts how managers and contractors can participate in the distribution phase of the self-configuration approach. When the assignment process starts, managers announce the list of services to the contractors. Contractors evaluate these services and submit bids on those for which they are suited. Then, the managers evaluate the bids. In the basic Contact Net Protocol, the parameter characterising this evaluation is the workload. Generally, the lower the workload of a node is, the more it is considered to be appropriate to receive the service. Our enhancement improves the awarding part by including trust, to enable that more trustworthy contractors always have a higher chance to receive services than less trustworthy contractors. Finally, the result of the service assignment is communicated to the contractors that submitted a bid.

Evaluation results [33] within our middleware show that the proposed self-configuration algorithm indeed provides better performance than the baseline Contract Net Protocol. The trust variation that is used to improve the availability of important services performs much better in all cases than the baseline algorithm, which underlines the effectiveness of our approach.

Regarding (2): In open environments, the issue of scalability is of particular importance for any self-configuring system. The self-configuration presented until now does not cover this issue. It was designed only for the sequential assignment of services on nodes and thus provides solutions that are not realistic to be applied in environments with many managers. To get a better comprehension of that problem, please consider the following example: Assuming two managers $m_1$, $m_2$ and one

[2]FIPA: Foundation for Intelligent Physical Agents – [Accessed: October 29, 2015] – http://www.fipa.org/specs/fipa00029/

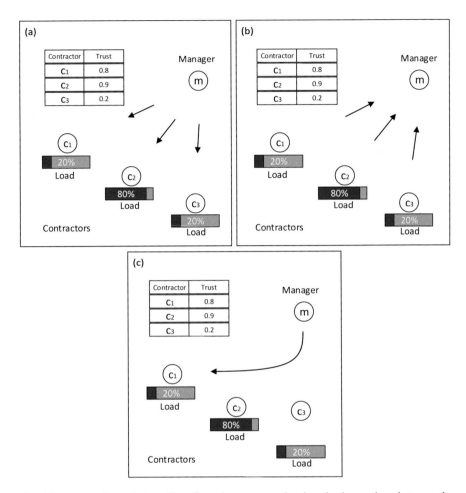

**Fig. 6.8** An overview of the self-configuration process showing the interactions between the manager and its contractors. Please note that each contractor in the network can be, at the same time and for different services, a manager of other contractors. (**a**) Announcement. (**b**) Bidding. (**c**) Awarding

contractor $c_1$. $m_1$ is responsible for assigning service $s_1$ and $m_2$ is responsible for assigning service $s_2$. Then, consider the following sequence of operations that are listed in Table 6.1.

Contractor $c$ receives both services $s_1$ and $s_2$, as expected. However, if both managers $m_1$ and $m_2$ perform their negotiations in parallel and without coordination, the outcome of the assignment could be wrong. Despite not having enough resources, contractor c uses the same bid value submitted as before to receive the service $s_2$. Because of this race condition, we need to incorporate coordination strategies into our self-configuration algorithm in order to further improve its scalability performance. Investigating and developing such strategies was the aim of our

**Table 6.1** Simplified example run of the self-configuration process that can exhibit a race condition between managers $m_1$ and $m_2$

| Manager $m_1$ | Contractor $c$ | Manager $m_2$ |
|---|---|---|
| Sends an announcement to c for a service $s_1$ | | Sends an announcement to $c$ for a service $s_2$ |
| | Evaluates the given services with respect to its workload and sends a bid to $m_1$ and $m_2$ | |
| Sends an award message to c informing it to be the most appropriate | | |
| | | Chooses $c$ to award him the contract for $s_2$, **while the latter submitted bid has recently become obsolete!** |

work in [34] and the outcome of this research is a simultaneous self-configuration algorithm which gives managers in our system the possibility to perform several distribution phases at the same time. To quantify our approach, evaluations have been conducted. The evaluation results [34] show that the simultaneous self-configuration attests an excellent time performance to assign services on nodes than the sequential approach. At least 50 % self-configuration time improvement was achieved and thus only for the context of two managers. However, the drawback of our approach is that it produces message overhead to coordinate the managers. But, this overhead is not excessive, in most cases lower than 1 % compared to the sequential approach, and is thus considered to be acceptable in use by our middleware.

Regarding (3): Reconfiguration is a main characteristic of modern distributed self-configuring systems. Managers have to assess at runtime whether contractors are operating correctly or not. Fault-tolerant techniques applied to our self-configuration algorithm are given in [35]. If one of the contractors failed, managers detect the failed node and trigger a reconfiguration in the system to re-establish the balance between nodes again. The reconfiguration is applied even well in situations in which nodes join the system. This can occur at any time during the self-optimisation process. Managers identify the entering of nodes and reconfigure themselves to regain an acceptable assignment state in the system.

### 6.4.3.2   The Trust-Aware Self-Optimisation

Self-x systems should be able to dynamically adapt their behaviour in response to changes in their environment. At runtime, they should have the ability to deal with situations not anticipated at design time, since not every situation can be considered when designing the system. After the initial service distribution that is given using the self-configuration process, nodes must be able to constantly observe their current resource consumptions as well as the trustworthiness of nodes they are cooperating with, identify unacceptable situations and reconfigure themselves to regain an acceptable state. Therefore, in [36] a self-optimisation algorithm is presented to optimise the allocation of services on nodes during runtime. The algorithm does not only consider pure load-balancing but also takes trust into account to improve the assignment of important services to trustworthy nodes. More precisely, it uses different optimisation strategies to determine whether a service should be transferred to another node or not.

Figure 6.9 illustrates how the self-optimisation property works in our system, using a simple example of just two nodes. Suppose that node $n_j$ sends an application message to another node $n_i$ at a certain point during runtime. It appends onto the outgoing message (a) its recently observed trust behaviour of node $n_i$, (b) its current workload and (c) some additional information (i.e. importance level and consumption) about services which are running on it. Based on this information, node $n_i$ decides which of the following optimisation strategies should be performed (given in Table 6.2):

The trust optimisation strategy is used in situations in which the workload of both nodes is similar but their trust values differ, as illustrated in Fig. 6.10. Important services are relocated to the more trustworthy node and unimportant services to the less trustworthy node. The workload balance, however, should still be maintained.

The second strategy is the load optimisation strategy, presented in Fig. 6.11. This strategy aims at finding a pure load balancing between nodes. Since $n_i$ and $n_j$ are

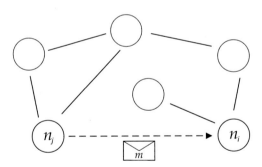

**Fig. 6.9** Cooperative self-optimisation in the TEM middleware. The optimisation process is initiated by an application message going from node $n_j$ to another node $n_i$. This message contains – as piggy-back – all relevant information allowing both nodes $n_j$ and $n_i$ to optimise their current states in the system at runtime

**Table 6.2** Type of strategies the nodes can use to optimise their current states in the system

| Workload similar | Trust similar | Optimisation strategy |
|---|---|---|
| True | False | Trust optimisation |
| False | True | Load optimisation |
| False | False | Trust and load optimisation |
| True | True | No optimisation |

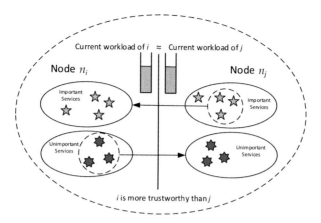

**Fig. 6.10** The trust strategy is depicted in a simplified form to optimise the state of nodes by relocating the assignment of their services at runtime. Please note that important services are represented by the *green stars*, whereas the unimportant services are depicted with *red starlets*

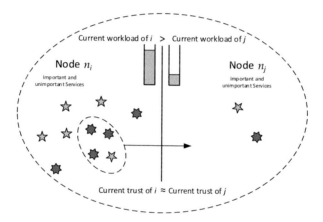

**Fig. 6.11** The illustration shows how pure load-balancing can be achieved between nodes. Important services are represented with the *green stars*, whereas the unimportant services are depicted with *red starlets*

cqually trustworthy with respect to a certain threshold, there is no need to consider trust by the relocation of services.

The trust and load optimisation strategy allows for providing workload balancing with additional consideration of the services' priority to avoid hosting important services on untrustworthy nodes (see Fig. 6.12).

Finally, the *No Optimisation* strategy is used to ensure termination when no further optimisation can take place, e.g. if both nodes $n_i$ and $n_j$ are well optimised in terms of trust and workload, as shown in Fig. 6.13. However, this termination is determined only locally. A global termination is reached if the system as a whole becomes optimised.

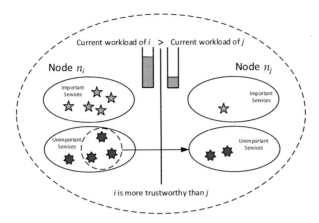

**Fig. 6.12** A simplified overview of the trust and load optimisation strategy. Please note that important services are represented with the *green stars*, whereas the unimportant services are depicted with *red starlets*

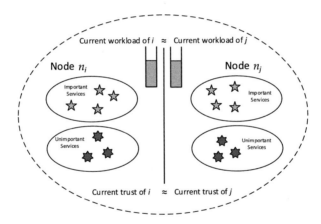

**Fig. 6.13** Illustration of the non-optimisation strategy used to determine the local termination of the algorithm. Please note that important services are represented with the *green stars*, whereas the unimportant services are depicted with *red starlets*

Experiments have been conducted based on simulations [37] to evaluate the effectiveness of the introduced trust-aware self-optimisation algorithm. The evaluation results showed that the proposed approach can improve the availability of important services during runtime. However, it makes a small deterioration (i.e. by about 7 %) regarding load-balancing. This is due the fact that solutions of this kind represent a trade-off problem in which it is impossible to make any trust distribution better without making at least the load balancing distribution worse. Moreover, the evaluation results showed that the trust-aware self-optimisation approach is only for use in situations in which no conflicting trust values between nodes occur. Such conflicts are caused, for example, by collecting trust values independently from

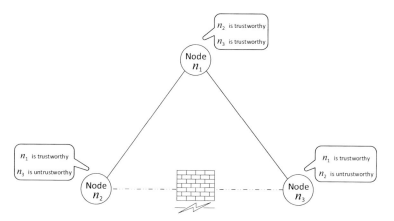

**Fig. 6.14** The conflicting trust values problem simplified within an example of just three nodes

the neighbours of a node that can contradict each other. Figure 6.14 visualises this problem in a short example of three nodes.

Let us consider a network with the three nodes $n_1$, $n_2$ and $n_3$. Let us now suppose that a shielding wall is set between the two nodes, i.e. $n_2$ and $n_3$, preventing communication and thus producing poor trust values between them, while the third node $n_1$ is not affected. In this case, $n_2$ considers node $n_3$ as untrustworthy and thus not being able to properly host services. Hence, it wants to relocate important services running on $n_3$ to another trustworthy node, while contractor $n_1$ sees no need for action. Such situations cause consistency conflicts during runtime between nodes and must be resolved. Therefore, in [38] a conflict resolution mechanism is proposed as an extension to the self-optimisation algorithm to deal with the trust conflict issue. In the testbed, an average conflict reduction of 97.5 %, 53.42 % and 6.47 % were achieved by the best-case, average-case and worst-case scenarios of the conflict resolution algorithm, respectively.

### 6.4.3.3  The Trust-Aware Self-Healing

Self-healing can be defined as the property that enables a system to perceive services that are not operating correctly and, without human intervention, make the necessary adjustments to restore them using self-configuration and self-optimisation principles. Two ways of thinking have to be considered in the self-healing process, namely *proactive* and *reactive*. The proactive measure enables the system to detect node instability prior to failure which is recognised through degradation of a node's trust value, and then to transfer all running services by using self-optimisation techniques to more trustworthy nodes. The strategies used for the service transfer are mainly the same as those described in Sect. 6.4.3.2 and thus are not further discussed here. More interesting is the reactive measure. This enables nodes to save recovery information periodically during failure-free execution. Then upon failure, which has to be detected by using a failure detector, a node uses the already saved information to restart from an intermediate state called snapshot, thus reducing the amount of lost computation. In the following, the underlying algorithms of the reactive measure are explained.

**Failure detectors:** Failure detectors play a crucial role in the development of robust and dependable self-x systems. Assuming that a contractor might crash, the manager has to be able to detect a contractor's failure and take appropriate recovery actions, otherwise the services running on it might block the whole system. Hence, it is important for the manager to regularly monitor its contractors, even if it is a non-trivial task. The main reason for this is the diversity of failures. When a contractor node in asynchronous and distributed environments is not working correctly, it is very difficult for the manager to know the specific cause with certainty: it may be due to a crash failure, execution failure or reachability failure. While there are slight discrepancies in the literature regarding their definitions, in the following the failure models are defined:

1. **Crash failure:** Contractors are considered to execute their services correctly. If a failure occurs at a certain time, the contractor stops permanently. This models a crash of contractor that never recovers by itself. Furthermore, contractors are not able to indicate their failures and stop to send any messages.
2. **Reachability failure:** The contractor is operating correctly but communication channels loose managers' contracts. Consequently, network partitions emerge in the system, which can lead to outdated or duplicated service results if the partitions are merged again into one network.
3. **Execution failure:** The contractor does not halt. It can send messages and answer that it is alive when asked. However, the services which are running on it report wrong results. Services can recover afterwards to the last stored correct state.

Regarding (1) and (2): A well-known technique to cope with crash failures is the *keep-alive* approach [39, 40], in the literature also known under the name of the *heartbeat* approach [16]. In this technique, contractors periodically send an alive messages to managers responsible for their monitoring. If, for example, a manager $m$ does not receive such a message from its contractor $c$ after an expiration of time $\Delta_{Timeout}$, it adds $c$ to its list of suspected contractors, as seen in Fig. 6.15. If $m$ later receives an alive message from $c$, then $m$ removes $c$ from its list of suspected contractors. This technique is defined by two parameters:

- The frequency period $\Delta_c$ is the time frequency at which alive messages are sent from $c$ to $m$.
- The timeout delay $\Delta_{Timeout}$ is the time between the last reception of an alive message from c and the time where $m$ starts suspecting $c$, until an alive message from $c$ is received.

Adjusting $\Delta_c$ and $\Delta_{Timeout}$ during runtime makes a trade-off in the system. If these parameters are chosen too short, then failures are detected quickly (i.e. short failure detection delays) but more alive messages are sent in the network. A

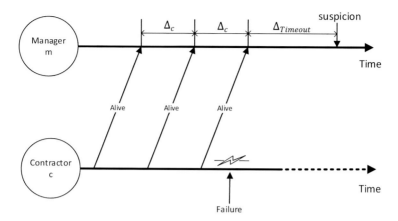

**Fig. 6.15** The most common approach used in literature to monitor the failure of contractors. This is based on the *pull* model in which contractors regularly unicast a message saying they are alive

longer choice of these parameter values results in a larger failure detection delay but less communication overhead. Because of this trade-off problem, it is obvious that an optimal solution minimising the two criteria simultaneously could never be reached in practice. Our contribution are robust approaches [41] that provide good but not necessarily optimal solutions to this trade-off problem. They make use of trust concepts to reduce the expected detection delay of failures and their subsequent message cost by allowing more trustworthy contractors to be monitored less frequently than the untrustworthy ones. However, the difference between our approaches arises in the way to determine $\Delta_c$ and $\Delta_{Timeout}$ either discrete, continuous or continuous-discrete. The facet of trust considered in this part of the work concerns the availability aspect. For this reason the trust values of contractors are determined based on their uptime in the last interaction steps. Evaluation results showed that the continuous-discrete approach performs best. It can adapt faster to changing trust conditions in the network than the two other approaches and is therefore considered suitable for our TEM middleware.

Having detected a failure, the next barrier is to determine its type. This can be either a crash failure or reachability failure between the manager and the contractor. In order to determine which one of these failures has occurred, the manager needs at least the help of two other nodes, i.e. $helper_1$ and $helper_2$. As shown in Fig. 6.16, both helpers send to the contractor the "*Are you alive?*" messages. If no response is received by both helpers (i.e. $helper_1$ and $helper_2$) from the contractor within a configurable time period, then a crash failure is confirmed. If one of the two helpers receives a response from the contractor then a reachability failure is confirmed.

Regarding (3): An important task for the manager is to check whether a contractor is reporting wrong results or not. For masking such execution failures, several approaches are known in literature. One approach which has received much attention in the recent years is the *redundant execution* [42–44]. This approach

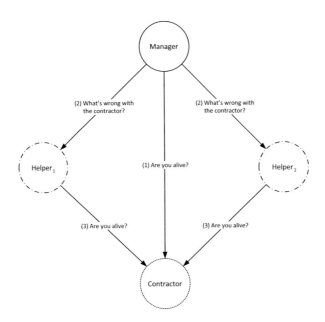

**Fig. 6.16** Simplified illustration of the detection model showing how to distinguish between crash and reachability failure by making use of helpers. *Solid circle* represents the manager, *dashed circle* represents the helpers, and *dotted circle* represents the contractor. Please note that in the practice, the manager would expect to have more helpers than only the two ones depicted here

enables to detect an execution failure by executing a service at least two times from different contractors and comparing the results. If the results are similar, then the service is run without failure, otherwise an execution failure has happened during the execution. One drawback, however, is that some services cannot be handled by redundant execution, e.g. I/O-based services that might not return the same result in different runs. But as it goes beyond the scope of this work it is not further discussed here.

**Service recovery:** As clarified in the introduced failure model, contractors in our system are subject to crash failures. Keeping that fact in mind, a manager has to store the stepwise results of its contractors in a trustworthy place in order to get them back in case of failure. This has the benefit to later reduce the recovery time by restarting the services not from the beginning but rather from an intermediate state. To ensure this, a robust data storage is needed for our system that must obey to the following identified research points:

- *How to adjust the amount of replicas in the system during runtime in order to guarantee a good availability of service data, characterised for example by five nines availability ≈99.999 %?*
  The answer of this question results, as expected, in a trade-off problem between performance overhead and availability. It is easy to see in Fig. 6.17 that the use of a higher number of replicas generally increases the availability of the stored

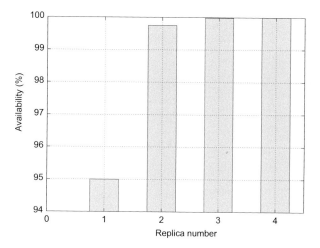

**Fig. 6.17** Example showing the number of replica required for an average nodes' availability of 95 %

data. However, this availability is only improved until three replicas have been reached. A greater number than 3 does not improve the availability any more but makes performance worse, since more replicas imply more resource consumption and higher management cost. Therefore, we provided an approach that enables us to calculate the minimum number of replicas needed for a desired degree of availability taking into account the average availability of nodes. First results of this approach attest a very good reduction of performance overhead in the network. More results related to large size networks are, however, left for future work.

- *How to distribute the replicas in a way that the more important replicas are always hosted only on most available nodes, while at the same time achieving load balancing between nodes?*
  This issue can be reduced with minor variations to the same problem that we have addressed in Sects. 6.4.3.1 and 6.4.3.2: Instead of using the reliability facet, the system focuses on the availability facet by observing the uptime of nodes. The self-configuration algorithm then uses these availability values to perform an initial distribution of replicas on nodes. At runtime, we make use of self-optimisation techniques to continuously optimise their assignments.

**Consistency limitation due to a Split-Brain Problem:** One limitation of the service recovery that we faced during the evaluation process is the Split-Brain Problem [45]. This represents a state in which nodes in the network are partitioned into clusters. And each one believes it is the only active cluster in the network. Figure 6.18 provides a better comprehension of that problem.

Assume we have one contractor $c_1$ that operates to report some service results to manager $m$. Let us further assume that $m$ can no more communicate with its contractor $c_1$, due to a reachability failure which can happen at any time in our

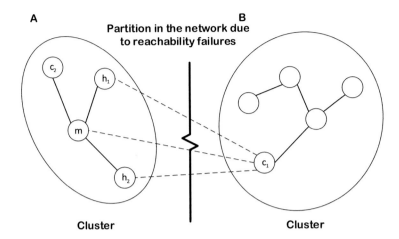

**Fig. 6.18** Simplified illustration of a network partition isolating a manager $m$ from its contractor $c_1$ due to a reachability failure in the network. Once the problem is resolved, an automatic reconciliation will be required in order to bring the network in a consistent state again

system. In such case, manager $m$ asks helpers $h_1$ and $h_2$ to check whether $c_1$ is alive or not, as explained above. The two helpers cannot reach $c_1$. Consecutively, $m$ believes that $c_1$ has crashed. It uses the data storage to recover all services which were running on $c_1$ and to restart them on another contractor $c_2$. Until now, the system seems to run correctly. However, a problem arises when the partition between the two clusters is lost and $m$ is not aware of it, leading to inconsistency in its service results. In the literature, there are many different approaches to deal with the split-brain problem. The most common one is the Quorum approach [46, 47], which consists of selecting the cluster with a majority of votes. A disadvantage of this method is that it does not operate if clusters in the system have the same number of votes causing a non-determinism in the solutions computed. Therefore we are interested in providing a better approach that is able to consider additional constraints (beside the voting constraint) such as the last version of services, the number of run services, the workload and trust of contractors and so on. More research related to this is left for future work.

## 6.5 Application Case Studies

The trust aware self-x properties introduced in this chapter concern basic middle-ware concepts to provide guarantees of reliability, availability and scalability for the TEM. Apart from these properties, the TEM implements mechanisms that allow the application running on top of it based on the trust metrics to measure uncertainty at runtime and to take the trustworthiness of the applications' entities into account when making decisions. Within the OC-Trust research group several application

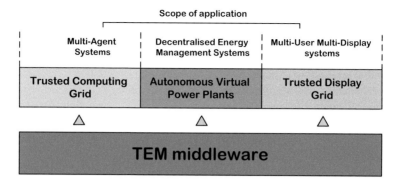

**Fig. 6.19**  The TEM used as basis for the construction of trustworthy self-organising applications

case studies are investigated for the TEM. The first case study comprises an application from the domain of multi-agent systems called the Trusted Computing Grid. The second application case study, the Autonomous Virtual Power Plants, stems from the domain of decentralised energy management systems. And the last case study is the Trusted Display Grid taken from the domain of multi-user multi-display systems (see Fig. 6.19). All these case studies have the main goal to utilise trust at the application level. They are implemented on the TEM to make use of the trust metrics and to profit from the robustness of TEM provided at the middleware level by means of the self-x algorithms described above.

**The Trusted Computing Grid:** The first application case study that profits from the TEM middleware is the Trusted Computing Grid. This consists of a great number of client computers with different resources that work together in a grid to cooperatively process computationally intensive tasks, e.g. face recognition [48] or ray tracing [49]. Each client in the grid takes on one of two roles related to the execution of an individual task: *submitter* or *worker*. A *submitter* is responsible for breaking down the task into work units, scheduling the execution of work units, and collecting the results of their execution. A *worker* is responsible for the actual execution of work units. However, not every worker in the grid is equally interested to process work units. There are, for example, some workers that might plan to exploit the system by accepting work units and cancelling their processing, so called *Egoistic Workers* [50]. By making use of trust, the submitters can identify those untrustworthy workers and form Trusted Communities (TCs) [51]. This represents a community formed by workers and submitters with strong mutual trust relationships that aims to reduce the probability of receiving invalid results. Each Trusted Community is managed by an elected trustworthy manager, called the *Trusted Community Manager* (TCM), which has as goal to maintain the stability of community members using self-x properties. This TCM is an example for an important service in the TEM middleware, since its failure can deteriorate the entire TC.

**The Autonomous Virtual Power Plants:** Another example of application that profits from the TEM middleware is the Autonomous Virtual Power Plants [52]. This is a power management system composed of a variety of power plants which provide either *dispatchable* or *non-dispatchable* power production. The dispatchable production is made by power plants whose output can be determined in advance such as coal or atomic power plants. In contrast, the non-dispatchable production is made by power plants whose output is unpredictable like wind turbines or solar power plants. One of the main challenges posed here is to maintain the balance between power production and consumption at all times. This is a non-trivial task for non-dispatchable power plants since their production depends on the availability of natural resources like sunlight, air, or wind, that cannot be controlled by humans. The Autonomous Virtual Power Plants application overcomes this issue by integrating trust to allow an automatic regulation of non-dispatchable power plants, so that the dispatchable power plants can be used only as needed [53, 54]. This allows the formation of Autonomous Virtual Power Plants (AVPPs), that group dispatchable and non-dispatchable power plants together based on the Observer/Controller architectural pattern [55]. If an observer identifies during runtime that the organisational structure of an AVPP is not suited, e.g. because maybe one or more AVPPs cannot maintain the power balance any more, the controller performs a new organisation of AVPPs in order to bring back the power balance optimised in the system again [56]. The autonomous organisation of AVPPs is an essential aspect of this application case study and is therefore considered as an example for an important service in the TEM middleware.

**The Trusted Display Grid:** The third application case study that profits from the TEM middleware is the Trusted Display Grid [57]. This allows users to interact in the system with multiple self-organising displays at the same time. The displays are divided into two types of usage: *private* and *public*. Private displays are those that can protect the personal data of users from external observation like smart phones and tablets. In contrast, public displays are those that everyone can use, whose data is public and can be shown in presence of other people like Microsoft Surfaces.[3] The major challenge here is to self-organise the transfer of data between public and private displays at runtime. However, such an organisation is a non-trivial task. This is because the displays should continuously protect the users' privacy on the one hand and on the other hand maintain the user's acceptance. Otherwise, the user might abandon the system. The Trusted Display Grid tackles this problematic situation by using the User Trust Model (UTM) [58], which allows the displays to monitor the interaction of users, to measure their current trustworthiness, and to apply appropriate self-organising mechanisms to increase the users' trust as well as usability in the system. This UTM is essential for the operability of the Trusted Display Grid and is therefore treated as an important service by the TEM middleware.

---

[3]Microsoft Surface – [Accessed: October 21, 2015] – http://www.microsoft.com/en-us/pixelsense/whatissurface.aspx.

## 6.6  Conclusion

In this chapter, a middleware architecture for trustworthy self-x properties in open distributed systems is presented. The design of the architecture relies on trustworthy algorithms to provide guarantees of reliability, availability and scalability to service-oriented middlewares. The baseline middleware used in this work is $OC\mu$. We have explained how the trustworthy self-x layer can be easily integrated into $OC\mu$ to make it more robust in the face of untrustworthy components. The resulting middleware is TEM, a trust-enabling middleware that can profit from the advantage of trust and OC principles at the same time. The TEM makes use of different trust metrics, i.e. such as direct trust, reputation, and confidence to monitor the behaviour of nodes in the system at runtime. This monitoring is very important to guide and control the self-organisation process between nodes by means of trust-aware self-x properties. The self-x properties examined in this work are self-configuration, self-optimisation, and self-healing. We believe that these properties are fundamental for the design of every autonomous, scalable and fault-tolerant service-oriented middleware. The self-configuration is related to the ability to perform an initial distribution of services on nodes taking the resource requirement and importance level of services into account. The self-optimisation focuses on optimising the allocation of services at runtime by monitoring the trust and resource consumption of nodes. And the self-healing aspect is concerned with the ability to handle failures of nodes in order to guarantee that all services running on them stay available even in case of network partitions. We applied the TEM middleware to different application case studies and clarified how uncertainty in open environments can be mastered by using trust. Due to the fact that future application services will become more autonomous, we expect to see more self-x systems based on our (or a similar) architecture. The future design of self-x middlewares will increase the demand of trustworthy self-x properties to ensure robustness in the system. The architecture presented in this chapter is a step in this direction.

For future work, we plan to investigate more sophisticated self-protecting mechanisms for the TEM that might further increase its robustness against trust manipulation. For this purpose, we have to analyse and study the most common security threats present in the field of trust in distributed environments such as the ones presented in [59] to get a deeper understanding of that issue. Of course, such investigation could also include other related fields such as Cloud Computing and peer-to-peer systems. Based on this study, we have to build self-protecting solutions that can be applied in our trustworthy self-x layer. It is important to note that the found solutions should also be characterised by low overhead in order to be integrated in TEM – no self-protection at any cost.

**Acknowledgements**  This research is partly sponsored by the research unit *OC-Trust* (FOR 1085) of the German Research Foundation. The TEM was devised and developed in cooperation with Rolf Kiefhaber, a former researcher at the University of Augsburg. The authors would like to thank all OC-Trust members who have contributed by providing background information about the application case studies implemented on TEM.

# References

1. Schmeck, H.: Organic computing – a new vision for distributed embedded systems. In: Proceedings of the Eighth IEEE International Symposium on Object-Oriented Real-Time Distributed Computing (ISORC05), Seattle (2005)
2. Horn, P.: Autonomic computing: IBMs perspective on the state of information technology. IBM Corporation, pp. 1–39 (2001). http://www.ibm.com/autonomic/pdfs/autonomiccomputing.pdf
3. Steghöfer, J.-P., Kiefhaber, R., Leichtenstern, K., Bernard, Y., Klejnowski, L., Reif, W., Ungerer, T., André, E., Hähner, J., Müller-Schloer, C.: Trustworthy organic computing systems: challenges and perspectives. In: Xie, B., Branke, J., Sadjadi, S., Zhang, D., Zhou, X. (eds.) Autonomic and Trusted Computing, vol. 6407, pp. 62–76. Springer, Berlin/Heidelberg (2010). ISBN: 978-3-642-16575-7
4. Roth, M., Schmitt, J., Kiefhaber, R., Kluge, F., Ungerer, T.: Organic computing middleware for ubiquitous environments. In: Organic Computing: A Paradigm Shift for Complex Systems, pp. 339–351. Springer, Basel (2011)
5. Lund, A., Betting, B., Brinkschulte, U.: Design and evaluation of a bio-inspired, distributed middleware for a multiple mixed-core system on chip. In: 18th International Symposium on Real-Time Distributed Computing Workshops, Auckland (2015)
6. Nickschas, M., Brinkschulte, U.: CARISMA – a service-oriented, real-time organic middleware architecture. J. Softw. **4**, 654–663 (2009)
7. Smith, R.G.: The contract net protocol: high-level communication and control in a distributed problem solver. Trans. Comput. (1980). ISBN:978-0-7695-4322-2
8. Seinturier, L., Merle, P., Rouvoy, R., Romero, D., Schiavoni, V., Stefani, J.-B.: A component-based middleware platform for reconfigurable service-oriented architectures. Softw.: Pract. Exp. **42**, 559–583 (2012)
9. Hoffmann, M., Wittke, M., Hähner, J., Müller-Schloer, C.: Spatial partitioning in self-organizing smart camera systems. J. Sel. Top. Signal Process. **2**, 480–492 (2008)
10. Jaenen, U., Spiegelberg, H., Sommer, L., von Mammen, S., Brehm, J., Hähner, J.: Object tracking as job-scheduling problem. In: Seventh International Conference on Distributed Smart Cameras (ICDSC), Palm Springs (2013)
11. Tomforde, S., Jänen, U., Hähner, J., Hoffmann, M.: Cloud services – towards an intelligent cloud-based surveillance system. In: Proceedings of the 10th International Conference on Informatics in Control, Automation and Robotics, Reykjavik (2013)
12. Dwork, C., Lynch, N.: Consensus in the presence of partial synchrony. J. Assoc. Comput. Mach. **35**, 288–323 (1988)
13. Schmitt, J., Roth, M., Kiefhaber, R., Kluge, F., Ungerer, T.: Realizing self-x properties by an automated planner. In: International Conference on Autonomic Computing, Karlsruhe (2011)
14. Trumler, W., Klaus, R., Ungerer, T.: Self-configuration via cooperative social behavior. In: Autonomic and Trusted Computing (ATC), pp. 90–99. Springer, Berlin/Heidelberg (2006)
15. Trumler, W., Pietzowski, A., Satzger, B., Ungerer, T.: Adaptive self-optimization in distributed dynamic environments. In: First International Conference on Self-Adaptive and Self-Organizing Systems (SASO 2007), Boston, pp. 320–323 (2007)
16. Satzger, B.: Self-healing distributed systems. PhD thesis, Universität Augsburg (2008)
17. Satzger, B., Pietzowski, A., Trumler, W., Ungerer, T.: A lazy monitoring approach for heartbeat-style failure detectors. In: International Conference on Availability, Reliability and Security, Barcelona (2008)
18. Richter, U., Mnif, M., Branke, J., Müller-Schloer, C., Schmeck, H.: Towards a generic observer/controller architecture for organic computing. In: GI Jahrestagung (1), 112–119 (2006)
19. Satzger, B., Ungerer, T.: Grouping algorithms for scalable self-monitoring distributed systems. In: International Conference on Autonomic Computing and Communication Systems, Turin (2008)

20. Kiefhaber, R.: Calculating and aggregating direct trust and reputation in organic computing systems. PhD thesis, University of Augsburg (2014)
21. Kiefhaber, R., Satzger, B., Schmitt, J., Roth, M., Ungerer, T.: Trust measurement methods in organic computing systems by direct observation. In: The 8th IEEE/IFIP International Conference on Embedded and Ubiquitous Computing (EUC 2010), Hong Kong, pp. 105–111 (2010)
22. Kiefhaber, R., Anders, G., Siefert, F., Ungerer, T., Reif, W.: Confidence as a means to assess the accuracy of trust values. In: The 11th IEEE International Conference on Trust, Security and Privacy in Computing and Communications (TrustCom 2012), Liverpool (2012)
23. Kiefhaber, R., Hammer, S., Savs, B., Schmitt, J., Roth, M., Kluge, F., André, E., Ungerer, T.: The neighbor-trust metric to measure reputation in organic computing systems. In: The 5th IEEE Conference on Self-Adaptive and Self-Organizing Systems Workshops (SASOW 2011), Ann Arbor, pp. 41–46 (2011)
24. Kiefhaber, R., Jahr, R., Msadek, N., Ungerer, T.: Ranking of direct trust, confidence, and reputation in an abstract system with unreliable components. In: The 10th IEEE International Conference on Autonomic and Trusted Computing (ATC-2013), Vietri sul Mere (2013)
25. Anders, G., Siefert, F., Msadek, N., Kiefhaber, R., Kosak, O., Reif, W., Ungerer, T.: TEMAS – a trust-enabling multi-agent system for open environments. Technical report, Universität Augsburg (2013)
26. Hsieh, F.-S., Chiang, C.Y.: Workflow planning in holonic manufacturing systems with extended contract net protocol. In: 22nd International Conference on Industrial, Engineering and Other Applications of Applied Intelligent Systems, Tainan (2009)
27. Kinnebrew, J.S., Biswas, G.: Efficient allocation of hierarchically-decomposable tasks in a sensor web contract net. In: Conference on Web Intelligence and Intelligent Agent Technology, Milan, vol. 02, pp. 225–232 (2009)
28. Goswami, K., Gupta, A.: Resource selection in grids using contract net. In: 16th Euromicro Conference on Parallel, Distributed and Network-Based Processing, Toulouse, pp. 105–109 (2008)
29. Deshpande, U., Gupta, A., Basu, A.: Performance improvement of the contract net protocol using instance based learning. In: 5th International Workshop – Distributed Computing, Kolkata (2003)
30. Dellarocas, C., Klein, M., Rodriguez-Aguilar, J.A.: An exception-handling architecture for open electronic marketplaces of contract net software agents. In: Proceedings of the 2nd ACM Conference on Electronic Commerce, Minneapolis (2000)
31. Kodama, J., Hamagami, T., Shinji, H., Tanabe, T., Funabashi, T., Hirata, H.: Multi-agent-based autonomous power distribution network restoration using contract net protocol. Electr. Eng. Jpn. **166**, 56–63 (2009)
32. Bozdag, E.: A survey of extensions to the contract net protocol. Technical report, Delft University of Technology (2008)
33. Msadek, N., Kiefhaber, R., Fechner, B., Ungerer, T.: Trust-enhanced self-configuration for organic computing systems. In: 27th International Conference on Architecture of Computing Systems ARCS2014, Luebeck (2014)
34. Msadek, N., Kiefhaber, R., Ungerer, T.: Simultaneous self-configuration with multiple managers for organic computing systems. In: The 2nd International Workshop on Self-Optimisation in Organic and Autonomic Computing Systems (SAOS14) in Conjunction with ARCS 2014, Luebeck (2014)
35. Msadek, N., Kiefhaber, R., Ungerer, T.: A trustworthy, fault-tolerant and scalable self-configuration algorithm for organic computing systems. J. Syst. Archit. **61**, 511–519 (2015)
36. Msadek, N., Kiefhaber, R., Ungerer, T.: A trust- and load-based self-optimization algorithm for organic computing systems. In: International Conference on Self-Adaptive and Self-Organizing Systems (SASO), London (2014)
37. Msadek, N., Kiefhaber, R., Ungerer, T.: Trustworthy self-optimization in organic computing environments. In: International Conference on Architecture of Computing Systems (ARCS), Porto (2015)

38. Msadek, N., Stegmeier, A., Kiefhaber, R., Ungerer, T.: A mechanism for minimizing trust conflicts in organic computing systems. In: International Workshop on Self-Optimisation in Organic and Autonomic Computing Systems (SAOS), Porto (2015)
39. Dedinski, I., Hofmann, A., Sick, B.: Cooperative Keep-alives: an efficient outage detection algorithm for P2P overlay networks. In: Seventh IEEE International Conference on Peer-to-Peer Computing, Galway (2007)
40. Price, R., Tino, P., Theodoropoulos, G.: Still alive: extending keep-alive intervals in P2P overlay networks. J. Mobile Netw. Appl. **17**, 378–394 (2012)
41. Msadek, N., Ungerer, T.: Trust-Based Monitoring for Self-Healing of Distributed Real-Time Systems (2016, submitted for publication)
42. Alexandersson, R., Öhman, P., Karlsson, J.: Aspect-oriented implementation of fault tolerance: an assessment of overhead. In: 29th International Conference on Computer Safety, Reliability, and Security, SAFECOMP 2010, Vienna, 14–17 Sept 2010 (0302-9743), vol. 6351, pp. 466–479 (2010)
43. Enokido, T., Aikebaier, A., Takizawa, M.: An energy-efficient redundant execution algorithm by terminating meaningless redundant processes. In: International Conference on Advanced Information Networking and Applications, Barcelona (2013)
44. Aidemark, J., Vinter, J., Folkesson, P., Karlsson, J.: Experimental evaluation of time-redundant execution for a brake-by-wire application. In: International Conference on Dependable Systems and Networks, Washington, DC (2002)
45. Bailis, P., Kingsbury, K.: The network is reliable: an informal survey of real-world communications failures. ACM J. Queue **12**(7), 20:20–20:32 (2014). http://doi.acm.org/10.1145/2639988.2639988. doi:10.1145/2639988.2639988
46. Shirriff, K.W.: Method and system for establishing a quorum for a geographically distributed cluster of computers. In Patent US7016946 B2 (2006)
47. Ueda, Y., Kojima, H., Tsuchiya, T.: On the availability of replicated data managed by hierarchical voting. In: 3rd International Conference on Information Science and Cloud Computing Companion, Guangzhou (2013)
48. Roberto, B.: Template Matching Techniques in Computer Vision: Theory and Practice. Wiley, Chichester (2009)
49. Glassner, A.: An Introduction to Ray Tracing. The Morgan Kaufmann Series in Computer Graphics. Academic, London (1989)
50. Edenhofer, S., Stifter, C., Jänen, U., Kantert, J., Tomforde, S., Hähner, J., Müller-Schloer, C.: An accusation-based strategy to handle undesirable behaviour in multi-agent systems. In: International Conference on Autonomic Computing, Grenoble (2015)
51. Klejnowski, L., Bernard, Y., Anders, G., Müller-Schloer, C., Reif, W.: Trusted community – a trust-based multi-agent organisation for open systems. In: Proceedings of the 5th International Conference on Agents and Artificial Intelligence (ICAART), Barcelona (2013)
52. Steghöfer, J.-P., Anders, G., Siefert, F., Reif, W.: A system of systems approach to the evolutionary transformation of power management systems. In: Proceedings of INFORMATIK 2013 – Workshop on Smart Grids, Koblenz, vol. P-220. Bonner Köllen Verlag (2013)
53. Anders, G., Schiendorfer, A., Siefert, F., Steghöfer, J.-P., Reif, W.: Cooperative resource allocation in open systems of systems. ACM Trans. Auton. Adapt. Syst. **10**, 11:1–11:44 (2015). ISSN:1556-4665
54. Kosak, O., Anders, G., Siefert, F., Reif, W.: An approach to robust resource allocation in large-scale systems of systems. In: 2015 IEEE 9th International Conference on Self-Adaptive and Self-Organizing Systems (SASO), Cambridge, pp. 1–10 (2015)
55. Steghöfer, J.-P., Eberhardinger, B., Nafz, F., Reif, W.: Synthesis of observers for autonomic evolutionary systems from requirements models. In: Workshop on Distributed Autonomous Network Management Systems, Belgium (2013)
56. Anders, G., Siefert, F., Reif, W.: A heuristic for constrained set partitioning in the light of heterogeneous objectives. English. In: Duval, B., van den Herik, J., Loiseau, S., Filipe, J. (eds.) Agents and Artificial Intelligence, vol. 9494, pp. 223–244. Springer (2015). ISBN:978-3-319-27946-6

57. Wißner, M., Hammer, S., Kurdyukova, E., André, E.: Trust-based decision-making for the adaptation of public displays in changing social contexts. J. Trust Manag. **1**, 1–23 (2014)
58. Hammer, S., Wißner, M., André, E.: Trust-based decision-making for smart and adaptive environments. User Model. User-Adapt. Interact. **25**, 267–293 (2015)
59. Mármol, F.G., Pérez, G.M.: Security threats scenarios in trust and reputation models for distributed systems. Comput. Secur. **28**, 545–556 (2009)

# Chapter 7
# From Trust and Forgiveness to Social Capital and Justice: Formal Models of Social Processes in Open Distributed Systems

Jeremy Pitt

**Abstract** Open systems typically occur in a wide range of applications, from virtual organisations and vehicular networks to cloud/grid computing and reconfigurable manufacturing. All these applications encounter a similar problem: how does a system component reliably complete its own tasks, when successful task completion depends on interaction and interoperation with other, potentially unreliable and conflicting, components. One solution to this problem is *trust*: depending on a second party requires a willingness to expose oneself to risk, and to the extent that this 'willingness' can be quantified or qualified, it can be used to inform a binary trust decision. Therefore, a formal model of the social relationship underpinning such trust decisions is essential for conditioning bipartite interactions between components in an open system. However, there are a number of issues that follow from this – for example: what is to be done when the outcome of the trust decision is contrary to expectation? Are there positive externalities that can be derived from a successful trust decision? and: How can we ensure that outcomes of collective decision-making in such circumstances are, in some sense, 'correct' and/or 'fair'. Our answers to these question have been found in the formalisation of other social relations, respectively forgiveness, social capital and justice. This chapter presents a survey of the development of formal models of social relations, from trust to justice via forgiveness and social capital, all of which address the issue of reliable interoperation in open systems.

**Keywords** Open systems • Trust • Forgiveness • Social capital • Justice

J. Pitt (✉)
Department of Electrical and Electronic Engineering, Imperial College London, Exhibition Road, London, SW7 2BT, UK
e-mail: j.pitt@imperial.ac.uk

© Springer International Publishing Switzerland 2016
W. Reif et al. (eds.), *Trustworthy Open Self-Organising Systems*,
Autonomic Systems, DOI 10.1007/978-3-319-29201-4_7

## 7.1  Introduction

We are interested in *open systems* which involve cooperating (and potentially conflicting) components, interacting asynchronously, in parallel, and peer-to-peer; with no centralised controller, and with potentially inconsistent beliefs.[1] Such open systems typically occur in a wide range of applications, from virtual organisations and vehicular networks to cloud/grid computing and reconfigurable manufacturing; and have been intensively studied in the fields of multi-agent systems [1], autonomic computing [2], and (of course) organic computing [3].

In all these applications, and the focal point of these studies, similar problems are encountered. One is resource allocation, how to ensure that a 'fair' and efficient distribution of common-pool resources can be achieved, especially in an economy of scarcity (when there are insufficient resources to satisfy everyone's requirements). However, this is preceded by another common problem: if a component is going to join such a system and pool its resources in the expectation of receiving a fair and efficient allocation, how does it decide whether it is 'safe' or 'worthwhile' to join? More generally, in the context of an open system: how does a component reliably complete its own tasks, when successful task completion depends on interaction and interoperation with other, potentially unreliable and conflicting, components?

One solution to this problem is *trust*: depending on a second party requires a willingness to expose oneself to risk, and to the extent that this 'willingness' can be quantified or qualified, it can be used to inform a binary trust decision. Therefore, a formal model of the essentially social relationship underpinning such trust decisions is required for conditioning bipartite interactions between components in an open system. Theories of cognition which explain how humans make trust decisions in various contexts, offer insights into and understanding of the process, which can then be formalised as algorithms and data structures and used as the basis for operationalisation to solve an engineering problem – i.e. how autonomous components can make trust decisions in open systems.

Furthermore, there are a number of issues that follow from this – for example: what is to be done when the outcome of the trust decision is wrong, or rather, contrary to expectation – in other words, the trust has been misplaced? As previously mentioned, the system components may be competing, or may be unreliable, and so may fail to comply with a mutually agreed system specification, or with the terms and conditions of a quality-of-service contract. However, there may be many reasons for this non-compliance, from inadvertence, through necessity, to (unfortunately) sheer malice. A second issue is: are there positive externalities that can be derived from a successful trust decision? A positive externality is generally considered to be

---

[1]Note this is different from open systems as defined from a systems theory perspective, i.e. a system which has interactions with its environment through some boundary; and from a computing perspective, where open systems are also defined as systems based on interoperability through open standards, or dynamic systems with unrestricted access and components that join and leave the system – although the open systems in which we are interested can exhibit all these features.

a benefit that is derived by a third party as a result of an economic transaction. But, what if there were positive externalities that were to be gained: from fixing incorrect trust decisions, for example; or as a result of using relational, rather than purely transactional, information. And a third issue involves ensuring that the outcomes of collective decision-making in such circumstances are, in some sense, 'correct' and/or 'fair' (in the sense that each component receives equal treatment according to some metric, within the constraint of efficiency – there is no benefit in having a mechanism that computes the 'fairest' possible distribution of resources, if all those resources are consumed in the computation, or are no longer needed by the time the computation has completed).

In addressing the initial problem, our first step was to define a formal model of trust, as discussed in Sect. 7.3, which is used to answer the basic question: how does one component engage with another, in an open system, if it really must (i.e. sitting out is not an option). This trust model is based on a formal characterisation of a socio-cognitive theory of trust, complemented by economic reasoning. Following on from this, our proposed solutions to the three issues have been found in the formalisation of other social relations, respectively forgiveness (Sect. 7.4), social capital (Sect. 7.5) and justice (Sect. 7.6). As a consequence, the chapter contributes both a historical survey of the development of a series formal models of social processes, from trust to justice via forgiveness and social capital, but also could be considered as a (preliminary) handbook of formal (social) methods, or social design patterns, for addressing the issues of 'reliable' interoperation in open systems.

## 7.2 Background: Open Systems

Open systems, as identified and defined by Hewitt [4], comprise autonomous components of heterogenous provenance interacting asynchronously, in parallel and peer-to-peer. Interaction implies that it is reasonable to assume there is a common language, a specification of correct behaviour and interfaces that facilitate interoperation; on the other hand, autonomy and heterogeneity imply that it is not reasonable to assume that the components share a common objective, nor to assume that there is a centralised controller that is directing or determining the actions of components, nor to assume that their behaviour will necessarily comply with the specification.

Based on these assumptions, five salient features of open systems are identifiable:

- *Co-dependence* and *competition*: each component is reliant on other components for successful accomplishment of its own goals, but those other components may themselves be unreliable, for example, if the components are competing for the same (scarce) resources;
- *Mutability*: the environment, network topology and constituent components can vary rapidly and unpredictably; therefore, each component will frequently be

exposed to 'first encounter' problems, i.e. how to interact in a situation or with a
component that has not been previously encountered;

- *Partiality* and *uncertainty of knowledge*: because interactions are asynchronous,
  in parallel, and peer-to-peer, this implies that there is no single source of 'true'
  knowledge. Therefore, each component only has a partial (and possible subjective) knowledge of the overall system and some of it components; furthermore
  the union of these knowledge bases may be inconsistent (this does not mean that
  it is necessary to 'give up' logic for open systems [5]);
- *Expectation of error*: actuality (what is the case) and ideality (what ought to be
  the case) do not necessarily coincide; in other words, the components may fail
  to comply according to the system specification – but for a variety of causes, for
  example by accident, necessity, or design. It is necessary to distinguish between
  these causes in order to recover from them; and
- *Self-organisation*: there is no central controller, and there is no operator intervention; therefore, the nodes have to resolve difference, deal with first encounters,
  cope with uncertainty and recover from errors *by and between themselves*.

One approach to addressing these issues is to observe how similar problems have
been resolved in natural (biological or social) systems, and formalise such solutions
in an appropriate calculus suitable for engineering a computational solution to be
used in (or by the components of) an artificial system.

This has, in fact, been the approach of the synthetic method underlying research
in artificial societies and artificial life [6]. The main steps involve generalising some
observed phenomena to produce a theory, from which an artificial system can be
constructed and used to test predicted claims. The outcome of applying the synthetic
method is to engineer an artificial system, and the resulting animation, experiments
or performance serves to support or refute the theory.

Several other attempts to apply ideas from the social sciences to the design of
computational systems (see, e.g. [7]) have followed a similar pattern. Furthermore,
researchers in biologically-inspired computing, notably those concerned with artificial immune systems [8] have developed a comparable approach. However, in
[9], another adaption of the synthetic method was proposed. In this approach, a
distinction was made between the social sciences source and engineering artificial
societies. The transition from theory to artificial system was no longer direct and
included the application of an intermediate step. In addition, the results of observed
performance were not used to justify or refute the source theory, but were instead
used to adjust the formalisms underpinning the artificial system.

This methodology, called *sociologically-inspired computing*,[2] is illustrated in
Fig. 7.1. The first step is to formulate a theory by defining, for example in

[2]The term 'sociologically-inspired' was chosen as a parallel to 'biologically-inspired', although
it is not, perhaps, such a good term. We take inspiration not just from sociology, but from across
the social and natural sciences, and indeed have formalised theories from linguistics, philosophy,
law, psychology, cognitive science, physiology, economics, and political science in our search for
computable solutions to engineering problems.

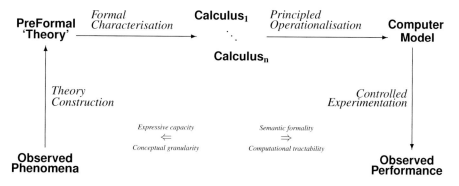

**Fig. 7.1** Methodology for sociologically-inspired computing

natural language, the terms and principles that are used to denote or describe the observed social phenomena. The second step of formal characterisation leads from the (predominantly) informal representations of the source theory, to formal representations, expressed in a formal language or 'calculus' of some kind (where by 'calculus' it is meant any system of calculation or computation based on the manipulation of symbolic representations). The third and final step is systematic, controlled experimentation with a computational model of an artificial system derived from the formal representation.

As explained in [9], there are (at least) two types of formal representation. Firstly, there are those representations that aim to provide an analysis of conceptual structure, identifying the fundamental elements of which complex concepts are composed, and articulating the principles governing their composition and inter-relations. Crucially, these representations, being used for a conceptual characteri-sation of the theory, are *theory-facing* constrained primarily by considerations of expressive capacity, and not those of computational tractability. Secondly, there are those representations that are more suitable to the development of software models and simulations: this is the basis of a computational framework for the theory. However, the key points to note about these representations is that they should be informed and guided by the conceptual characterisations of a theory-facing representation, but they may well involve some degree of simplification, or approximation, and there may be some abstractions that can be tolerated in a theory-facing representation, but not in an *implementation-facing* one. It is expected, though, that the designer should be fully aware of how the conceptual characterisation is being approximated, or how the computational framework is being enriched (i.e. it is a not a matter of 'theory hacking' in a preferred formalism).

The final step of principled operationalisation is concerned with moving from the computational framework to a model of the artificial system, with algorithmic intelligence of the components embedded in identifiable functions and processes. This step may also be selective or approximate, but it too is principled in that it is conducted knowing which selections and approximations have been made, and why.

This methodology has, in part, emerged from addressing the features of open systems. We begin in the next section with a formalisation of a socio-cognitive theory of trust, in order to deal with issues of uncertainty and unreliability (in 'recurring encounter' situations) and mutability (leading to 'first encounter' situations).

## 7.3  Trust

A particular feature of open systems is co-dependence: one component has to rely on one or more other components in order to successfully complete its own tasks. For example, in an ad hoc network, one node has to rely on a network of other nodes to transmit its messages across that network [10]; in a distributed supply chain, one manufacturing component has to rely on the timely delivery and quality of the goods delivered in order to satisfy its own commitments to the chain [11]; in desktop grid computing, components have to delegate tasks to each other [12]; and so on.

This requires a decision to be made about the reliability of the network, other suppliers, etc. This is, essentially, decision-making under uncertainty, because the decision-maker has no control over the autonomous behaviour of the components on which it chooses to rely. Furthermore, a decision *has* to be made: inaction implies inevitable failure to complete one's own task.

This is a *trust* decision, loosely defined as a willingness (or necessity) to expose oneself to risk, with the intention to reduce the doubt involved in the decision and so mitigate the risks involved. However, this assessment of risk concerning reliance on someone or something outside one's control is a potentially 'expensive' computation; furthermore it is one that needs to be performed frequently and in some cases replicated – in which case it would be pointless to repeat the computation, but in any case there would be new information (i.e. the outcome of the previous interaction).

Therefore, in dealing with such a trust decision, a framework is required which takes into account Weisberg's [13] two dimensions of uncertainty: doubt and ambiguity. Doubt measures the degree of belief in a proposition; ambiguity reflects an understanding of that proposition. Doubt is derived from those aspects that cannot be controlled, such as randomness, chaos or non-observability; ambiguity stems from having only a partial understanding of the situation. Doubt, according to Weisberg, can be quantified, typically by statistical measures; but ambiguity is essentially qualitative and requires logical reasoning.[3]

In retrospect, this combination of doubt and uncertainty (although not couched in those terms) is a feature of the trust framework developed by Neville and Pitt [14],

---

[3] Although Weisberg's key, and highly cogent, point is that in the pursuit of the elimination of doubt by data analytics and machine learning, some researchers appear to have neglected ambiguity and choose to remain *wilfully ignorant* of this component of uncertainty.

ten years prior to the publication of Weisberg's book. Effectively, this framework tried to deal with the quantitative element of doubt about the outcome by means of *economic* reasoning, i.e. in terms of utilities, cost/benefit analysis, and on on; and the qualitative element of ambiguity in the process by means of *socio-cognitive* reasoning, i.e. in terms of confidence in beliefs, experiences, recommendations, the interpretation of signals (such as reputation), and so on. The resulting trust-decision framework brought together both socio-cognitive and socio-economic reasoning.

Applying the methodology of the previous section, the socio-cognitive reasoning element of this framework was based on the formalisation of a trust theory from cognitive science. In this case, computational representation of an agent's trust belief is based on the formal model of Castelfranchi and Falcone [15]. The essential conceptualisation is as follows: the degree to which agent $A$ trusts agent $B$ about task $\tau$ in (state of the world) $\Omega$ is a subjective probability $\mathbf{DoT}_{A,B,\tau,\Omega}$. This is the basis of agent $A$'s decision to rely upon $B$ to "get $\tau$ done". The framework incorporates this stance, but computes 'trust' as this (subjective) probability of one agent's expectation regarding the performance of another, as a product of its direct experiences of that other party, and from the recommendations of its peers (i.e. reputation), in both cases qualitative information used to reduce ambiguity.

The economic model used by a decision-making agent focuses on estimating the utility gained by the agent from a successful outcome of the trust decision, and estimating the utility lost in the event of an unsuccessful outcome. In situations where there may be a number of possible partners from whom to select (e.g. a trading partner in a supply chain, next hop in an ad hoc network, etc.), the agent should choose to trust the potential partner with the highest positive expected utility $\mathscr{E}$, i.e.:

$$\mathscr{E} = \mathbf{DoT}_{A,B,\tau,\Omega} \times \mathbf{U}(\text{succ})_{A,B,\tau,\Omega} + (1 - \mathbf{DoT}_{A,B,\tau,\Omega}) \cdot \mathbf{U}(\text{fail})_{A,B,\tau,\Omega}$$

An overview of the operation of the framework, as illustrated in Fig. 7.2, is as follows (for a detailed description, including formulas and algorithms, see [14]).

Given an opportunity (or requirement) to trust a peer (process (1) in Fig. 7.2), the agent uses its economic model to calculate its outcome utilities (2,3). These outcome utilities are the economic influence on the decision to trust (5), and represent the payoffs of accepting the risk in relying on the peer. The other parameter in the decision to trust is the agent's trust belief (4) conditioned by its confidence in that belief (14), this being the agent's subjective evaluation of the probability of a successful outcome of trusting the peer. The agent's trust belief, is computed from the combination of the agent's belief about its direct experiences (8) and the reputation of the potential trustee (10). The relative influence of these beliefs on the trust belief is determined by the agent's confidence in their respective accuracies (7). Direct experience represents a distillation of its set of prior first hand interactions with the trustee into one belief (9). Likewise, the agent's opinion of the reputation of the potential trustee is informed by the recommendations of its peers (11). The credibility assigned to an experience or recommendation, and hence its weight of influence during the distillation process, is a function of the currency of the belief

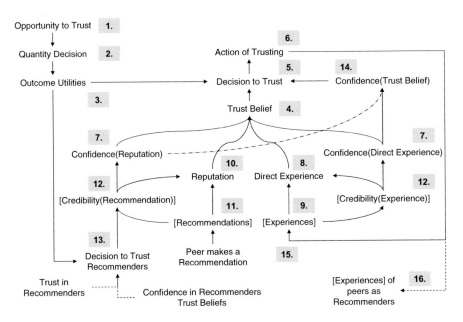

**Fig. 7.2** Trust Framework based on Socio-{economic, cognitive} Reasoning

and it is also dependent upon the agent's decision to trust the source of the belief
(12). This opportunity to trust a peer as a source of recommendations is handled
in the same manner as defined here for the generic case (13). The agent will look
to its experiences of the peer as a recommender and at what its peers recommend
about them as recommenders. We will assume that the agent can trust itself not to
lie about or distort its own experiences (although we do not rule out the possibility
of self-deception).

In the cases where the resultant trust belief is enough to decide to trust the
potential trustee, and given there are no better opportunities available, the agent
will act upon its decision (6). The resultant experience of the trustee is added to
the agent's set of prior experiences (15). Experiences are also formed about those
agents that have made recommendations referring to the trustee and subsequently
the agents that recommended them and so on (16).

The trust framework has been tested in a producer-consumer scenario with
unreliable producers. For details of the simulation, experiments and results, see
[16], but the main result was that consumer decision-making with the fully-featured
trust framework produced a close approximation to a 'safe' market (i.e. one with no
malicious or unreliable producers). The other interesting feature of the framework
was its anytime computation based on 'sufficient confidence': this demonstrated
that the agents' reasoning shifts over time and experience from 'risk' trust, an
'expensive' computation for decision-making in first encounters, to 'reliance' trust,
which short-cuts such computations (by the confidence metric) for $n$th encounters,

i.e. sufficient prior direct experience is such that there is an expectation of a beneficial outcome without needing to consider others' recommendations.

Of course, this is open to exploits, but this is a characteristic of 'stings' in human commercial transactions. However, the fact a trust decision, based on a trust relationship, *can* be exploited, raises another question – *what happens when the outcome of the trust decision is wrong, or is contrary to expectation?* One answer to this question is proposed in the next section.


## 7.4  Forgiveness

Trust was (informally) defined as a willingness to expose oneself to a risk; indeed, the computation of the 'degree of trust' (in the trust framework of the previous section) explicitly took into account the utility of successful and unsuccessful outcomes. In this case, as in many trust frameworks in the multi-agent systems literature [17], 'trust' is a measure of probability, or an indicator of the doubt involved in a certain transaction or relationship. Therefore, many of these trust frameworks attempt to reduce the level of doubt – but it is impossible to eliminate it altogether, otherwise it would hardly be a trust decision. Therefore, if there is always some risk of an unsuccessful outcome, the key question becomes, as previously posited, what is a component in an open system to do, when it misplaces its trust, so that the outcome of its trust decision is wrong, or contrary to expectation? Critically, this does not imply that the use of trust itself is necessarily misguided, and that the entire trust framework should be abandoned, but instead some complementary mechanism for dealing with a particular trust breakdown is required.

A possible explanation for the trust breakdown is that there has been a violation of a norm, or from the truster's perspective, a violation of the *expectation* that the trustee's behaviour will comply with a norm, which is believed to be 'in force'. This follows from the Jones [18] account of trust, where it is suggested that the act of trusting has two components, a *belief* component and an *expectation* component, and that one ordinarily says of a particular situation that "*A* trusts *B*" if *A* has the *belief* that there is a norm, or rule (to be complied with in this situation), and *A* has the *expectation* that *B*'s behaviour will indeed comply with the norm.

Typically, then, in multi-agent systems research, and indeed in social system for e-commerce, the reaction to a trust breakdown has been to damage or diminish the reputation of the violator. Notice, though, that reputation is a factor that is part of the trust decision framework, and as such is a quantitative punishment mechanism which only serves to reduce doubt. It does not do anything to deal with the *ambiguity*, i.e. taking into account the truster's understanding of the situation, or why it is that the trustee has violated the norm, or how serious the offence was, or any of many other factors that pertain to the complexity of a trusting relationship.

Therefore, what is required instead is a *qualitative repair* mechanism, i.e. one that tries to take the ambiguity into account, and instead try to restore the system to a (kind of) homeostatic equilibrium. In fact, there is a well-established social

mechanism for achieving precisely this effect – *forgiveness* [19]. Forgiveness is
a pro-social motivational change in someone who has incurred a transgression.
It implies giving up resentment and desire to punish someone. When people
forgive, they become motivated to engage in relationship-constructive, rather than
relationship-destructive, actions towards the offender. Forgiveness is influenced
by psychological processes such as empathy for the transgressor, attributions and
appraisals, and rumination about the transgression.

In social systems, forgiveness allows the truster (victim of the violation) to distinguish between intentional and unintentional violations (and a range of infractions
in between), to consider the seriousness of the offence, and to take into account
the dependence on whether this was a 'risk' trust vs. a 'reliance' trust decision
(one might be more forgiving towards someone with whom one had an established
beneficial relationship, than someone who violated in a 'first encounter' situation).
Forgiveness is also known to stimulate voluntary acts of recompense from the
violator.

Consequently, in 'technical' systems, we require a forgiveness framework which
reduces negative predisposition towards offender, and accentuates positive motivations for self-repair. In [20], just such a forgiveness framework was proposed
and developed. Based on a survey of the psychological literature on forgiveness, a
conceptual model was proposed which begins with a negative evaluation, that is then
subject to four positive motivations – empathy, reparation, judgement of offence
and prior beneficial historical relationship – which might reverse an initial negative
reaction into a positive one (see Fig. 7.3).

The four positive motivations for forgiveness were broken down into 11 constituent signals as follows:

- judgement of offence: offence severity, offence frequency, intent;
- reparation: apology, actions of repair;
- beneficial historical relationship: benefits utility, benefits frequency; and
- empathy: visible acknowledgement, prior familiarity, similarity, propensity to
  embarrassment.

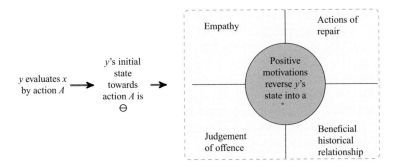

**Fig. 7.3** Conceptual model for forgiveness

This conceptual model was formalised in a computational forgiveness framework as follows. With the exception of 'propensity to embarrassment', each constituent signal, a formula was specified to identify the 'strength' of the signal (see [20] for full details). For example, the signal $j$ for the frequency of a particular offence was computed by:

$$j = \frac{\left(\frac{n_{offence\_kind}}{n_{offences}} + \frac{n_{offences}}{n_{collaborations}}\right)}{2}$$

where $n_{offence\_kind}$ denotes the number of the offender's offences of the current kind, $n_{offences}$ is the offender's total number of offences across time, and $n_{collaborations}$ is the offender's total collaborations within the community. Note that two aspects of frequency are encapsulated in this formula: the frequency of the current offence is computed with the first division and the frequency of the offender's total past offences is computed with the second division. Among other possibilities, this formula intends to capture the instances where an agent has infrequently violated a particular norm but at the same time frequently violates many others, i.e. it is trying to accommodate different aspects of ambiguity in the appreciation of the situation. The same holds for the other signals (note that 'propensity to embarrassment' resisted formulation in this way, although some attempts have been made to define a formal model of 'digital blush', e.g. [21]).

Each constituent signal was then input into a fuzzy inference system (FIS), each of which consisted of rules of the following form:

```
IF severity IS low
AND frequency IS low
AND intent IS high
THEN judgement_of_offence IS 0.4
```

There were four such FIS, one each positive motivation of the conceptual model, which were combined in a fifth FIS to output a final forgiveness decision $d$, as in Fig. 7.4. (Note that the weight of each input to FIS1 is equally divided between the four positive motivations (hence 25 %); furthermore the weight on each signal input

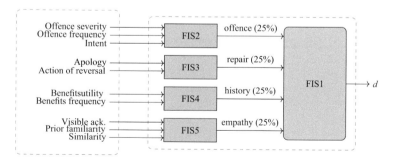

**Fig. 7.4** Fuzzy inference system for computing forgiveness decisions

to FIA2–FIS4 was equal. This was a design decision based on assumption that the import of the ten signals and the four motivations were equally strong. That need not be the case; moreover, a learning agent could quite reasonably modify the weights at runtime according to experience. There is nothing in the framework that dictates these weights should be equal or immutable.)

The computational framework for forgiveness has been used as a decision-support system for unintentional violations in computer-mediated communication (CMC) [22]. This showed that it is possible to enhance CMC interface design with mechanisms to encourage pro-social behaviour (in this case, avatars which exhibited shame or embarrassment at non-compliance), suggesting that it is not simply anonymity that encourages anti-social online behaviour, but the absence of cues that activate self-awareness in a social setting. The framework has also been used in a socio-technical system to improve pro-social behaviour and reduce workplace civility in, for example, open plan offices [23].

One of the other features of forgiveness is that it can even *increase* the strength of a social relationship (in the same way that a broken bone re-knits more strongly).[4] This is because not only can the truster rely on the trustee, but it can also rely on being able to resolve an issue if the trust relationship is misplaced. As a result, qualitative social value can be created, even in an open system, which transcends purely quantitative transactional information. These social values are, in fact, parameters to trust decisions, forgiveness decisions, and so on, and can be formalised as social capital, as discussed in the next section.

## 7.5   Electronic Social Capital

Consider a decentralised community energy system (CES), such as that described in [24], where there are a number of inter-connected 'smarthouses', each with their own renewable energy generation mechanism, but no local storage mechanism, and a number of domestic appliances which need to be operated. When generation and consumption are in balance, all is fine; unfortunately, at some times, if generation exceeds consumption then it needs to be burnt off, which is wasteful and potentially harmful, and at other times, if generation is less than consumption, then the house will experience a blackout.

Therefore, smarthouses aggregate together to form CES. However, these CES require a method of lowering the consumption peaks by flattening the demand, reducing the difference between peaks and troughs in electricity usage by creating a levelled usage pattern that lessens the deviation from the average usage. One way

---

[4]It has been pointed out that previously broken bones also ache in stressful situations, such as cold weather – a reminder of the break. This may be stretching the analogy, but forgiving and somehow not quite forgetting, so that caution could be exercised in important situations, could be a beneficial feature of a future forgiveness framework.

of doing this is to create an 'internal market' in the CES, where the smarthouses trade energy. An alternative way is a self-organising flexible demand system where smarthouses can offer, demand and exchange an amount of electricity for a period of time in an exchange arena.

Such an exchange arena is presented in [25, 26]. In these works, the smarthouses in a CES require resources at specific time-slots, but are allocated, by some pre-defined method some other set of time-slots. However, in the exchange arena, they can exchange these time-slots. The key factor in the exchange is that a successful exchange counts as a *favour*, and that if an exchange makes it better for both smarthouses, that counts as *two* favours. Favours could then be used to gain a preferred allocation, Experiments showed that a CES consisting of 96 'selfish' smarthouses, which only agreed to exchange time-slots if it made its own allocation better (but not otherwise, even if no worse) were outperformed in the long term by a CES consisting of 96 'pro-social' smarthouses, using the favour-based exchange arena.

The favour-based exchange arena demonstrates that in the absence of a centralised controller, command structure, or other form of orchestration, an open system can nevertheless use both mutually-agreed *conventional* rules, and equally intangible mutually-agreed social relations (such as 'owing a favour'), as incentives to participate, contribute, or select an action which serves the collective, rather than individual, utility.

Furthermore, successful trust and forgiveness decisions in a two-party interaction can, as we have seen, also create a positive externality of benefit to third parties. For example, in a producer-consumer market of products or services with $m$ producers and $n$ consumers, it is mutually believed by all $m+n$ participants that there are some norms, and each has the same expectation, that others' behaviour will comply with those norms. As a consequence of a successful interaction between one producer-consumer pair, and of a failed interaction which is subsequently repaired, the belief in and expectations of the norms are reinforced, and so are more useful to other producer-consumer pairs in subsequent transactions.

This is *social capital*, which has been described as "the features of social organisation, such as networks, norms and trust, that facilitate coordination and cooperation for mutual benefit" [27], and more recently as the "attribute of individuals that enhances their ability to solve collective action problems" [28]. In this latter work, Ostrom and Ahn observed that social capital has multiple forms, of which they identified three:

- *'trustworthiness'*, as distinct from trust, and related to reputation, being a shared understanding of someone's willingness to honour agreements and commitments;
- *social networks*, including strong and weak ties, identifying both channels through which people communicate or other social relations; and
- *institutions*, identified as sets of conventional rules by which people voluntarily and mutually agree to regulate their behaviour.

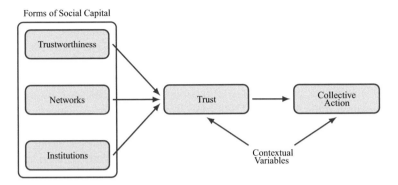

**Fig. 7.5** Ostrom and Ahn's social capital model

They also suggested that *trust* itself was the 'glue' that enabled these various forms of social capital to be leveraged for solving collective action problems (see Fig. 7.5), for example, the sustainability of a common-pool resource. Social capital generates 'reliance' trust, as mentioned earlier, and, where reliance trust can be seen as a complexity-reducing decision-making short-cut which also helps resolve collective action problems.

In the context of this social capital model, it is interesting to consider how to define electronic social capital for open systems, as a conventional incentivisation mechanism for cooperation that creates positive externalities which reinforce the very same incentives. Therefore, in [26], a formal framework was proposed to represent and reason about (an electronic version of) social capital. The framework comprises an observation model in which actions enhance or diminish the different forms of social capital, and a decision-making model which uses the information from the forms of social capital to decide to cooperate or not with another agent.

Figure 7.6 shows a schematic view of the framework. Agents sense from the environment different events that they translate into Social Capital Information. This information is the input of the Social Capital Framework and includes information about when an agent cooperates or not; what messages are sent or received and all the institutional actions such as joining, leaving, sanctioning, etc. The three forms of social capital (Trustworthiness, Networks and Institutions) will store the information received and aggregate it. When the agent needs information about another agent or an institution, it will query the Social Capital Decision Module which will combine all the information from the forms of social capital into a value from zero to one, where zero is *no cooperation* and one is *full cooperation*.

To evaluate the Social Capital Framework we defined a theoretical scenario called Cooperation Game. The Cooperation Game is a strategic game were a population of agents is repeatedly randomly paired to play a game against each other. At every round, each player has a randomly designated opponent and a two-player strategic game to play. Once paired, players must choose either to *Cooperate*, *Defect* or *Refuse to play* (in this scenario, we allow 'sitting out' as an option). Then, the payoff

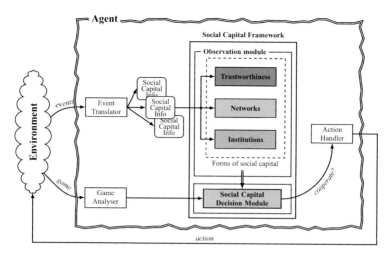

**Fig. 7.6**  Social Capital Framework

matrixes are applied and they receive or lose points depending on what they have played. If one of the players refuses to play, the game is cancelled and agents do not receive or lose any points. A global count of points is kept for all the players and it is used to evaluate their performance over the time.

An experimental testbed has been implemented to evaluate the social capital framework in this scenario, which was used to compare the performance of different types of agents' behaviours in different environments (represented by the games). The experimental results show that the use of social capital incentivises cooperation and enhances collective action: the use of any combination of the three forms of social capital results in higher cooperation amongst agents, outperforming the dominant strategy that would be suggested by a game theoretic analysis.

However, it was also concluded that while social capital is fine as a concept, as a term it is potentially misleading, as it suggests something that can be owned, traded or (even worse) 'spent'. Therefore, to define social capital in terms of concrete attributes runs the risks of commodifying the concept, with the concomitant loss of the actual 'value' or leverage that social capital has or can achieve (cf. [29]). In other words, it is more important not to focus so much on what social capital is, but on what social capital does; and what it does is to coordinate expectations [30] and provide a basis for community governance [31]. Therefore, any framework for electronic social capital which can be used to support successful collective action in self-organising open systems will need not just to define, in computational form, the attributes that agents need to represent and reason with, but also the processes by which those same agents can coordinate their expectations and govern their communities.

Accordingly, in [32], there was further investigation into using alternative economic arrangements for addressing demand-side self-organisation in decentralised community energy systems, generally focusing on relational rather than transactional information, and specifically on a formal representation of electronic social capital rather than market-based approaches, such as auctions.

This work has now developed a new framework for electronic social capital in multi-agent systems, based on this understanding of what social capital does rather than on what social capital is. As stated above, one function it 'does' is to coordinate expectations, so reducing the complexity of decision-making in collective action situations. To examine this proposition, a simulator was developed for an open, self-organising multi-agent system playing the unscrupulous diners' dilemma, an $n$-player game [33].

This simulator was developed using PreSage-2, a large-scale multi-agent platform for simulation and animation [34]. This allows the definition of different types of agent participating in the game: these experiments had three types: random players which arbitrarily chose their action; dominant strategy agents which selected the Nash equilibrium action; and social capital players, which use some form (or forms) of social capital as an input to their decision-making process. The three forms were trustworthiness, social networks, and institutions, and social players could use some combination of all three. Experiments were run with different populations of types of agents, averaging 50 simulation runs per population distribution to average out the effects of randomness and non-linearity in the system. The aim of the experiments was to investigate, *inter alia*, the performance of agents using social capital in a heterogenous population, the effects of scale, and a comparative evaluation of different combinations of social capital.

Full details of the experimental results can be found in [32], but the general observations that follow from these simulations were that the use of social capital in $n$-party collective action situations is:

- optimal in the long-term, as agents using the social capital framework outperform agents using the dominant strategy or other simplistic strategies;
- computable, as all the framework updating mechanisms are 'offline' and the algorithms for computing the social capital metrics are mostly linear (note there is no known polynomial-time algorithm for finding the Nash equilibrium in general $n$-player, $k$-strategy games [35]); and
- scalable, because the complexity of individual social decision-making is independent of the size of the collective population.

The significance of this work is that it shows, as with trust, forgiveness (both as above), and with models of Elinor Ostrom's institutional design principles for self-organising common-pool resource management [36], how formal representations of social concepts and processes could be used to regulate interactions between autonomous agents in a relational economy based on reciprocity (rather than a purely transactional one based on prices), which is also computable and scalable. This has positive implications for self-organisation in large-scale collective action situations, precisely those encountered in the decentralised community energy systems with which we began this section.

## 7.6 Computational Justice

So far, we have considered the formalisation of social concepts, processes and relations that are directly related to individual decision making (trust and forgiveness) or to creating positive externalities which are of benefit to individuals within a community setting. In this section we will consider the formalisation of a social concept which aims to formalise an abstract social concept that relates to the well-being of the collective itself. This concept is *justice*.

Consider again an open system in which there is co-dependence, i.e. a mutual reliance between components. Very often, this reliance stems from the need for *sharing* or *pooling* of resources. For example in a sensor network there are several common-pool resources (e.g. battery power, CPU time, bandwidth, memory, etc.) which need to be allocated and which, even under normal load conditions, could become scarce (i.e. enough resources for some; insufficient resources for all). Precisely the same issues arise in cloud computing, grid computing, vehicular networks, virtual organisations and reconfigurable manufacturing; indeed all the different types of open system application that were considered in Sect. 7.2.

Managing and distributing common-pool resources, particularly under conditions of scarcity, has been a continuous or recurring social problem for thousands of years. The issue of sustainable common-pool resource management has been studied from the perspectives of economic and political science by Elinor Ostrom, whose pioneering (and Nobel Prize-winning) work specified eight institutional design principles for sustainable common-pool resource management based on the self-organisation of conventional rules [37]. Recent work has shown how these principles can be given an axiomatic specification in computational logic – which is in turn executable [36], providing the foundations for a new type of *self-organising rule-oriented system* (SOROS).

In general, given a set of components needing to share resources, an allocation scheme which maps resources to those components, and a set of rules for determining that allocation scheme, some natural questions arise: Is this allocation fair? Is the allocation method effective? Is it efficient? Are the decision makers accountable? To what extent did those affected by the rules participate in their selection? Was any punishment for non-compliance with the rules proportional to the severity of the offence? Such questions have been the subject of much inter-disciplinary research, including computational social choice [38], multi-agent systems [39] and communications [40], as well as studies in law, health, politics and organisational psychology [41], but these remain open questions.

Some insight into a general solution can be derived from an analysis of the key features of resource allocation in open systems. These are:

- Self-determination: the rules for resource allocation, and indeed the rules for choosing them, are determined by the entities themselves, i.e. those who are affected by the rules participate in the formation, selection and modification;
- Expectation of error: as before behaviour contrary to a mutually-agreed specification should be expected, be it by accident, necessity or malice; in addition,

there must be provision for monitoring to detect non-compliant behaviour, and
for the non-repudiable enforcement of sanctions for non-compliance should be
implemented;

- Economy of scarcity: there may be sufficient resources to keep all the components 'satisfied' in the long term, even if there are insufficient resources to
  keep all the components 'optimised' in the short term; in economic terms, the
  components are satisfiers (content is good enough) rather than optimisers (only
  interested in content with maximal utility);
- Endogenous resources: all the resources are generated from within the system, so
  that computing the allocation, and associated tasks like monitoring, sanctioning
  etc. must be 'paid for' from the same resources to be allocated; and
- No full disclosure: as before, components are autonomous, heterogeneous and
  their internal states cannot be checked, only their observable actions; but the
  range of actions does include communication with each other.

In [42], it is argued that answers to these questions can be uniformly found in
the formal characterisation of different aspects of **justice**, and that these different
aspects need a principled operationalisation as policies for system management. The
different aspects of justice that are proposed include:

- **Natural** justice: do agents participate in the decision-making affecting them?
- **Distributive** justice: how to distribute resources fairly?
- **Retributive** justice: how to punish non-compliant behaviour, proportionately?
- **Procedural** justice: is a procedure fit-for-purpose? Is it engaging/open/efficient?
- **Interactional** justice: subjectively, how fair do the components themselves
  consider their treatment to be, by the rules and the decision makers?

For example, Elinor Ostrom's research, introduced previously, provides an
explanation of how people can resolve the problem of sustainable common-pool
resource management by the formation of self-governing institutions [37]. Ostrom's
institutional design principles can be specified and operationalised by axiomatising
the design principles in computational logic which in turn provides an executable
specification for algorithmic self-governance [36]. One of these principles is
effectively that of self-determination, that those affected by a set of mutually-agreed,
conventional rules get to participate in their formation, selection and modification,
so this axiomatisation directly contains an element of natural justice.

This approach has been extended in [43] to incorporate a theory of distributive
justice based on legitimate claims due to Rescher [44]. Rescher observed that
distributive justice had been held, by various sources, to consist of treating people
wholly or primarily according to one of seven canons (established principles
expressed in English), these being the canons of equality, need, ability, effort, productivity, social utility and supply-and-demand. However, each canon has different
properties and qualities, satisfying different (and possibly inconsistent) notions of
utility, fairness, equity, proportionality, envy-freeness, efficiency, timeliness, etc.

Rescher's analysis showed that each canon, taken in isolation, was inadequate
as the sole dispensary of distributive justice. He proposed instead that distributive

justice could be represented by the canon of claims, which consists of treating people according to their legitimate claims, both positive and negative. Then the issue of "which is the preferred canon of distributive justice" can be displaced by questions of: what are the legitimate claims in a specific context, how can plurality be accommodated, and how can conflicts be reconciled.

These were the questions addressed in [43], who showed that agents participating in an open provision and appropriation system, who could self-organise the legitimate claims, could, even under an economy of scarcity, achieve a fair resource allocation (as measured by the Gini index) in the long term, even if none of the individual allocations were at all fair, using the same fairness metric. The allocation was also fairer than alternative allocation schemes based on random assignment, rationing or strict queuing. Thus distributive justice was effectively axiomatised as an intrinsic fairness property of the SOROS.

Another one of Ostrom's principles was concerned with the congruence of the provision and appropriation rules and the state of the prevailing environment. However, there are numerous difficulties with assessing that congruence, even as a binary measure, let alone a degree of congruence (which would offer some assurance that a change from one configuration of the rules to another would be an improvement). In [41], it was proposed to equate congruence with *fitness for purpose*, and measure fitness for purpose using a computational framework for procedural justice.

Taking ideas from law, public health and organisational psychology, fitness for purpose was evaluated according to three principles, and each principle was computed according to a set of metrics. The three principles, and the metrics used to compute a value for each were:

- Participation principle: purposeful activities in which agents take part in relation to governance (not just voting). Metrics included:

  - *Empowerment*: what is the distribution of (institutionalised) power within the institution?
  - *Inclusivity*: how many of the agents affected by the rule have a saying on how to choose it?
  - *Representation*: are the decisions made solely by agents affected by the rule, or is there any external influence?
  - *Decision frequency*: how often a decision about the rule is made, in relationship to its application frequency?

- Transparency principle: the amenability of procedures to be subject of investigation and analysis to establish facts of interest (e.g. who is making the decisions? Do they benefit disproportionately? Are they accountable? Can their decisions be reviewed?) Metrics included:

  - *Justifiability*: is membership of decision-making bodies disclosed, are their procedures available, and are their workings revealed?
  - *Accountability*: do those who make the decisions benefit equally (rather than excessively) from the outcomes, and are they liable if they go wrong?

- *Equal Suffrage*: to what extent is the principle of 'one agent, one vote' upheld, or do some agents have multiple votes?
- *Temporality*: are decisions appealable, and are they repealable?

• Balancing principle: determining the proportionality of relative benefits and burdens. Metrics included:

- *Cost*: what is the cost (in whatever 'currency', which could be time) of operating a procedure?
- *Accuracy*: does the procedure ensure the correct outcome [45]?
- *Consistency*: does a procedure produce equal outcomes for different individuals under the same circumstances?

The relationship between different aspects of justice and the key features of resource allocation is illustrated in Fig. 7.7. For example, to address the feature of self-determination, we need to ensure participation, inclusivity and consultation (e.g. through voting), which are all elements of natural justice. Similarly, to deal with the range of different types of error and the enforcement of punishments for them, we need a system of graduated sanctions (typically proportional to the severity of the offence), and a system of dispute resolution (e.g. for appeals against punishments): these are all features of retributive justice. Insufficiency of resources and the requirement of 'fair' allocation mechanisms are issues for distributive justice. In systems with endogenous resources, where applying the rules of natural, distributive and retributive justice have to be 'paid for' from the very resources that are to be distributed, the issue of efficiency comes to the fore (amongst other issues, for example, the participation, transparency and balancing principles discussed above), and is a concern for procedural justice. Finally, where the 'internals' of

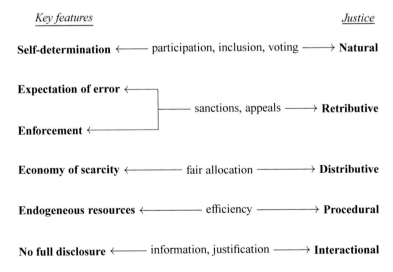

**Fig. 7.7** Computational justice and the key features of resource allocation in open systems

decision-making (of individuals, or committees) cannot be inspected, then it is possible to aggregate subjective self-assessments of fairness or treatment into a collective assessment; this is a matter for interactional justice.

However, the relationships depicted in Fig. 7.7 are, as yet, incomplete, although see [42] for more details. We have described here some initial works on formalising natural, distributive and procedural justice, while the formalisation of retributive and interactional justice is currently ongoing research.

## 7.7   Summary and Conclusions

In this chapter, we have reviewed three computational frameworks for decision-making in open systems. These frameworks were based on trust, forgiveness and social capital; and each was derived from a formalisation of a theory from, respectively, cognitive science, psychology and socio-economics, using the methodology of sociologically-inspired computing. The computational frameworks were shown to support bipartite decisions concerning reliance on a second party (trust), an autonomic mechanism for restoring social relations in the event of a trust breakdown, and to support collective action through the creation of positive externalities in the form of social capital. These computational frameworks can, we believe, be used by autonomous components to interoperate in open systems which are significantly more trustworthy, reliable, and robust compared to alternative approaches.

From the foundations provided by these three frameworks, we then offered some contributory ideas to a new programme of research on *computational justice*, which lies at the intersection of Computer Science and Economics, Philosophy, Psychology and Jurisprudence. As exemplified in Fig. 7.7, it encompasses the study of formal and/or computational models of judicial processes and systems and the formal representation, organisation and administration of rules or policies. Effectively, and ambitiously, we are trying to apply the methodology of sociologically-inspired computing to the concept of justice. This is accomplished by importing concepts from the Social Sciences into computing applications, but interesting outcomes can be expected when these ideas are exported back into the social systems that originally inspired them. For example, the role of electronic social capital and its relation to cryptocurrencies, in the creation of values, incentives and alternative market arrangements based on relational rather transactional arrangements, needs to be fully explored in the development of a new generation of complex, adaptive, collective socio-technical systems, such as those to be found in smart grids [46].

Therefore, the programme for computational justice ensures that the specification of conventional rules for an open system provides the basis for algorithmic self-governance which embodies such values as sustainability, inclusivity, and fairness and democratic indices. As a corollary, we would additionally contend that self-organising rule-oriented systems (SOROS) have the potential to support the design and (autonomous) operation of not just open distributed systems, but also computer-mediated socio-technical systems, which also take into account these qualitative social values – in other words, it is the basis of value-sensitive design [47] for socio-technical systems.

At the core of this research programme is the intention to support the design, development and deployment of self-organising socio-technical systems to create digital communities for computer-supported collective action. This may be for the specific objective of avoiding a problem, such as depletion or exploitation of a resource such as water, energy (for example, in a community energy system [24]), or knowledge commons [48]; hyper-localised solutions to problems of incivility in sharing a communal living space [23]; or synchronised behaviour to incentivise individual benefits, e.g. participatory sensing, fitness activities, etc.

Underpinning all of these applications, is the both the implicit and explicit concern for *values*. For example, in resource management, there is an explicit concern for sustainability of the common-pool resource, but also an implicit concern for the 'fairness' in the distribution of the resources. Therefore, applying the methodology of value-sensitive design (VSD), which effectively puts values (rather than functionality or usability) as the primary design focus, to the development of such socio-technical systems, is a proposition that warrants further consideration in future research.

**Acknowledgements** The work reported in this chapter is the product of numerous collaborations dating back more than ten years. Much of work on open systems in general and agent societies has been done with Alexander Artikis, and the methodology reported in Sect. 7.2 is joint work with Andrew Jones and Alexander Artikis. The work on the computational trust framework is joint with Brendan Neville; the work on the computational forgiveness framework is joint with Mina Vasalou; and the work on the computational social capital framework is joint with Patricio Petruzzi. The research programme on computational justice was initiated with Dídac Busquets and Régis Riveret. Needless to say, I am duly grateful for these valuable collaborations.

This chapter has benefitted greatly from the careful reading and the very helpful comments of the three anonymous reviewers, and many thanks for these encouraging remarks. The editors have been correspondingly helpful in the preparation and production of this chapter, for which again many thanks.

The work reported here has been supported by a number of European and UK projects, including ALFEBIITE (EU FET IST-1999-10298), HUMAiNE (EU NoE IST-2002-507422), Marie Curie Intra-European Fellowships ITS4SIT (FP7 274057) and NORMS4SRA (FP7 331472), and APS (EPSRC Autonomic Power System Grand Challenge I031650).

# References

1. Pitt, J., Artikis, A.: The open agent society: retrospective and prospective views. Artif. Intell. Law **23**, 241–270 (2015)
2. Sterritt, R., Parashar, M., Tianfield, H., Unland, R.: A concise introduction to autonomic computing. Adv. Eng. Inform. **19**, 181–187 (2005)
3. Müller-Schloer, C., Schmeck, H., Ungerer, T. (eds.): Organic Computing—A Paradigm Shift for Complex Systems. Springer, Birkhäuser Basel (2011)
4. Hewitt, C.: Offices are open systems. ACM Trans. Inf. Syst. **4**, 271–287 (1986)
5. Kowalski, R.: Logic-based open systems. In: Representation and Reasoning, pp. 125–134. www.doc.ic.ac.uk/~rak/papers/open.pdf (1988)

6. Steels, L., Brooks, R.: The Artificial Life Route to Artificial Intelligence: Building Situated Embodied Agents. Lawrence Erlbaum Ass, New Haven (1994)
7. Edmonds, B., Gilbert, N., Gustafson, S., Hales, D., Krasnogor, N. (eds.): Socially inspired computing. In: Proceedings of the Joint Symposium on Socially Inspired Computing (AISB), Hatfield (2005)
8. Andrews, P., Polack, F., Sampson, A., Stepney, S., Timmis, J.: The CoSMoS process, version 0.1: a process for the modelling and simulation of complex systems. Technical Report YCS-2010-453. University of York (2010)
9. Jones, A., Artikis, A., Pitt, J.: The design of intelligent socio-technical systems. Artif. Intell. Rev. **39**, 5–20 (2013)
10. Cho, J.-H., Swami, A., Chen, I.-R.: A survey on trust management for mobile ad hoc networks. IEEE Commun. Surv. Tutor. **13**, 562–583 (2010)
11. Easwaran, A., Pitt, J.: Supply chain formation in open, market-based multi-agent systems. Int. J. Comput. Intell. Appl. **2**, 349–363 (2002)
12. Klejnowski, L., Niemann, S., Bernard, Y., Müller-Schloer, C.: Using trusted communities to improve the speedup of agents in a desktop grid system. In: Proceedings 7th International Symposium on Intelligent Distributed Computing (IDC), pp. 189–198. Springer, Cham (2013)
13. Weisberg, H.: Willful Ignorance. Wiley, Hoboken (2014)
14. Neville, B., Pitt, J.: A computational framework for social agents in agent mediated e-commerce. In: Omicini, A., Petta, P., Pitt, J. (eds.) Engineering Societies in the Agents World (ESAW) IV, pp. 376–391. Springer, Berlin/New York (2003)
15. Falcone, R., Castelfranchi, C.: Social trust: a cognitive approach. In: Trust and Deception in Virtual Societies, pp. 55–90. Kluwer Academic, Dordrecht/Boston (2000)
16. Neville, B., Pitt, J.: A simulation study of social agents in agent mediated e-commerce. In: Falcone, R. (ed.) AAMAS Trust Workshop, pp. 83–91. www.doc.ic.ac.uk/~rak/papers/open.pdf (2004)
17. Pinyol, I., Sabater-Mir, J.: Computational trust and reputation models for open multi-agent systems: a review. English. Artif. Intell. Rev. **40**, 1–25 (2013). ISSN:0269-2821
18. Jones, A.: On the concept of trust. Decis. Support Syst. **33**, 225–232 (2002)
19. McCullough, M.E.: Forgiveness: who does it and how do they do it? Curr. Dir. Psychol. Sci. **10**, 194–197 (2001). ISSN:0963-7214
20. Vasalou, A., Pitt, J., Piolle, G.: From theory to practice: forgiveness as a mechanism to repair conflicts in CMC. In: Proceedings iTrust IV. Lecture Notes in Computer Science, vol. 3986, pp. 397–411. Springer, Cham (2006)
21. Pitt, J.V.: Digital blush: towards shame and embarrassment in multi-agent information trading applications. Cognit. Technol. Work **6**, 23–36 (2004)
22. Vasalou, A., Hopfensitz, A., Pitt, J.: In praise of forgiveness: ways for repairing trust breakdowns in one-off online interactions. Int. J. Hum.-Comput. Stud. **66**, 466–480 (2008)
23. Santos, M., Pitt, J.: Emotions and norms in shared spaces. In: Balke, T., Dignum, F., van Riemsdijk, M.B., Chopra, A. (eds.) COIN, vol. 8386, pp. 157–176. Springer, Cham/Heidelberg/New York/Dordrecht/London (2013)
24. Pitt, J., Busquets, D., Bourazeri, A., Petruzzi, P.: Collective intelligence and algorithmic governance of socio-technical systems. In: Miorandi, D., Maltese, V., Rovatsos, M., Nijholt, A., Stewart, J. (eds.) Social Collective Intelligence, pp. 31–50. Springer, Cham (2014)
25. Petruzzi, P., Busquets, D., Pitt, J.: Self organising flexible demand for smart grid. In: 7th IEEE International Conference on Self-Adaptive and Self-Organizing Systems (SASO) Workshops, pp. 21–22. IEEE (2013)
26. Petruzzi, P., Busquets, D., Pitt, J.: Social capital as a complexity reduction mechanism for decision making in large scale open systems. In: 8th IEEE International Conference on Self-Adaptive and Self-Organizing Systems (SASO), pp. 145–150. IEEE (2014)
27. Putnam, R.D.: The prosperous community: social capital and public life. Am. Prospect **13**, 35–42 (1993)
28. Ostrom, E., Ahn, T.: Foundations of Social Capital. Edward Elgar Pub., Cheltenham (2003)

29. Pitt, J., Nowak, A.: The reinvention of social capital for socio-technical systems. IEEE Technol. Soc. Mag. **33**, 27–33 (2014)
30. Peyton Young, H.: Social norms. In: Durlauf, S., Blume, L. (eds.) The New Palgrave Dictionary of Economics, 2nd edn. Palgrave Macmillan, New York (2008)
31. Bowles, S., Gintis, H.: Social capital and community governance. Econ. J. **112**, F419–F436 (2002)
32. Petruzzi, P., Busquets, D., Pitt, J.: A generic social capital framework for optimising self-organised collective action. In: 9th IEEE International Conference on Self-Adaptive and Self-Organizing Systems (SASO). IEEE (2015)
33. Glance, N.S., Huberman, B.A.: The dynamics of social dilemmas. Sci. Am. **270**, 76–81 (1994)
34. Macbeth, S., Busquets, D., Pitt, J.: Principled operationalization of social systems using Presage-2. In: Gianni, D., D'Ambrogio, A., Tolk, A. (eds.) Modeling and Simulation-Based Systems Engineering Handbook, pp. 43–66. CRC Press, Boca Raton (2014)
35. Papadimitriou, C.H., Roughgarden, T.: Computing equilibria in multi-player games. In: Proceedings 16th Annual ACM-SIAM Symposium on Discrete Algorithms (SODA), pp. 82–91 (2005)
36. Pitt, J., Schaumeier, J., Artikis, A.: Axiomatization of socio-economic principles for self-organizing institutions: concepts, experiments and challenges. Trans. Auton. Adapt. Syst. **7**, 39 (2012)
37. Ostrom, E.: Governing the Commons: The Evolution of Institutions for Collective Action. Cambridge University Press, Cambridge, UK (1990)
38. Chevaleyre, Y., Endriss, U., Lang, J., Maudet, N.: A short introduction to computational social choice. In: Proceedings of the 33rd Conference on Current Trends in Theory and Practice of Computer Science (SOFSEM), pp. 51–69. SpringerVerlag, Berlin/Heidelberg (2007)
39. Jong, S., Tuyls, K.: Human-inspired computational fairness. Auton. Agents Multi-Agent Syst. **22**, 103–126 (2011). ISSN:1387-2532
40. Lan, T., Kao, D., Chiang, M., Sabharwal, A.: An axiomatic theory of fairness in network resource allocation. In: INFOCOM, pp. 1343–1351 (2010)
41. Pitt, J., Busquets, D., Riveret, R.: Procedural justice and 'Fitness for Purpose' of self-organising electronic institutions. In: PRIMA. Lecture Notes in Computer Science, vol. 8291, pp. 260–275. Springer, Cham (2013)
42. Pitt, J., Busquets, D., Riveret, R.: The pursuit of computational justice in open systems. English. AI Soc. **30**, 359–378 (2013). ISSN:0951–5666
43. Pitt, J., Busquets, D., Macbeth, S.: Distributive justice for self-organised common-pool resource management. ACM Trans. Auton. Adapt. Syst. **9**, 14:1–14:39 (2014)
44. Rescher, N.: Distributive Justice. Bobbs-Merrill, Indianapolis (1966)
45. Rawls, J.: A Theory of Justice. Harvard University Press, Harvard (1971)
46. Pitt, J., Diaconescu, A.: Structure and governance of communities for the digital society. In: 2015 IEEE International Conference on Autonomic Computing (ICAC), pp. 279–284. IEEE, Piscataway (2015)
47. Friedman, B., Kahn Jr., P., Borning, A., Kahn, P.: Value sensitive design and information systems. In: Human-Computer Interaction and Management Information Systems: Foundations, pp. 348–372. ME Sharpe, Armonk (2006)
48. Macbeth, S., Pitt, J.: Self-organising management of user-generated data and knowledge. Knowl. Eng. Rev. **FirstView**, 1–28 (2014)

# Chapter 8
# Trust & Self-Organising Socio-technical Systems

**Cristiano Castelfranchi and Rino Falcone**

**Abstract** We present our theory on trust and its components and dimensions, and apply it to trust in complex dynamic socio-technical systems and to their self-organising emergent results. Specifically, we apply our theory to ICT-based systems, where a "Social Order" is no longer fully "spontaneous" due to the invisible hand impinging on individual and selfish-decisions. In such contexts, a social order is rather based on programmed interactions, algorithmic procedures and big data. Since trust cannot be fully programmable and predictable, how can we build it in this complex and dynamic system? Some of our research questions sound: is it necessary that folks "understand" the underlying mechanisms they are relying on? What kind of information about forecasts or future projections should be provided and adjusted? What kind of role do simulation, serious games play on learning to understand and expect? Will there be algorithms working on the micro-processes and producing the emergent organisation, and if yes, how effective and reliable will they be? There are at least two different levels of trust in complex systems and in their functioning processes: trust in the emergent order and trust in the micro-layer rules. Are the systems rules and resulting equilibriums fair, equity inspired, in relation to the interests of the involved groups/subjects? A complex and cognitive model of trust is needed for this analysis.

**Keywords** Trust modelling • Trust dimensions • Hybrid systems • Spontaneous order • Self-organisation

## 8.1 Premise

We will present some of the main features of our socio-cognitive theory of trust and its components (expectations, evaluations, desires, perceived risks) and bases, and apply this model to trust in complex dynamic socio-technical systems and to their self-organising emergent results. The aim is to discuss how we can build trust in

C. Castelfranchi (✉) • R. Falcone
Institute for Cognitive Sciences and Technologies, National Research Council, via San Martino della Battaglia 44, Roma, Italy
e-mail: cristiano.castelfranchi@istc.cnr.it; rino.falcone@istc.cnr.it

© Springer International Publishing Switzerland 2016                               209
W. Reif et al. (eds.), *Trustworthy Open Self-Organising Systems*,
Autonomic Systems, DOI 10.1007/978-3-319-29201-4_8

ICT-based socio-technical systems, in particular in self-organising hybrid systems, where the "Social Order" (Hayek) is no longer fully "spontaneous", but it is rather based on programmed interactions, algorithmic procedures, and big data [1, 2].

### 8.1.1  Two Challenges

(A) Any new technology we create or introduce in work or society actually is not just technology but it is a whole new Socio-Technical System. Sometimes this facet is not explicit enough.[1]

"Socio-Technical System" means that any new technology implies, requires, or introduces not only new skills and competencies, but also new representations, expectations, goals and beliefs. It also implies or introduces new scripts, with their roles and norms; new forms of interaction and conventions among the social actors, and new relations among people or between people and the artificial system, imposed or allowed by that specific technology [9]. We must hence specify the "cognitive" and interactive side of the new system [5]. This sounds like a challenge in the current computational and network revolution: we are indeed building a New Kind of Society, which is trans-local, connected, participatory; but also hybrid (human and artificial intelligences interact with each other) and mirror (a mix of virtual and physical world and actions).

(B) Moreover, this new complex Socio-Technical (and mental) System is not just planned and designed. It is a complex, dynamic system, with 'emergence' and 'self-organisation' producing a "spontaneous" Social Order (von Hayek). Its dynamic equilibrium is not necessarily good for all the actors [10].

### 8.1.2  Human Centred Systems and Trust

The kinds of systems we have introduced so far should be designed in a human centred and user-friendly way. In order to go towards this direction:

(a) machines should understand and incorporate human social interaction and organisation to support them and mediate;
(b) machines (i.e. agents) should emulate human social interaction and organisation for good multi-agent or hybrid interactions, organisations, and so forth. These

---

[1]Consider for example the excellent definition of "Organic Computing System" in Müller-Schloer's document on "Organic Computing Initiative" (2004): an "Organic Computing system is a technical system which adapts dynamically to the current conditions of its environment. It is self-organising, self-configuring, self-optimising, self-healing, self-protecting, self-explaining, and context-aware". See also [3–8].

emulations should include interpersonal aspects (e.g. trust and reputation), conventional and normative aspects and institutional aspects (e.g. roles).

Even though these propositions incorporate the main reasons of the new growing AI paradigm (that has to say, Artificial Social Intelligence), (a) and (b) are not sufficient for our crucial challenge, which is focused on how to build users' trust in those systems and in the Cyber-Society, specifically:

– trust among people or organisations mediated by the technology;
– trust towards the tools and the infrastructure itself.

We do definitely agree with the central claim of the Call for paper of the "Trustworthy Self-Organising Systems" WS (Budapest, 2010): "The nature of self-organising systems demands that issues of trust and its different facets become a primary concern."[2]

Substituting trust with other concepts and mechanisms in the cooperative framework (e.g. short-cuts, tricks, and ad hoc solutions) sounds to us like a wrong move, as well as identifying it with simplified, but reductive 'measures' like probability or uncertainty. Trust is frequently modelled as a simple index, a number, a dimension, a mere subjective probability. In our view [11, 12], though, trust is not just an evaluation of the probability of a desirable result, or a perceived (un-)certainty. Trust is a complex cognitive attitude and representation, which cannot be simplified in such terms. It is an expectation about a specific outcome, and more specifically it is the combination of a belief about the future and of a goal (i.e. a desire or a need). It is also understood as the possible decision to rely on a certain result and on the 'agent' or process Y that should produce it. It can be seen as the evaluation of Y's features and qualities such that one can count-on Y. In our view, it also deals with the acceptance and exposure to risks. Trust is based on information, beliefs, and evidences, and it is not simply a matter of 'faith'. On the other hand, mistrust is not simply a low level of trust: it is rather a negative evaluation and a bad expectation. Trust is also context dependent and dynamic. Therefore, we need to ask ourselves what are the main bases and origin of trust evaluations and decisions, as well as what are the main trust dynamic processes. Moreover: what are the relations between trust in Y and trust in the context and in the circumstances? Or between trust and control (e.g. of Y's behaviour)? What connects the different aspects of 'uncertainty' and trust? This kind of questions goes mainly unanswered and probably unasked in the current research. However, if trust is deeply analysed and understood within the

---

[2]We also agree with the main claims there: [what matters is] "the human as the user of self-organising and self-adaptive systems and the usability of such systems"; "Functional correctness, security, safety, and reliability are facets that have to be ensured for the system's components as well as for the system as a whole. The classical notions of trust and reputation in MAS also apply to this relationship between system components. The relationship between the system and the user is influenced by the transparency and consistency of the system towards the user and most importantly by its usability, i.e. the way the user is informed about self-organising processes and is allowed to interact with the system.". However, we see additional problems in this, like the participatory and hybrid nature of the system, or the hidden interests of the "spontaneous" order.

various and disconnected disciplines, what kind of framework shall we adopt? May we just import models and theories from sociology, economics, psychology, etc. without trying to unify them and without considering the new original domain in which we should embed a comprehensive model of trust?

As we mentioned, trust has different facets and components and one has to model many of them, with their specific principles dynamics and metrics. In particular, trust is not reducible to functional correctness, safety and security (which is crucial in contexts that contemplate artefacts and tools) and to reputation, and privacy.

Perceived trustworthiness (see Sect. 8.2(a)) and the perception of the system as a whole do also matter in defining trust. We would also like to highlight that "the relationship between the system and the user is influenced by the transparency and consistency of the system towards the users [. . . ] and by its usability". With this statement, several new problems arise, especially concerned with how to manage the users' perception of risks or of uncertainty. One of the mission of the systems should be that of providing new scenarios to people, new scripts and new social norms. These latter should not be aimed to merely simplify people's reasoning, information search, decisions, and behaviours, but they should also give them reliance on the others, coordination, and reduction of uncertainty in certain social domains. Even in self-organising dynamic systems we have to perceive and presuppose a natural 'suspension' of uncertainty and the assumption of normality [13]. Consider that trust is instrumental only in principle (and in its function). It is actually an end itself, it is a human need: the need to have trustworthy relations and environments, regardless of their use and exploitation (e.g. receiving help, support, and exchanges). It is a need for feelings of safety and possibility.[3]

Having this said, how shall we give transparency and right expectations, and how shall we correct wrong expectations? How can possible failures be explained, or accounted for?

"Visualization of self-organisation process" (cited Budapest Call) is a good idea in our view. Although, we claim that simulation, experiments, predictions and serious games could also be exploited. Let us now be more specific on what we mean by trust towards technology.

## 8.2   Trust & Technology

Trust is not just a social attitude towards humans. It can also be applied to tools, technologies and functional objects. It is not intended or felt towards these objects' designers or producers, but rather towards the working devices themselves [11, 14]. This also applies to multi-agent complex dynamics and results, like traffic in a given city, or performances on the markets. As for ICT and its systems, trust is frequently

---

[3]Consider the celebrated sentence of Epicurus: "It is not our friends' help that helps us, it is the confidence of their help."

and wrongly identified with – or reduced to – a problem of security, whereas security issues are just one of trust's components (see Sect. 8.2(i)). There is also a point of view coming from sociology (ex. [15]) and economics (ex. [16]), which conceives trust as necessarily mutual and respondent. In our model though, trust is not only interpersonal and it is not only addressed towards other persons. It can also be felt, intended or addressed towards a certain process or mechanism (e.g. I can trust a given drug or not), and towards a specific technology. In this sense, trust also includes beliefs and expectations regarding the effectiveness of a specific object or device. For example, they can be thoughts on how reliable it is, or on how accessible and friendly it feels. The opposite (but complementary) side of trust, in this sense, deals with the perceived risk and the perceived unreliability or unmanageability of technology. We may not only trust technology, but also a lot of abstract and non-personal entities, like categories of people, institutions, organisations, rules, roles, etc. [11, 17, 18].

Trust in computers and in networks is just the final evolution of the process of abstraction and depersonalization of trust that characterizes modernity [19]. Concerns on trustworthy systems in the current literature are higher than those regarding trust. We would like to stress the fact that these are indeed two different concepts, which share a non-trivial and bidirectional relationship:

(a)  on the one hand, what matters in social systems and in socio-technical systems is not just trustworthiness (henceforth: TW), but also perceived TW. Objective TW is not enough for organisation interaction, political systems, and even for the market (that's why we have marketing). Moreover, objective TW is not sufficient to create perceived TW; in fact, we can perceive TW – then have trust – even when TW is not there (e.g. credit cards, WEB, etc.).

(b)  On the other hand, the members or users' trust in the system is a crucial component of its TW and of its correct functioning. This is especially true for hybrid systems where the global result is due to the information processing and the actions of both humans and AI systems. However, we still need a correct dialectic between the emergence (e.g. of a self-organising TW infrastructure, rules, conventions and scripts) and the immergence of cognitive mediators of trust and TW in the agents' minds. Trust is the immergent needed result of the TW system, and a condition for its emergence.

There are four different (but not independent) possible perspectives on this:

(i)  A trustworthy technology that deserves and elicits trust dispositions. In this sense, trust is not merely a matter of security, as engineers currently believe: it is rather a mental model of what is happening, of dependability, emotion, personalization, transparency, and participation.

(ii)  A technology (e.g. agents), which can co-construct social trust relationships with the users, as well as confidence, social bonds, and empathy.

(iii)  A technology that is capable to support social trust relations in communities and social networks, and to create new trust dimensions among humans (e.g. institutions).

(iv) A technology that elicits trust dispositions both at the micro-level and at the macro-level; this aspect is particularly important for the self-organising, emergent result, that nobody can directly decide about (see Sect. 8.4).

## 8.2.1  Trust, Security and Safety

A conceptualization of trust and how trust can be used in artificial societies is a different subject of study from the techniques applied to secure network protocols and cryptography. Security techniques can guarantee identification of individuals and privacy of transmission, but they cannot guarantee that an interaction partner has the competence he/she claims, or that he/she is honest about his/her intentions. Security can be useful in the case of intrusiveness identification, which is a crucial aspect of trust [20]. However, security is just one of the many components of trust, like perception of dangers and risks. Trust must give us tools for acting in a world that continues to be insecure in principle: it has to provide us the means to act efficaciously when we have to rely on someone in risky situations. Trust can be seen as an open system where new possible partnerships can arise; and at the same time, it is a complex system with non-linear and non-local effects. We cannot reduce trust to safety and security,[4] since:

> on the one hand, what matters is 'perceived' safety, and,
> on the other hand, building a trustful environment and atmosphere and trustworthy agents is one of the bases for safety, and vice versa. Perceived unreliability elicits cheating and bad actions, whereas collective distrust creates dangers (e.g. panic).

## 8.3  A Socio-cognitive Model of Trust

The Socio-Cognitive model of trust is based on a portrait of the mental state of trust in cognitive terms (i.e. beliefs, goals). This is not a complete account of the psychological dimensions of trust, but it represents the most explicit, reason-based, and conscious form. We will not consider the more implicit forms of trust (e.g. trust by default, not based upon explicit evaluations and beliefs, or derived from previous experience or other sources) or the affective dimensions of trust, which are not based on explicit evaluations, but on emotional responses and on an intuitive, unconscious appraisal.

The word "trust" means different things, which are all systematically related to each other. In particular, three crucial concepts have been recognized and

---

[4]To see how strong such identification was, see for example [21]; the review of "Trust on the Internet", a book on Internet security, which focuses solely on the topic of security.

distinguished, not only in natural language, but also in the scientific literature. Trust is:

- a mere mental attitude (prediction and evaluation) towards another agent, or we may say "a simple disposition";
- a decision to rely upon the other (i.e. an intention to delegate and trust, which makes the trustor vulnerable in some way);
- a behaviour (i.e. the intentional act of trusting, and the consequent relation between the trustor and the trustee).

In each of the above concepts, different sets of cognitive ingredients are involved in the trustor's mind. The model is based on the BDI (Belief-desire-intention) approach for mind modelling that is inspired to Bratman's philosophical model. In this trust model only an agent endowed with both goals and beliefs can trust another agent. Let us consider the trust of an agent X towards another agent Y about the (Y's) behaviour/action $\alpha$ relevant for the result (goal) g when:

> X is the (relying) agent, who feels trust; it is a cognitive agent endowed with internal explicit goals and beliefs (the trustor);
> Y is the agent or entity which is trusted (the trustee);
> X trusts Y about g/$\alpha$ and for g/$\alpha$.

In this model, Y is not necessarily a cognitive agent (e.g. an agent can – or cannot – trust that a chair will sustain his weight when he/she is seated on it). On the contrary, X must always be a cognitive agent: so, in the case of artificial agents, we should be able to simulate these internal explicit goals and beliefs. For all the three notions of trust above defined (trust disposition, decision to trust, and trusting behaviour) we claim that someone trusts someone else only with regards to some specific goal (i.e. the general, basic teleonomic notion, that's to say any motivational representation in the agent: desires, motives, will, needs, objectives, duties, utopias, are kinds of goals). An unconcerned agent does not really "trust": he/she just has opinions and forecasts. Moreover, trust itself consists of beliefs. Since Y's action is useful to X (i.e. trust disposition), and X decided to rely on it (i.e. decision to trust), this means that X might delegate (i.e. act of trusting) some action or goal in his/her own plan to Y. This is the strict relation between trust disposition, decision to trust, and delegation. Our model includes two main basic beliefs (we are considering the trustee as a cognitive agent too):

- Competence Belief: a sufficient evaluation of Y's abilities, insofar as X should believe that Y is useful for a certain goal, that Y can produce or provide the expected results, or that Y can play such a role in X's plan or action.
- Willingness Belief: X should think that Y is not only capable of doing a certain action or task, but he/she should also think that Y actually will do what he/she needs under given circumstances. This belief makes the trustee's behaviour predictable.

Another important basic belief for trust is: Dependence Belief: X believes that either he/she needs Y, or X depends on Y (strong dependence), or at least X believes that it is better for X to rely rather than not rely on Y (weak dependence). In other terms, when X trusts someone, X is in a strategic situation: X believes that his/her rewards and the results of his/her projects depend on the actions of another agent Y. The willingness belief hides a set of other beliefs on the trustee's reasons and motives for helping. In particular, X believes that Y has some reasons to help him/her (or to adopt his/her goal), and that these reasons will probably prevail – in case of conflict – on other reasons, which may be negative for him/her. Notice that reasons to adopt a certain goal are of several different kinds: from friendship to altruism, from morality to fear of sanctions, from exchange to common goals (e.g. cooperation), and so on. This explain why, for example, it is important to have common culture, shared values, or the same acknowledged authorities between trustors and trustees. Another important characteristic of the socio-cognitive model of trust we propose is the distinction between trust 'in' someone or something that has to act and produce a given performance thanks to their internal characteristics, and the global trust in a global process and in its result. This latter aspect is also affected by external factors like opportunities and interferences. Trust in Y (e.g. 'social trust' in a strict sense) seems to consist in the two first prototypical beliefs identified as the basis for reliance: competence (which, in the case of cognitive agents, includes knowledge and self-confidence), and disposition (which is based on willingness, persistence, and engagement). An evaluation about external opportunities is not really an evaluation about Y (at most the belief about its ability to recognize, exploit and create opportunities is part of our trust 'in' Y). We should also add an evaluation about the probability and consistence of obstacles, adversities, and interferences. Trust can also implicitly or explicitly imply the subjective probability of the successful performance of a given behaviour D. Agents decide whether to rely on Y depending on this subjective evaluation of risk and opportunity. No matter what the probability index is based on, trust always derives from those beliefs and evaluations. In other terms, the global, final probability of the realization of a goal g (i.e. the probability of the successful performance of D), should be seen separately as the probability of Y performing the action well (internal attribution), the probability of having the appropriate conditions (external attribution) for the performance and for its success, and the probability of not having interferences and adversities (external attribution). The specification of these different probabilities and attributions is important because:

– the trustor's decision might be different with the same global probability or with the same risk, depending on intrinsic factors (i.e. personality traits);
– trust composition (i.e. internal vs external) produces completely different intervention strategies. Manipulating the external variables (e.g. circumstances, infrastructures) is completely different from manipulating internal parameters.

The idea that trust is gradable is widespread in common sense, in social sciences and in Artificial Intelligence. However, since no real definition and cognitive characterization of trust is given, the quantification of trust is often quite ad hoc and arbitrary and the introduction of this notion or predicate seems to us semantically empty without a proper account of its concept. On the contrary, in the socio-cognitive model of trust we attempt to propose, we find a strong coherence between the cognitive definition of trust, its mental ingredients, its value, and its social functions, whereas the latter are based on the former. A degree of trust of X in Y is grounded on the cognitive components of X's mental state of trust. More precisely, the degree of trust is a function of the subjective certainty of the pertinent beliefs. The degree of trust is used to formalize a rational basis for the decision of relying and betting on Y. A "quantitative" aspect of another basic ingredient is relevant: the value, importance or utility of the goal g. In sum, the quantitative dimensions of trust are based on the quantitative dimensions of its cognitive constituents. Trust is a dynamic phenomenon in its intrinsic nature. It changes with experience, as well as with the different sources it is based on, with the emotional state of the trustier, with the environmental changes of the context in which the trustee is supposed to perform, and so on. In other words, trust is an attitude that depends from dynamic phenomena; therefore it is itself a dynamic entity. From the point of view of the dynamic studies of trust, it is relevant to underline how the above basic beliefs might change during the same interaction or during several interactions: for example, the abilities of the trustee could change, or the trustor's beliefs on them may change; the reasons for willing may change too, as well as the relations of dependence between the trustor and the trustee. We have considered two main aspects of the dynamics of trust:

(i)  the traditional problem of trust reinforcement on the basis of successful experiences (and conversely, its decreasing in case of failures);

(ii) the fact that in the same situation trust is influenced by trust itself in several complex ways.

The first case considers the well-known phenomenon that trust evolves in time and has a history: X's trust in Y depends on X's previous experience, including learning with Y itself or with other (similar) entities. We analysed some results where trust in the trustee decreases with positive experiences (i.e. when the trustee realizes the delegated task) and increases with negative experiences (i.e. when the trustee does not realize the delegated task). The problem here is the attribution phenomenon to different parts of the trust experience. Since trust is not simply an external prediction coming from an observer, or an expectation about a certain fact, we also considered a case where trust is influenced by trust itself in several complex ways that may occur in the same situation. We also took into account how trust creates reciprocal trust, and distrust elicits distrust, and vice versa: how X's trust in Y could induce lack of trust or distrust in Y towards X, while X's diffidence can make Y more trustful in X.

## 8.4  What Trust to Build Towards Self-Organising Systems and Orders?

In our view, desirable features of trust towards a self-organising social system [22] are the following ones:

(A)  The emergent outcome should:

- fulfil its task in a satisfactory way;
- be more efficient in terms of time and costs than the traditional, spontaneous dynamics;
- not expose people to too frequent and non-forewarned failures, impasses, or crises;
- guarantee a reliable structure that can monitor (top-down and bottom-up from stakeholders), readjust, and make predictions via simulation (see Sect. 8.6);
- produce a system whose logics and functioning can be 'understandable' and dependable for folks;
- produce a system of which people can be informed of.

However, there is an additional problem in social domains:

(B)  What are the 'rules' applied in the micro-process in order to obtain such a global result? Do we also trust that the 'rules' and 'principles' of the designed 'invisible hand' are acceptable? In the distribution of power or water, for instance, are there systematic unfair treatments of some subjects, despite having a globally good result? What and whose are the 'interests' protected by this kind of mechanism?[5]

People should trust both levels of the self-organisation process: the result and the mechanism; and the second one implies some 'transparency' and 'negotiation' of the underlying criteria.

### 8.4.1  "Kripta"[6] of Trust in a Computer-Mediated Social System

Let us be more explicit on the problems that trust presents in complex systems with a series of very specific, yet unanswered questions. Trust in complex dynamic socio-

---

[5]Not only the design is never neutral but is in favour of the interests of one party over another, with conflicting interests [23], but also the algorithms managing a MA equilibria and dynamics have the same – but more hidden – feature.

[6]"Kripta" is the nice term – introduced by Bacharach and Gambetta [24] – to explain that trust presupposes and it is ascribed to some non-observable, hidden 'quality' of the trustee. We can observe her/his/its behaviour ("manifesta") but we rely on its control-devices. In our model, the "internal" attribution of trust and its ascription to 'inner' qualities are particularly important: they can be motivational (e.g. honesty, values, or friendship), cognitive (e.g. expertise, or competence), and also performative (e.g. skills).

technical-systems and their self-organising emergent results is different from trust in ICT-based systems where such a social order is no longer fully "spontaneous" (due to the "invisible hand" impinging on individual and selfish-decisions) because it is based on programmed interactions, algorithmic procedures and collected data.[7]

The issue is: how can we build trust in this kind of complex dynamic systems and their outcomes, given that they cannot be fully programmable and predictable? In particular, our questions sound:

> Is it necessary that folks "understand" the underlying mechanism they are relying on? And what does this mean for us? Trust is not necessarily based on a real technical understanding of how a given tool works. For example, it is not necessary that people really technically understand how a device works; however, it's important for them to have a meaningful "mental model" of that device's mechanisms and processes, because that is what gives them the proper expectations, and valid approximated ideas about the steps and contexts of the process.

> What kind of information about forecasts or "future projections" should be provided, and adjusted? And what role do simulation or serious games play in the learning processes that lead to understanding and expecting?

> What kind of information should folks (i.e. not only technicians and authorities) receive about the obtained results, about their limits, or taken risks? How much direct experience is needed in order to achieve regular and locally good results for those folks? How much information about failures, (e.g. their frequency and reasons) is needed in their context?

> What forms of 'control' should be introduced in the process and used for goals such as monitoring and prediction? The system should have a cycle of 'adjustment', which should be based on feedbacks and bottom-up hints from people.

> How to build and maintain trust in the designers, in the authorities, in technicians, signallers or in the stakeholders of this techno-social dynamic system?

> How effective and reliable will be the programming algorithms working on the micro-processes and producing the emergent organisation?

> Are there alerts for unexpected evolutions? How reliable are they? On what are they based, and how frequent are they? Are adequate, and reliable information provided? And are there rules or recommendations for readjusting or protecting purposes in case of undesired emergences?

---

[7]See also the so called "Algorithmic Economy"; e.g. http://www.forbes.com/forbes/welcome/; http://blogs.gartner.com/peter-sondergaard/the-internet-of-things-will-give-rise-to-the-algorithm-economy/

## 8.4.2  Not Just 'External' but 'Systemic' Trust

While coping with a chaotic system (e.g. traffic in a city), cognitive agents usually do not have a clear representation of its complexity and dynamics. Complexity is not in our common sense, and it is not simple to understand. People frequently ascribe the cause of an emerging problem (e.g. a serious stoppage at a crossroad) to the bad conduct of specific local actors (e.g. the traffic cop, that stupid driver, that group of cars...) and they tend to distrust them. This is not so counterintuitive, if we think of it: that agent can and has to act only locally, in order to solve his personal problems. Even if he had a good understanding of such chaotic system and of possible unpredictable hitches, he/she will in any case just act locally and on the basis of his/her trust in the other present agents.

Anyway, this relation between the local individual action and limited understanding and representation, gives us some suggestion on what to do in order to build trust in complex emerging orders and hidden devices.

- First off, one should improve the knowledge and understanding of complex systems, by educating people to realize their peculiar nature (e.g. with serious games, or by seeing possible simulations and predictions, or by having a global monitoring of the current situation).
- Secondly, creating some possibility of communication from local stakeholders towards some 'authorities' – in order to signal problems, inform about local dynamics, or suggest local solutions – may also be very important. It would also create an important situation of three-party trust relation [11], on two layers: trust among the local agents producing the phenomenon, and trust towards the meta-level agency, especially if that 'authority' (e.g. a policeman) had intervention instruments to re-program the systems, and to readjust it.
- People's trust should also be built by means of monitoring and governing devices (e.g. computational and ICT apparatus), which notify people about the "good usual order", and which give people experience of critical situations and unpredicted, but well managed and solved crises. This would increase the trust in the 'system', especially in authorities and machinery.

We would also like to stress the difference between 'internal' vs. 'external' attribution: trust in the agents' willingness and capacity is crucially separated from trust in the external environmental conditions that might favour or hinder the success of the agent's action. When we deal with a multi-agent open environment and with the need for a good emergent coordination and 'order', the problem of 'external' attribution shows yet another aspect. Coordination is frequently based on rules, conventions and norms the agents have to follow in order to produce the desired 'organisation' and emergent result. These two faces of trust can be completely independent.

Suppose that all the involved agents are absolutely reliable as for respecting the rules of the game; however, suppose that these rules are bad, not really well designed to produce the desired global coordination and result. In this scenario, agents are trustworthy but it would be impossible to trust 'the system', because it is impossible to trust the 'mechanism' that produces that order. The opposite situation may also arise: the rules and coordination artefacts in a given context may be excellent, but the agents are not reliable whereas they systematically violate the rules and produce a chaotic result. Or even, since the rules are bad and we do not trust and rely on them, we trust agents who can intelligently violate them in order to solve the problem locally.[8]

Trust is not just generically in the external 'context' of the agents' actions, but it is rather in the 'system'. For self-organising systems, we have to build a 'systemic' trust, with its various components: in the agents, in the authorities, in the infrastructure, in the rules and procedures, and in their complementarity. It is relevant to also remind the difference between simple ignorance, uncertainty, "lack of trust" versus true "distrust". As we said, distrust is a form of negative trust; that is, in our model, a negative evaluation about competence or reliability of Y. It is the ground of a possible decision to avoid, not to delegate and not to rely on someone. The systems must not only create trust in potential partners, organisations, etc. It also has to create negative evaluations and decisions of avoidance [26] (see also [? ]). However, it is crucial to remark that in order to induce possible distrust judgements in the users, those users have to positively trust the system and its reliability. If there is no 'systemic trust', but 'lack of trust' or 'distrust' in the system, no reduction of uncertainty is possible, neither in the positive, nor in the negative direction.

## 8.5  The Emergent Equilibriums Are Not Necessarily the Best and Fair

In our view, trust towards complex self-organising Socio-Technical Systems implies another serious problem. A spontaneous social order is such in the sense of an "emergent" and self-organising equilibrium. However, this does not prevent it from being biased, slanted, or systematically favouring certain subjects at the expenses of the others [10]. We are not claiming that it can no longer be spontaneous,[9] but steered, or that there are hidden intelligences controlling and orienting the economic and social emergence. Unfortunately, this is not the main, basic explanation of the tendentious nature of the organising society; even the influence and control of political power over society dynamics is limited. There is not just a problem of hidden powers intentionally governing the economy: local, non-intentional, distributed decisions and actions will let emerge that "order" like a microphysics

---

[8]On the possible usefulness of violations in any organisation, see [25].

[9]In the paper on "Making visible the invisible hand" [27] the title of a section sounds "The pseudo-spontaneous order"; despite its rhetorical efficacy, in the text there is no claim that the emerging social order is fully "manoeuvred".

determines macro-properties. And to say it with an example, to reveal, monitor, and correct complexity is more difficult than to "occupy Wall Street".

**A 'functional' (bad) equilibrium** – A misunderstanding on this issue is frequent: an emerging equilibrium that is not so good for the participating actors may be a functional equilibrium. This reminds people of the wonderful problem of the Prisoner Dilemma, where the equilibrium that emerges from the locally rational choices of the two actors (Nash' equilibrium) is not the best result possible for both of them in that strategic situation (Pareto's optimality). They are "prisoners" of their local view. This is a crucial problem and an important example for social policies, but it is not our problem. There are two relevant differences in the tendentious result of the spontaneous social order.

(a) We do not simply have one shot or repeated games that culminate with such a bottom-up result. We have a self-organising collective outcome, caused by feedbacks on its micro-layer (i.e. minds and behaviours of the actors). In such a way, it also reproduces and maintains itself. In our vocabulary, this is a "functional" outcome. There is not only a bottom-up process, but also a top-down process; there is a dialectical circularity. That outcome becomes the "end" (A. Smith) of the individuals' behaviours, and their function [28].

(b) Secondly, the problem is about the systematic advantage of some participants (endowed with local and personal or structural and social powers). The "political" problem is not how to make the participants aware of the limits of their choice and help them to achieve a better solution for both. The problem is how to get a more equitable equilibrium that limits the power of dominating social groups. This is not a matter of a "technical" solution but of a political solution: it is the decision to change the result of a basic "social conflict", or a conflict of "interests", even if unaware and not understood. This problem of "hidden/covert interests" is frequently ignored; it seems that since that order is "spontaneous", then it is also necessarily "neutral".

For example, in Veits' work (within the "Global Brain" project) we find the claim that "distributed governance in a world of views is the next phase in the cognitive development of human society" thanks to the development of a Global Brain [29]. In our view, this perspective is not completely incorrect, but we find it rather simplistic and optimistic. It ignores the conflictive side of social relations and of societies, which are not due to lack of information or limited rationality. Society is not an "organism" where the "organs" do necessarily cooperate. Thus, also the interesting claims that a Distributed Governance System "needs to facilitate the following functions: (a) Allow for the co-existence of diverse worldviews and social institutions. (b) Provide an effective medium of communication, dialogue and co-evolution. (c) Propagate successful experiments and containing failures (antifragility)" are shareable but partial. In fact, the problem is not just to build or provide an 'infrastructure', or a medium for the governance; what we should build is a hybrid/symbiotic (i.e. human and AI systems) governing system and we want to know its hidden, implemented principles, which produce the resulting equilibriums in the emergent global 'order'. Thus,

> for computer-mediated social orders and systems, one has to explain for whose advantage that order is established, which group/class is favoured, and if there are other fairer orders.
> See also on that Pitt and Artikis' work on the design of Self-Governing Institutions (for example, [14]) on the basis of Ostrom's and Rescher's principles of Commons and Justice, axiomatised in computational logics.[10]
> One should introduce and publicize that there are binds within and in the system, as well as norms and rules that prevent some undesirable individual and collective conducts, conventions, roles, and scripts that facilitate functional cooperative aggregations.
> It should be showed how the awareness, the rules, the norms, and the individual commitment improve the collective outcome.
> Trust should be built not just in relation to personal goals and advantages, but also in relation to public goods, or common plans.

## 8.6  Making Visible the Invisible Hand by MA-Based Social Simulation

We claim that a very special role for users' trust and understanding of self-organising systems will be played by Social Simulation (and serious game and virtual reality) systems.

### 8.6.1  Social Simulation as Social Imagination and Prediction

Intelligent "Agents" (both agent-based social simulation and agents embedded in smart environments) will play a crucial role for the intelligent management of social phenomena, especially for complex and emergent dynamics. They will mediate human negotiation or situated collective planning, and provide the computational support for coordination, cooperation and conflict. In particular, predictive and imaginative simulations will be crucial. This means, models should be run in order to diagnose and anticipate possible trends and effects of different policies or of current social movements (see also [30]). Computer modelling and simulations should be run to predict observable phenomena and to understand the underlying psycho-social mechanisms. All this is crucial for an effective intervention policy dealing with complex systems, not just with 'organisations'.

---

[10]According to us, the authors are a bit optimistic as for: (i) the computational governance of complex and self-organising hybrid systems; (ii) the role of cooperation, common interests, social capital, etc. whereby they ignore the crucial and positive role of 'conflicts'.

However, a fundamental challenge for the future – in our view – is the following one:

> How can we systematically integrate the simulations of social phenomena with the real-time feedback coming from everyday social context?

In one decade (or a bit more), we will see a generalized and structural use of computer simulations (especially agent-based) as the required ground for all the decisions to be taken in relation to strategies or policies, in a number of different domains: military, environmental, economic, financial, urban, demographic, energetic, educational, health, logistic. Indeed, no political or managerial complex decision can be taken without grounding it on fine grain predictions of effects and possible developments and outcomes. Moreover, the latter will be enabled by computer modelling and simulations of the relevant phenomena and by long-term unfolding and 'governable' dynamics [27]. Social 'planning', or at least an intelligent government and orientation of spontaneous social dynamics should become reliable and unavoidable. It requires fine-grained predictions based on "simulations", and should combine the opportunistic, bottom-up, local adjustments of such predictions and of the imagined policies themselves.

## 8.6.2 A Top-Down and Bottom-Up Model with Feedback from the Field

The simulated predictive model (although based on previously collected empirical data) cannot just be top-down and centralized, and simply "applied" to the field. One will need to combine the simulation and its predictions, and their implementation in the real domain, with possible timely feedbacks from the territory, due to intelligent sensors or witnesses. This should happen in order to immediately readjust the simulations on the basis of the real feedback and the subsequent policy or intervention; and so on, cyclically (Fig. 8.1).

This cycle will increase the realism of the model. "What is needed is the normal "cycle" of learning for problem-solving and ability acquisition: Objective $\implies$ hypothesis about possible actions (planning/problem-solving) $\implies$ attempt and feedback $\implies$ possible failures $\implies$ interpretation/understanding $\implies$ re-planning (new adjusted solution) $\implies$ ...

No learning without possible (predicted) failures and their monitoring for revising models and replanning behaviours. Babies do that; why not nations[27]?" On the other hand, the model should be highly flexible and adjustable to reflect no trivial dynamics. The solution (and its design) cannot be the same in every domain, since the degree of complexity and of possible information (e.g. stakeholders) and intervention differ from one domain to the other (e.g. traffic is not like an epidemic, or an unforeseen leakage of toxic substances). In other terms, also the simulative "mind" has to be "situated", distributed, and externalized. Computer modelling and simulation can be a revolution of the "collective cognition"; but this collective

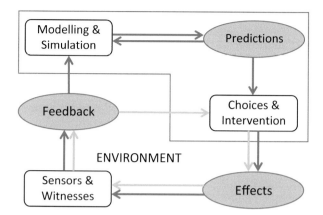

**Fig. 8.1** The Monitoring and Adjusting cycle (Two possible sub-cycles: Simulation => predictions and on such basis => interventions, policies. An executive cycle: To look at the real effects of a policy, and on the basis of this feedback from the environment readjust the policy, change the intervention. Or the combination of both, by re-simulating on the basis of the external feedbacks and then changing the policy.) according to [27]

cognition must be "situated" anyway, as well as it should be context-dependent and opportunistic, based on data of the "here" and "now" of its environment, and continuously adapted to the field, not fully and rigidly planned. It must be also "distributed", with various subjects and local simulation sub-systems. Their criteria, ends, priorities and data must be complemented and integrated with very powerful and flexible computational instruments, such as unifying ontologies; factor models; Big Data, etc. This approach provides the "social simulation"[11] with a double experimental ground:

- the real "experimental" data coming from the model of simulation, with expected and unexpected results;
- the "field study" of what is really happening when we apply a given simulated policy or when we observe a given simulated phenomenon.

### 8.6.3 Inventing the Future

Simulation is not only, and not mainly, for predictions. As Alan Kay once suggested, "the best way to predict the future …is to invent it"; the "Artificial Collective Imagination" that we are building is for that too. On the one hand, we need to imagine what is possible and probable and will probably happen, on the other

---

[11] For the use of simulation to test collective decision making models see in this book Ch. 17 Lucas and Payne.

hand, we also have to imagine what is impossible, and what might be or become possible: action consists in creating new conditions and modifying the possibility and probability of future events. We need imagination to explore creative solutions in problem solving and in designing; this cannot be well done in reality, but it surely can be done on representations, virtually, as an architect would do on drawings and scale models. Simulation is not only useful for predictions also because strict predictions are impossible in complex dynamics like social systems. We should not forget that predictions are frequently imprecise and wrong and predicting events is impossible in principle, especially due to complex dynamics. Events are unpredictable, like earthquakes. However:

i. is seismology a useless science since earthquakes cannot be precisely and reliably predicted? We do not think so. Also approximated and probabilistic predictions can be very useful (e.g. for prevention, or proportional investments);
ii. we need long-term and global predictions, but also very short term and operational predictions in guiding and monitoring specific actions like motor-prediction in motor-action. These predictions are there for immediate matching and for immediate adjustment of both acting and prediction.

The comparison between what is expected and what is actually there, between anticipated and perceptual information, allows us to systematically and quickly react to the unexpected, with its threats and opportunities. Do we need at the collective level an analogous process of attention? We need to build not only imagination, but also artificial "attentional systems", not by pre-programmed inspections and controls, but by timely signalling and focus changing in monitoring, interpreting, and predicting.

### 8.6.4   Empowering People

It is not simply a matter of feedbacks from the field and from people, from various signallers and indicators, in different times, and of continuous readjusting of the model and of the simulation. A more politically and technically advanced model is conceivable on technological bases, implying rooms for negotiation and decisions. For any given social phenomena, there is always a variety of stakeholders with different interests. Therefore, the solution of the problem can never be merely technical and predefined. We rather have to deal with new forms of participatory evaluation. The solution requires processes, space, time, and modalities of political negotiation between the various subjects, interests, and points of view. Social research and scientists cannot provide strict predictions, as well as no recipes, or ready solutions. They can just give us the evaluation of possible pros and cons of the various alternatives, and a critical attitude about our certainties and preferences. The decision is always – overtly or less – political, not technical. Those "who have a say" should be inserted in the very "model" of the "social planning"; this would not simply imply feedback, re-simulation, or re-planning (see Fig. 8.1). This would also imply a model that includes "re-decision" phases and places: who decides? And – more importantly – on the basis of what kind of re-discussion and re-negotiation of the involved interests? How shall we give room, how support, and mediate different agreements and decisions in the processes [27]? ICT will provide us new opportunities for participation, transparency of political decisions and practices of e-democracy, which are necessary to deeply understand and manage complex social phenomena. Other functions of Social Simulation – In this perspective, it is clear that other uses of computer simulation will also be important. Such virtual environments can be used as a "laboratory" for experience and understanding: for example, problem-focused and data-based realistic sociological "serious games". We also find they may provide an educational role of learning-by-doing, of understanding by looking and possible outcomes of our proposals and moves. We cannot have a real participatory discussion, project, and decision process based on spontaneous judgements, opinions, prejudices, group-psychology and even demagogy. Circulating real information is crucial, and we need it to improve real understanding and knowledge. Networking and information circulation and discussion should serve also to educate, to argue, to increase our knowledge. Using simulations, by trial and errors, predictions and unexpected results can also be effective and useful. Before deciding, real feedbacks and readjusting, simulating hypotheses might be a very important instrument for bottom-up, participatory proposals.

## 8.7   Concluding Remarks

Our clearest conclusion sounds as follows: we need a complex and multidimensional model of trust, not just a vague notion or a simple measure. We need a model that can explicitly specify who is trusting whom, for what needs and expectations and in what contexts. This model should also deal with trust in different environments and how these environments support or interfere with trust. We need a model that specifies the dynamics of trust: transitivity, inference (e.g. from classes to individuals, from roles to players) and feedback. This model should also take into account the following dynamics: trust and reputation; trust and direct experience; trust and security; attribution of hidden 'qualities'; degree of trust as evaluation; decisions to trust and rely on; perceived risks; belief/reason-based trust versus felt trust; and trust, autonomy and control. Reductionist approaches are simpler and faster to formalize. However, they seem to us to be not adequate to model and manage real problems and dynamics. As for the specific issues of complex systems, computational self-organisation and emergent 'orders', let us simply underline our critical remarks on a prevailing and rather optimistic view:

- on the one hand, a self-organising order might be quite (and not accidentally) unbalanced and unfair (see Sect. 8.5);

- on the other hand, also the users' role must also be stressed: "the human as the user of self-organising and self-adaptive systems and (then) the usability of such systems" (cited Budapest Call).

Are we so sure that humans will actually be the users of those emergent, collective, self-organising systems? Can we, as humans, consider ourselves the "users" of a "spontaneous social order" like the market, or of political systems? This was the very ideological claim of von Mises [31], who said that consumers command in the market – a claim that does not take while marketing, manipulation or oligopolies into account. Similarly, are we the "users" of political power? Or are we just the submitted 'subjects' of such mechanisms and the exploited micro-mechanisms that maintain them? Why or how this should be different in a computationally managed, self-organising socio-technical system? This is important not only for a different (and prudent) philosophical, social and moral view of what we are building. We find this important also in order to have a less reductive view of a needed "transparenc". In order to have confidence and reliance in this kind of systems we also need to feel or know that the systems rules and resulting equilibriums are fair and equity inspired. We want to know that the system is correct in relation to the interests of the involved groups and subjects, and that the system is open and sensible to our reactions, criticisms, problems, and possible conflicts. Transparency has to be bidirectional and about listening.

We need to ask ourselves: was the system designed to empower its users? With empowerment we mean:

(a) not just "usability", "user friendliness";
(b) not just in an individualistic perspective: empowering the separated users; but empowering users as "demos", as a collective agent.

# References

1. Omicini, A., Contucci, P.: Complexity and interaction: blurring borders between physical, computational, and social systems. English. In: Badica, C., Nguyen, N., Brezovan, M. (eds.) Computational Collective Intelligence. Technologies and Applications, vol. 8083, pp. 1–10. Springer, Berlin/Heidelberg (2013). ISBN:978-3-642-40494-8
2. Pezzulo, G., Hoffmann, J., Falcone, R.: Anticipation and anticipatory behavior. Cognit. Process. **8**, 67–70 (2007)
3. Anders, G., Siefert, F., Steghöfer, J.-P., Reif, W.: Self-Organizing Systems, pp. 90–102. Springer, Berlin/Heidelberg (2014)
4. Nafz, F., Ortmeier, F., Seebach, H., Steghöfer, J.-P., Reif, W.: A universal self-organization mechanism for role-based organic computing systems. In: Nieto, J.G., Reif, W., Wang, G., Indulska, J. (eds.), Autonomic and Trusted Computing, pp. 17–31. Springer, Berlin/Heidelberg (2009)
5. Noriega, P., Padget, J., Verhagen, H., d'Inverno, M.: The challenge of artificial socio-cognitive systems. In: COIN. AAMAS, Paris (2014)
6. Sollner, M., Pavlou, P., Leimeister, J.M.: Understanding trust in IT artifacts – a new conceptual approach. In: Academy of Management Annual Meeting, New York (2013)

7. Steghöfer, J.-P., Kiefhaber, R., Leichtenstern, K., Bernard, Y., Klejnowski, L.: Trustworthy organic computing systems: challenges and perspectives. In: Xie, B., Branke, J., Sadjadi, S.M., Zhang, D., Zhou, X. (eds.) Autonomic and Trusted Computing, pp. 62–76. Springer, Berlin/Heidelberg (2010)
8. Steghöfer, J.-P., Behrmann, P., Anders, G., Siefert, F., Reif, W.: HiSPADA: self-organising hierarchies for large-scale multi-agent systems. In: IARIA'13, Lisbon (2013)
9. Aslanyan, Z., Ivanova, M.G., Nielson, F., Probst, C.: Modeling and analysing socio-technical systems. In: 1st International Workshop on Socio-Technical Perspective in IS Development (STPIS), Stockholm, vol. 1374, pp. 121–124 (2015)
10. Castelfranchi, C.: For a Pessimistic Theory of the Invisible Hand and Spontaneous Order. https://www.academia.edu/823483/For_a_Pessimistic_Theory_of_the_Invisible_Hand_and_Spontaneous_Order (2001)
11. Castelfranchi, C., Falcone, R.: Trust Theory. A Socio-Cognitive and Computational Model. Wiley, Chichester (2010)
12. Falcone, R., Castelfranchi, C.: Social trust: a cognitive approach. In: Castelfranchi, C., Yao-Hua, T. (eds.) Trust and Deception in Virtual Societies, pp. 55–90. Kluwer Academic Publishers, Dordrecht (2001)
13. Garfinkel, H.: A conception of, and experiments with, 'trust' as a condition of stable concerted actions. In: Harvey, O.J. (ed.) Motivation and Social Interaction, pp. 187–238. Ronald Press Co., New York (1963)
14. Pitt, J., Artikis: A.: The open agent society: a retrospective and future perspective. In: COIN. AAMAS, Istanbul (2015)
15. Rutter, J.: Sociology of trust towards a sociology of E-trust. Int. J. New Prod. Dev. Innov. Manag. **3**, 371–385 (2001)
16. Pelligra, V.: Under trusting eyes: the responsive nature of trust. In: Gui, B., Sugden, R. (eds.) Economics and Social Interaction: Accounting for Interpersonal Relations. Cambridge University Press, Cambridge (2005)
17. Falcone, R., Castelfranchi, C.: Socio-cognitive model of trust. In: Encyclopedia of Information Science and Technology. IGI Global, Hershey (2005)
18. Falcone, R., Piunti, M., Venanzi, M., Castelfranchi, C.: From Manifesta to Krypta: the relevance of categories for trusting others. ACM Trans. Intell. Syst. Technol. **4**, 1–24 (2013)
19. Giddens, A.: Modernity and Self-Identity. Self and Society in the Late Modern Age. Stanford University Press, Stanford (1991)
20. Gollmann, D.: Security in Socio-technical Systems (2011)
21. Clegg, A.: Trust on the Internet. Telecomun. Policy **22**, 159–160 (1998)
22. Hassas, S., Marzo-Serugendo, G.D., Karageorgos, A., Castelfranchi, C.: On Self-Organising Mechanisms from Social, Business and Economic Domains (2006)
23. Fry, T.: Design as Politics. Berg Publishers, New York (2010)
24. Bacharach, M., Gambetta, D.: Trust as type detection. In: Castelfranchi, C., Tan, Y.-H. (eds.) Trust and Deception in Virtual Societies, pp. 1–16. Springer, Netherlands (2001)
25. CastelFranchi, C.: Engineering social order. In: Omicini, A., Tolksdorf, R., Zambonelli, F. (eds.) Engineering Societies in the Agents World, pp. 1–18. Springer, Berlin/Heidelberg (2000)
26. Cofta, P.: Trust, Complexity and Control: Confidence in a Convergent World. Wiley, Hoboken (2007)
27. Castelfranchi, C.: Making visible "the Invisible Hand". The mission of social simulation. In: Adamatti, D., Dimuro, G., Coelho, H. (eds.) Interdisciplinary Applications of Agent-Based Social Simulation and Modeling. IGI Global, Hershey pp. 1–19 (2014)
28. Castelfranchi, C.: The theory of social functions. Challenges for multi-agent-based social simulation and multi-agent learning. J. Cognit. Syst. Res. **2**, 5–38 (2001)
29. Veitas, V.: A World Views: The Cognitive Development of the Global Brain. http://www.slideshare.net/vveitas/dsg-short-presentation (2014)
30. Zia, K., Ferscha, A., Riener, A., Wirz, M., Roggen, D., Kloch, K., Lukowicz, P.: Pervasive computing in the large: the socionical approach. In: Adjunct Proceedings of the Eighth International Conference on Pervasive Computing, Helsinki, p. 6 (2010)
31. Von Mises, L.: In: Press, Y.U. (ed.) Bureaucracy. https://mises.org/library/bureaucracy (1944)

# Chapter 9
# To Trust or Distrust: Has a Digital Environment Empowered Users to Proceed on Their Own Terms?

Natasha Dwyer and Stephen Marsh

**Abstract** We claim that the wider trust research area (academics and industry practitioners) strive to develop systems that are both trustworthy and foster trust. Evaluation methods follow this pursuit and measure for the presence of trust. However, if considered from a user's perspective and if a digital environment is instead designed to empower users about their trust choices, then trust and distrust are valid options. How can environments, designed to empower users in their trust responses (referred to in this chapter as TEU environments), be evaluated? Practitioners need to be able to gauge their progress. In this chapter, we outline how a practitioner can work around some of the complexities surrounding the design of TEU environments and we present one evaluation method. To understand whether a TEU environment is indeed empowering a user regarding trust, we suggest investigating whether there is a change in a user's level of uncertainty. A reduction in uncertainty is a proxy for both trust and distrust. When uncertainty is reduced a user is clearer about what to do and is not caught up in a cycle of exploring possibilities. Survey questions allowing responses on a Likert scale are one means to evaluate change.

**Keywords** Usability • Usable security • Information trustworthiness • Evaluating • Trust evidence

## 9.1 Introduction

Currently the wider trust research area (academics and industry practitioners), working in the interests of organisations and governments, value environments that promote trusting behaviour and fostering of trust [1]. This may be because,

N. Dwyer (✉)
College of Arts, Victoria University, Melbourne, VIC, Australia
e-mail: Natasha.Dwyer@vu.edu.au

S. Marsh
Faculty of Business and Information Technology, University of Ontario Institute of Technology, Oshawa, ON, Canada
e-mail: stephen.marsh@uoit.ca

© Springer International Publishing Switzerland 2016
W. Reif et al. (eds.), *Trustworthy Open Self-Organising Systems*,
Autonomic Systems, DOI 10.1007/978-3-319-29201-4_9

as reflected in Fukuyama's famous line 'trust greases the wheels' [2], a state of trust results in higher productivity. Evaluation methods reflect this pursuit of trust, measuring for the presence and intensity of trust. When the goal is to promote trust, the approach towards measurement is clear: measure the level of trust before and after an interaction or intervention [3].

If instead, as we explain in this chapter, a practitioner considers the design of a digital environment from a user's perspective and with the user's interests at heart, then both trust and distrust may be valid choices [4]. For instance, there may be a good reason why a user should purchase from a particular vendor. Measuring whether trust has occurred does not reveal much beyond whether the user was coerced to engage with a system. It does not indicate whether the user was able to make the trust choice that was in his or her interests, which is the type of experience we want to design. Once the needs of the user are in the foreground, the role of context in a trust scenario is emphasised. Context is different for every user and is central to how trust and distrust are regarded [5].

Rather than systems that pretend to be trustworthy or foster and enhance trust, designers and developers are now creating digital systems (such as sets of web pages and mobile apps) that empower the user about trust choices, which we describe as TEU environments. Examples of TEU environments are dating sites that help users negotiate fraught relations [6] or an application that allows individuals to self-select and come together to develop a creative project [7]. Nurse et al. [8] present a model in which users can plug in their individual trust preferences and, at appropriate times, receive a graph suggesting future actions.

The aim of this chapter is to develop a means to evaluate whether systems that are designed to be TEU are indeed empowering users confronting trust choices. Developers, researchers, designers and others interested in working in users' interests have some means to interrogate their work. We argue that the lens to understand whether an environment empowers a user is to investigate whether uncertainty has been reduced. Trust researchers agree that there are several results of trust and distrust [9]. A reduction in uncertainty is common to both the experience of trust and distrust and is an outcome that is beneficial for the user. The user is clearer about how best to proceed, which we define as a form of empowerment. In contrast, without a state of either trust or distrust, a user may be caught up in a cycle of assessing possibilities and considering how he/she should act, in other words, keep wondering about whether he/she should be either trusting or distrusting. Such a cycle is resource intensive for an individual [9]. To assess trust and distrust from a user's perspective, we draw on the work of Cofta [9] who distilled work across the trust research area and argues that users look for evidence to trust across several dimensions. In short, the dimensions are continuity (how long a trustee has existed in a community), competence (does a trustee have the skills to deliver on an interaction?) and motivation (does the trustee have a commitment to working in the trustor's interests).

Often when theory meets practice there are complexities, and this issue is no exception. This chapter outlines some of the issues practitioners need to tackle. We first review how trust in a digital environment is usually valued and measured.

Examples of alternative design approaches that attempt to empower trust for the user are outlined. We then identify challenges associated with evaluating TEU environments. Finally, we suggest one path: to measure whether uncertainty has been reduced for the user. The technique of surveys arranged around Likert scale statements is an established means to gauge attitude change. Survey statements focusing on different areas of trust evidence can help a designer access the nuances of users' understanding of a TEU.

## 9.2   Our Perspective

This chapter takes a social science perspective, more specifically, a user experience design (UX) viewpoint. UX is the design and communication of a system from a user's perspective and overlaps with other practices such as interaction design, accessibility, usability and human computer interaction (HCI) [10]. Within the social sciences, trust is broadly understood as a context-bound relationship within which the trustor, in a position of vulnerability, is confident that another party (the trustee) will respond in the trustor's interest. However, static definitions of trust do not contribute much when considering the design of trust and distrust in a practical setting, as the notion of trust is only meaningful when understood in context. The difficulty of defining trust was raised by Luhman [11], who pointed to society as the place where trust interactions are grounded. The notion of context is stressed by social scientists, because this emphasises the shift in an understanding of trust depending on who you are, where you are and the moment in time [12]. All disciplines conceptualise and define trust depending on the outcome sought by the researcher and the research area [13]. An outcome sought by the social science discipline is to problematise a situation, i.e. to problem-set rather than problem solve [14]. To study trust and distrust in digital environments from a social science perspective is to explore power relations, design, choice, and control across the Internet, which are significantly underexplored to date [15]. If issues of power are not acknowledged or interrogated, then there is the risk that what is in the interests of the most powerful is assumed as what is best for all. There are many challenges for the designers of TEU environments.

Our motivation is to gather data to inform a project we are undertaking, 'Device Comfort', which is a personal interface that speculates about states of interactions in an environment and its owner's current context [16]. Working on behalf of the individual, the interface is designed specifically for the purpose of health and wellbeing and can manage an individual's health data, aggregated from a range of sources. The interface unites several sources of information, such as nearby devices and the predilections of the user to present to the user an overall 'comfort level'. What the user does with this guidance is ultimately up to the user. The idea is to provide an opportunity for the user to have a 'second thought'. Developing measures of success for this interface was the original impetus for this chapter. Before they begin development, designers can benefit from a sense of the measurements for success and outcomes for users they should aim for in their projects. Usually the activities of evaluating and measuring are regarded as the domain of more quantitative-orientated disciplines. However, all developers need to have a sense of how well their projects are functioning and need to access the power of numbers to indicate change. The issue of evaluation and trust is a practical concern for designers and developers of digital environments. The intended audiences of this chapter are those who wish to apply theory about users and trust in practice in order to create websites, 'apps' and other digital outputs.

## 9.3   A Problem of Bias and Emphasis

Design is never neutral; it always works in the interests of one party over another [17]. Unsurprisingly, owners of digital environments design their spaces so that their business models and agendas are served. Although some practitioners of 'user-centred' design claim that they put the user first, this prioritisation is debatable, Blythe et al. [18] argue that in fact their claim is unfounded and the label 'user-centred' design is simply a marketing device. When owners of a digital environment employs design strategies for their space in order to increase the success of their mission and their engagement with users, one of the first qualities they seek is trustworthiness and the trust of their users (regardless of whether trust is deserved). Trust is so often touted as the magical 'make or break' component of a design [1].

The academic trust research area also values a result of trust (not distrust) and emphasises the study of trust (rather than distrust). Trust is regarded as beneficial and a success while distrust is considered a negative state and an outcome to be avoided [1, 19]. Blyth et al. [18] argue that the acceptance of business and commercial values is the default position of the wider human computer design industry and is due to the close links between academia and industry.

The valuation of trust and a positive outcome for organisations and businesses can be seen in the use of language and the prioritisation of goals by researchers and practitioners. For instance, the area of virtual work systems and trust is shaped by the work of Mayer et al. [20] who define trust as 'the willingness to be vulnerable to the actions of another party' and cooperation, which complements the goals of management [21], is seen as a measure of trust [20]. A popular theme in the research area is how trust can propagate within virtual team environments [22].

E-commerce practitioners look to the speed and number of sales as indicators of trust [23, 24]. We see this commercial interest translate into guidelines for designers to give an interface the appearance of trust, regardless of the nature of the contents (for instance [25]). A popular recommendation is to develop a 'professionally designed' site, one that a designer with traditional graphic skills has created in order to provide an aura of authority (for instance [26] and [27]). Other researchers provide detail of what might constitute a professional appearance. Colour, it is also argued, plays a role in  the formation of a professional site, for instance, the use of blue can promote trust as does the avoidance of black [28]. Inclusion of photographs of company people on a website, incorporating their names, can also build a trustworthy picture, especially photographs of people in 'everyday situations'. The idea is to engineer 'human warmth' into a digital environment [29].

If we take a user's perspective, we know that there are good reasons for us not to trust what is presented to us in digital environments. There are very good reasons why an employee should not collaborate in the virtual workplace, even if it is in the interest of the company. For instance, management may favour one particular employee and a virtual workplace is designed to hand this employee all intellectual property at the expense of other employees [30]. In the domain of e-commerce, sometimes a user should not buy the advertised product or engage with a particular service. The product may not be what it should be or may be a ruse for a user to provide credit card details [31].

## 9.4   TEU Environments

Trust and distrust differs depending on who you are, as the following example illustrates. Let us assume that an individual has recently been diagnosed with a certain medical syndrome that could be a life threatening condition. The individual is exhibiting new symptoms. As it is the weekend, there is nobody for the individual to turn to and the individual logs into a portal focusing on the condition. The site includes a range of content including written advice and discussion, videos and advertising material. The trust issue for the user is working out whose advice to follow. It is difficult for the user to determine who owns the site. The material may be marketing a particular medication that may be unsuitable. On the other hand, advocates of a philosophy may be providing advice that is also biased and not what is in this individual's interests. From the perspective of other stakeholders, the individual's vulnerability is an opportunity for profit. Researchers exploring this case from a commercial perspective could explore whether the design increased the visitation rates of the site, whether the individual recommended the site to others, or bought products or services. From our perspective, the TEU position, we are interested in whether the site enabled a user to make the choice about her problem that was in his/her interests guided by his/her beliefs, expectations, customs and the other elements shaping the context that Zack and McKenney outline [32]. The context could include factors such as risk, visual design elements, and presentation of language. This example demonstrates how difficult it is to empower a user to form trust or distrust on his/her own terms. Designers develop solutions to these problems for users, for instance, providing tools for users to decode the bias behind the visual design of a site or to organise their observations about trustworthiness.

In contrast to a commercial design that attempts to convince its audience that it is the correct choice, a trust empowering design enables users to form their own choices. In addition to the examples provided in the introduction, we are seeing the rise of 'trustware', systems that attempt to assist individuals form trust perceptions about others by allowing users to translate the reputation they have developed in one network to another [33]. Some examples of these systems include TrustCloud[1] and Legit.[2] The demand for trustware is increasing as the sharing economy grows [34]. As the phenomenon of strangers sharing valuable resources continues, there needs to be means for individuals to work out with whom who they should interact. Although 'start-up' entrepreneurial business models are currently highly influential in the design of the systems, this area of technology design is in its infancy [34]. In the near future we will see a diverse range of trustware approaches, and perhaps systems dedicated to specific industries, such as health. An example is a system that helps individuals to negotiate smoking cessation advice provided by a range of sources. Approaches to evaluation are needed to assess these designs, examining whether users are able to form the trust choices that are in their interests.

## 9.5   Complexities of Designing TEU Environments

TEU environments need to engage with a range of potential users' interpretations of the contexts they encounter. Trust and context are strongly interlinked. Trust is a social construction that is only meaningful when understood in context, i.e. the 'here and now' (cf. [35]). A user's interpretation of context is shaped by a whole range of factors, such as power relations, social conventions, traditions, expectations, habits and memory [32]. Suchman [36] in her landmark work 'Plans and Situated Actions' argues that technological developments that ignore context result in unsuccessful technology that is not accepted by its user base. As we review in this section, recognising the unavoidable link between trust and context adds levels of complexity when considering the design and evaluation of environments intended to empower individual users.

Drawing on the authority of sources of advice deemed as trustworthy, without any further exploration, is problematic. The practice of designers, governments and companies assuming that they know what is best for users and telling them what to do is known as 'benevolent paternalism' [37]. Often the exponents of benevolent paternalism try to distinguish themselves from commercial practices that seek to convince users to adopt a certain behaviour in order to increase the profits of a company. But there are still problems with 'benevolent paternalism'. Advice can be biased, for instance, motivated by political and religious agendas. Advice provide by authorities cannot provide an indisputable answer on every occasion for all people. As authorities can disagree over the solution to seemingly uncontroversial issues, there is no guidance to suggest which authority is correct. For instance, following from the example provided above of the user with a medical condition, an individual could seek advice from three online doctors about different treatments. There are

---

[1] https://trustcloud.com

[2] https://www.legit.com

two different medications for the condition. One doctor may prescribe one type of medication. Another doctor may prescribe the second medication. The third doctor may prescribe a combination. So, it is clear that it is difficult to decide which advice should dominate. The consequence in this scenario is medication that may not suit the patient's needs. However, Srnicek and Williams [38] point out that to refuse all advice is misguided and does not take advantage of the expertise available to us in the modern world. Such a rejection of authority does not recognise the nuances by which individuals are controlled in society. Designing trust empowering systems is a political and complicated exercise.

An evaluation of a design incorporating a 'benevolent paternalism' perspective may test for whether the presentation of information in a digital environment allowed the user to make the 'correct' decision regarding a medical condition. But when one acknowledges the role of context, we can see how the 'pre-prepared' approach is limited. Defenders of 'benevolent paternalism' may argue that right or wrong answers can be successful for the majority of the population. However, we argue that it is impossible to know when and how such judgments can be applied, due to the role of context, and thus 'benevolent paternalism' is a questionable design strategy.

When the importance of context is acknowledged, the potential of a digital system or an authority to pre-determine right or wrong answers for individual users in a trust scenario is limited. Context, i.e. the environment in which understandings are made, can only be constructed between people as they read it, participate within it, and work out how they might function in a specific situation. Trusting and distrusting are not entirely rational thought processes: they are a combination of subjective and objective thinking. The response depends on the individual. As Möllering [39] writes, there is an element of trust that is always unaccountable and 'mystical', otherwise what is being discussed is not trust and could more aptly be described as 'calculation'. When one of the elements in a context is altered, then the outcome may be different. This is why Marsh et al. [40] suggest that TEU environments should allow users to monitor and intervene, so that users can have a role in interpreting their contexts.

It is also problematic for designers to simply draw on the authority of 'trustworthy' sources, otherwise known as second-hand trust [41]. There is no such thing as a consistently reliable trustworthy source. The generators of what might once have been considered trustworthy or even truthful information, governments and non-government organisations, no longer wield the same respect as in the past [42]. The authority, bias and competence of these sources are now questioned on a regular basis [43]. Additionally, as users of digital environments, we know that spammers continually attempt to replicate what might be regarded as a trustworthy agent. The problem of assessing trustworthiness is multi-layered. A trust-empowering interface should not attempt to provide a definitive answer, but instead aim to keep a 'case open' ready to receive new developments.

## 9.6 Isolating a Means to Evaluate for Trust Empowerment

The creation of a TEU environment, a system that empowers its users to negotiate trust on their own terms, requires resolution of many design challenges. How can we measure whether a digital environment does indeed empower users to negotiate trust on their own terms? As we argue, measuring the presence of trust is not appropriate; distrust may be a valid option for a certain user in a specific context. Additionally, we cannot test that users have made the 'correct' trust choice, as the capacity to judge another's trust perception is limited. Evaluating whether a design includes elements we think empower trust is not ideal, it is the user's perspective that is relevant.

We argue that one way to assess the ability of an environment to trust empower the user is for researchers to measure the level of uncertainty before and after interaction, and by implication, the level of certainty, as we will explain shortly. Certainty is a subjective sense of conviction or validity about one's attitude or opinion [44]. Certainty is when a user knows what he or she would like to do and what is important to him or her. By uncertainty, we mean that the user is unclear about what to do or how to proceed. In our scenario, a reduction in uncertainty as result of interacting with a TEU environment would mean that the user is clearer about what trust choice is best suited to their needs. The experience of the interaction with the digital system has assisted the user to negotiate and interrogate trust. It is the quality of assistance that we value, as this type of experience 'empowers' users rather than simply supporting their current status. The aim of the evaluation is to see if uncertainty is reduced as a result of an interaction. In this section we explain why attitude certainty, which we argue is a proxy for both trust and distrust, is an appropriate way to measure trust empowerment. In the following section, we explain how a change in uncertainty levels can be measured.

Trust researchers agree that trust and distrust have an impact on cooperation, including willingness for vulnerability, confidence, and a reduction of uncertainty (as documented in [45]). Measuring how much a user is willing to cooperate or be vulnerable focuses on what the user might be agreeable to, or arguably, how much a user can be exploited. The notion of confidence does center more on the user's interests, but can be coopted to suit the demands of commerce and government. According to [46], this is due to the impact of the 'New Management Era', the movement to streamline the public sector in the U.K. and the U.S. Confidence is regarded as a means to move forward with more reforms. Thus, we argue that the concept of 'confidence' is not suited to our purposes because some users may associate the term with managerial approaches.

We argue that studying if there is a reduction in uncertainty for the user is the most suitable means to explore the success of a TEU empowerment. It is a result orientated to a user's interests and the term does not have strong societal connotations, such as the word confidence. A reduction in uncertainty is a result of both trust and distrust. Focusing on the possibility of a reduction allows an interrogation of whether a trustee has received a benefit of both trust and distrust.

Without trust and distrust, the user is caught up in the cycle of exploring possibilities [5]. With trust and distrust, some future possibilities are foreclosed, as Clark [15] says, there is a 'call to action'. Distrust is at least as important as trust in this view. Although often seen as a negative state, distrust can in fact resolve a complex scenario, closing down possible paths for the individual to choose as well as protecting the individual from negative consequences. Thus we use a reduction in uncertainty as a proxy for trust empowerment, a means to understand whether a user of a digital environment has indeed been empowered regarding trust. Researchers use proxies to explore the notions of trust and distrust as neither concept can be directly observed [47], for instance, [48] use the presence of cohesion in a team as a proxy for trust, while [49] use the occurrence of an alliance of two parties.

Jøsang et al. (see [50]) also emphasise the role in uncertainty in trust interactions. In their view, subjective logic, probability calculations that work with uncertainty, can help solve trust problems. Their response is to develop an oeuvre of algorithms that draw on a range of users' opinions in order to dissipate the impact of uncertainty. The design work we attempt aims to engage the user in an active role within a digital system. In contrast, Jøsang et al. seek to automate decisions on behalf of the user. A TEU system could allow a user to choose which interactions are handled automatically and which ones require further interrogation and customisation. This is a research issue for further investigation.

## 9.7 How Can Uncertainty Levels Be Measured?

We argue that a change in the user's uncertainty levels before and after interacting with a digital environment can be a proxy for whether trust empowerment has occurred. In this section, we explore means to understand whether a digital environment has reduced it. There are well-developed techniques to evaluate the strength of attitude. One way is to ask the participant to self-report via a survey undertaken before and after an experience. The two results are compared. The field of Psychology has well-developed survey techniques to undertake these measurements and determine how strongly a respondent holds an opinion via self-report. Several fields have drawn on these techniques including Marketing and Political Science (see [51] for an overview). Likert and Thurstone are notable early attitude researchers, they developed the Likert scale to quantifiably measure attitudes [52]. A common argument by survey practitioners is that strong attitudes are more likely to exist across time, influence behaviour, and predict behaviour than are attitudes that are not as certain [53]. The work of Maio and Haddock [53], who have surveyed the field of the psychology of attitudes, argue that a measurement of attitude strength is an indication of a reduction in uncertainty. Thus there is the potential for suitable construct validity, when an operationalisation measure does indeed study the variable under consideration.

To develop survey questions revolving around trust, we recommend that survey writers work from the three dimensions of trust that the field agrees: competence, motivation, and continuity [4]. The evidence users seek in order to proceed in a trust interaction fall into these categories and analysing a design in terms of these dimensions allows us to understand an environment from a user's perspective. The dimensions of trust are interlinked and overlap but can be described as follows. Competence refers to whether the trustee has the ability and skill to fulfill the requirements of the interaction [45]. Motivation has to do with shared interest: Does the trustee have an interest in working towards the welfare of the trustor? Finally, the dimension of continuity is about whether there is possibility of a connection between the trustor and trustee beyond the current encounter. Do the trustor and trustee belong to similar communities? Will their paths cross again? The important point to note is that we do not seek to test for the presence and strength of continuity, competence and motivation but how clear a respondent is about their perception and conviction regarding these dimensions. By studying whether a user is more certain about different dimensions of trust evidence, we can see if a TEU environment has indeed empowered a user about trust.

We now turn to the survey content to evaluate the 'Device Comfort' initiative, an interface that assists users with health decisions in different everyday situations. The interface aggregates advice from different locations and helps the user interpret the advice in accordance with the user's preferences. We wish to explore whether this element does empower the user regarding trust.

The following survey statements are examples of what we will use to evaluate the performance of our interface. Each statement, which forms a survey question, focuses on one of the three dimensions of trust evidence as argued by Cofta [9]. By isolating this evidence into the three dimensions, we can gain insight into the nuances of trust and investigate whether there is a shift in just one dimension of trust, for instance, 'continuity' or whether there is a more generalised trust impression change. Such insights are invaluable to designers because the guidance can inform the design of one interface element over another. Participants in our study will be asked to reflect on their perception of an advice provider at different points in time. They will be asked the following questions:

- The advice provider has the appropriate expertise and background to provide advice. (To determine the dimension of competence)
- The advice provider has a desire to work in my interests. (To determine the dimension of motivation)
- The advice provider has been a member of relevant communities for a long time. (To determine the dimension of continuity)

To close the survey and to ascertain how certain the respondent is, we draw on the work of attitude researchers [54, 55] (who have developed questions to be used with a Likert scale to gauge certainty). These questions provide an opportunity to compare the strength of a user's attitude so a change can be detected:

- I am sure that my attitude towards the advice provider is correct.
- I feel confident that my attitude towards the advice provider is the most accurate attitude possible.

- I believe that if someone challenged my views on the advice provider I would be able to easily defend my point of view.
- I do not think that my attitude towards the advice provider is going to change.

Naturally, there are limitations to the survey approach and there are questions that require further exploration. Social science literature debates the issues, which are often context specific (see [56] for an overview). For instance, how many survey items gather a suitable amount of data about an interaction? What are the criteria? How much reduction in uncertainty is considered a success and does this change across contexts? If so, why? Organising users to complete a survey is difficult to achieve. The completion of two surveys by each participant is even more difficult. The survey needs to be administered at a time when the participant is mindful of the experience of the digital system.

Additionally, an increase in attitude strength across the two surveys may be a result of a participant's familiarisation with the context, in which they are placed in for the research. Experimental researchers often encounter this issue. Can an intervention really change behaviour in the fashion intended or are the results the effect of the participants simply being involved in a study that has primed them to think in certain ways [53]? Familiarity is part of the trust equation and familiarity breeds trust [11]. There is, however, a predictive validity issue. Is the process really isolating a shift in uncertainty? Is the approach measuring the effect of trust and distrust or other variables, such as familiarity or memory, entering into the equation that could interfere with the results? Refining the boundaries of trust, familiarity, and attitude strength is another task for future research.

A future direction is to explore the potential of social network data, rather than surveys, to evaluate whether a digital environment empowers trust. Social networks can harness public comments written by users of social media sites (such as Facebook and Twitter). Conclusions can be drawn about how different sets of users are responding to new events and products. Sometimes users utilise the hashtag (#) as a means to signal to others that they want their comments to be linked to other discussions around a certain topic. The practice of sentiment analysis, which draws assumptions about how users are thinking and feeling from their social media activity, may provide precedents for exploring if a user is feeling more or less certain about their trust interactions.

## 9.8 Conclusion

Often industry and academia value an outcome of trust for their projects and evaluation methods follow a similar path. Yet an outcome of trust may not suit the user of a project. From the user's perspective, distrust may be as valuable as trust. Some practitioners create projects that work in users' interests and empowering them regarding trust (which we refer to as TEU environments). These practitioners need measures to understand the impact of their designs. Arriving at an evaluation method is not straightforward proposition. Assessing whether trust has formed is not appropriate, as is testing for right and wrong answers in connection to trust.

In order to evaluate whether a TEU is successful, we suggest evaluating whether a reduction in uncertainty for the user has occurred as a result of interacting with an environment. A reduction in uncertainty is one of the side effects shared by both trust and distrust that is commonly agreed upon in the research area. A reduction in uncertainty levels can be measured via surveys administered before and after a user interacts with a TEU environment. The work of attitude researchers provides guidance into the use of Likert scales in a survey to identify a shift in attitude.

# References

1. Ashleigh, M., Meyer, E.: Deepening the understanding of trust: combining repertory grid and narrative to explore the uniqueness of trust. In: Lyon, F. (ed.) Handbook of Research Methods on Trust. Edward Elgar Publishing, Cheltenham (2012)
2. Fukuyama, F.: Trust: The Social Virtues and the Creation of Prosperity. Free Press, New York (1995)
3. Lewicki, R., Brinsfield, C.: Measuring trust beliefs and behaviours. In: Lyon, F. (ed.) Handbook of Research Methods on Trust. Edward Elgar Publishing, Cheltenham (2012)
4. Cofta, P.: The trustworthy and trusted web. Found. Trends Web Sci. **2**, 243–381 (2011)
5. Goffman, E.: Frame Analysis: An Essay on the Organization of Experience. Harvard University Press, Cambridge (1974)
6. Basu, A., Dwyer, N., Naicken, S.: A concordance framework for building trust evidences. In: 2012 Tenth Annual International Conference on Privacy, Security and Trust (PST), pp. 153–154. IEEE, Paris (2012)
7. Möllering, G.: Trusting in art: calling for empirical trust research in highly creative contexts. J. Trust Res. **2**, 203–210 (2012)
8. Nurse, J., Agrafiotis, I., Goldsmith, M., Creese, S., Lamberts, K.: Two sides of the coin: measuring and communicating the trustworthiness of online information. J. Trust Manag. **1**, 1–20 (2014)
9. Cofta, P.: Trust, Complexity and Control: Confidence in a Convergent World. Wiley, Hoboken (2007)
10. Gothelf, J.: Lean UX: Applying Lean Principles to Improve User Experience. O'Reilly Media, Sebastopol (2013)
11. Luhmann, N.: Trust and Power. Wiley, Chichester (1979)
12. Dwyer, N.: Traces of digital trust: an interactive design perspective. PhD thesis. Victoria University (2011)
13. Langheinrich, M.: When trust does not compute–the role of trust in ubiquitous computing. In: Seattle Workshop on Privacy at UBICOMP, Seattle (2003)
14. Schön, D.: The Reflective Practitioner: How Professionals Think in Action. Basic Books, New York (1983)
15. Clark, D.: The role of trust in cyberspace. In: Harper, R. (ed.) Trust, Computing, and Society, pp. 17–38. Cambridge University Press, New York (2014)
16. Marsh, S., Briggs, P., El-Khatib, K., Esfandiari, B., Stewart, J.: Defining and investigating device comfort. J. Inf. Process. **19**, 231–252 (2011)
17. Fry, T.: Design as Politics. Berg, Oxford (2010)
18. Blythe, M., Bardzell, S., Bardzell, J., Blackwell, A.: Critical issues in interaction design. In: Proceedings of the 22nd British HCI Group Annual Conference on People and Computers: Culture, Creativity, Interaction, vol. 2, pp. 183–184. British Computer Society, Liverpool (2008)

19. Harper, R.: Reflections on trust, computing, and society. In: Harper, R. (ed.) Trust, Computing, and Society, pp. 299–339. Cambridge University Press, New York
20. Mayer, R., Davis, J., Schoorman, F.: An integrative model of organizational trust. Acad. Manag. Rev. **20**, 709–734 (1995)
21. Pyöriä, P.: Managing telework: risks, fears and rules. Manag. Res. Rev. **34**, 386–399 (2011)
22. Verburg, R., Bosch-Sijtsema, P., Vartiainen, M.: Getting it done: critical success factors for project managers in virtual work settings. Int. J. Proj. Manag. **31**, 68–79 (2013)
23. Weisberg, J., Te'eni, D., Arman, L.: Past purchase and intention to purchase in e-commerce: the mediation of social presence and trust. Internet Res. **21**, 82–96 (2011)
24. Hajli, M.: A research framework for social commerce adoption. Inf. Manag. Comput. Secur. **21**, 144–154 (2013)
25. Egger, F.: From interactions to transactions: designing the trust experience for business-to-consumer electronic commerce. PhD thesis. Eindhoven University of Technology (2003)
26. Swaak, M., de Jong, M., de Vries, P.: Effects of information usefulness, visual attractiveness, and usability on web visitors' trust and behavioral intentions. In: IEEE International Professional Communication Conference (IPCC 2009), pp. 1–5. IEEE, Waikiki (2009)
27. Djamasbi, S., Siegel, M., Tullis, T., Dai, R.: Efficiency, trust, and visual appeal: usability testing through eye tracking. In: 43rd Hawaii International Conference on System Sciences (HICSS), pp. 1–10. IEEE, Honolulu (2010)
28. Alberts, W., van der Geest, T.: Color matters: color as trustworthiness cue in web sites. Tech. Commun. **58**, 149–160 (2011)
29. Hassanein, K., Head, M.: Building online trust through socially rich web interfaces. In: Proceedings of the 2nd Annual Conference on Privacy, Security and Trust, Fredericton, New Brunswick, pp. 15–22 (2004)
30. Connaughton, S., Daly, J.: Strategies for leading virtual teams. In: Pauleen, D. (ed.) Virtual Teams: Projects, Protocols and Processes. Idea Group Pub., Hershey (2004)
31. Kumar, A., Chaudhary, M., Kumar, N.: Social engineering threats and awareness: a survey. Eur. J. Adv. Eng. Technol. **2**, 15–19 (2015)
32. Zack, M., McKenney, J.: Social context and interaction in ongoing computer-supported management groups. Organ. Sci. **6**, 394–422 (1995)
33. Botsman, R.: TED Talk: The currency of the new economy is trust. TED Talk. http://www.ted.com/talks/rachel_botsman_the_currency_of_the_new_economy_is_trust.html (2012)
34. Botsman, R., Rogers, R.: Beyond zipcar: collaborative consumption. Harv. Bus. Rev. **88**, 30 (2010)
35. Maynard, D., Clayman, S.: The diversity of ethnomethodology. Annu. Rev. Sociol. **17**, 385–418 (1991)
36. Suchman, L.: Plans and Situated Actions: The Problem of Human-Machine Communication. Cambridge University Press, New York (1987)
37. Thaler, R., Sunstein, C.: Nudge: Improving Decisions About Health, Wealth, and Happiness. Yale University Press, London (2008)
38. Srnicek, N., Williams, A.: Inventing the Future: Postcapitalism and a World Without Work. Verso, Brooklyn (2015)
39. Möllering, G.: Trust, institutions, agency: towards a neoinstitutional theory of trust. In: Bachmann, R., Zaheer, A. (eds.) Handbook of Trust Research, pp. 355–376. Edward Elgar Publishing, Cheltenham (2006)
40. Marsh, S., Basu, A., Dwyer, N.: Rendering unto Caesar the things that are Caesar's: complex trust models and human understanding. In: Proceedings of the 6th International Conference on Trust Managaement: Trust Management VI. Surat, pp. 191–200. Springer, Heidelberg (2012)
41. Alcade, B.: Trusted third party, who are you. In: Proceedings of the 4th International Conference on Trust Management: Trust Management IV, Morioka, pp. 49–59. Springer (2010)
42. Bødker, H.: Rethinking journalism: trust and participation in a transformed news land-scape. Digit. Journal. **1**, 399–400 (2013)
43. Luxon, N.: Crisis of Authority: Politics, Trust, and Truth-Telling in Freud and Foucault. Cambridge University Press, Cambridge (2013)

44. Festinger, L.: Conflict, Decision, and Dissonance. Stanford University Press, Stanford (1964)
45. Cofta, P.: Designing for trust. In: Whitworth, B. (ed.) Handbook of Research on Socio-technical Design and Social Networking Systems, pp. 388–401. IGI Global, Hershey (2009)
46. Riggs, W.: Lessons in leading: developing a culture of innovation in public sector planning and governance. Focus: J. City Reg. Plan. Dep. **11**, 24 (2014)
47. Möllering, G., Bachmann, R., Hee Lee, S.: Introduction: understanding organizational trust-foundations, constellations, and issues of operationalisation. J. Managerial Psychol. **19**, 556–570 (2004)
48. Diallo, A., Thuillier, D.: The success of international development projects, trust and communication: an African perspective. Int. J. Proj. Manag. **23**, 237–252 (2005)
49. Gulati, R.: Does familiarity breed trust? The implications of repeated ties for contractual choice in alliances. Acad. Manag. J. **38**, 85–112 (1995)
50. Jøsang, A.: A Probabilistic logic under uncertainty. In: Proceedings of the Thirteenth Australasian Symposium on Theory of Computing, vol. 65, pp. 101–110. Australian Computer Society, Inc., Ballarat (2007)
51. Bruner, G., Hensel, P., James, K.: Marketing Scales Handbook: Multi-Item Measures for Consumer Insight Research. American Marketing Association, Chicago (2001)
52. Edwards, A., Kenney, K.: A comparison of the Thurstone and Likert techniques of attitude scale construction. J. Appl. Psychol. **30**, 72 (1946)
53. Maio, G., Haddock, G.: The Psychology of Attitudes and Attitude Change. Sage, Thousand Oaks (2009)
54. Bizer, G., Tormala, Z., Rucker, D., Petty, R.: Memory-based versus on-line processing: implications for attitude strength. J. Exp. Soc. Psychol. **41**, 646–653 (2006)
55. Carpenter, C., Boster, F.: The relationship between message recall and persuasion: more complex than it seems. J. Commun. **63**, 661–681 (2013)
56. Wellington, J.: Educational Research: Contemporary Issues and Practical Approaches. Bloomsbury Publishing, London (2015)